# HOW TO DRAW PLANES

# DESSINER LES AVIONS PAS À PAS

# FLUGZEUGE ZEICHNEN – SCHRITT FÜR SCHRITT

# VLIEGTUIGEN TEKENEN – STAP VOOR STAP

# CÓMO DIBUJAR AVIONES PASO A PASO

# COMO DESENHAR AVIÕES PASSO A PASSO

# HOW TO DRAW PLANES

# DESSINER LES AVIONS PAS À PAS

# FLUGZEUGE ZEICHNEN – SCHRITT FÜR SCHRITT

# VLIEGTUIGEN TEKENEN – STAP VOOR STAP

# CÓMO DIBUJAR AVIONES PASO A PASO

# COMO DESENHAR AVIÕES PASSO A PASSO

**KÖNEMANN**
is an imprint of Frechmann Kolón GmbH
www.frechmann.com



**Editorial project:**
**LOFT Publications**
Barcelona, Spain
Tel.: +34 932 688 088
Fax: +34 932 687 073
loft@loftpublications.com
www.loftpublications.com

logos
Edito e distribuito in Italia da:
2014 © Logos edizioni
Strada Curtatona 5/2
41126 Modena, Italy
Tel: 059 412 648
commerciale@logos.info
libri.it
logosedizioni.it

**Editorial coordinator:** Cristian Campos
**Illustrations and texts:** Sergio Guinot
**Art director:** Emma Termes Parera
**Layout:** Lourdes Bao Navarro
**Translations:** Cillero & de Motta

ISBN 978-3-86407-466-0 (GB)
ISBN 978-3-86407-464-6 (D)
ISBN 978-3-86407-467-7 (NL)
ISBN 978-3-86407-465-3 (E)
ISBN 978-3-86407-468-4 (PORT)
ISBN 978-88-576-0478-7 (Logos, Italy)

Printed in Spain

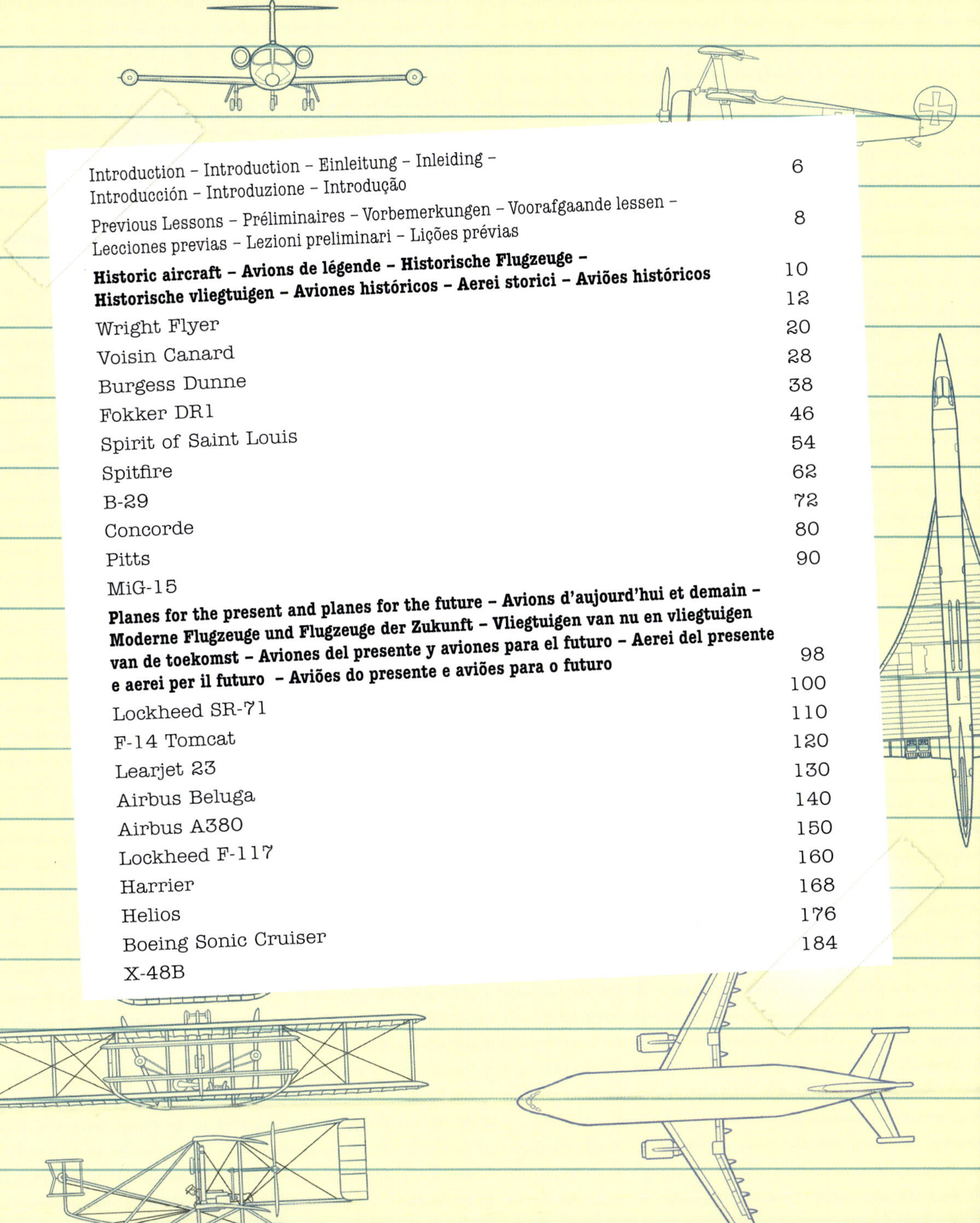

## Introduction

Let's learn to draw airplanes together. Sit by me as we fly through the most characteristic models in the history of aviation. This book will teach you the main features of these flying machines and you will learn how to draw any kind of plane, whether real or fiction, giving it the appearance of a solid, believable, and functional aircraft.

We will find ourselves mid-air with all kinds of difficulties and problems to solve, both technical and aesthetic, for which we will find the solution so that you gain plenty of experience and improve as an illustrator.

There are other journeys, but not like this one. There are other adventures, but not as much fun as this. Are you ready? Come on board!

## Introduction

Vous allez entamer un voyage parmi les plus grands modèles de l'histoire de l'aviation. Grâce à ce livre, vous connaîtrez les principales caractéristiques de ces machines volantes et vous apprendrez à dessiner tous types d'avions, réels ou imaginaires, sous forme d'aéronefs réalistes, solides et fonctionnels.

Votre voyage sera parsemé de multiples difficultés et de problèmes techniques ou esthétiques qu'il vous faudra résoudre grâce à des solutions qui vous permettront d'acquérir l'expérience nécessaire et de vous perfectionner en tant qu'illustrateur.

Il existe bien des voyages mais nul n'est semblable à celui-ci. Il existe bien des aventures mais nulle ne saura vous divertir comme celle-ci. Vous êtes prêt ? Alors n'attendez plus, montez à bord !

## Einleitung

Lernen Sie mit uns, wie man Flugzeuge zeichnet. Nehmen Sie Platz und unternehmen Sie mit uns eine Reise, auf der Sie die berühmtesten Modelle aus der Geschichte der Luftfahrt kennen lernen. Mithilfe der vorliegenden Bandes werden Sie Näheres über die wichtigsten Merkmale dieser Flugmaschinen erfahren und lernen, wie man – wirklich existierende oder fiktive – Flugzeuge aller Art glaubhaft darstellt.

Während unseres Fluges werden Sie auf technische wie auch ästhetische Schwierigkeiten und Probleme treffen, die es zu lösen gilt… und wir halten zahlreiche Tipps und Tricks parat, damit Sie an Erfahrung gewinnen und zu einem besseren Zeichner werden.

Es gibt viele andere Reisen, doch keine ist wie diese. Und es gibt auch viele andere Abenteuer, aber keines ist so unterhaltsam wie unseres. Sind Sie bereit? Dann kommen Sie an Bord!

## Inleiding

Laten we samen leren hoe vliegtuigen getekend moeten worden. Ga naast me zitten en laten we we samen langs de meest kenmerkende modellen van de luchtvaartgeschiedenis vliegen. Aan de hand van dit boek leer je wat de hoofdkenmerken van deze vliegende machines zijn en leer je elk soort echt of denkbeeldig vliegtuig te tekenen en deze op een solide, geloofwaardig en functioneel luchtvaartuig te laten lijken.

We nemen een hoge vlucht met alle technische en esthetische problemen vandien, waarvoor wij een oplossing willen geven zodat je voldoende ervaring opdoet als illustrator.

Er zijn andere reizen, maar niet deze. Er zijn andere avonturen, maar niet zulke leuke als deze. Ben je er klaar voor? Kom dan aan boord!

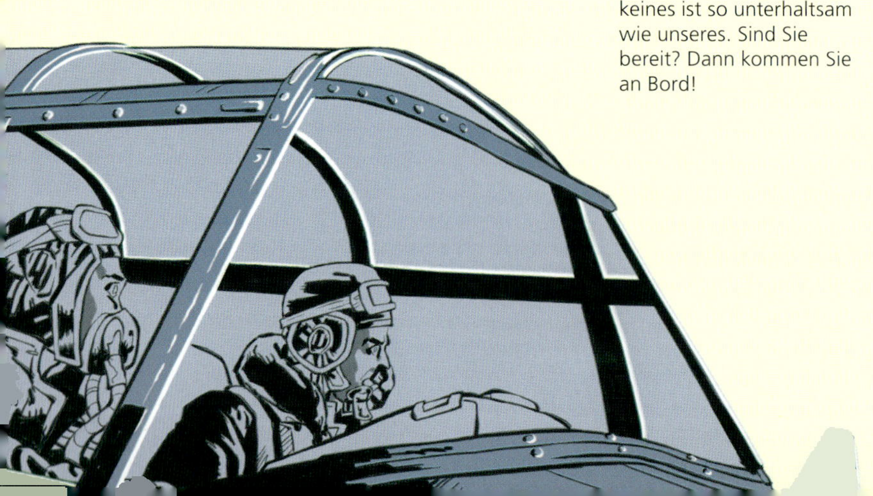

## Introducción

Aprendamos juntos a dibujar aviones. Siéntate a mi lado y pilotemos este viaje por los modelos más característicos de la historia de la aviación. Con este libro conocerás cuáles son las características principales de estas máquinas voladoras y aprenderás a dibujar cualquier tipo de avión, real o ficticio, haciendo que parezca una aeronave sólida, creíble y funcional.

Nos encontraremos en pleno vuelo con todo tipo de dificultades y problemas por resolver, técnicos y estéticos, a los que daremos solución para que adquieras la suficiente experiencia y mejores como ilustrador.

Hay otros viajes, pero no son este. Hay otras aventuras, pero no tan divertidas como esta. ¿Estás listo? ¡Sube a bordo!

## Introduzione

Impariamo insieme a disegnare aeroplani. Siediti accanto a me e partiamo insieme per un volo attraverso i modelli più caratteristici della storia dell'aviazione. Con questo libro conoscerai le caratteristiche principali di queste macchine volanti e imparerai a disegnare qualsiasi tipo di aereo, reale o immaginario, facendo in modo che sembri un velivolo solido, credibile e funzionale.

Durante questo volo ci imbatteremo in ogni sorta di difficoltà e problemi da risolvere, sia tecnici che estetici, a cui troveremo soluzione per farti acquisire l'esperienza sufficiente e farti migliorare come illustratore.

Ci sono altri viaggi, ma nessuno è simile a questo. Ci sono altre avventure, ma nessuna è divertente come questa. Sei pronto? Allora sali a bordo!

## Introdução

Vamos aprender juntos a desenhar aviões. Senta-te ao meu lado e pilotemos esta viagem pelos modelos mais característicos da história da aviação. Com este livro conhecerás quais são as características principais destas máquinas voadoras e aprenderás a desenhar qualquer tipo de avião, real ou fictício, fazendo com que pareça uma aeronave sólida, credível e funcional.

Encontrar-nos-emos em pleno voo com todo o tipo de dificuldades e problemas por resolver, técnicos e estéticos, aos quais daremos solução para que adquiras a experiência suficiente e melhores como ilustrador.

Há outras viagens, mas não são esta. Há outras aventuras, mas não tão divertidas como esta. Estás pronto? Sobe a bordo!

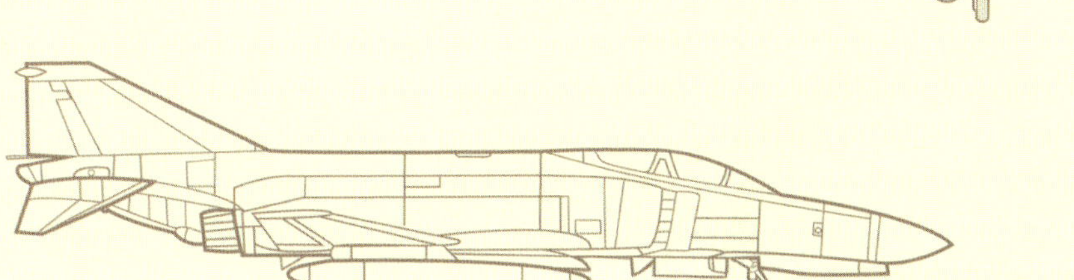

## Previous lessons

The skeleton and outline are simplifications that serve as the base for your drawing.

The sketch is a preparation for the penciling, and aims to achieve the correct volume for the elements of the skeleton and the outline.

The penciling step can include anything from a detailed sketch to an almost complete ink drawing. The penciling should include all the elements that will feature in the final drawing.

Inking is represented by several shades, according to the desired effect. In all the examples, the ink color variations were created using software.

Lighting and shading are often represented over a fictitious gray base for easier visualization.

The base color is not always realistic, as it attempts to explain different concepts to the reader.

The finished drawing is a combination of all the stages, which are shown separately in this book so that each can be understood easily, but they should be visualized at the same time with the saturation and opacity adjusted.

The extras are surprises, contributions by the author, with tricks and artistic touches for the reader that will make reading more pleasurable.

The order of the steps for each exercise do not need to follow those of this book. There are many ways of reaching your the final goal, and you should discover which one best suits your qualities and the drawing technique you choose (freehand or computer drawing).

## Préliminaires

Le squelette et le schéma sont des simplifications servant de base pour notre dessin.

L'ébauche est une préparation pour le crayonné, une recherche du volume approprié des éléments du squelette et du schéma.

Le crayonné peut à la fois être une ébauche très détaillée ou un dessin à l'encre presque achevé. Il doit comporter tous les éléments du dessin final.

L'encrage est réalisé avec différentes couleurs, selon l'effet recherché. Dans tous les cas, les variations de couleur de l'encre ont été réalisées avec des programmes informatiques.

Les ombres et les lumières sont généralement réalisées sur des bases fictives de gris afin de mieux les visualiser.

La base de couleur n'est pas toujours réaliste car elle a pour but d'expliquer au lecteur différents concepts.

Le dessin final est l'union de toutes les phases, qui sont présentées dans ce livre de façon indépendante pour une meilleure compréhension de chacune. Toutefois, il est nécessaire de les visualiser comme un ensemble ajusté en termes de saturation et d'opacité.

Les extras sont des surprises de l'auteur, des petits trucs et astuces ou des clins d'œil au lecteur, qui rendront plus agréable encore la lecture de ce livre.

Pour chaque exercice, l'ordre des étapes ne doit pas nécessairement être celui indiqué dans ce livre. Il existe de nombreuses façons d'atteindre l'objectif final et il nous faut découvrir celle qui correspond le mieux à nos qualités et à la technique de dessin choisie (à la main sur papier ou sur ordinateur).

## Vorbemerkungen

Beim Skelett und beim Grundschema handelt es sich um vereinfachte Darstellungen, die als Ausgangspunkt für die Zeichnung dienen.

Die Skizze ist ein vorbereitender Schritt. Die Buntstiftzeichnung kann eine detaillierte Skizze oder auch eine fast vollendete Tuschezeichnung sein. Die Buntstiftzeichnung muss alle Elemente enthalten, die in der fertigen Darstellung erscheinen sollen.

Tuschezeichnungen werden je nach gewünschter Wirkung in mehreren Farbnuancen gestaltet. Die Farbabstufungen wurden hier mit Computerprogrammen erarbeitet. Licht und Schatten werden oft auf einem fiktiven grauen Hintergrund dargestellt, um ihre Wirkung besser verdeutlichen zu können.

Die grundlegende Färbung fällt nicht immer wirklichkeitsgetreu aus, da sie darauf abzielt, verschiedene Konzepte zu veranschaulichen. Die fertige Zeichnung vereint alle Arbeitsschritte, die einzeln vorgestellt werden.

Bei den zusätzlichen Details handelt es sich um Tipps und Tricks des Autors, die das Studium der einzelnen Seiten noch unterhaltsamer gestalten.

Die Reihenfolge der einzelnen Übungsschritte muss nicht unbedingt der vorgestellten entsprechen. Das Ziel kann auf vielerlei Wegen erreicht werden. Der Leser muss herausfinden, welche Vorgehensweise und Zeichentechnik seinen Fertigkeiten am besten entspricht.

## Voorafgaande lessen

Het ontwerp en het schema zijn vereenvoudigingen die als basis voor onze tekeningen dienen.

De schets is een voorbereiding voor de potloodtekening, het zoeken naar het juiste volume van de elementen van het ontwerp en het schema.

Een potloodtekening kan een goed gedetailleerde schets tot een bijna afgeronde inkttekening zijn. De potloodtekening moet alle elementen bevatten die in de eindtekening zijn opgenomen.

Inkttekeningen worden in verschillende tinten, naargelang het gewenste effect, afgebeeld. De variaties in inktkleur zijn in alle gevallen met computerprogramma's uitgewerkt.

Licht en schaduwen worden vaak voor een betere visualisatie op fictieve grijze ondergronden uitgebeeld.

De basiskleur is niet altijd realistisch. Hiermee wordt geprobeerd om de lezer verschillende concepten uit te leggen.

De afgeronde tekening is de verbinding van alle fases die in dit boek afzonderlijk worden getoond, zodat elke fase beter te begrijpen is, maar moeten tegelijk gevisualiseerd en qua verzadiging en ondoorschijnendheid aangepast worden. De extra's zijn door de schrijver van het boek geïntroduceerde verrassingen, kleine trucs of knipogen naar de lezer die het lezen van dit werk aangenamer maken.

Men hoeft zich niet per se aan de volgorde van de verschillende stappen van elke oefening uit dit boek te houden. Er zijn vele manieren om het einddoel te bereiken en we moeten zelf ontdekken welke het best bij onze vaardigheden en bij de gekozen tekentechniek (uit de vrije hand op papier of met de computer) passen.

## Lecciones previas

El esqueleto y el esquema son simplificaciones que nos sirven de base para nuestro dibujo.

El boceto es una preparación para el lápiz, una búsqueda del volumen adecuado de los elementos del esqueleto y el esquema.

El lápiz puede ser desde un boceto bien detallado hasta una tinta casi terminada. Debe incluir todos los elementos que incluirá el dibujo final.

Las tintas se representan en varios tonos, según el efecto deseado. En todos los casos, las variaciones en el color de la tinta se han realizado con programas informáticos.

Las luces y sombras se representan a menudo sobre bases grises ficticias para su mejor visualización.

El color base no siempre es realista, pues busca explicar diferentes conceptos al lector.

El dibujo acabado es la unión de todas las fases, que en este libro se muestran separadas para una mejor comprensión de cada una, pero que deben visualizarse a la vez y ajustadas en saturación y opacidad.

Los extras son sorpresas que aporta el autor del libro, pequeños trucos o guiños al lector que harán más amena la lectura de esta obra.

El orden de los pasos de cada ejercicio no debe ser necesariamente el de este libro. Existen muchas maneras de llegar al objetivo final, y debemos descubrir cuál es la que mejor se adapta a nuestras cualidades y a la técnica de dibujo escogida (a mano sobre papel o por ordenador).

## Lezioni preliminari

Lo scheletro e lo schema sono semplificazioni che servono come base per il disegno.

Il bozzetto è preparatorio per le matite; è una ricerca del volume adeguato degli elementi dello scheletro e dello schema.

Le matite possono andare da un bozzetto molto dettagliato fino a un ripasso quasi completo. La fase a matita deve includere tutti gli elementi che compariranno nel disegno finale.

Il ripasso a china viene eseguito in vari toni, a seconda dell'effetto desiderato. In tutti i casi, le variazioni di colore della china sono state realizzate con programmi informatici.

Le luci e le ombre spesso si rappresentano su una base grigia fittizia per migliorare la visualizzazione.

Il colore di base non è sempre realistico, in quanto serve a spiegare al lettore concetti diversi.

Il disegno finito è l'unione di tutte le fasi, che in questo libro sono mostrate separatamente per una migliore comprensione, ma che devono essere visualizzate simultaneamente e calibrate in saturazione e opacità.

Gli extra sono sorprese offerte dall'autore, piccoli trucchi o consigli che renderanno più divertente la lettura di quest'opera.

L'ordine delle fasi di ogni esercizio non deve seguire necessariamente quello del libro. Esistono molti modi per raggiungere l'obiettivo finale: spetta a noi scoprire qual è quello più adatto alle nostre qualità e alla tecnica di disegno scelta (a mano sulla carta o al computer).

## Lições prévias

O esqueleto e o esquema são simplificações que nos servem de base para o nosso desenho.

O esboço é uma preparação para o lápis, uma procura do volume adequado dos elementos do esqueleto e do esquema.

O lápis pode ser desde um esboço bem detalhado até uma tinta quase terminada. Deve incluir todos os elementos que incluirá o desenho final.

A tinta representa-se em vários tons, segundo o efeito desejado. Em todos os casos, as variações na cor da tinta foram realizados com programas informáticos.

As luzes e as sombras representam-se com frequência sobre bases cinzentas fictícias para sua melhor visualização.

A cor base nem sempre é realista, pois procura explicar diferentes conceitos ao leitor.

O desenho acabado é a união de todas as fases, que neste livro se mostram separadas para uma melhor compreensão de cada uma, mas que devem visualizar-se ao mesmo tempo e ajustadas em saturação e opacidade.

Os extras são surpresas que nos traz o autor do livro, pequenos truques ou sugestões cúmplices ao leitor que tornarão mais agradável a leitura desta obra.

A ordem dos passos de cada exercício não deve ser necessariamente a deste livro. Existem muitas maneiras de chegar ao objectivo final, e devemos descobrir qual é a que melhor se adapta a nossas qualidades e à técnica de desenho escolhida (à mão sobre papel ou por computador).

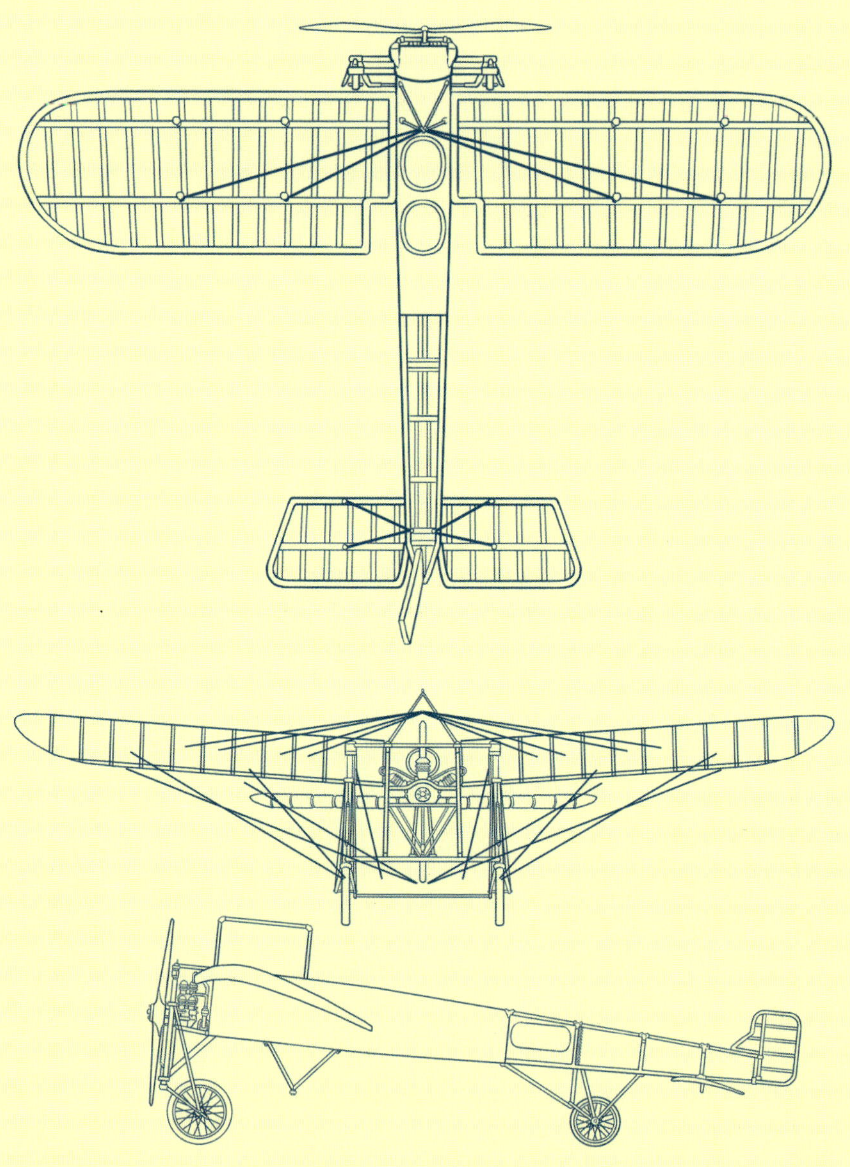

## Historic aircraft

Including all the planes that have set the course of the history of aviation in one book is an impossible task. But if not all of them are here, there is no doubt that all of the ones here are included among them. All the aircraft presented in this first chapter are classics of the history of aeronautics: decisive, pioneering, and revolutionary planes.

## Avions de légende

Il est impossible de rassembler en un seul volume tous les avions ayant marqué l'histoire de l'aviation. Néanmoins, si tous ceux qui existent ne sont pas dans ce livre, tous ceux qui y sont présentés existent. Tous les aéronefs exposés dans la première partie de cet ouvrage sont des grands classiques de l'histoire de l'aéronautique : précurseurs, pionniers et révolutionnaires.

## Historische Flugzeuge

Alle Flugzeuge, die die Geschichte der Luftfahrt geprägt haben, in einem einzigen Band unterzubringen, ist völlig unmöglich. Doch auch wenn nicht jedes einzelne der so zahlreichen Modelle vorgestellt werden kann, so handelt es sich bei den hier präsentierten Flugzeugen um die großen Klassiker der Luftfahrtgeschichte: Wegbereitende Flugmaschinen, Vorreiter und revolutionäre Entwicklungen.

## Historische vliegtuigen

Het is onmogelijk om alle vliegtuigen die in de luchtvaart geschiedenis hebben gemaakt in één boek op te nemen. Hoewel niet alle vliegtuigen in het boek staan, horen alle vliegtuigen die erin staan erbij. Alle luchtschepen die wij in het eerste deel van dit werk laten zien zijn klassiekers van de geschiedenis van de luchtvaartkunde: beslissende, baanbrekende en revolutionaire vliegtuigen.

## Aviones históricos

Incluir en un solo volumen todos los aviones que han marcado la historia de la aviación es tarea imposible. Pero si no están todos los que son, sin duda son todos los que están. Todas las aeronaves que presentamos en la primera parte de esta obra son grandes clásicos de la historia de la aeronáutica: aviones decisivos, pioneros y revolucionarios.

## Aerei storici

Includere in un unico volume tutti gli aerei che hanno segnato la storia dell'aviazione è impossibile. Tuttavia, la selezione qui presente è sicuramente molto rappresentativa. Tutti i velivoli che presentiamo nella prima parte di quest'opera sono grandi classici della storia dell'aviazione: aerei determinanti, pionieristici e rivoluzionari.

## Aviões históricos

Incluir num só volume todos os aviões que marcaram a história da aviação é tarefa impossível. Mas se não estão todos os que são, sem dúvida que todos os que estão o são. Todas as aeronaves que apresentamos na primeira parte desta obra são grandes clássicos da história da aeronáutica: aviões decisivos, pioneiros e revolucionários.

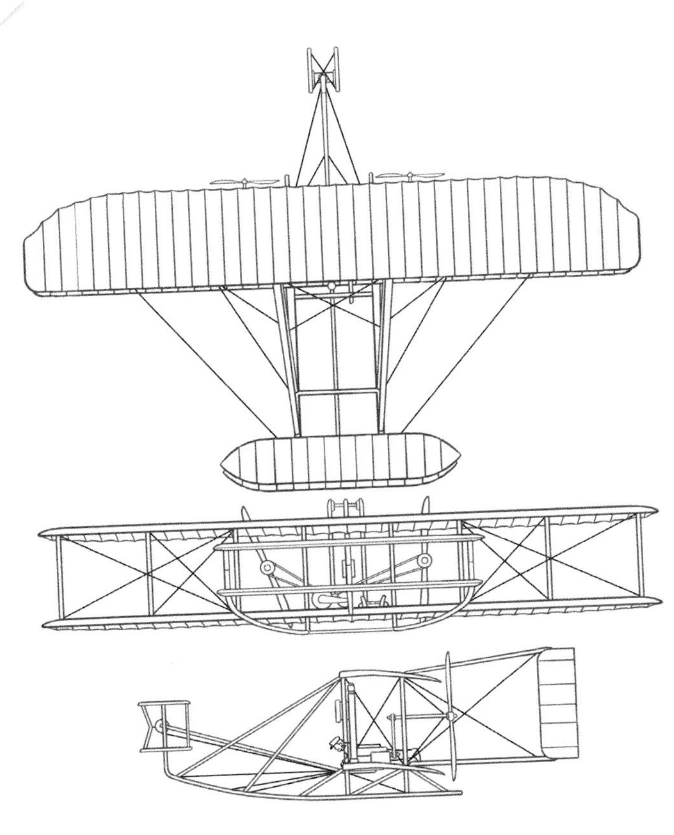

# Wright Flyer

# 1

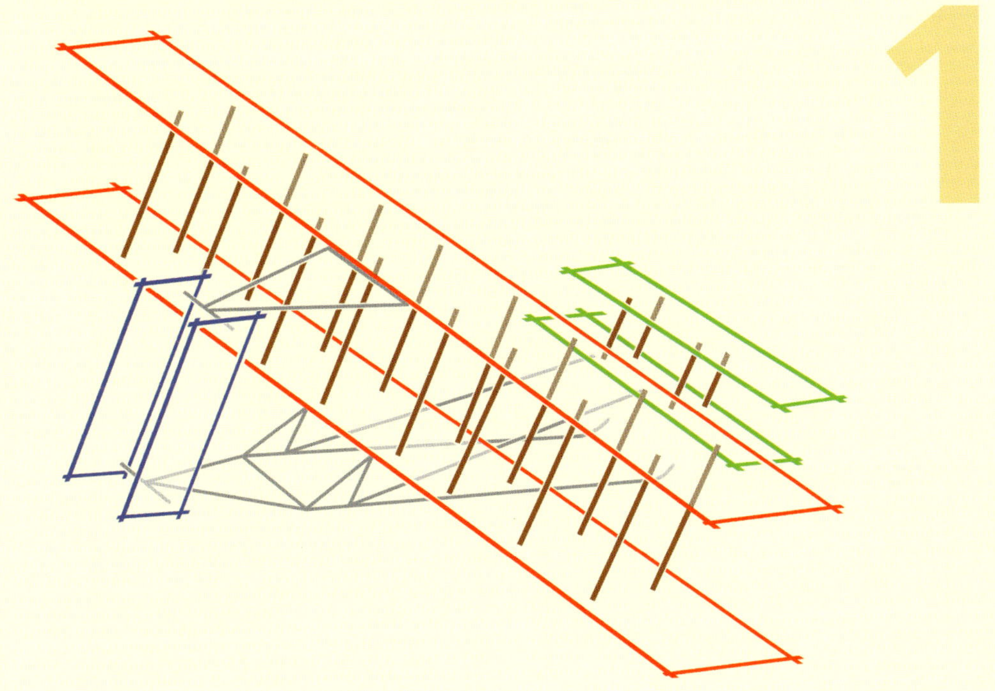

The use of different colors gives you a clearer understanding of the outline. Here the wings are in red, held together by brown wooden struts. The rudder is in blue, the front elevator is in green, and the base frame is in gray.

L'utilisation de différentes couleurs nous permet de mieux comprendre notre schéma. Ici, les ailes sont rouges, reliées par des barres en bois marron ; la gouverne arrière est bleue ; l'élévateur avant est vert et la structure de base est grise.

Durch die Verwendung mehrere Farben wird das Grundschema leichter verständlich. In diesem Fall wurden die Tragflächen rot gestaltet, die hölzernen Verbindungsstangen braun, das hintere Seitenruder blau, das vorn angebrachte Höhenruder grün und die Grundstruktur grau.

Het gebruik van diverse kleuren stelt ons in staat om het schema beter te begrijpen. In dit geval zijn de vleugels in het rood getekend en zijn deze met stokken van bruin hout aan elkaar verbonden. Het richtingsroer is blauw, het hoogteroer vooraan is groen en de basisstructuur is grijs.

Usar varios colores nos permite entender mejor nuestro esquema. En este caso, tenemos las alas en rojo, unidas por bastones de madera marrones, el timón trasero azul, el elevador delantero verde y la estructura base de color gris.

Utilizzare diversi colori ci permette di capire meglio il nostro schema. In questo caso abbiamo le ali in rosso, collegate da montanti in legno di color marrone, il timone posteriore in blu, l'equilibratore anteriore in verde e la struttura di base in grigio.

Usar várias cores permite-nos entender melhor o nosso esquema. Neste caso, temos as asas a vermelho, unidas por bastões de madeira castanhos, o timão traseiro azul, o elevador dianteiro verde e a estrutura base de cor cinzenta.

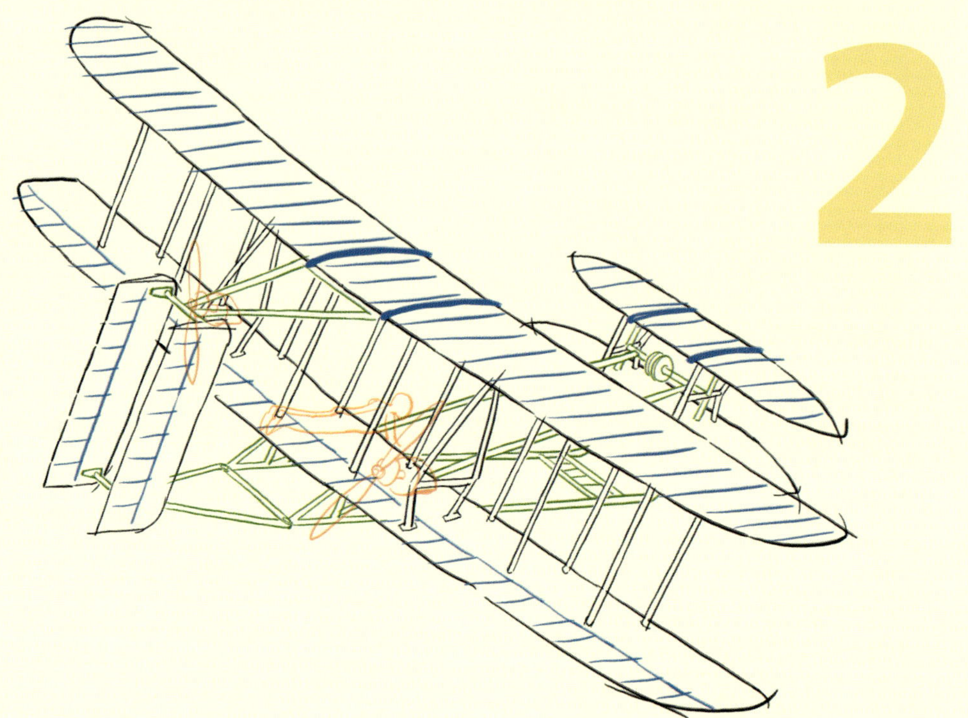

2

Penciling enables you to give shape to each of the parts of the outline (black and green) and we include details inside each piece (blue). Now is the time to add some elements that were not included in the basic outline.

Sur le crayonné, donnez forme aux différentes pièces et ajoutez-y des détails (en bleu) qui ne figurent pas dans le schéma de base.

Mithilfe von Buntstiften erhalten die einzelnen Elemente des Grundschemas ihre konkreten Formen (schwarz und grün). Außerdem werden die Einzelheiten der verschiedenen Bestandteile eingezeichnet (blau). Ferner werden in diesem Schritt einige Elemente hinzugefügt, die nicht im Grundschema enthalten sind.

Met potlood geven we elk van de onderdelen van het schema vorm (zwart en groen) en voegen we details aan elk onderdeel toe (blauw). Op dit moment moeten een aantal elementen worden toegevoegd die niet zijn opgenomen in het basisschema.

Con el lápiz damos forma a cada una de las piezas del esquema (negro y verde) e incluimos detalles dentro de cada pieza (azul). Es el momento de añadir algunos elementos que no incluimos en el esquema básico.

Con la matita diamo forma a ognuna delle parti dello schema (nero e verde) e includiamo i dettagli all'interno di ogni parte (blu). È il momento di aggiungere alcuni elementi che abbiamo tralasciato nello schema di base.

Com o lápis damos forma a cada uma das peças do esquema (preto e verde) e incluímos detalhes dentro de cada peça (azul). É o momento de acrescentar alguns elementos que não incluímos no esquema básico.

3

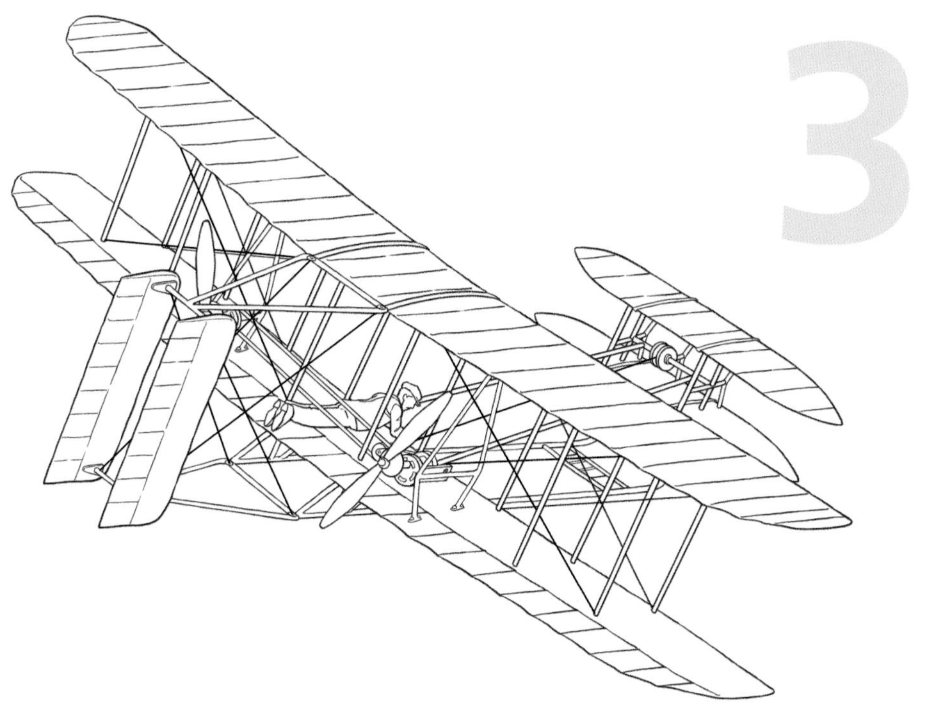

The inking uses thin strokes that are as curved as possible, taking into account the fragility of the aircraft. The bracing and rigging wires have been added in this step as they are simple straight lines that need no prior preparation.

Les lignes, aussi fines et courbes que possible, reflètent la fragilité de l'appareil. Les câbles de fixation et de tension sont ajoutés durant cette étape ; il s'agit de simples lignes droites ne nécessitant pas d'esquisse préalable.

Die Strichführung sollte möglichst dünn und geschwungen erfolgen, um die Zerbrechlichkeit des Flugzeugs zu verdeutlichen. In diesem Schritt werden außerdem die Halte- und Spannseile hinzugefügt (einfache gerade Linien, die keine Vorbereitung erfordern).

De inktlijnen zijn dun en zo veel mogelijk gebogen, zodat de breekbaarheid van het vaartuig naar voren komt. In deze fase zijn de bevestigings- en spankabels toegevoegd aan de hand van simpele rechte lijnen die niet van tevoren hoeven te worden geschetst.

Las tintas son finas y curvadas en lo posible, dando cuenta de la fragilidad de la nave. Se han añadido en esta fase los cables de sujeción y tensión, por ser simples líneas rectas que no necesitan preparación previa.

Il tratto a china è sottile e ricurvo ove possibile, per trasmettere la fragilità di questo aeroplano. In questa fase sono stati aggiunti i cavi di sostegno e di tensione, i quali, essendo semplici linee rette, non richiedono una precedente preparazione.

As tintas são finas e curvilíneas dentro do possível, exibindo a fragilidade da nave. Acrescentaram-se nesta fase os cabos de fixação e tensão, por serem simples linhas rectas que não necessitam preparação prévia.

# 4

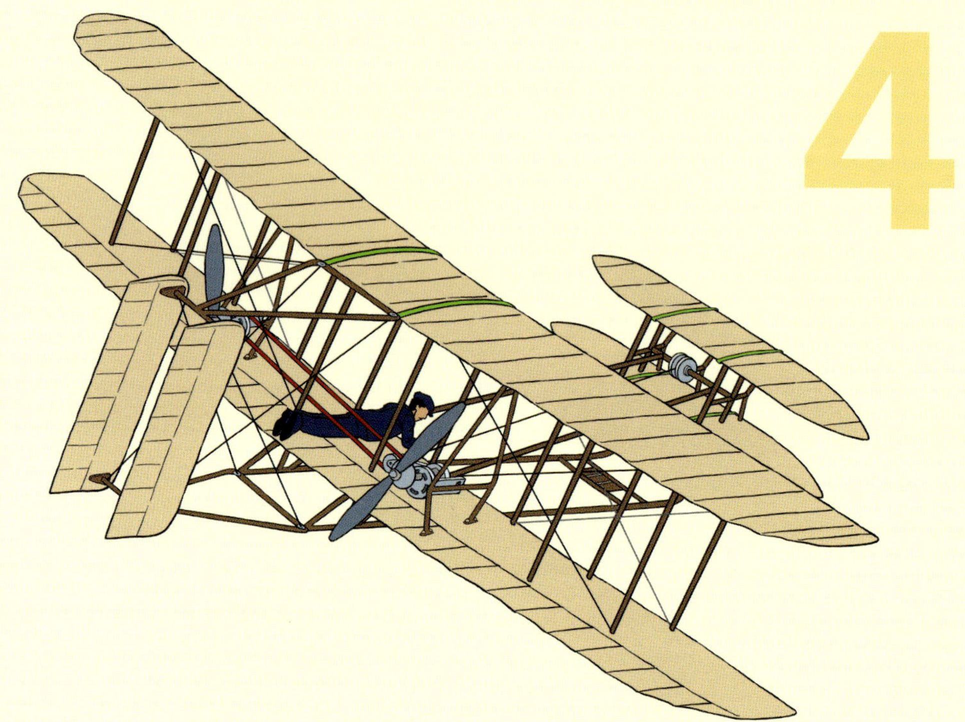

The base colors are natural and low tech: soft browns and ochers, which give the feeling of fragility. Only the propeller blades and the pilot's suit have elaborate colors representing metal and fabric.

Les couleurs de base sont naturelles et peu technologiques, dans des tons marron et ocre pâle, qui apportent une impression de fragilité. Les seules couleurs représentant des métaux et tissus très élaborés sont celles des ailes de l'avion et de la tenue du pilote.

Bei den grundlegenden Farben handelt es sich um Naturtöne (Braun und Ocker), die die Zerbrechlichkeit der Konstruktion unterstreichen und wenig technologischen Fortschritt vermitteln. Nur die Propeller und der Anzug des Piloten sind in Farben gehalten, die für Metalle und hochwertige Stoffe stehen.

De basiskleuren, bruin en zachte okerkleuren, zijn natuurlijk en niet erg technologisch en stralen breekbaarheid uit. Alleen de schoepen en het pak van de piloot hebben kleuren die metaal en bewerkte stoffen uitbeelden.

Los colores base son naturales y poco tecnológicos, marrones y ocres suaves, que dan sensación de fragilidad. Sólo las aspas y el traje del piloto tienen colores que representan metales y tejidos muy elaborados.

I colori di base sono naturali e poco tecnologici, marroni e ocra delicati, che trasmettono una sensazione di fragilità. Solo le pale delle eliche e la tuta del pilota sono colorati in modo da raffigurare rispettivamente il metallo e un tessuto molto elaborato.

As cores base são naturais e pouco tecnológicas, castanhos e ocres suaves, que dão a sensação de fragilidade. Apenas as pás e o vestuário do piloto têm cores que representam metais e tecidos muito elaborados.

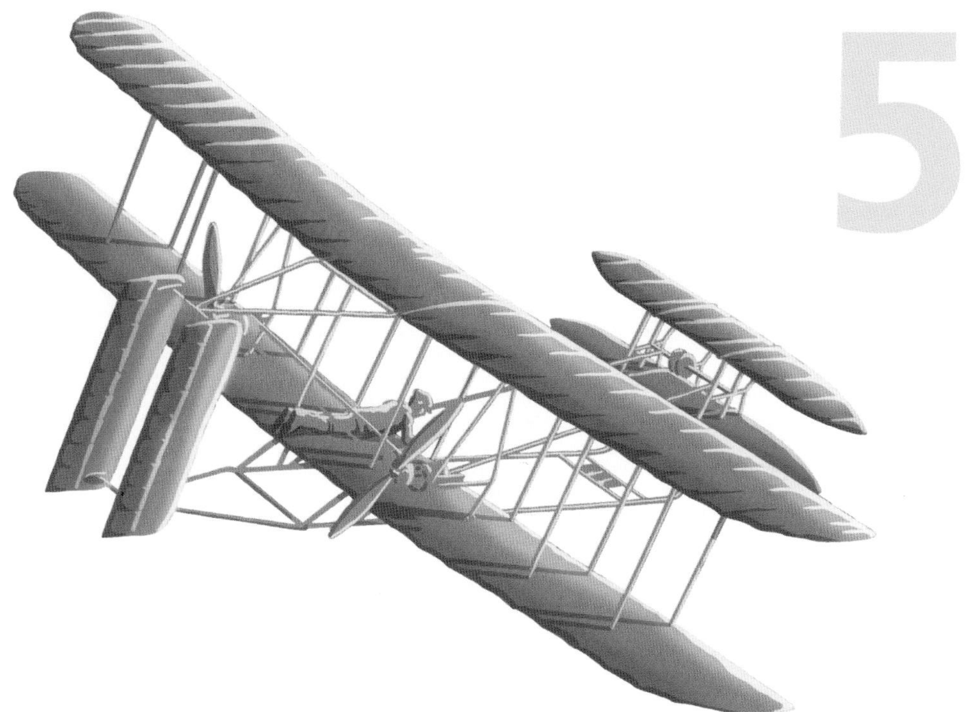

5

With the light source at the front, the light penetrates the wings like tentacles. The shadows cast by the rear are smaller, and the shadows cast by the struts add three-dimensionality.

Partant de l'avant, les lumières s'étendent sur les ailes, tels des tentacules. Les ombres de la partie postérieure sont plus petites et celles projetées par les barres apportent un aspect tridimensionnel.

Durch die von vorn scheinende Lichtquelle fällt das Licht tentakelförmig auf die Tragflächen. Die Schatten im hinteren Bereich sind kleiner, die Schatten der Verbindungsstangen vermitteln eine dreidimensionale Wirkung.

De lichtbron komt van voren waardoor het licht als tentakels om de vleugels wordt geworpen. De schaduwen aan de achterkant zijn kleiner en de door de stokken geworpen schaduwen zorgen voor een driedimensionaal effect.

Con el foco de luz delante, las luces penetran como tentáculos en las alas. Las sombras en la parte posterior son más pequeñas, y las sombras arrojadas por los bastones aportan tridimensionalidad.

Con la sorgente luminosa posta sul davanti, le luci penetrano nelle ali come tentacoli. Nella parte posteriore le ombre sono più piccole, e le ombre portate dei montanti aggiungono tridimensionalità.

Com o foco de luz à frente, as luzes penetram como tentáculos nas asas. As sombras na parte posterior são mais pequenas, e as sombras arrojadas pelos bastões concedem tridimensionalidade.

# 6

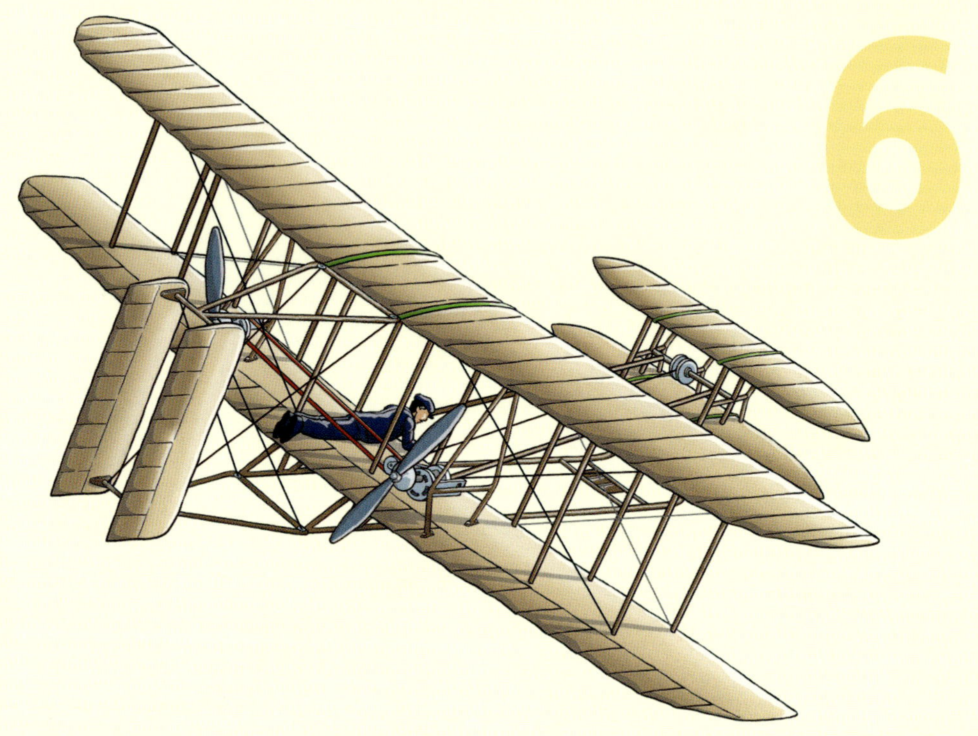

The finished drawing shows the flight of this plane, also known as Flyer I. It is a light, gentle, and calm flight, directly into the brilliant future of aviation.

Le dessin final représente le vol de cet avion connu comme le Flyer I. Il s'agit d'un vol léger, doux et paisible vers l'avenir brillant de l'aviation.

Die fertige Zeichnung zeigt das unter der Bezeichnung „Flyer I" bekannte Flugzeug in der Luft. Es fliegt leicht, sanft und friedlich auf direktem Wege in die glorreiche Zukunft der Luftfahrt.

De afgeronde tekening laat de vlucht van dit vliegtuig, ook wel bekend als Flyer I, zien. Het is een lichte, soepele en vreedzame vlucht, rechtstreeks richting de briljante toekomst van de luchtvaart.

El dibujo acabado muestra el vuelo de este avión, también conocido como Flyer I. Es un vuelo ligero, suave y apacible, directo hacia el brillante futuro de la aviación.

Il disegno finito mostra il volo di questo aeroplano, noto anche come Flyer I. È un volo leggero, morbido e delicato, diretto verso il brillante futuro dell'aviazione.

O desenho acabado mostra o voo deste avião, também conhecido como Flyer I. É um voo leve, suave e aprazível, directo para o brilhante futuro da aviação.

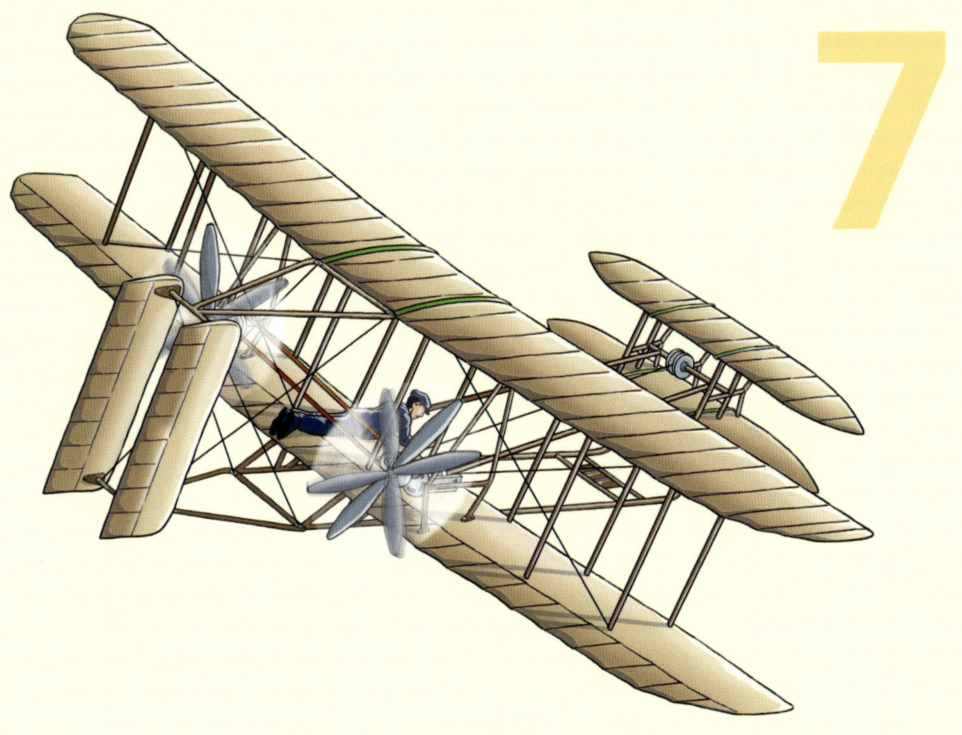


The extra detail is an effect that is easy to recreate using a computer. The propeller blade is repeated in different positions and several white lines are added between them. A Gaussian blur effect is applied to the whole image.

Le détail supplémentaire est un effet facile à obtenir avec l'aide d'un ordinateur. Nous dupliquons l'hélice dans différentes positions entre lesquelles nous ajoutons plusieurs lignes blanches. Puis nous ajoutons à l'ensemble un effet de flou gaussien.

Als zusätzliches Detail kann mithilfe des Computers ein einfacher Spezialeffekt eingefügt werden. Die Propellerflügel werden in verschiedenen Positionen dupliziert, zwischen ihnen werden mehrere weiße Linien eingezeichnet. Anschließend wird ein Gaußscher Weichzeichner angewendet.

Het extra detail is een effect dat met behulp van een computer gemakkelijk wordt verkregen. Kopieer de vleugel in verschillende standen en voeg diverse witte strepen ertussen aan toe. We geven het geheel een Gaussiaans vervagend effect.

El detalle extra es un efecto fácil de conseguir con la ayuda del ordenador. Duplicamos el aspa en distintas posiciones y añadimos varias líneas blancas entre ellas. Al conjunto le aplicamos un efecto de desenfoque gaussiano.

Il dettaglio extra è un effetto facile da realizzare con l'aiuto del computer. Duplichiamo le pale in diverse posizioni e vi inframmezziamo varie linee bianche. All'insieme applichiamo un effetto di sfocatura gaussiana.

O detalhe extra é um efeito fácil de conseguir com a ajuda do computador. Duplicamos as pás em diferentes posições e acrescentamos várias linhas brancas entre elas. Aplicamos ao conjunto um efeito de desfocagem gaussiana.

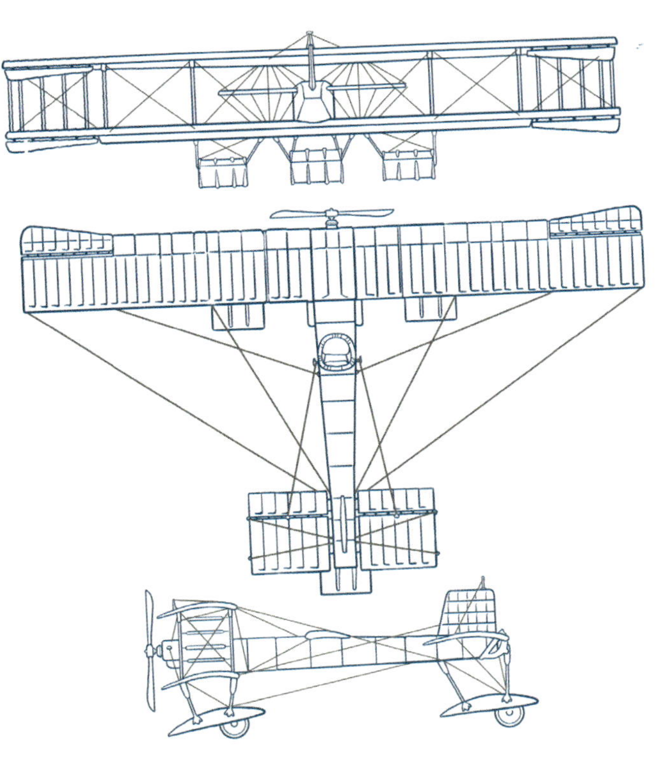

# Voisin Canard

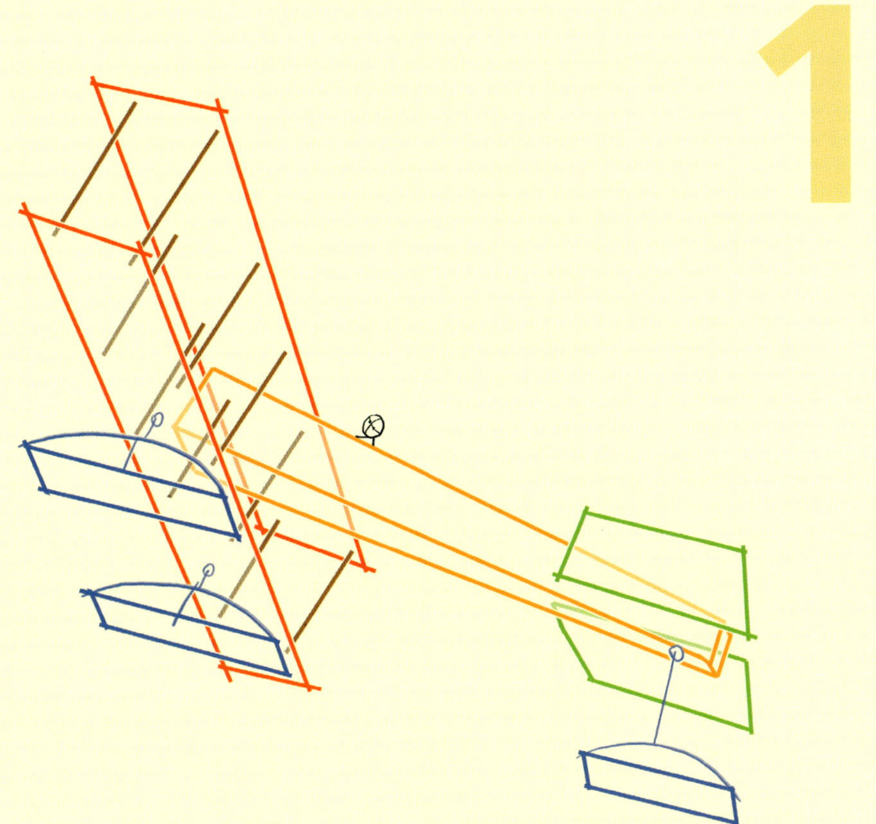

1

Start the plane by outlining simple geometric shapes that enable you to make a mental note of the structure, allowing you to draw it by heart from any perspective.

Le fait de commencer le dessin de l'avion avec un schéma composé de figures géométriques simples vous permet de garder à l'esprit sa structure et de pouvoir facilement le dessiner de mémoire depuis n'importe quelle perspective.

Zu Beginn werden einige geometrische Formen gezeichnet, um die Grundstruktur des Flugzeugs zu verdeutlichen. Dadurch wird das Zeichnen aus dem Kopf aus unterschiedlichen Perspektiven enorm erleichtert.

Begin het vliegtuig met een schema van eenvoudige geometrische figuren waardoor we mentaal de structuur ervan kunnen onthouden en het gemakkelijker is om het vliegtuig vanuit welk perspectief dan ook uit ons hoofd te tekenen.

Comenzar el avión con un esquema de figuras geométricas sencillas nos permite retener mentalmente su estructura y nos facilitará dibujarlo de memoria desde cualquier perspectiva.

Cominciare l'aeroplano con uno schema costituito da figure geometriche semplici ci permette di imprimere nella mente la struttura e ci consente di disegnarlo a memoria da ogni prospettiva.

Começar o avião com um esquema de figuras geométricas simples permite-nos reter mentalmente a sua estrutura e facilitar-nos-á desenhá-lo de memória de qualquer perspectiva.

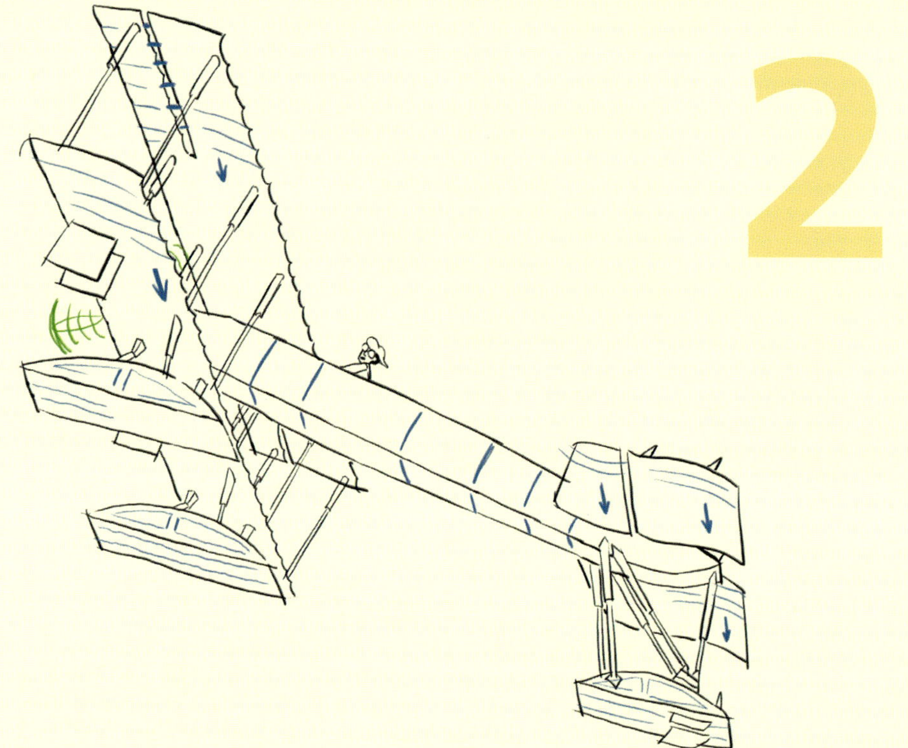

# 2

If you are in a hurry to finish the drawing, why not make a detailed sketch that serves as penciling? If there are repeated features, it will not be necessary to draw all of them. Add a mark (blue arrows) making it clear which concept will be followed.

Si vous devez finir rapidement un dessin, vous pouvez prendre le risque de réaliser une ébauche détaillée qui vous servira de crayonné. Si des éléments se répètent, il n'est pas nécessaire de tous les dessiner. Il suffit d'ajouter un signe (des flèches bleues) mettant en évidence le concept à suivre.

Wenn Sie eine Zeichnung besonders schnell fertigstellen möchten, können Sie eine detaillierte Skizze erstellen, die gleichzeitig als Buntstiftzeichnung dient. Sich wiederholende Elemente müssen nicht in ihrer gesamten Anzahl eingezeichnet werden. Durch Hinzufügen eines Symbols (blaue Pfeile) wird angezeigt, welche Elemente sich wiederholen.

Als je haast hebt om een tekening af te ronden, neem dan risico's en maak een gedetailleerde schets die als potloodtekening fungeert. Als er elementen worden herhaald hoeven ze niet allemaal getekend te worden. Voeg een signaal (blauwe pijlen) toe waardoor het te volgen concept duidelijk wordt.

Si tienes prisa por acabar un dibujo, arriésgate a realizar un boceto detallado que sirva como lápiz. Si hay elementos repetidos, no es necesario dibujarlos todos. Añadiremos una señal (flechas azules) que nos deje claro el concepto que debemos seguir.

Se vuoi terminare in fretta un disegno, prova a realizzare un bozzetto dettagliato invece delle matite di base. Se vi sono elementi ripetuti non è necessario disegnarli tutti. Aggiungeremo un simbolo (frecce blu) che chiarisce il concetto da ripetere.

Se tens pressa em acabar um desenho, arrisca-te a realizar um esboço detalhado que sirva como lápis. Se há elementos repetidos, não é necessário desenhá-los todos. Acrescentaremos um sinal (setas azuis) q ue nos deixe claro o conceito a seguir.

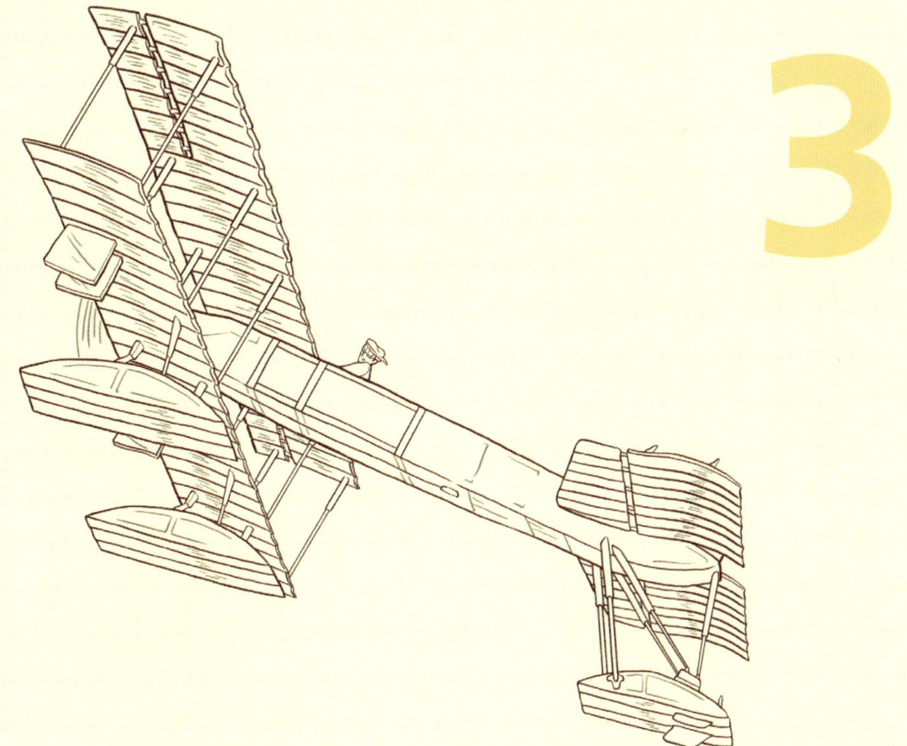

3

The inking is soft and done freehand to avoid giving the sense of rigidity, except for the wing struts, which should give a greater impression of strength.

L'encrage léger est réalisé à main levée afin d'éviter toute sensation de solidité ou de technologie, excepté pour les bâtons qui soutiennent les ailes, sensés apporter une plus grande impression de robustesse.

Die Tuschezeichnung mit sanfter Strichführung wurde frei Hand erstellt, um eine zu starre und technische Wirkung zu vermeiden. Nur die Verbindungsstangen zwischen den Tragflächen vermitteln Robustheit und Stärke.

De inkttekening is zacht en met de hand omhoog uitgewerkt om een te stijve of technologische indruk te vermijden, behalve bij de stokken die de vleugels ondersteunen. Deze geven een gevoel van stevigheid.

La tinta es suave y ha sido realizada a mano alzada para evitar una sensación demasiado rígida o tecnológica, excepto en los bastones que sostienen las alas, que pretenden dar una mayor sensación de firmeza.

Il ripasso a china è leggero e si realizza a mano libera per evitare una sensazione troppo rigida o tecnologica, tranne che nei montanti che sostengono le ali, i quali devono trasmettere una sensazione di maggior fermezza.

A tinta é suave e foi realizada à mão livre para evitar uma sensação demasiado rígida ou tecnológica, excepto nos bastões que sustentam as asas, que pretendem dar uma maior sensação de firmeza.

4

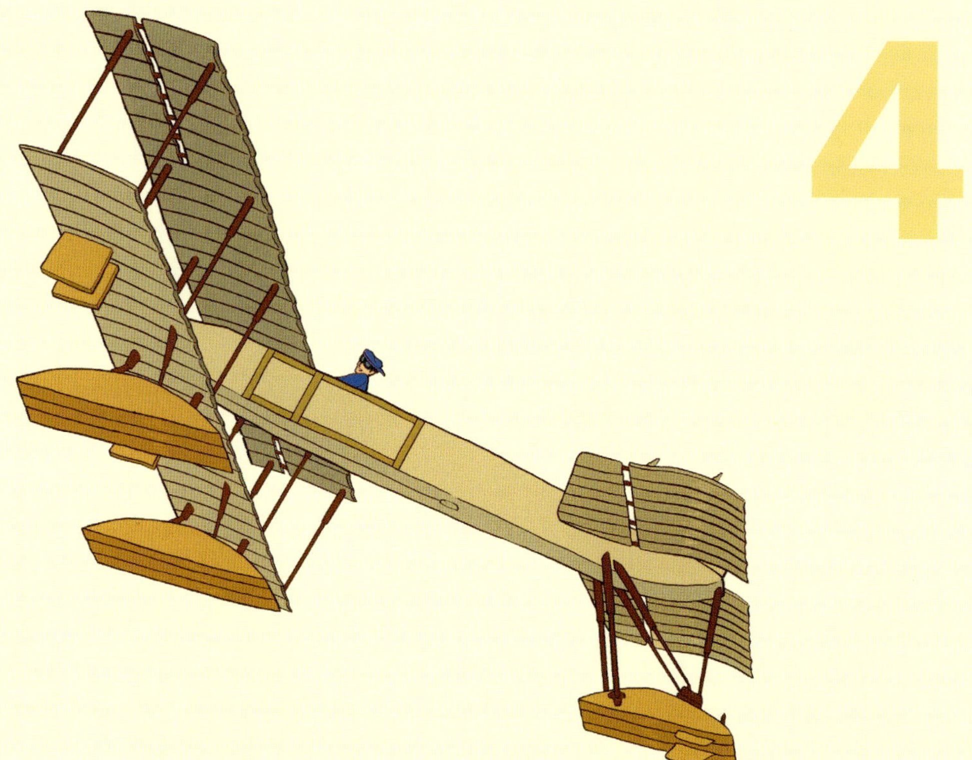

The base colors for this airplane are also brown and orange shades, highlighting its low-tech nature. The different hues also add volume, marking the each of the different surface planes with regard to the sun.

Les couleurs de base de cet avion sont également marron et orangé, peu technologiques. Les nuances de chaque couleur apportent du volume en distinguant les différents plans de chaque surface par rapport au sol.

Bei den grundlegenden Farben dieses Flugzeugs handelt es sich ebenfalls um Braun- und Orangetöne, die wenig technologischen Fortschritt vermitteln. Die einzelnen Farbabstufungen verleihen der Zeichnung Volumen und kennzeichnen die einzelnen Ebenen hinsichtlich der Sonneneinstrahlung.

De basiskleuren van dit vliegtuig, eveneens bruin en oranje, zijn niet al te technologisch. De verschillende kleurschakeringen zorgen voor volume en markeren de diverse vlakken van elk oppervlakte ten opzichte van de zon.

Los colores base de este avión son también marrones y naranjas, poco tecnológicos. Los diferentes matices de cada color aportan volumen, marcando los distintos planos de cada superficie respecto al sol.

Anche in questo aereo i colori di base sono il marrone e l'arancio, poco tecnologici. Le diverse sfumature di ogni colore aggiungono volume, evidenziando i diversi piani di ciascuna superficie rispetto al sole.

As cores base deste avião são também castanhos e laranjas, pouco tecnológicos. As diferentes tonalidades de cada cor dão volume, definindo os diferentes planos de cada superfície em relação ao sol.

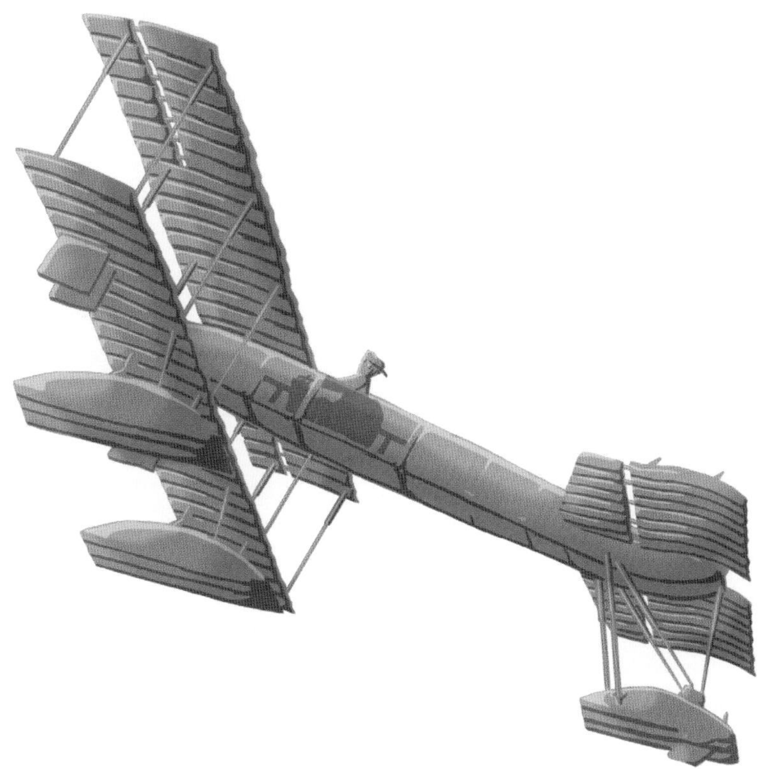

5

Keeping the light source at the front, the lighting and shading add visual impact, representing the volume formed for each wing segment and the floats.

Grâce à l'éclairage frontal, les ombres et les lumières confèrent un bel impact visuel au dessin et donnent du volume à chaque segment des ailes et des flotteurs.

Durch das Licht von vorne verleihen die Licht- und Schattenbereiche der Zeichnung mehr Tiefe. Auf diese Weise wird das Volumen jedes einzelnen Segments an Tragflächen und Schwimmern unterstrichen.

Met de lichtbron aan de voorkant, zorgen licht en schaduwen voor opzichtigheid en beelden zij het volume uit dat op elk segment van de vleugels en de drijvers wordt gevormd.

Teniendo el foco de luz al frente, las luces y sombras aportan vistosidad, representando el volumen que se forma en cada segmento de las alas y los flotadores.

Tenendo la sorgente luminosa di fronte, le luci e le ombre creano vistosità, rappresentando il volume che si forma in ogni segmento delle ali e dei galleggianti.

Tendo o foco de luz à frente, as luzes e as sombras chamam à atenção, representando o volume que se forma em cada segmento das asas e dos flutuadores.

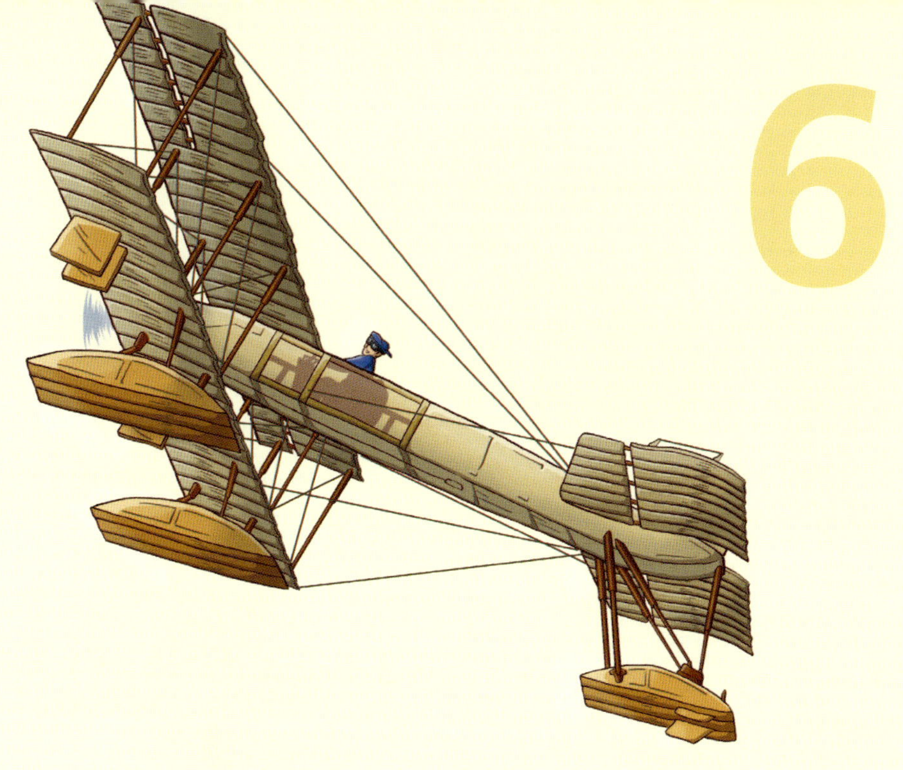

6

Two small details have been added to the finished drawing on separate layers: the bracing cables and the propeller. These details could have been added at any time during the previous steps.

Deux petits détails ont été ajoutés sur le dessin final en couches séparées : les câbles de tension et l'hélice. Ces détails auraient pu être intégrés lors des étapes précédentes.

Die fertige Zeichnung wird in separaten Ebenen mit zwei weiteren Details versehen – den Spannkabeln und dem Propeller. Diese Einzelheiten hätten auch problemlos in einem der vorhergehenden Schritte eingefügt werden können.

Aan de afgeronde tekening zijn in aparte lagen twee kleine details toegevoegd: de spankabels en de propeller. Deze details zouden ook op elk moment van de voorgaande fases kunnen zijn toegevoegd.

Al dibujo acabado se le han añadido dos pequeños detalles en capas aparte: los cables de tensión y la hélice. Estos detalles podrían haberse añadido también en cualquier momento de las fases anteriores.

Al disegno finito sono stati aggiunti due piccoli dettagli su livelli separati: i tiranti e l'elica. Questi dettagli potrebbero essere stati aggiunti anche in qualsiasi momento durante le fasi precedenti.

Ao desenho acabado acrescentaram-se dois pequenos detalhes em camadas à parte: os cabos de tensão e a hélice. Estes detalhes poderiam ter-se acrescentado também em qualquer momento das fases anteriores.

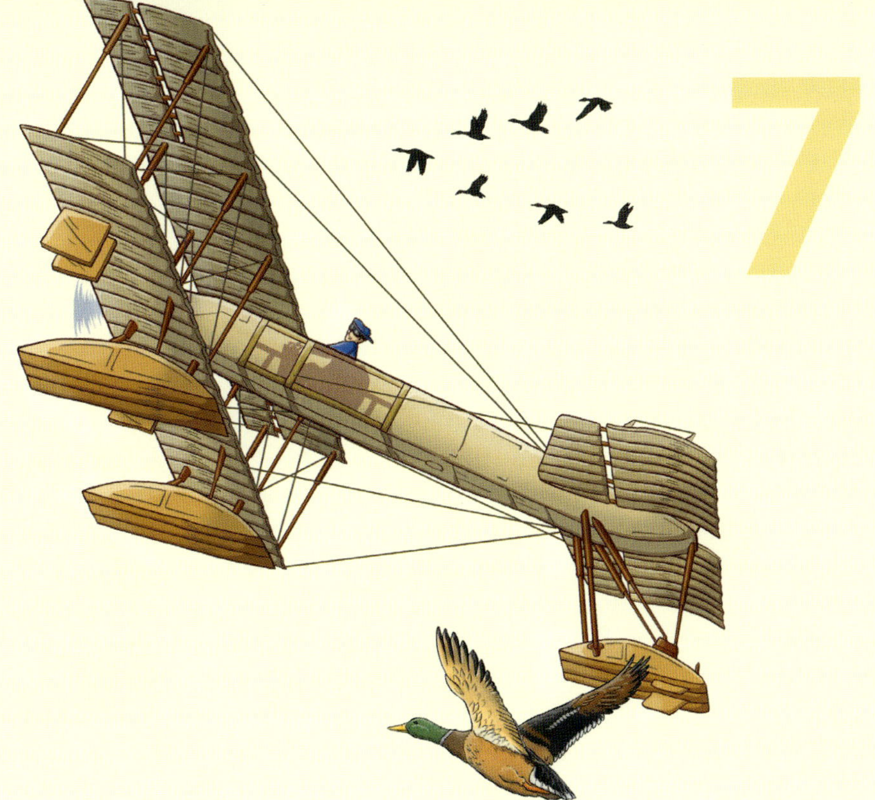


The extra in this exercise is a trick for the reader, playing on the name of the plane, to show that with a few features you can create a story that might have been true at some point in the past.

L'extra de cet exercice est une plaisanterie destinée au lecteur, un jeu de mot avec le nom de l'avion, afin de montrer qu'il est possible de créer une histoire avec très peu d'éléments, une histoire qui aurait pu se produire dans le passé.

Bei dieser Übung wurde als Anspielung auf den Namen des Flugzeugs ein witziges Extra eingefügt. Dadurch wird verdeutlicht, dass schon durch ein paar kleine Details eine ganze Geschichte entstehen kann, die sich möglicherweise sogar in der Vergangenheit so ereignet hat.

De toegift van deze oefening is een grap waarbij gespeeld wordt met de naam van het vliegtuig, om de lezer te laten zien dat er met weinig elementen een verhaal kan worden gecreëerd dat, wellicht, in het verleden ooit werkelijkheid geweest zou kunnen zijn.

El extra de este ejercicio es una broma al lector, jugando con el nombre del avión, para mostrar que con pocos elementos podemos crear una historia, que, quizá, pudo haber sido realidad en algún momento del pasado.

L'extra di questo esercizio è una strizzatina d'occhio al lettore: giocando con il nome dell'aereo, si dimostra che con pochi elementi possiamo creare una storia, la quale magari può anche essere successa nel passato...

O extra deste exercício é uma brincadeira para o leitor, brincando com o nome do avião, para mostrar que com poucos elementos podemos criar uma história, que, quem sabe, pode ter sido realidade nalgum momento do passado.

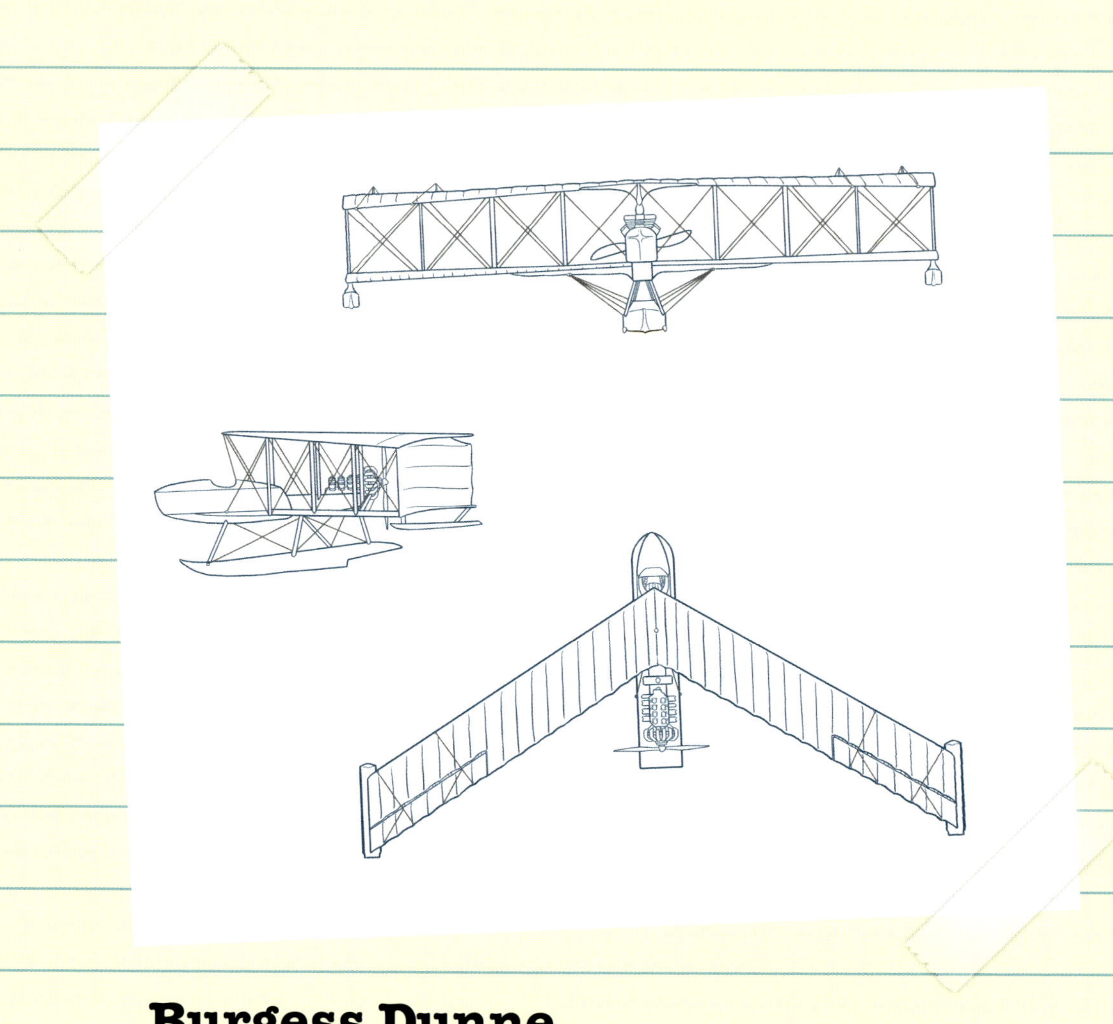

# Burgess Dunne

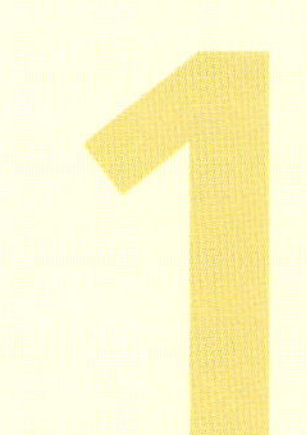

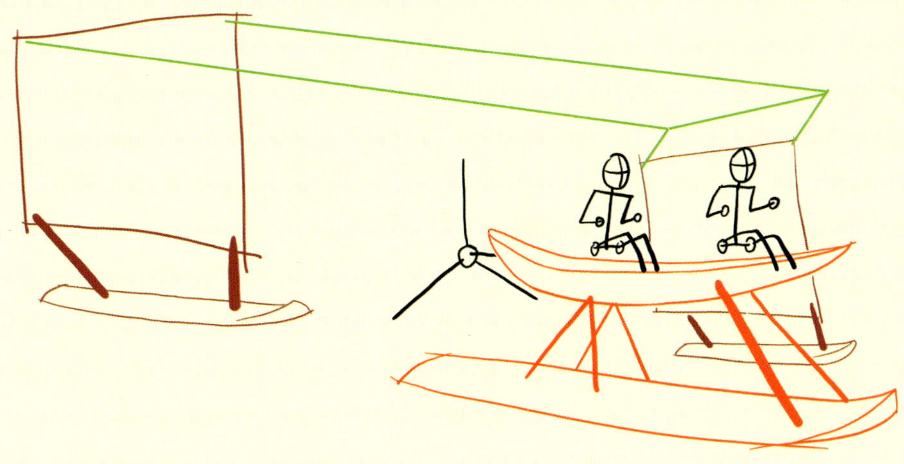

Making as simple a skeleton as possible will help you achieve a good placement of the elements of this aircraft, but feel free to add any details that you picture clearly in your mind.

Réaliser un squelette aussi simple que possible permet de bien placer les différentes parties. Toutefois, n'hésitez pas à détailler davantage les éléments qui vous sont familiers.

Durch das Zeichnen eines möglichst vereinfachten Skeletts kann man die einzelnen Elemente richtig positionieren. Wenn Sie bestimmte Merkmale vor ihrem geistigen Auge bereits klarer sehen, können Sie diese ruhig etwas detaillierter einzeichnen.

Het maken van een zo simpel mogelijk ontwerp helpt om een goede positie van de elementen te bereiken, maar je bent vrij om de elementen die je je duidelijker voorstelt gedetailleerder te tekenen.

Realizar un esqueleto lo más simple posible nos ayuda a conseguir una buena situación de los elementos, pero debes sentirte libre de darle más detalle a aquellos elementos que veas más claros en tu mente.

Realizzare uno scheletro il più semplice possibile ci aiuta ad ottenere una buona ubicazione degli elementi. Tuttavia, devi sentirti libero di dettagliare di più gli elementi che vedi in modo più chiaro nella tua mente.

Realizar um esqueleto o mais simples possível ajuda-nos a conseguir uma boa posição dos elementos, mas deves sentir-te livre para dar mais detalhe àqueles elementos que vejas mais claros na tua mente.

2

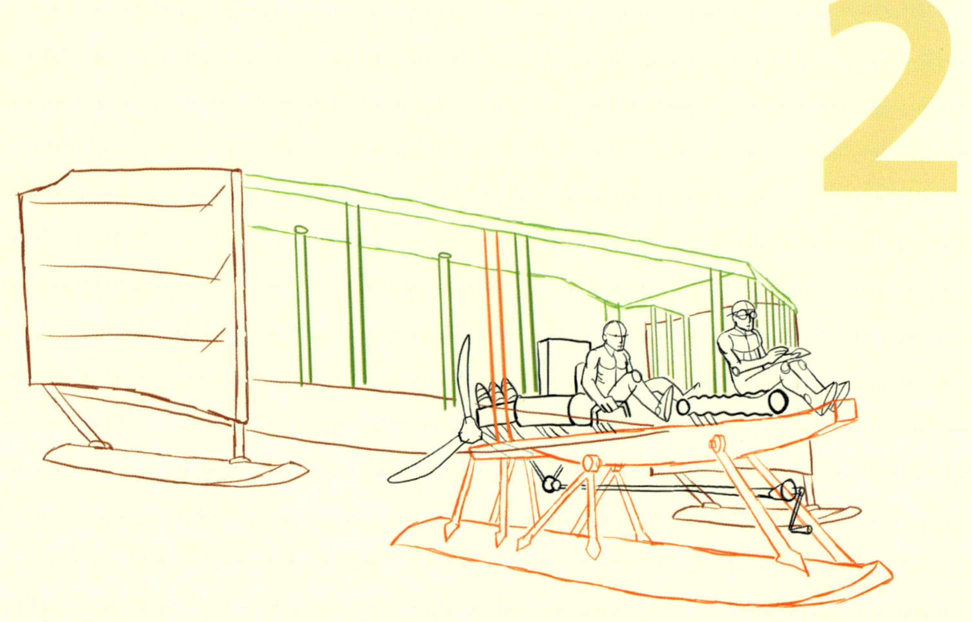

Some elements are incorporated into the outline in more detail. Others are simply empty spaces where several elements will go. Although it is an outline, erase and repeat any elements that you are not sure of.

Certains éléments sont intégrés au schéma de façon détaillée. D'autres sont des espaces vides qui pourront contenir des ajouts ultérieurs. Bien qu'il s'agisse d'un simple schéma, n'hésitez pas à effacer et recommencer les éléments qui ne vous conviennent pas.

Nun werden einige Bildelemente im Detail hinzugefügt. Andere Elemente, die aus mehreren Bauteilen bestehen, halten zunächst einmal den erforderlichen Platz im Bild frei. Auch wenn es sich nur um eine Schemazeichnung handelt, sollten Sie einzelne Elemente, die Sie nicht überzeugen, ausradieren und neu skizzieren.

Sommige elementen worden in detail in het schema opgenomen. Andere dienen er uitsluitend voor om ruimte te reserveren waarin later diverse onderdelen zullen worden getekend. Het gaat om een schema, maar desgewenst kun je de componenten waarvan je niet overtuigd bent uitwissen en herhalen.

Algunos elementos se incorporan al esquema de forma detallada. Otros son meras reservas de espacio, en las que incorporaremos varias piezas. Aunque sea un esquema, borra y repite los componentes que no te convenzan.

Alcuni elementi sono stati incorporati nello schema in modo molto dettagliato. Altri sono semplici demarcazioni di spazi in cui inseriremo varie parti. Benché si tratti di uno schema, cancella e ripeti le parti che non ti convincono del tutto.

Alguns elementos incorporam-se ao esquema de forma detalhada. Outros são meras reservas de espaço, nas quais incorporaremos várias peças. Embora seja um esquema, apaga e repete os componentes que não te convençam.

# 3

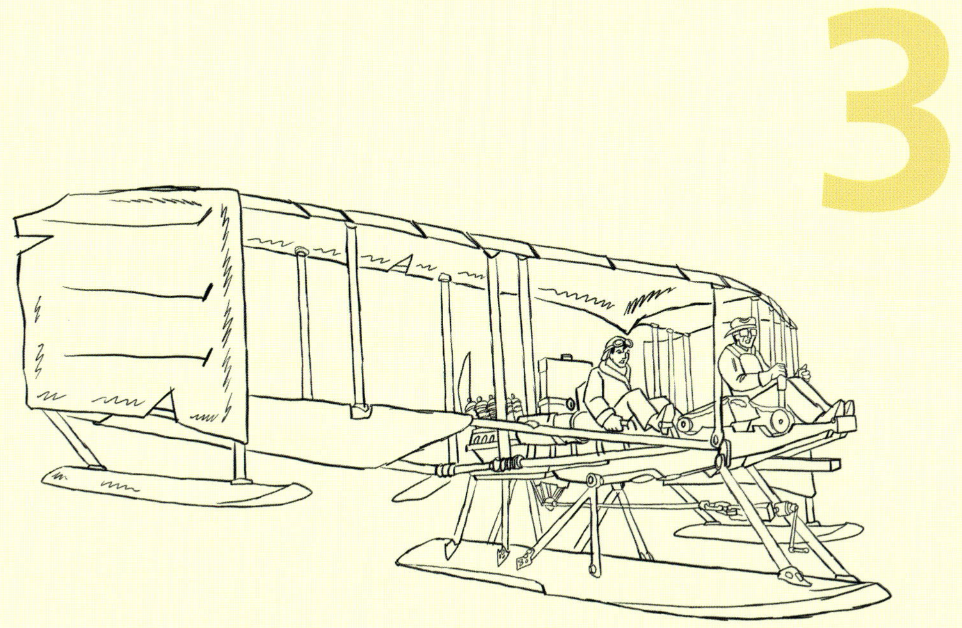

When you feel that an illustration will be complex, it is best to make a sketch knowing that you can improve it during the penciling step. Treat it like a simulation that prepares you to achieve quality penciling.

Lorsque vous sentez qu'une illustration sera compliquée, il convient de faire une ébauche avant de l'améliorer avec le crayonné. Cette simulation vous permet de préparer un crayonné de meilleure qualité.

Wenn man ahnt, dass sich eine Zeichnung kompliziert gestalten wird, sollte man zunächst eine Skizze anfertigen, die anschließend mithilfe von Buntstiften ausgearbeitet wird. Dabei handelt es sich um eine gute Übung, die als Vorbereitung für eine qualitativ ausreichende Buntstiftzeichnung dient.

Wanneer we aanvoelen dat een illustratie ingewikkeld wordt, is het beter om een schets te maken waarvan we weten dat die hij later in de potloodtekening beter zal worden uitgewerkt. Het is als een schijnhandeling die ons voorbereidt op een kwalitatief goede potloodtekening.

Cuando intuimos que una ilustración nos va a resultar complicada es mejor hacer un boceto sabiendo que después se mejorará con el lápiz. Es como un simulacro que nos prepara para obtener un lápiz con calidad suficiente.

Quando intuiamo che un'illustrazione ci risulta difficile, è meglio eseguire un bozzetto sapendo che in seguito lo si migliorerà nella fase a matita. È come una simulazione che ci prepara ad ottenere delle matite della qualità sufficiente.

Quando intuímos que uma ilustração se vai tornar complicada é melhor fazer um esboço sabendo que depois será melhorada com o lápis. É como um simulacro que nos prepara para obter um lápis com qualidade suficiente.

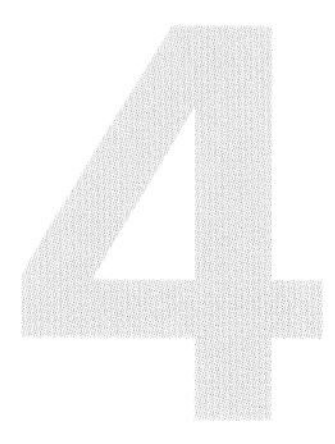

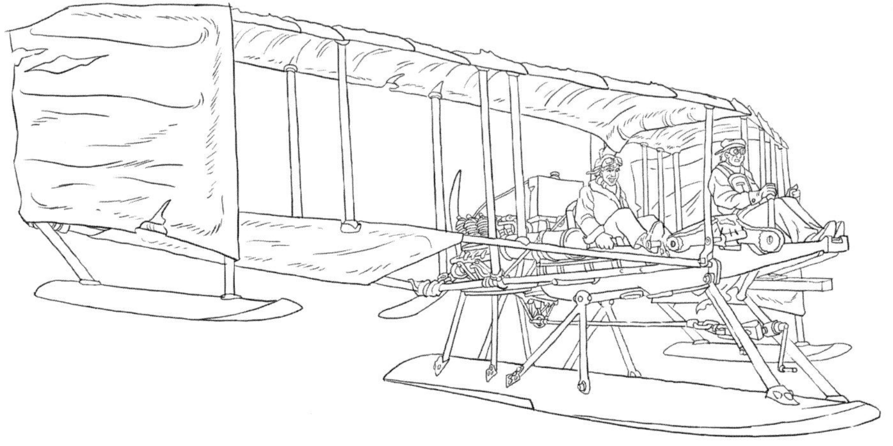

Making a good sketch will improve the quality of your penciling. Doing the first steps properly means creating a good base which, like the foundations of a building, provides a solid framework even if it is not seen.

Réaliser une bonne ébauche vous permettra d'accroître la qualité de votre crayonné. Pour exécuter correctement les premières étapes, il convient de mettre en place une base solide, semblable aux fondements d'un édifice, qui, même invisible, procurera de la solidité à la structure.

Durch eine gute Skizze wird die Qualität der anschließenden Buntstiftzeichnung verbessert. Wenn Sie die ersten Zeichenschritte gewissenhaft ausführen, schaffen Sie eine hervorragende Grundlage für die spätere Darstellung – gleich einem unsichtbaren Fundament, das dem darauf errichteten Gebäude Festigkeit und Widerstandskraft verleiht.

Een goede schets verbetert de kwaliteit van onze potloodtekening. De eerste fases goed uitwerken betekent de creatie van een goede basis die, net als de fundering van een goed gebouw, de structuur, ook al is dit niet te zien, stevigheid verleent.

Realizar un buen boceto mejorará la calidad de nuestro lápiz. Hacer correctamente las primeras fases supone crear una buena base que, como los cimientos de un buen edificio, está ahí dando solidez a la estructura aunque no se vea.

Realizzare un buon bozzetto migliorerà la qualità delle nostre matite. Svolgere correttamente le prime fasi significa porre delle buone basi che, come le fondamenta di un edificio, conferiscono solidità alla struttura anche se non si vedono.

Realizar um bom esboço melhorará a qualidade do nosso lápis. Realizar correctamente as primeiras fases pressupõe criar uma boa base que, como os alicerces de um bom edifício, existe para dar solidez à estrutura embora não se veja.

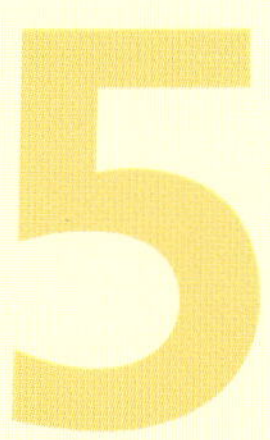

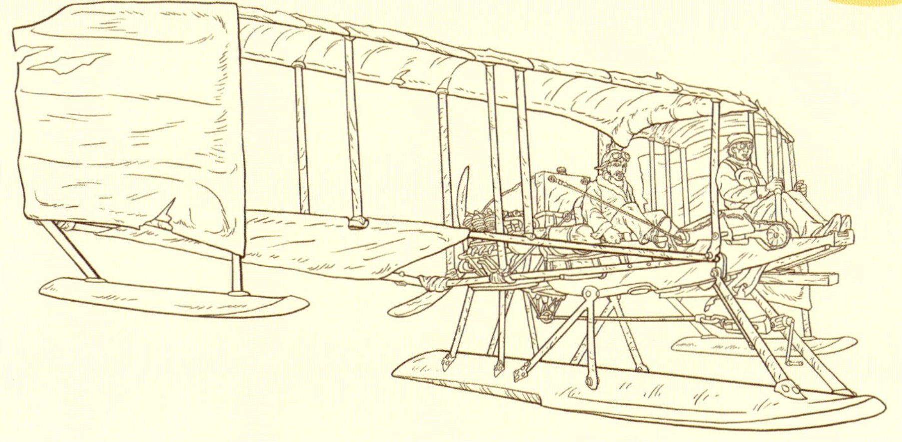

Here the inking is a good example of what it should be: an ordered revision of the penciling with the addition or removal of small details, depending on the creative freedom of the inker.

Vous avez ici un très bon exemple de ce que doit être un encrage : une révision ordonnée du crayonné, supposant l'ajout ou la suppression de certains détails, en accord avec la liberté créative de l'artiste.

In diesem Fall ist die Tuschezeichnung ein klares Beispiel dafür, wie dieser Arbeitsschritt aussehen sollte: Die Buntstiftzeichnung wurde überarbeitet und einige Kleinigkeiten wurden unter Berücksichtigung der künstlerischen Freiheit des Zeichners hinzugefügt bzw. gelöscht.

In dit geval is de inkttekening een duidelijk voorbeeld van wat ingekleurd moet worden: een herziening van de potloodtekening met de toevoeging of verwijdering van een klein detail, overeenkomstig de creatieve vrijheid van degene die inkleurt.

En este caso, la tinta es un ejemplo claro de lo que debe ser un entintado: revisión ordenada del lápiz con el añadido o la eliminación de algún pequeño detalle, de acuerdo a la libertad creativa del entintador.

In questo caso, le chine sono un chiaro esempio di quello che dovrebbe essere un ripasso a china: una revisione ordinata delle matite con l'aggiunta o l'eliminazione di qualche piccolo dettaglio, secondo la libertà creativa dell'inchiostratore.

Neste caso, a tinta é um exemplo claro do que deve ser uma arte-final: revisão ordenada do lápis com o acrescento ou a eliminação dalgum pequeno detalhe, de acordo com a liberdade criativa do arte-finalista.

# 6

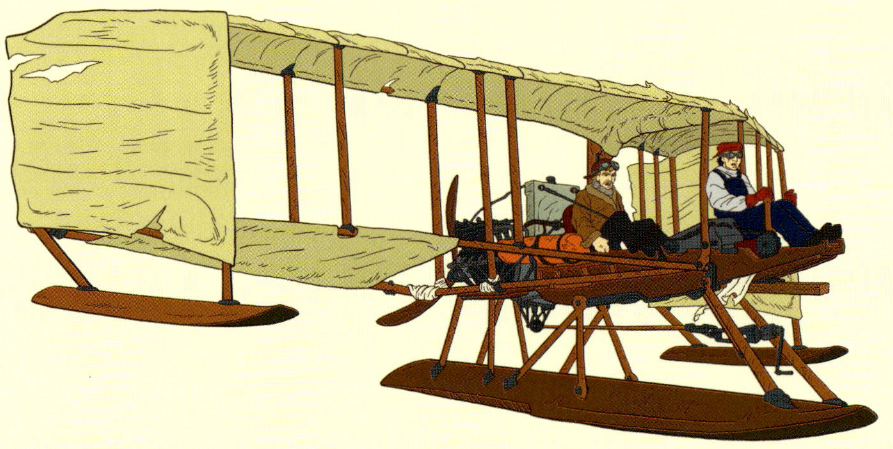

As the base colors of the skids and gondola are darker, they indicate greater solidity. The light colors of the wings show their fragility. Cold colors are used for metal parts.

Les couleurs de base des patins et de la nacelle, plus foncées, dénotent une grande solidité. Les ailes présentent une couleur plus claire reflétant leur fragilité. Les parties métalliques sont dotées de couleurs froides.

Die dunkleren Grundfarben der Schwimmer und der Gondel vermitteln Robustheit. Die Tragflächen werden heller gestaltet und wirken daher zerbrechlicher. Für Metallteile werden kalte Farben verwendet.

De basiskleuren van de drijvers en de gondel, die donkerder zijn, duiden op meer stevigheid. De vleugels hebben een lichtere kleur die op breekbaarheid duidt. Voor de metalen delen worden kille kleuren gebruikt.

Los colores base de los patines y la góndola, al ser más oscuros, indican mayor solidez. Las alas muestran un color más claro que indica fragilidad. En las partes metálicas se utilizan colores fríos.

I colori di base dei pattini e della gondola, essendo più scuri, indicano maggiore solidità. Le ali presentano un colore più chiaro che indica fragilità. Per le parti metalliche vengono usati colori freddi.

As cores base dos flutuadores e da gôndola, ao serem mais escuras, indicam maior solidez. As asas mostram uma cor mais clara que indica fragilidade. Nas partes metálicas utilizam-se cores frias.

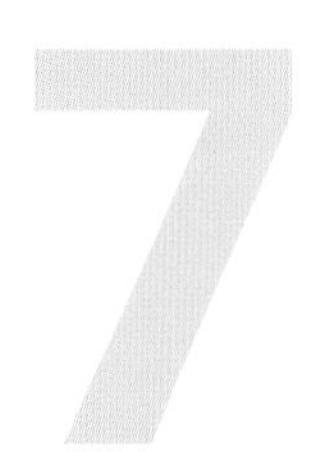

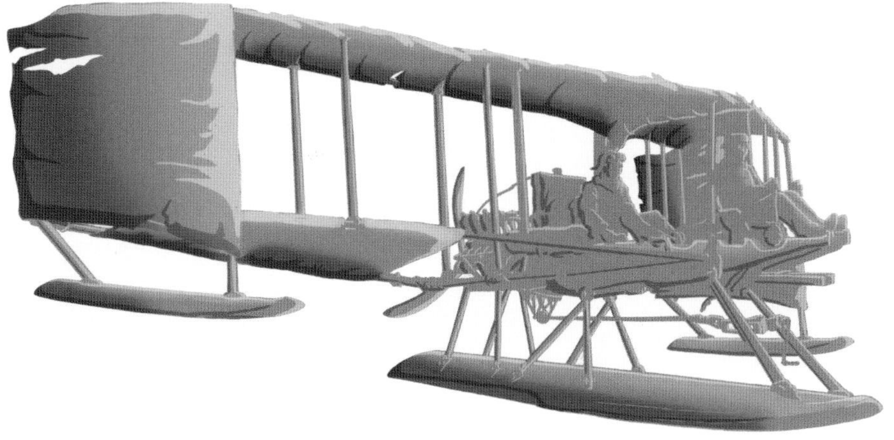

The lighting is provided on a single layer of whites with reduced opacity, representing the raised light source. Shading on two black layers with different levels of opacity add a dramatic touch to the scene.

Les lumières, réalisées avec une seule couche de blanc, faiblement opaques, mettent en évidence une source zénithale. Les ombres, réalisées sur deux couches de noir de différentes opacités, confèrent à la scène un aspect dramatique.

Die Lichtbereiche werden mithilfe einer Schicht Weiß mit leichter Transparenz eingearbeitet und zeigen die hohe Position der Lichtquelle. Die Schattenbereiche in zwei unterschiedlich transparenten schwarzen Ebenen verleihen der Szene eine besondere Dramatik.

Het licht is een enkele laag wit met een beperkte ondoorschijnendheid aangebracht en beeldt de verhoogde plaatsing van de lichtbron uit. De schaduwen, in twee lagen zwart met een verschillende ondoorschijnendheid, geven de scène een dramatisch karakter.

Las luces se han dado con una sola capa de blancos a opacidad reducida y representan la situación elevada del foco de luz. Las sombras, en dos capas de negro a distinta opacidad, aportan dramatismo a la escena.

Le luci sono state date con un solo livello di bianco a opacità ridotta e rappresentano la posizione elevata della sorgente luminosa. Le ombre, in due livelli di nero con diversa opacità, aggiungono drammaticità alla scena.

As luzes deram-se apenas com uma camada de brancos com opacidade reduzida e representam a colocação elevada do foco de luz. As sombras, em duas camadas de preto com diferente opacidade, concedem dramatismo à cena.

# 8

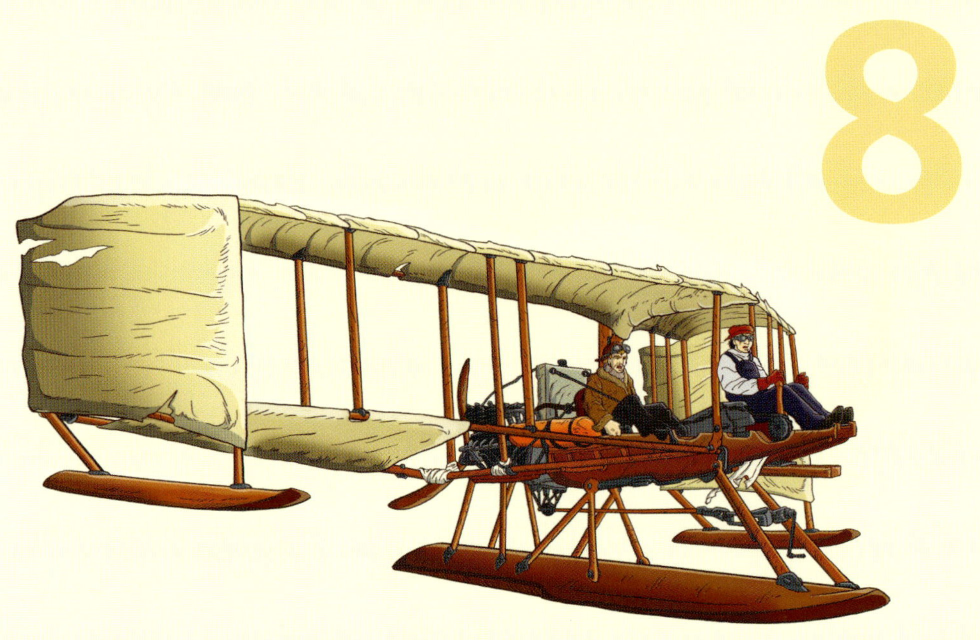

When uniting all the steps in a single image, you can see that everything fits very well, offering a colorful appearance with the tension provided by the darkness auguring a tragic outcome.

Toutes les phases, rassemblées sur une seule image, se combinent parfaitement, avec un aspect coloré contrasté par la tension de l'obscurité qui présage un dénouement fatal.

Bei der Verbindung aller Arbeitsschritte in einem einzigen Bild wird deutlich, dass alles gut zusammenpasst. Das Bild wirkt farbenfroh und gleichzeitig herrscht durch die dunklen Bereiche eine gewisse Spannung, die ein tragisches Ende des Flugversuchs vorhersagt.

Door alle fasen in één afbeelding samen te voegen zien we dat ze goed in elkaar passen en een kleurig aspect ontstaat, maar met de spanning van het duister dat een fatale afloop voorspelt.

Al unir todas las fases en una sola imagen vemos que encajan muy bien, dando un aspecto colorido, pero con la tensión de la oscuridad presagiando un desenlace fatal.

Unendo tutte le fasi in una sola immagine, vediamo che combaciano molto bene, dando un aspetto vivace, però con la tensione dell'oscurità che preannuncia un esito fatale.

Ao unir todas as fases numa só imagem vemos que encaixam muito bem, dando um aspecto colorido, mas com a tensão da obscuridade pressagiando um desenlace fatal.

# 9

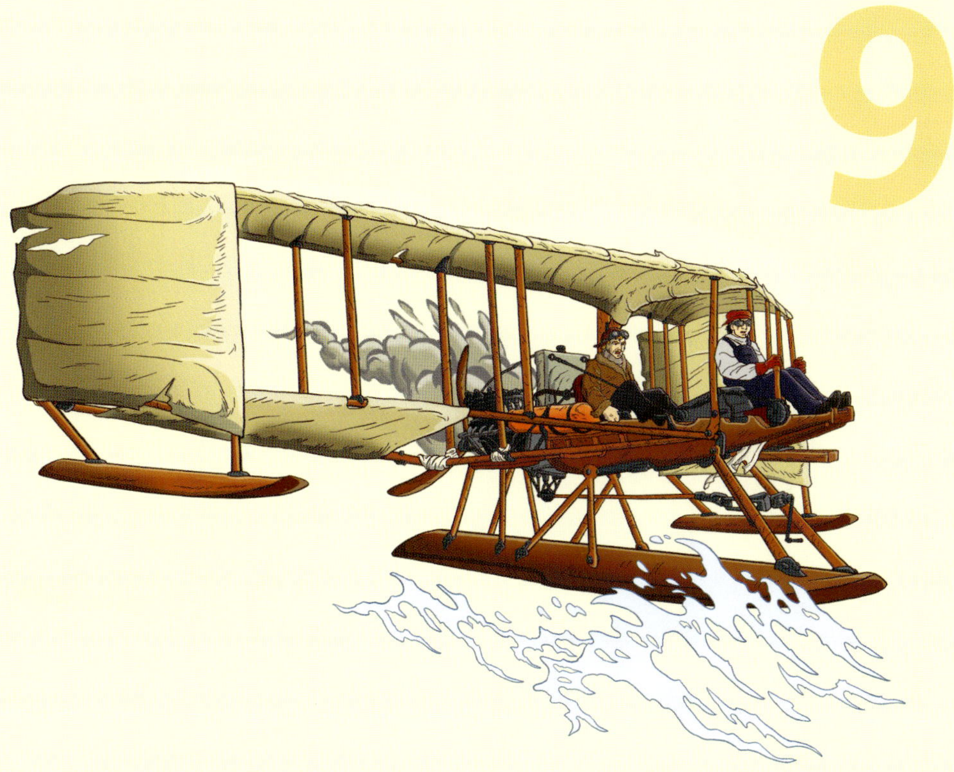

Minimum details in the setting help to tell a story. With the addition of a little swell and a the smoke from an explosion, the reader is almost compelled to imagine what happened in the lead up and what will take place in the following instants.

La création d'un contexte, aussi sommaire soit-il, permet de raconter une histoire. Avec une légère houle et une explosion de fumée, le lecteur peut imaginer ce qui vient de se passer et ce qui est sur le point de se produire.

Schon wenige Einzelheiten helfen dabei, mit einem Bild eine ganze Geschichte zu erzählen. Einige Wellen und eine Explosion mit Rauchentwicklung bringen den Betrachter dazu, sich vorzustellen, was zuvor gerade passiert ist und was sich in den nächsten Augenblicken ereignen wird.

Een minimale uitwerking van de omgeving helpt een verhaal te vertellen. Met wat golven en een walmende explosie wordt de lezer ertoe gezet om zich voor te stellen wat ervoor is gebeurd en wat er dadelijk gaat gebeuren.

Un mínimo entorno ayuda a contar una historia. Con un poco de oleaje y una humeante explosión, el lector se ve casi obligado a imaginar qué ha ocurrido en los momentos anteriores y qué ocurrirá durante los próximos instantes.

Un'ambientazione minima aiuta a raccontare una storia. Con un po' di onde e un'esplosione fumosa, il lettore è quasi costretto a immaginare che cosa è successo nei momenti precedenti e che cosa accadrà in quelli successivi.

Um mínimo ambiente ajuda a contar uma história. Com um pouco de ondulação e uma fumegante explosão, o leitor vê-se quase obrigado a imaginar o que ocorreu nos momentos anteriores e o que ocorrerá durante os próximos instantes.

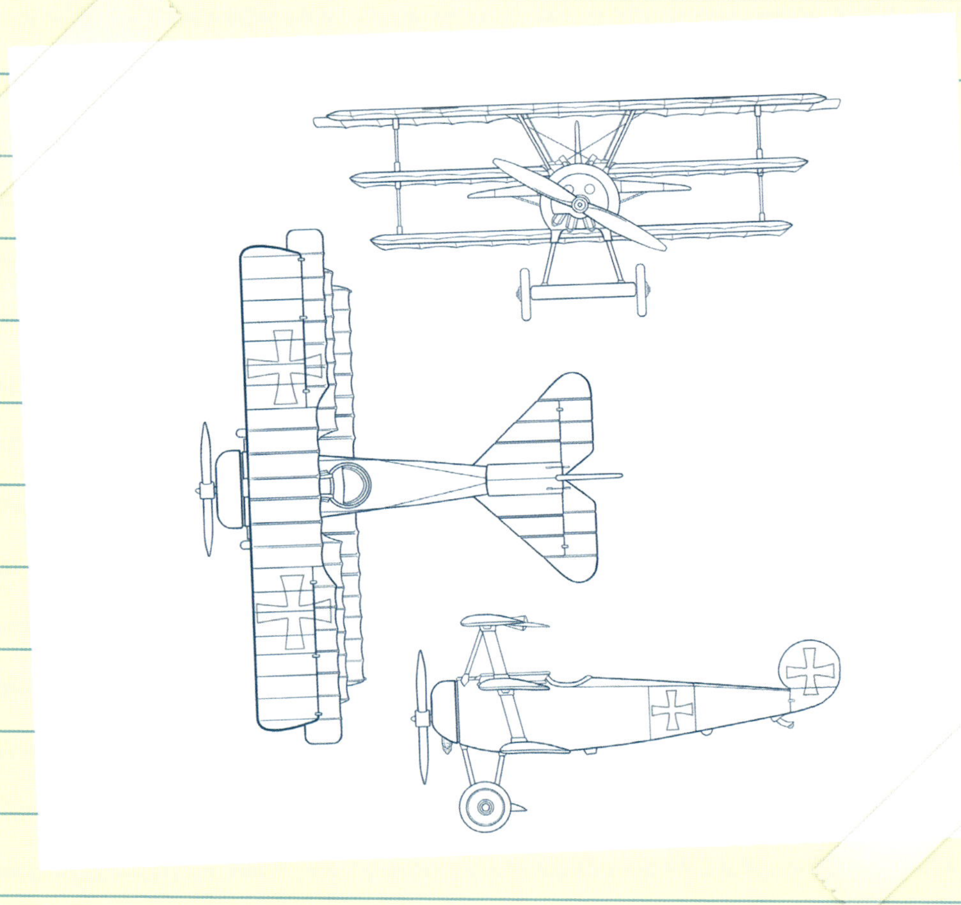

# Fokker DR 1

# 1

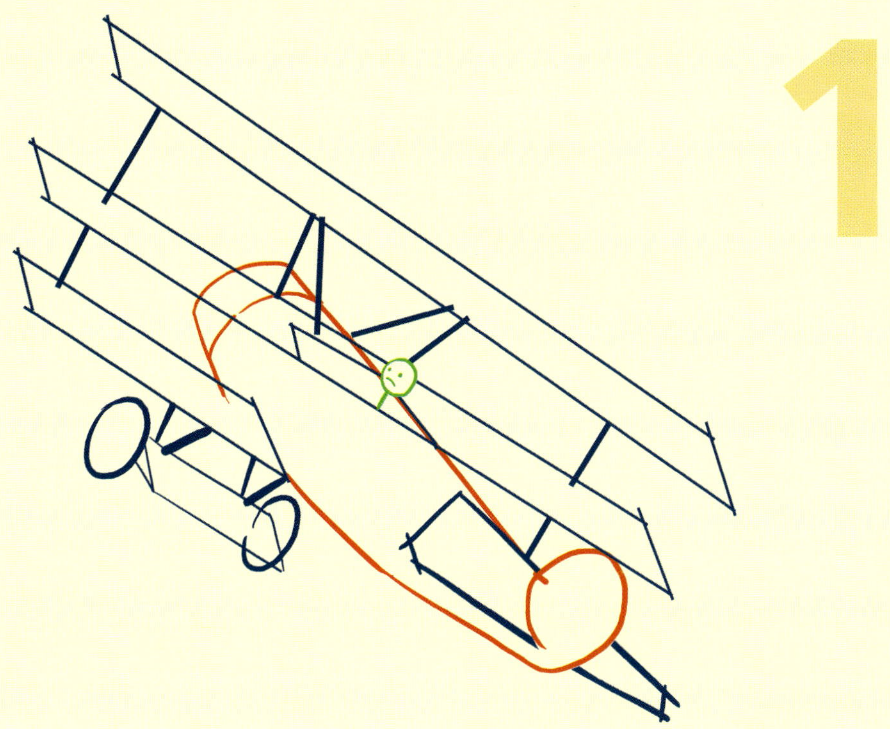

For your outline to work, you should always start with the large parallel planes – the three wings in this case. Positioning the remaining features in relation to them is much simpler than doing it the other way around.

Pour que votre schéma fonctionne, commencez toujours par dessiner les grands plans parallèles, en l'occurrence les trois ailes. Il est ensuite beaucoup plus facile de placer les autres éléments par rapport à ces plans.

Damit die Schemazeichnung richtig wird, sollte man stets mit den großen parallelen Flächen beginnen, wie in diesem Falle mit den drei Tragflächen. Die übrigen Elemente können dann ganz einfach (und erheblich praktischer als umkehrt) rund um diese Grundformen angeordnet werden.

Opdat het schema functioneert, moet altijd begonnen worden bij de grote parallelle vlakken, zoals in dit geval de drie vleugels. De rest van de elementen ten opzichte van elkaar plaatsen is veel gemakkelijker dan andersom.

Para que tu esquema funcione, comienza siempre por los grandes planos paralelos, como en este caso las tres alas. Situar el resto de los elementos respecto a ellos es mucho más sencillo que hacerlo al contrario.

Affinché il tuo schema funzioni, comincia sempre dai piani paralleli più grandi, in questo caso le tre ali. Situare i restanti elementi rispetto a questi è molto più facile che non il contrario.

Para que o teu esquema funcione, começa sempre pelos grandes planos paralelos, como neste caso as três asas. Colocar o resto dos elementos em relação a estes é muito mais simples que fazê-lo ao contrário.

# 2

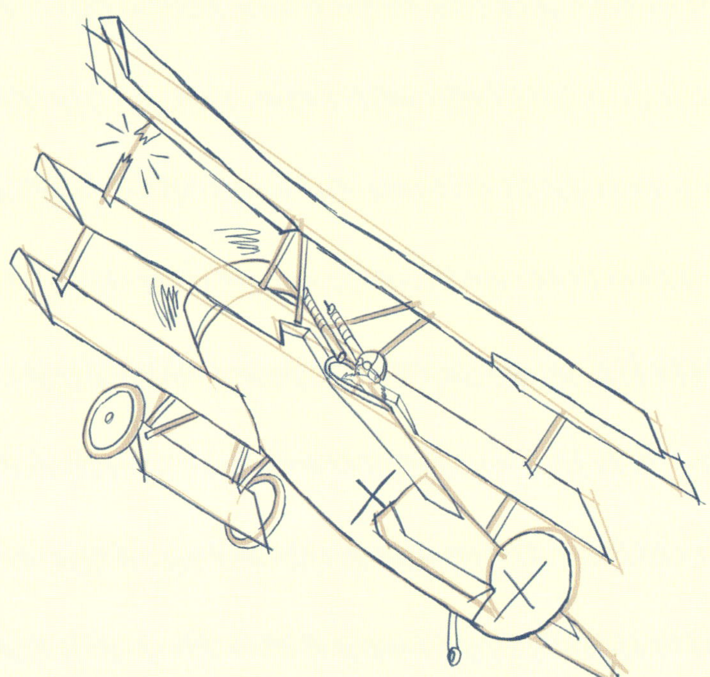

You can add narrative elements to the sketch, as well as giving volume to the basic structure of the aircraft. Here the left strut is broken and the pilot's gesture shows him turning his head in surprise.

L'ébauche vous permet déjà d'intégrer quelques éléments narratifs et de donner du volume à la structure de base de l'avion. Ici, vous pouvez représenter la cassure de la barre gauche et l'air surpris du pilote qui tourne la tête.

In die Skizze können bereits einige erzählerische Elemente eingebaut werden. Außerdem wird der Grundstruktur des Flugzeug Volumen verliehen. In diesem Falle wird die linke Verbindungsstange zerbrochen dargestellt, der Pilot dreht seinen Kopf und blickt erschrocken.

In de schets kunnen we verhalende elementen toevoegen en de basisstructuur van het vliegtuig volume geven. In dit geval wordt dit gedaan met de gebroken linkerstok en het gebaar van de piloot die zijn hoofd verbaasd omdraait.

En el boceto ya podemos aportar elementos narrativos, además de dar volumen a la estructura básica del avión: en este caso, el bastón izquierdo partido y el gesto del piloto, que gira la cabeza, sorprendido.

Nel bozzetto possiamo aggiungere già alcuni elementi narrativi, oltre a dare volume alla struttura di base del velivolo. In questo caso, il montante sinistro spezzato e il gesto del pilota, che gira la testa sorpreso.

No esboço já podemos fornecer elementos narrativos, para além de dar volume à estrutura básica do avião. Neste caso, o bastão esquerdo partido e o gesto do piloto, que gira a sua cabeça surpreendido.

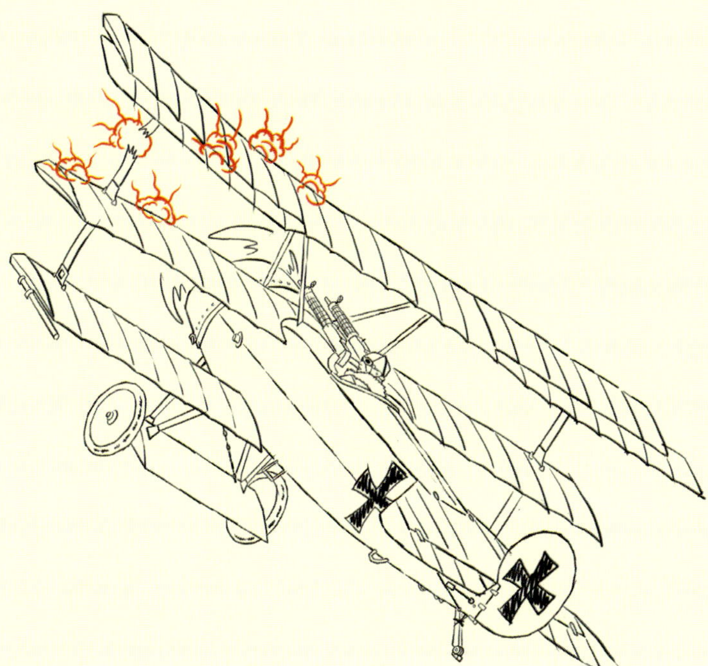

3

The penciling continues to add large and small elements, leaving everything ready for inking. The explosions (red) are on a separate layer so as not to hold up the inking process and to show that they need special attention.

Continuez d'ajouter sur le crayonné de nouveaux éléments, grands ou petits, de façon à préparer le terrain pour l'encrage. Les explosions (en rouge) sont réalisées sur une couche séparée afin de ne pas entraver l'encrage et d'indiquer qu'elles doivent recevoir un traitement particulier.

Bei der Buntstiftzeichnung werden weitere große und kleine Elemente hinzugefügt und die Darstellung wird für den nächsten Schritt – die Tuschezeichnung – vorbereitet. Die rot gekennzeichneten Explosionen werden in einer separaten Ebene eingezeichnet, um die Tuschezeichnung nicht zu stören und darauf hinzuweisen, dass diese Elemente eine besondere Behandlung erfordern.

Bij de potloodtekening worden nog meer grote en kleine elementen toegevoegd en wordt de weg vrijgemaakt voor het inkleuren. De explosies (rood) worden in een aparte laag aangebracht om het inkleuren van de rest niet te belemmeren en om aan te geven dat zij een specifieke behandeling vergen.

En el lápiz seguimos añadiendo elementos, grandes y pequeños, dejando el terreno listo para el entintado. Las explosiones (rojo) están en una capa aparte para no entorpecer el entintado y para señalar que debe recibir un tratamiento específico.

Nella fase a matita continuiamo ad aggiungere elementi, grandi e piccoli, preparando il terreno per il ripasso a china. Le esplosioni (rosso) sono in un livello separato per evitare interferenze con il ripasso e per evidenziare che devono ricevere un trattamento specifico.

No lápis continuamos a acrescentar elementos, grandes e pequenos, deixando o terreno pronto para a arte-final. As explosões (vermelho) estão numa camada à parte para não dificultar a arte-final e para sinalizar que deve receber um tratamento específico.

# 4

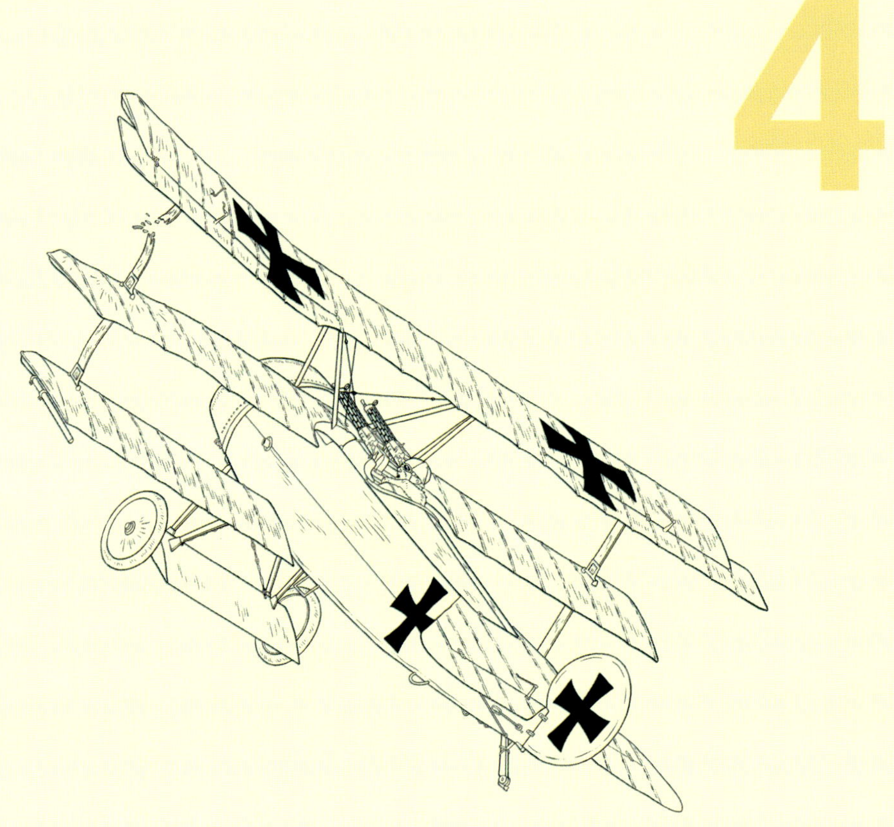

A small repeated detail in the inking can embellish the drawing a great deal: in this case, the small lines added to the wings increase the sensation of speed.

Un petit détail répétitif permet d'améliorer l'illustration : ici, les petits traits ajoutés sur les ailes augmentent la sensation de vitesse.

Ein kleines, sich wiederholendes Detail kann die Zeichnung erheblich verschönern: Hier verstärken die kleinen Striche auf den Tragflächen das Gefühl von Geschwindigkeit.

Een klein herhalend detail in de inkttekening kan het verfraaien van de tekening zijn: in dit geval de kleine aan de vleugels toegevoegde streepjes die het gevoel van snelheid verhogen.

Un pequeño detalle repetitivo en la tinta puede embellecer mucho el dibujo: en este caso, las pequeñas rayitas añadidas en las alas aumentan la sensación de velocidad.

Un piccolo dettaglio ripetitivo aggiunto nella fase di ripasso può abbellire di molto il disegno: in questo caso, i trattini aggiunti sulle ali aumentano la sensazione di velocità.

Um pequeno detalhe repetitivo na tinta pode embelezar muito o desenho: neste caso, as pequenas riscas acrescentadas nas asas aumentam a sensação de velocidade.

5

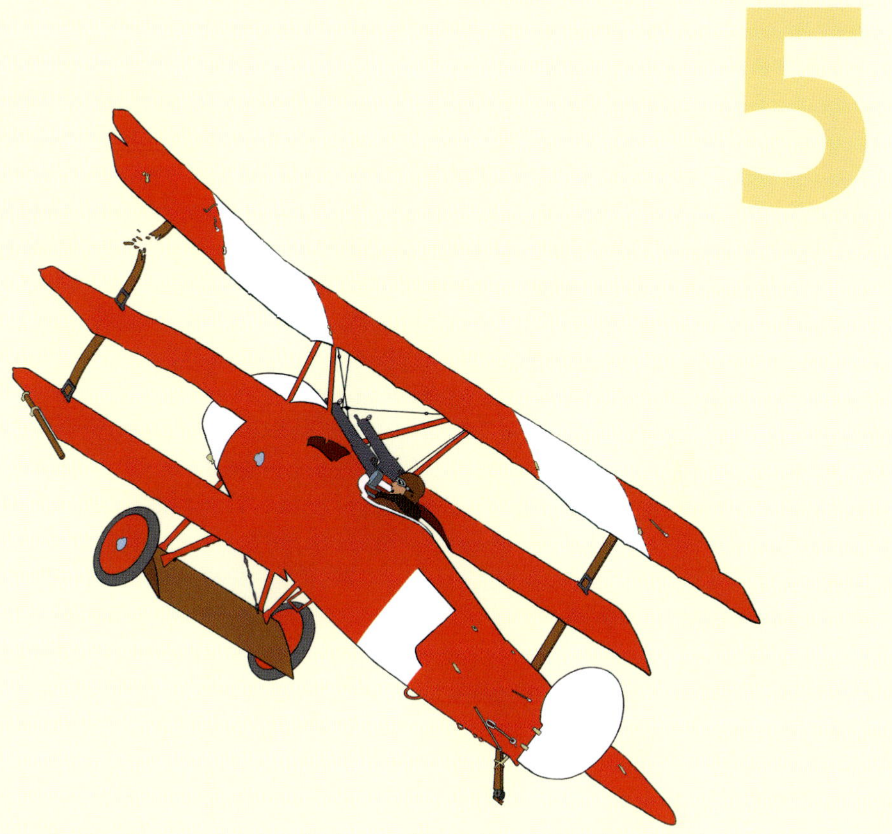

Red is the predominant base color, given that this color inevitably serves the character. Browns add fragility and grays represent artificial materials.

La base de couleur est principalement dominée par le rouge qui fait ressortir le personnage. Les tons marron apportent une certaine fragilité tandis que le gris évoque des matériaux artificiels.

Bei den Farben herrscht Rot vor, das der gesamten Szene Leben einhaucht. Die Brauntöne stehen für Zerbrechlichkeit, die Grautöne für künstliche Materialien.

Onder de basiskleuren heeft rood de overhand, omdat deze kleur onvermijdelijk ten dienste van het personage staat. De bruine tinten zorgen voor broosheid en de grijze kleuren staan voor kunstmaterialen.

Entre los colores base predomina el rojo, puesto que el coloreado está inevitablemente al servicio del personaje. Los marrones aportan fragilidad y los grises representan materiales artificiales.

Tra i colori di base predomina il rosso, poiché la colorazione è inevitabilmente al servizio del personaggio. I marroni danno la sensazione di fragilità e i grigi rappresentano i materiali artificiali.

Entre as cores base predomina a vermelha, uma vez que o colorido está inevitavelmente ao serviço da personagem. Os castanhos concebem fragilidade e os cinzentos representam materiais artificiais.

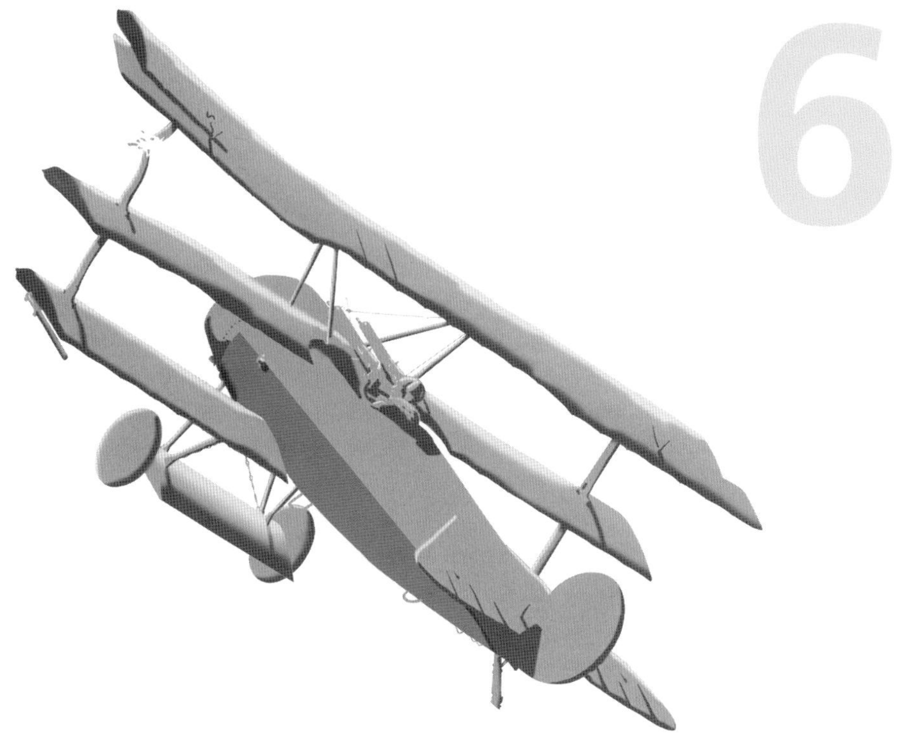


The light layer is only diffuse between the wheels, where a curved surface is applied. Although the intention was to use a single shading layer, it was necessary to add a second to show the lower plane of the fuselage.

La couche de lumière est diffuse entre les roues, où elle est appliquée à une surface courbe. Si une seule couche peut paraître suffisante, il paraît tout de même nécessaire d'en ajouter une seconde pour représenter le plan inférieur du fuselage.

Das Licht erscheint ausschließlich zwischen den Rädern diffus, da es dort auf eine gebogene Oberfläche aufgetragen wird. Auch wenn eigentlich nur eine Schattenebene eingearbeitet werden soll, so ist eine zweite schließlich nicht vermeidbar, damit der untere Bereich des Rumpfs korrekt dargestellt wird.

De lichtlaag is alleen tussen de wielen, waar een gebogen oppervlak wordt toegepast, vaag. Hoewel we slechts één schaduwlaag willen gebruiken, zal het uiteindelijk nodig zijn om een tweede laag toe te passen om het ondervlak van de romp af te beelden.

La capa de luz sólo es difusa entre las ruedas, donde se aplica a una superficie curva. Aunque pretendamos utilizar una sola capa de sombra, finalmente será necesaria una segunda para representar el plano inferior del fuselaje.

Il livello delle luci è sfumato solo fra le ruote, dove si applica a una superficie ricurva. Anche se volevamo utilizzare un singolo livello di ombre, alla fine ne è necessario un secondo per rappresentare il piano inferiore della fusoliera.

A camada de luz só é difusa entre as rodas, onde se aplica a uma superfície curva. Embora pretendamos utilizar uma só camada de sombra, no final será necessária uma segunda para representar o plano inferior da fuselagem.

# 7

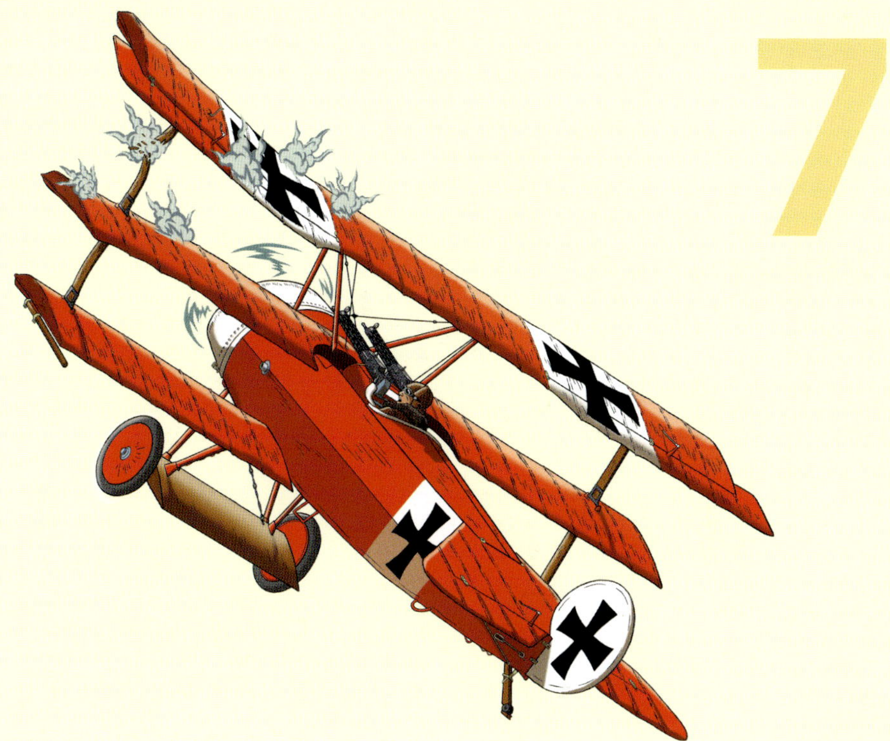

Zigzag lines are added to the finished drawing to represent the propeller in motion, and small spots in two shades of blue represent the hits received, providing the scene with action.

Sur le dessin final, ajoutez des lignes en zigzag pour représenter l'hélice en mouvement, ainsi que des petites taches bleues représentant les impacts reçus.

Die fertige Zeichnung wird mit einigen Zickzack-Linien versehen, die den sich drehenden Propeller darstellen. Kleine Flecken in zwei unterschiedlichen Blautönen verdeutlichen die Einschüsse am Flugzeug und verleihen der Darstellung mehr Dynamik.

In de afgeronde tekening brengen we wat zigzagstrepen aan die de bewegende schroef uitbeelden en kleine vlekjes in twee blauwtinten die de treffers uitbeelden en de scène van actie voorzien.

En el dibujo acabado añadimos una líneas en zigzag que representan la hélice en movimiento y unas pequeñas manchas con dos tonos de azul que representan los impactos recibidos, para aportar acción a la escena.

Nel disegno finito aggiungiamo alcune linee a zigzag che rappresentano l'elica in movimento e alcune piccole macchie con due tonalità di blu che rappresentano gli impatti ricevuti, conferendo azione alla scena.

No desenho acabado acrescentamos linhas em ziguezague que representam a hélice em movimento e umas pequenas manchas com dois tons de azul que representam os impactos recebidos, concedendo acção à cena.

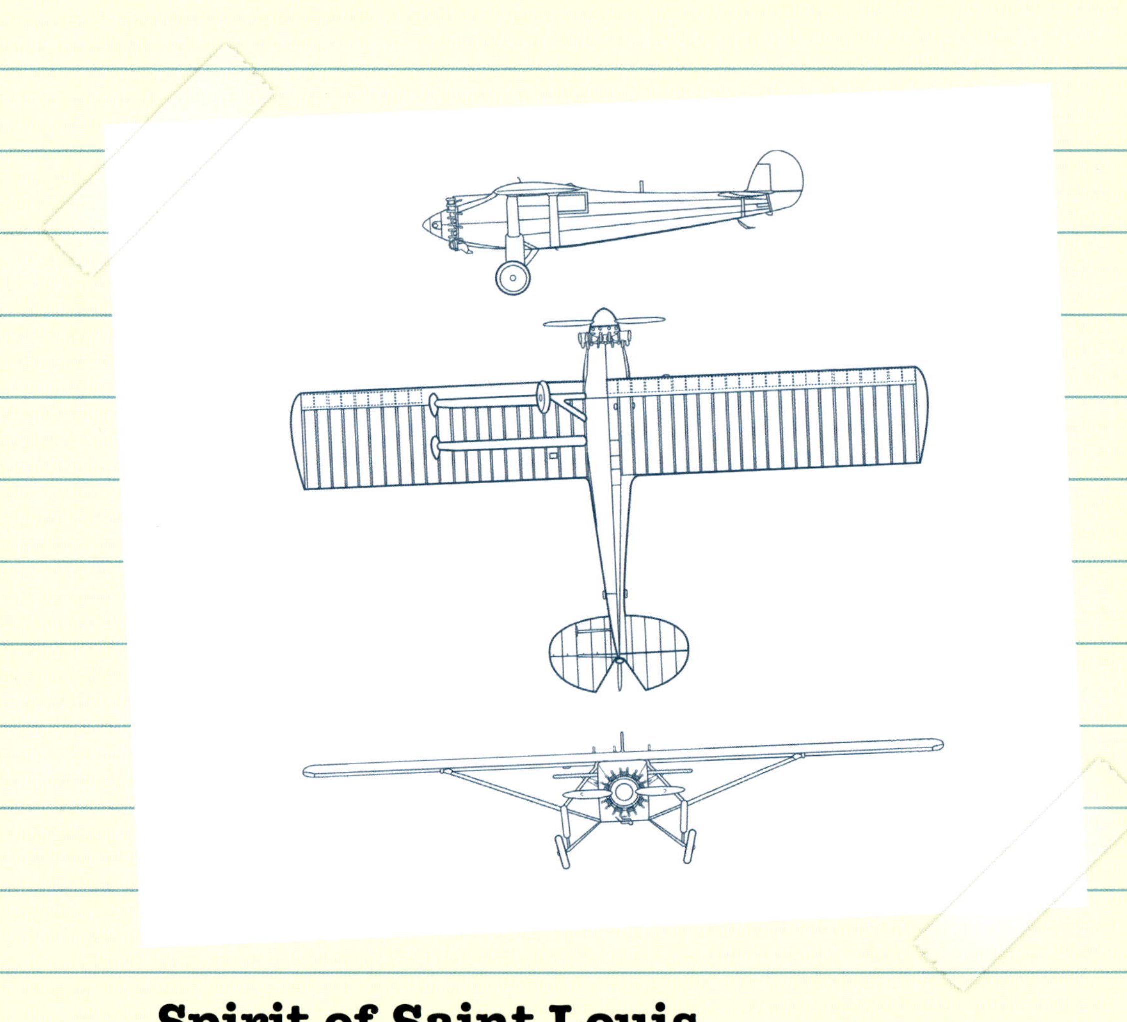

# Spirit of Saint Louis

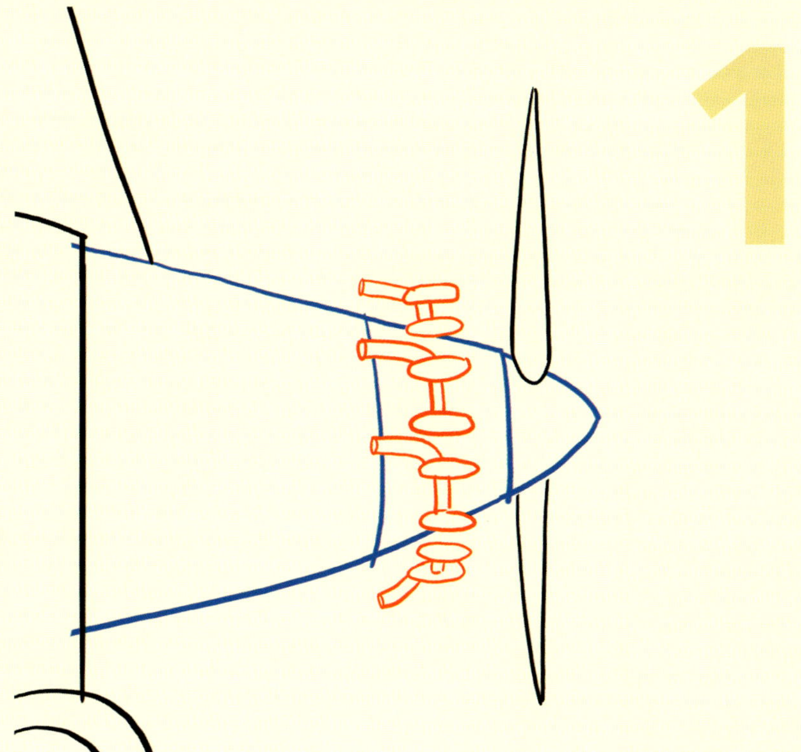

For illustrators, often unfamiliar with mechanics, the outline represents a study and understanding of the mechanisms of an airplane. Each of the four red pairs represents one of the nine engine cylinders.

Pour les illustrateurs, souvent étrangers au domaine de la mécanique, le schéma représente une étude et un moyen de compréhension des mécanismes de l'avion. Chacun des quatre éléments rouges représente l'un des neuf cylindres du moteur.

Illustratoren, die oftmals keine umfassenden Kenntnisse im Bereich Mechanik vorweisen können, nutzen das Grundschema gerne, um bestimmte Mechanismen des Flugzeugs genauer zu studieren und besser zu verstehen. Jedes einzelne der vier rot eingefärbten Paare an Bauelementen steht für einen der neun Zylinder des Motors.

Voor illustrators, die vaak geen verstand van mechaniek hebben, houdt het schema de bestudering en het begrip van de mechanismen van het vliegtuig in. Elk van de vier rode paren stelt een van de negen cilinders van de motor voor.

Para los ilustradores, en muchas ocasiones profanos en mecánica, el esquema representa un estudio y comprensión de los mecanismos del avión. Cada uno de los cuatro pares en rojo representa uno de los nueve cilindros del motor.

Per gli illustratori, spesso profani di meccanica, lo schema rappresenta una fase di studio e di comprensione dei meccanismi del velivolo. Qui ciascuna delle quattro coppie in rosso rappresenta uno dei nove cilindri del motore.

Para os ilustradores, em muitas ocasiões desconhecedores de mecânica, o esquema representa um estudo e compreensão dos mecanismos do avião. Cada um dos quatro pares a vermelho representa um dos nove cilindros do motor.

2

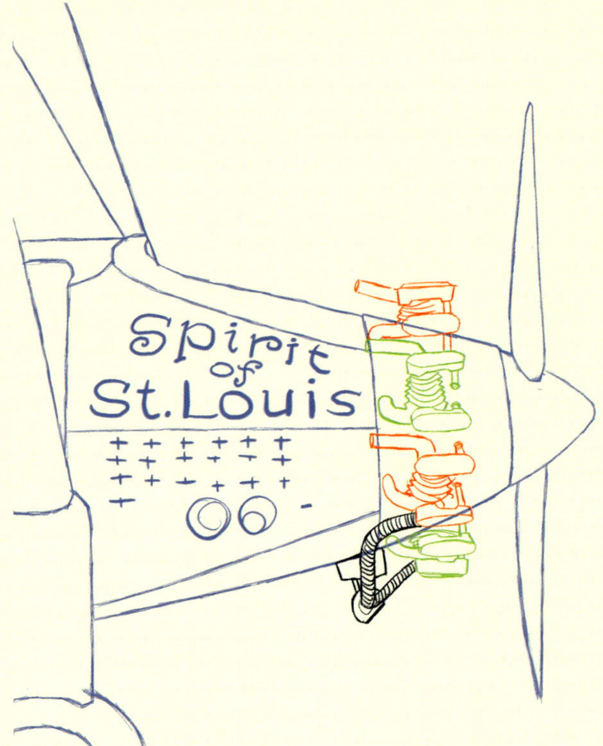


Sometimes the sketch is necessary for only one element. It was used here to give shape to each part of the fuselage, but had it not been for the complexity of the engine (separate layer and in different colors), it could have been done directly during penciling.

Il est parfois nécessaire de faire une ébauche pour un seul élément. Profitez-en pour modeler chaque partie du fuselage. Sans ce moteur complexe (réalisé sur une couche séparée à l'aide de différentes couleurs), vous auriez pu passer directement au crayonné.

Bisweilen ist einen Skizze allein aufgrund eines einzelnen Elements erforderlich. Hier wird die Skizze genutzt, um Teile des Rumpfs auszuarbeiten. Wäre der (in einer weiteren Ebene mehrfarbig gezeichnete) Motor weniger kompliziert, könnte man sich direkt der Buntstiftzeichnung widmen.

Soms is er een schets nodig voor maar één element. Ik maak er gebruik van om elk deel van de romp vorm te geven, maar was het niet vanwege de gecompliceerde motor (in elke afzonderlijke laag en met diverse kleuren), dan zou ik direct met de potloodtekening beginnen.

A veces el boceto es necesario por un único elemento. Aprovecho para dar forma a cada parte del fuselaje, pero, de no ser por el complicado motor (en capa aparte y con varios colores), me atrevería a realizar directamente el lápiz.

A volte il bozzetto è necessario per un solo elemento. Colgo l'occasione per modellare ogni parte della fusoliera, ma se non fosse per il complicato motore (in un livello separato e con vari colori) mi azzarderei a realizzare direttamente le matite.

Às vezes o esboço é necessário por um único elemento. Aproveito para dar forma a cada parte da fuselagem, mas se não fosse o complicado motor (em camada à parte e com várias cores) atrever-me-ia a realizar directamente o lápis.

3

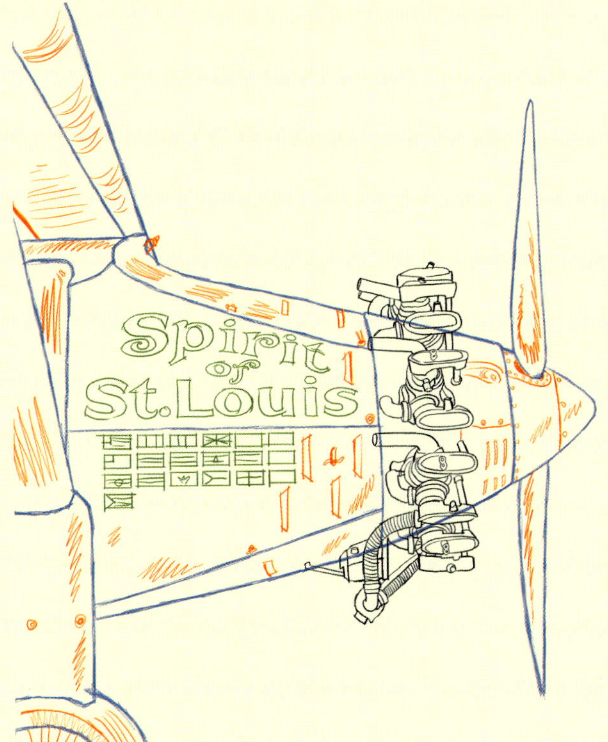


The penciling is done (in red) over the sketched fuselage, with texture lines, grooves, rivets, and decorative features (green) marked. The sketched engine layer is replaced with penciling that enables it to be inked.

Réalisez le crayonné sur l'ébauche du fuselage, en marquant les lignes de texture, les rainures et les rivets (en rouge) ainsi que les éléments décoratifs (en vert). Remplacez le calque d'ébauche du moteur par un crayonné qui pourra être encré.

Die Buntstiftzeichnung (in Rot) wird über die Skizze des Rumpfs gelegt. Dabei werden Linien zur Kennzeichnung von Texturen, Ritzen und Nieten eingearbeitet und es werden dekorative Elemente (in Grün) hinzugefügt. Die Motorskizze wird durch eine Bleistiftzeichnung ersetzt, welche die nachfolgende Tuschezeichnung vorbereitet.

Teken met potlood (rood) op de schets van de romp en markeer textuurstrepen, groeven en klinknagels, evenals de decoratieve elementen (groen). Vervang de schetslaag van de motor voor een potloodtekening die kan worden ingekleurd.

Realizamos el lápiz (rojo) sobre el boceto del fuselaje, marcando líneas de textura, ranuras y remaches, así como los elementos decorativos (verde). Sustituimos la capa del boceto del motor por un lápiz que permita ser entintado.

Realizziamo le matite (rosso) sul bozzetto della fusoliera, tracciando le linee dei materiali, le scanalature e la rivettatura, oltre che gli elementi decorativi (verde). Sostituiamo il livello del bozzetto del motore con un disegno a matita che possa essere ripassato a china.

Realizamos o lápis (vermelho) sobre o esboço da fuselagem, definindo linhas de textura, ranhuras e rebites, assim como os elementos decorativos (verde). Substituímos a camada do esboço do motor por um lápis que permita a arte-final.

# 4

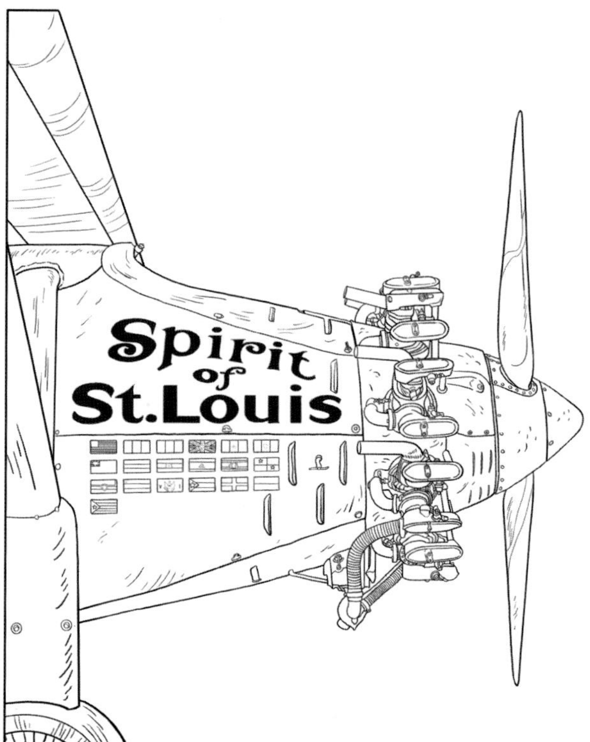


Inking adds a magical effect to illustrations. It orders the chaos of the preceding stages. Everything comes to life and finds its logic as part of the whole.

L'encrage a un effet magique sur les illustrations. Avec cette technique, le chaos des étapes précédentes laisse place à l'ordre, l'ensemble prend vie et chaque chose y trouve sa logique.

Bei der Tuschezeichnung geschieht etwas ganz Besonderes mit allen Darstellungen. Das Chaos der verschiedenen vorhergehenden Arbeitsschritte wird geordnet, die Zeichnung wirkt logisch und scheint lebendig zu werden.

Inkt heeft een magisch effect op de illustraties. Hiermee wordt de chaos van de voorgaande fases geordend en lijkt alles tot leven te komen en zijn logica binnen het geheel te vinden.

La tinta tiene un efecto mágico sobre las ilustraciones. Con ella, el caos de las fases anteriores se ordena y todo parece cobrar vida y encontrar su lógica dentro del conjunto.

La china ha un effetto magico sulle illustrazioni. Con essa, il caos delle fasi precedenti si ordina e tutto sembra prendere vita e ritrovare la sua logica.

A tinta tem um efeito mágico sobre as ilustrações. Com ela, o caos das fases anteriores ordena-se e tudo parece ganhar vida e encontrar a sua lógica dentro do conjunto.

# 5

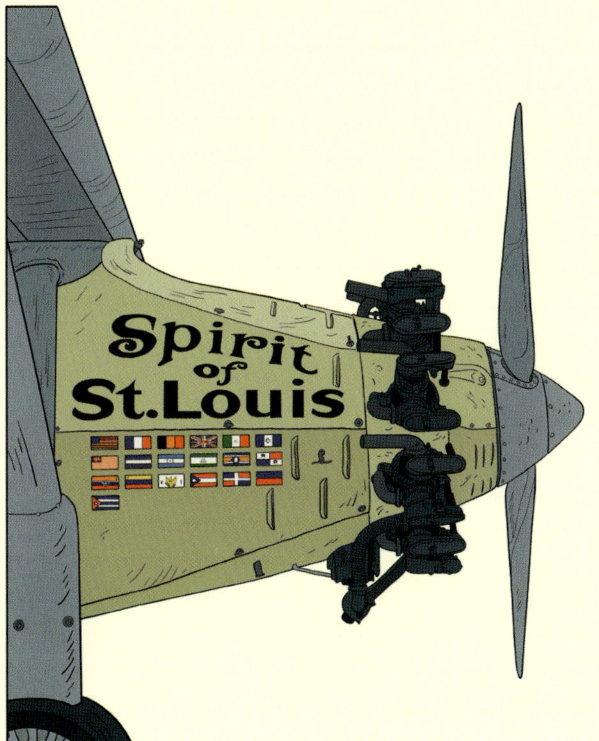


Given that this is a specific aircraft, the original colors are respected. It is important to point out that, with few exceptions, the shade of black should never be so dark as to prevent the inking from being visualized.

Comme il s'agit d'un avion spécifique, vous devez tenter de respecter les couleurs d'origine de l'appareil. Il est important de noter que, sauf exceptions, le noir ne doit jamais être foncé au point de masquer les tracés.

Da es sich hier um ein ganz spezielles Flugzeug handelt, wird versucht, seine Farben möglichst wirklichkeitsgetreu wiederzugeben. Wir betonen, dass die Farbe Schwarz – außer in Einzelfällen – nicht so dunkel sein sollte, dass sie die Tuschezeichnung vollständig überdeckt.

Aangezien het om een specifiek vliegtuig gaat, proberen we de oorspronkelijke kleuren van het luchtvaartuig te respecteren. Het is belangrijk om op te merken dat, uitzonderingen daargelaten, zwart nooit zo donker moet zijn dat de inkttekening verborgen blijft.

Dado que se trata de un avión específico, intentamos respetar los colores originales de la aeronave. Es importante destacar que, salvo excepciones, el negro nunca debe ser tan oscuro que impida visualizar las tintas.

Dal momento che si tratta di un aereo specifico, proviamo a rispettarne i colori originali. Va sottolineato che, tranne eccezioni, il nero non deve essere mai tanto scuro da impedire la visualizzazione del ripasso a china.

Dado que se trata de um avião específico, tentamos respeitar as cores originais da aeronave. É importante destacar que, salvo excepções, o preto nunca deve ser tão escuro que impeça visualizar as tintas.

6

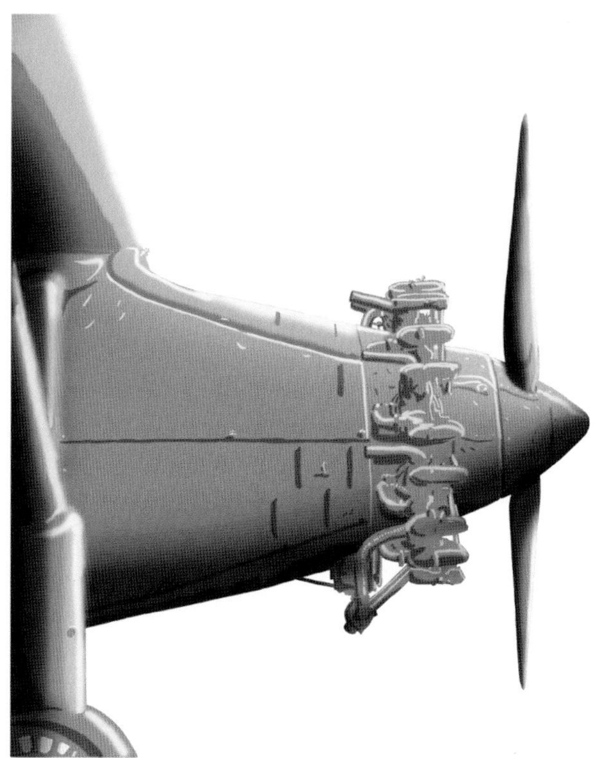

In order to add drama to this close up of the nose cone, lighting and shading is given particular contrast, appearing with degradation on larger surfaces and with specific edges on smaller ones.

Afin de donner un aspect dramatique au gros plan du nez de l'avion, apportez d'importants contrastes entre ombres et lumières, dégradées sur les grandes surfaces et plus concrètes sur les petites.

Um der Flugzeugnase eine besondere Dramatik zu verleihen, werden Licht- und Schattenbereiche mit deutlichen Kontrasten versehen. Auf großen Flächen sind diese Bereiche sanft abgestuft, an kleineren Elementen werden sie mit scharfen Rändern versehen.

Om te proberen een dramatisch karakter aan deze close-up van de neus van het vliegtuig te geven, worden het licht en de schaduwen duidelijk gecontrasteerd en lijken zij in de grote vlakken af te lopen en op de kleine vlakken concretere randen te hebben.

Para intentar dar dramatismo a este primer plano del morro del avión, contrastamos mucho las luces y las sombras, que aparecen en degradado en superficies grandes y con bordes concretos en las pequeñas.

Nel tentativo di conferire drammaticità a questo primo piano del muso dell'aereo, contrastiamo molto le luci e le ombre, che appaiono sfumate sulle superfici più grandi e ben delineate su quelle più piccole.

Para tentar dar dramatismo a este primeiro plano do nariz do avião, contrastamos muito as luzes e as sombras, que aparecem em esbatimento em superfícies grandes e com margens concretas nas pequenas.

# 7

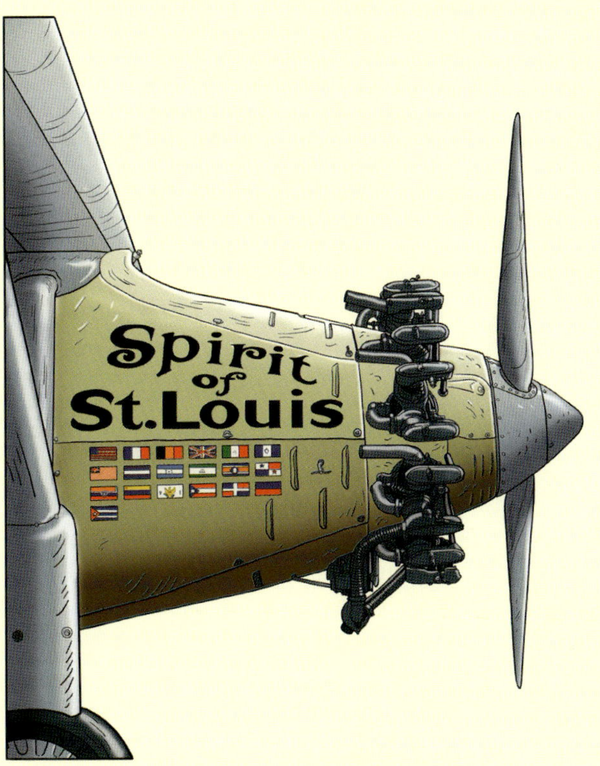


The lighting and shading fit well on the finished drawing without sacrificing the color or the inking. The illustration has a retro appearance with a certain melancholy and romantic feel.

Sur le dessin final, les ombres et les lumières sont en harmonie avec l'ensemble, sans nuire à la couleur ou aux tracés. Le tout présente un côté rétro chargé d'une certaine mélancolie et d'une touche de romantisme.

In der fertigen Zeichnung harmonieren Licht- und Schattenbereiche, ohne die Farbgebung oder die Tuschezeichnung zu beeinträchtigen. Das Gesamtergebnis ist eine Retro-Zeichnung, die eine gewisse Melancholie und Romantik ausstrahlt.

In de afgeronde tekeningen passen het licht en de schaduwen goed zonder dat kleur of inkt wordt opgeofferd. Het geheel ziet er retro uit met een zekere melancholische en romantische uitstraling.

En el dibujo acabado, las luces y las sombras encajan bien sin sacrificar el color o las tintas. El conjunto tiene un aspecto retro cargado de cierta melancolía y romanticismo.

Nel disegno finito, le luci e le ombre si adattano bene senza pregiudicare il colore o la china. L'insieme ha un aspetto rétro, carico di malinconia e romanticismo.

No desenho acabado, as luzes e as sombras encaixam bem sem sacrificar a cor ou as tintas. O conjunto tem um aspecto retro carregado dalguma melancolia e romantismo.

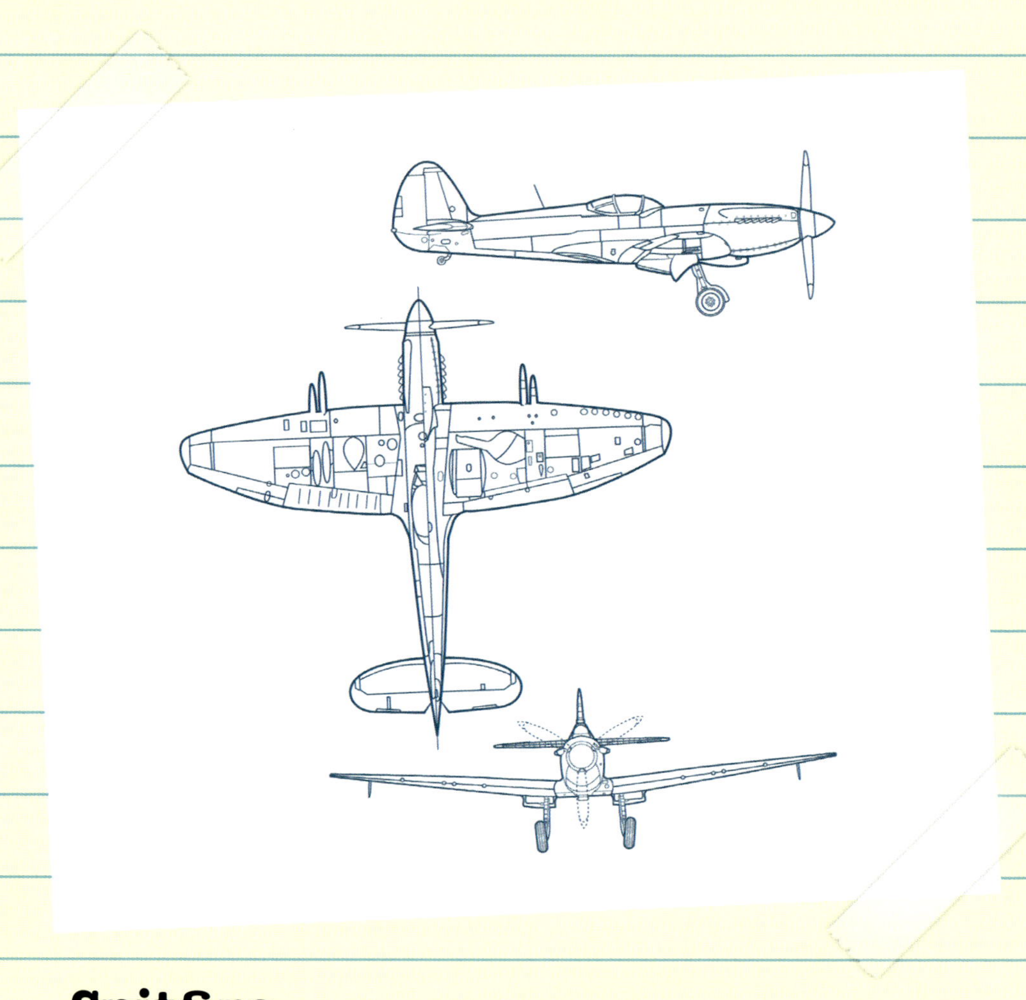

# Spitfire

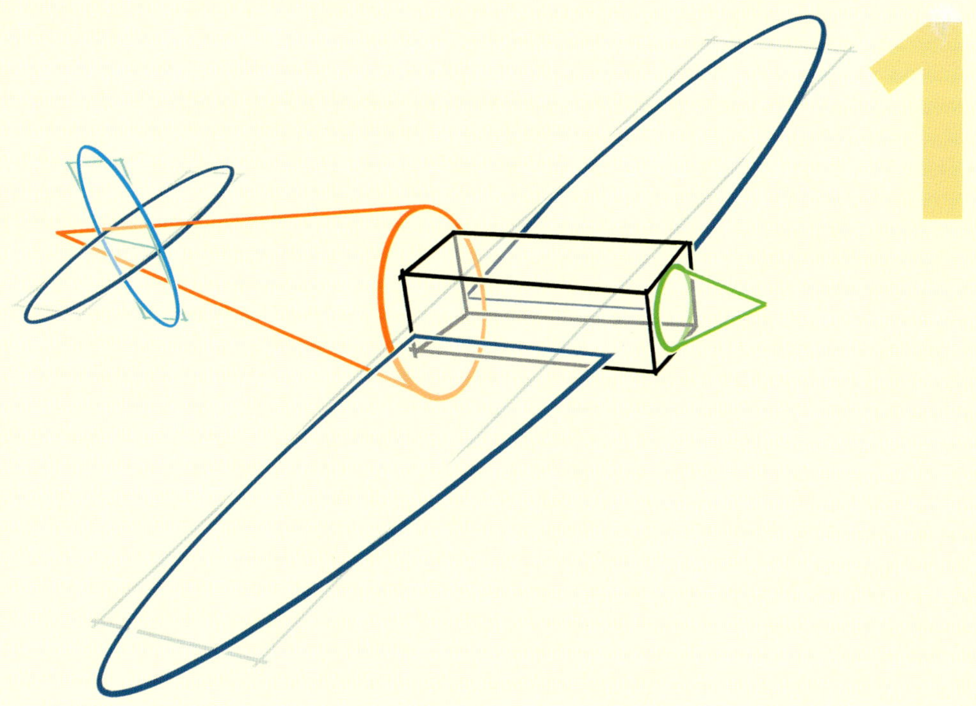

1

Even if it is your intention to illustrate on paper, when the skeleton is no more than a series of ellipses, cones, and hexahedrons, computer drawing programs can greatly simplify this step.

Même si vous souhaitez faire votre illustration sur papier, lorsque votre schéma n'est rien de plus qu'un squelette composé d'ellipses, de cônes et d'hexaèdres, les outils informatiques des programmes graphiques permettent de simplifier grandement cette étape.

Auch wenn Sie lieber auf Papier zeichnen: Sofern es sich beim Grundschema lediglich um ein Skelett aus Ellipsen, Kegeln und Hexaedern handelt, erleichtern Zeichen-programme auf dem Computer diesen Schritt um ein Vielfaches.

Wanneer ons schema niets meer of minder is dan enkel een skelet van ellipsen, kegels en zesvlakken, wordt deze stap enorm vereenvoudigt door werktuigen van grafische computerprogramma's ook al willen we de illustratie op papier maken.

Aunque queramos ilustrar en papel, cuando nuestro esquema no es más que un esqueleto de elipses, conos y hexaedros, las herramientas de los programas gráficos de ordenador simplifican mucho este paso.

Anche se vogliamo realizzare un'illustrazione su carta, quando il nostro schema non è altro che uno scheletro di ellissi, coni ed esagoni, gli strumenti offerti dai programmi di computer grafica semplificano enormemente questa fase.

Ainda que queiramos ilustrar em papel, quando o nosso esquema não é mais que um esqueleto de elipses, cones e hexaedros, as ferramentas dos programas gráficos de computador simplificam muito este passo.

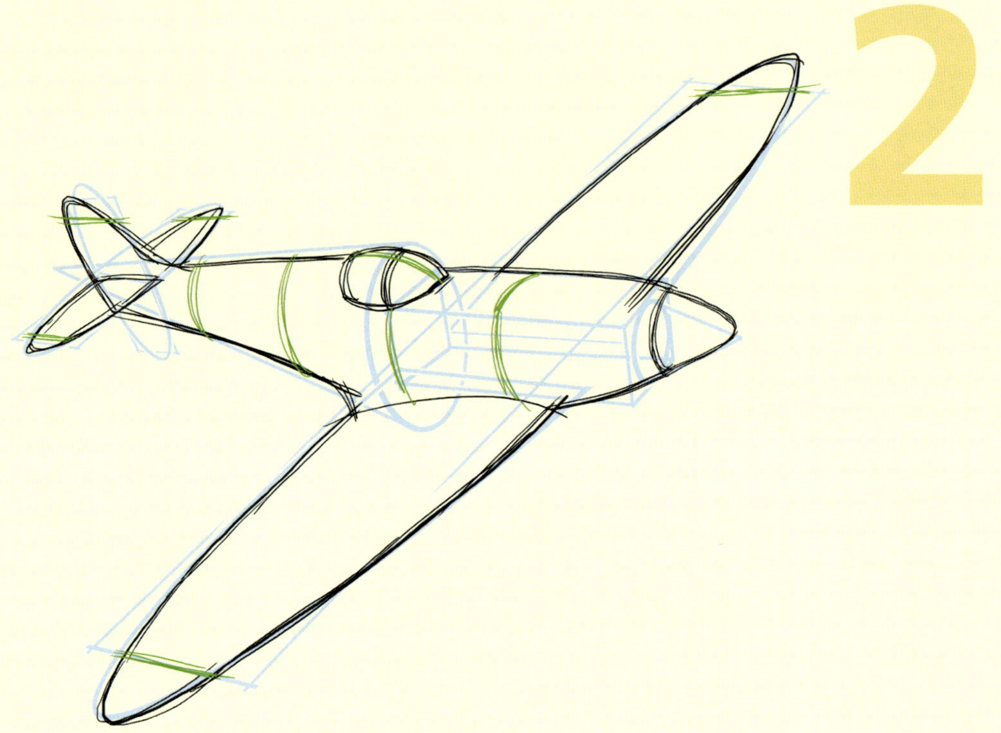


It is customary to make sketches with different lines when trying to achieve the right volume. We play with the pencil thinking "it's too narrow" or "it needs more curves". The best lines can be chosen later, but the most important thing is that all the good parts are there.

Pendant la recherche du volume, vous réalisez souvent des ébauches avec différentes lignes, tout en faisant tourner votre crayon en pensant : « trop étroit » ou « trop courbé ». Choisissez la meilleure : l'important est qu'elle soit là, quelque part.

Beim Anfertigen der Skizze macht man üblicherweise mehrere Striche und versucht, das passende Volumen für die Darstellung zu finden („zu schmal", „etwas mehr gebogen"...). Anschließend wählt man aus den verschiedenen Versuchen die beste Strichführung aus.

Het is gebruikelijk om schetsen te maken met diverse lijnen wanneer naar het juiste volume wordt gezocht en we bij de potloodtekening vormen uitproberen en denken "te smal" of "ronder". Daarna kiezen we de beste streep. Het belangrijkst is dat de goede streep er staat.

Es habitual hacer bocetos con varias líneas cuando se busca el volumen adecuado y jugamos con el lápiz pensando «demasiado estrecho» o «más curvado». Después elegiremos la mejor de las líneas, pero lo importante es que la buena esté ahí.

È abituale realizzare bozzetti con varie linee quando si cerca il volume appropriato, giocando con la matita e pensando: "troppo stretto" o "più curvo". Successivamente sceglieremo la linea migliore, ma la cosa importante è che fra tutte ci sia anche quella buona.

É habitual fazer esboços com várias linhas quando se procura o volume adequado e brincamos com o lápis pensando "demasiado estreito" ou "mais curvado". Depois elegemos a melhor das linhas, mas o importante é que a boa esteja lá.

# 3

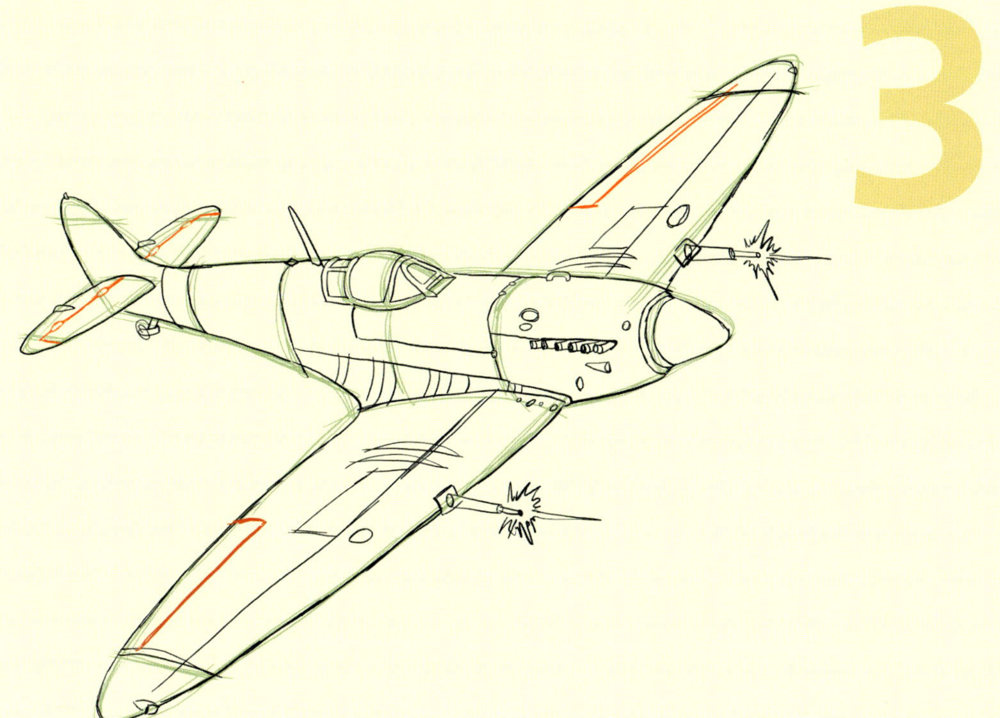

When penciling over the sketch (tracing on another sheet or on a new layer, reducing the opacity of the sketch layer), adding each detail can become a simple process that only requires patience.

Lorsque l'on dessine le crayonné sur l'ébauche (en calquant sur une autre feuille ou sur un nouveau calque, et en réduisant l'opacité du calque d'ébauche), l'ajout de chaque détail est un jeu d'enfant qui ne requiert que de la patience.

Legt man die Buntstiftzeichnung über die Skizze (sei es durch Abpausen oder mithilfe einer neuen Ebene und erhöhter Transparenz der Skizze), wird das Hinzufügen der einzelnen Details zu einem Leichten. Das Wichtigste dabei ist ausreichend Geduld.

Wanneer met potlood over de schets wordt getekend (door op een ander blad over te trekken of aan de hand van een nieuwe laag de opaciteit van de schetslaag te verminderen), verandert het toevoegen van elk detail in een eenvoudig spel dat enkel geduld vergt.

Al dibujar el lápiz sobre el boceto (calcando en otra hoja o en una capa nueva, reduciendo la opacidad de la capa boceto), añadir cada detalle se convierte en un sencillo juego que sólo requiere paciencia.

Quando si tracciano le matite definitive sul bozzetto (su un foglio separato o in un nuovo livello, riducendo l'opacità del livello del bozzetto), aggiungere ciascun dettaglio diventa un gioco da ragazzi che richiede solo un po' di pazienza.

Ao desenhar o lápis sobre o esboço (calcando noutra folha ou numa camada nova, reduzindo a opacidade da camada esboço), acrescentar cada detalhe converte-se num jogo simples que só requer paciência.

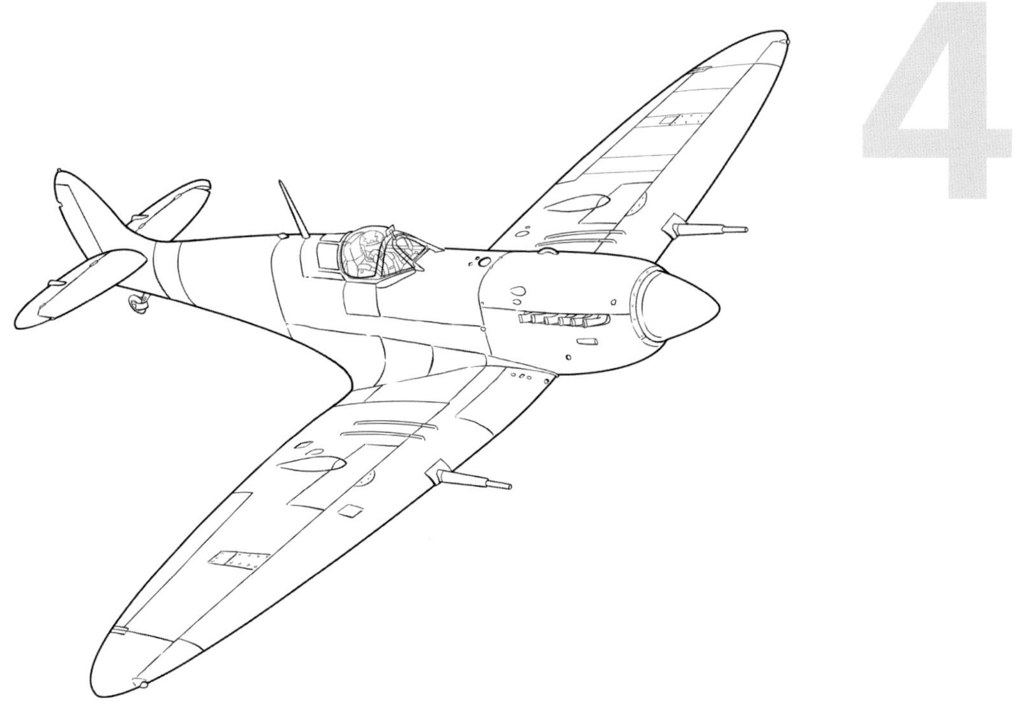


Using different brush thicknesses when inking is essential in most illustrations. A general rule is to use thicker ink lines for outlines and thinner ones for the interior.

Pour la majorité des illustrations, il est fondamental d'utiliser des tracés de contour d'épaisseur différente. Il existe une règle générale simple : utiliser des tracés plus épais pour les contours extérieurs et des tracés plus fins pour les lignes intérieures.

Für die meisten Zeichnungen ist die Verwendung unterschiedlich dicker Striche grundlegend. Die Grundregel hierfür lautet: Verwenden Sie dickere Linien für die Umrisse und feinere Linien für das Innere der Bildelemente.

Het gebruik van verschillende inktdiktes is in de meeste illustraties van groot belang. Een eenvoudige algemene regel is het gebruik van dikkere inktstrepen voor de buitenste lijnen en dunnere inktstrepen voor de binnenste lijnen.

Utilizar diferentes grosores de tinta es fundamental en la mayoría de las ilustraciones. Una regla general sencilla es utilizar tintas más gruesas para las líneas exteriores y tintas más finas para las interiores.

Utilizzare diversi spessori durante la fase di ripasso è fondamentale nella maggior parte delle illustrazioni. Una semplice regola generale è quella di utilizzare un tratto più spesso per le linee esterne e uno più sottile per quelle interne.

Utilizar diferentes espessuras de tinta é fundamental na maioria das ilustrações. Uma regra geral simples é utilizar tintas mais espessas para as linhas exteriores e tintas mais finas para as interiores.

## 5

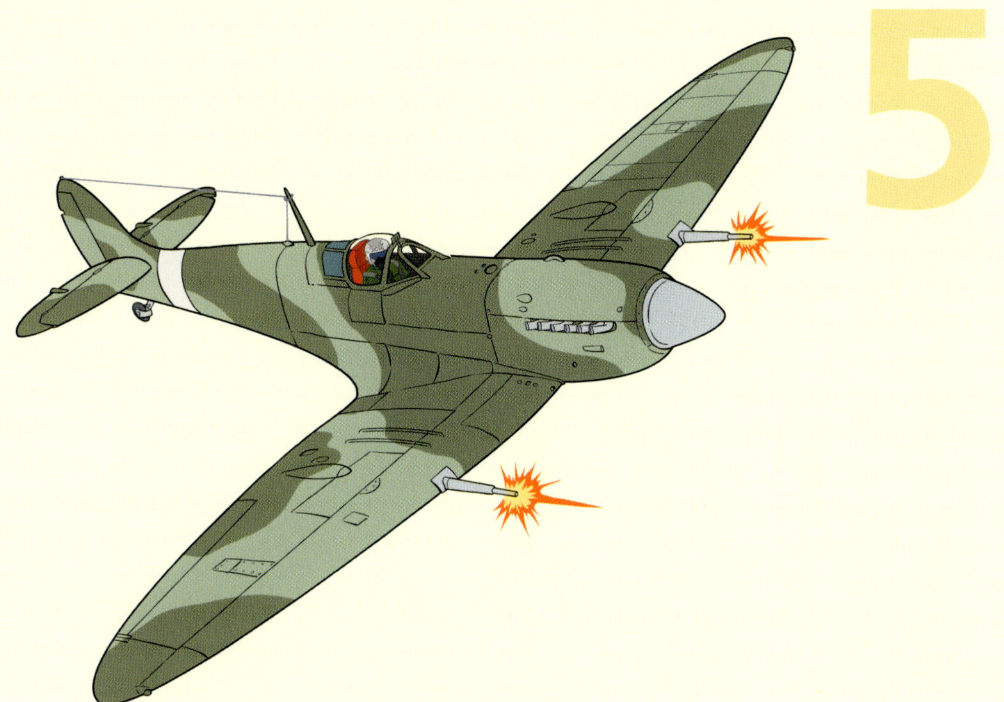

Except for a few details in gray to represent bare metal, the aircraft is painted in camouflage colors. These are based on dark splotches in a lighter shade of the same color.

À l'exception de quelques détails gris représentant le métal brut, l'appareil est peint avec des motifs de camouflage. Ceux-ci se composent de tâches foncées sur un ton plus clair de la même couleur.

Mit Ausnahme einiger in Grau gestalteter Details, die unbeschichtetes Metall darstellen, wird das Flugzeug mit Tarnfarben versehen. Das Tarnmuster besteht aus dunkleren Flecken auf einem helleren Ton der gleichen Farbe.

Met uitzondering van sommige grijze details die het naakte metaal uitbeelden, is het luchtvaartuig in camouflagekleuren geverfd. Deze zijn gebaseerd op donkere vlekken op een lichtere tint van dezelfde kleur.

Excepto algunos detalles grises, que representan el metal desnudo, la nave está pintada con colores de camuflaje, que se basan en manchas oscuras sobre un tono más claro del mismo color.

Tranne alcuni dettagli in grigio, che rappresentano il metallo nudo, l'aereo è dipinto con una livrea mimetica, basata su macchie scure sovrapposte a una tonalità più chiara dello stesso colore.

Excepto alguns detalhes cinzentos, que representam o metal despido, a nave está pintada com cores de camuflagem. Estas baseiam-se em manchas escuras sobre um tom mais claro da mesma cor.

# 6

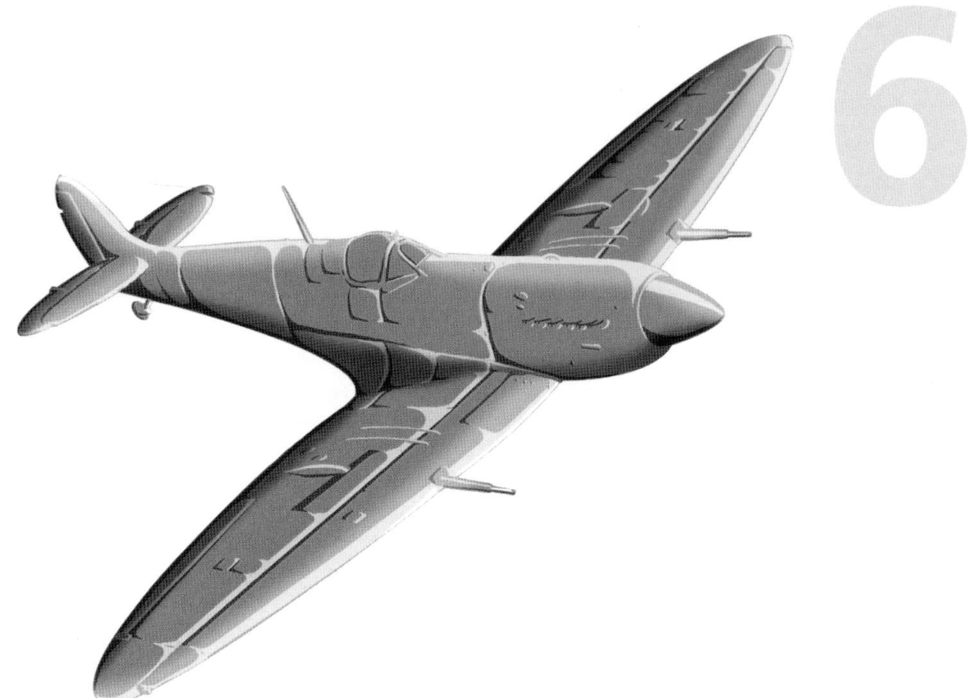

With the light source above the front of the plane, the lighting and shading is worked towards the rear in the form of Vs, helping to represent the plane's speed.

Avec une source lumineuse située face à l'avion, dans la partie supérieure, les ombres et les lumières se projettent vers l'arrière, en forme de pointes, ce qui aide à reproduire la sensation de vitesse.

Die Lichtquelle befindet sich schräg oben vor dem Flugzeug. Die Licht- und Schattenbereiche laufen in Richtung des hinteren Flugzeugteils spitz zu, wodurch die Geschwindigkeit des Tiefdeckers unterstrichen wird.

Met de lichtbron aan de bovenkant voor het vliegtuig, worden het licht en de schaduwen naar achteren geworpen, in de vorm van punten, wat helpt de snelheid van het luchtvaartuig uit te beelden.

Con el foco de luz en la parte superior delantera del avión, las luces y las sombras se lanzan hacia detrás, en forma de picos, ayudando a representar la velocidad de la aeronave.

Con la sorgente luminosa posta nella parte superiore frontale dell'aereo, le luci e le ombre sono proiettate all'indietro, con forma appuntita, contribuendo a rappresentare la velocità del velivolo.

Com o foco de luz na parte superior dianteira do avião, as luzes e as sombras lançam-se para trás, em forma de picos, ajudando a representar a velocidade da aeronave.

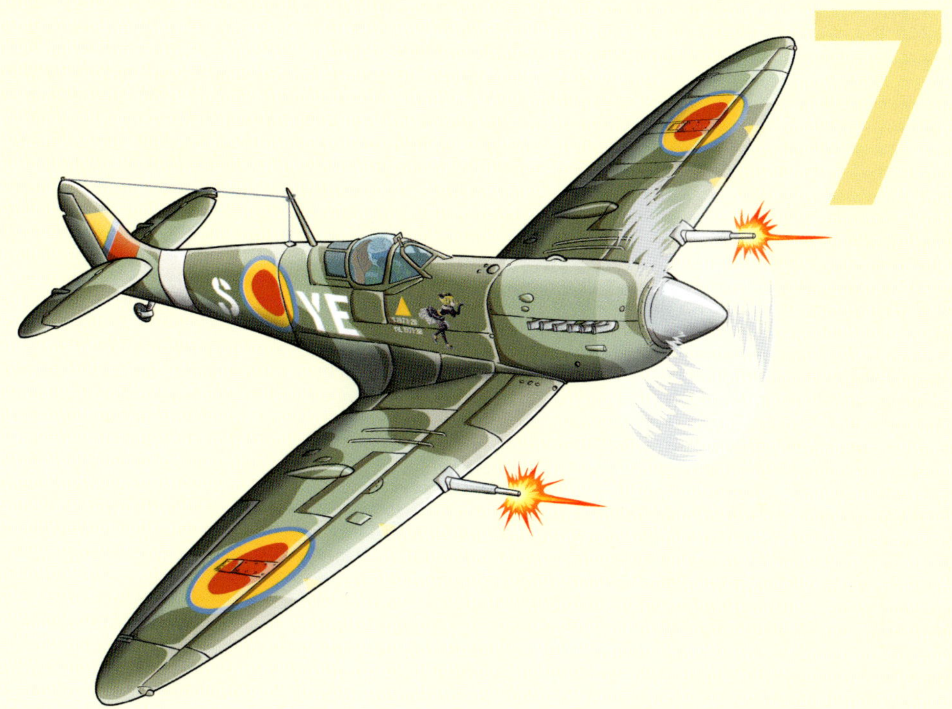


Taking advantage of the convenience offered by computer drawing programs and for placing features on different layers, different details such as letters and devices, the propeller, explosions, the cockpit glass, and the tail brace can be added to the drawing.

Grâce aux facilités procurées par le travail sur ordinateur et à la séparation des éléments sur différentes couches, vous pouvez ajouter sur le dessin final certains détails tels que les lettres et les dessins, l'hélice, les coups de feu, le verre de la cabine et le tendeur de la queue.

Anhand der praktischen Funktionen, die das Arbeiten mit dem Computer und mit unterschiedlichen Bildebenen bietet, können Details (wie z.B. Buchstaben, Symbole, der Propeller, das Mündungsfeuer, das Glas der Pilotenkanzel und das Spannseil) problemlos hinzugefügt werden.

Dankzij de faciliteiten die het werken met een computer en met elementen in verschillende lagen verstrekt, kunnen we op de afgeronde tekening details zoals letters en tekeningen, de propeller, de steekvlammen, de ruit van de cabine en de spanner van de staart toevoegen.

Gracias a las facilidades que proporciona trabajar con ordenador y con los elementos en diferentes capas, podemos añadir sobre el dibujo acabado detalles como letras y dibujos, la hélice, los fogonazos, el cristal de la cabina y el tensor de cola.

Grazie alle funzioni offerte dal computer, come i livelli, possiamo aggiungere sul disegno finito dettagli come lettere e disegni, l'elica, le scintille, il vetro della cabina e il tirante di coda.

Graças às facilidades que proporciona o trabalhar com computador e com os elementos em diferentes camadas, podemos acrescentar sobre o desenho acabado detalhes como letras e desenhos, a hélice, os clarões, o vidro da cabina e o tensor da empenagem.

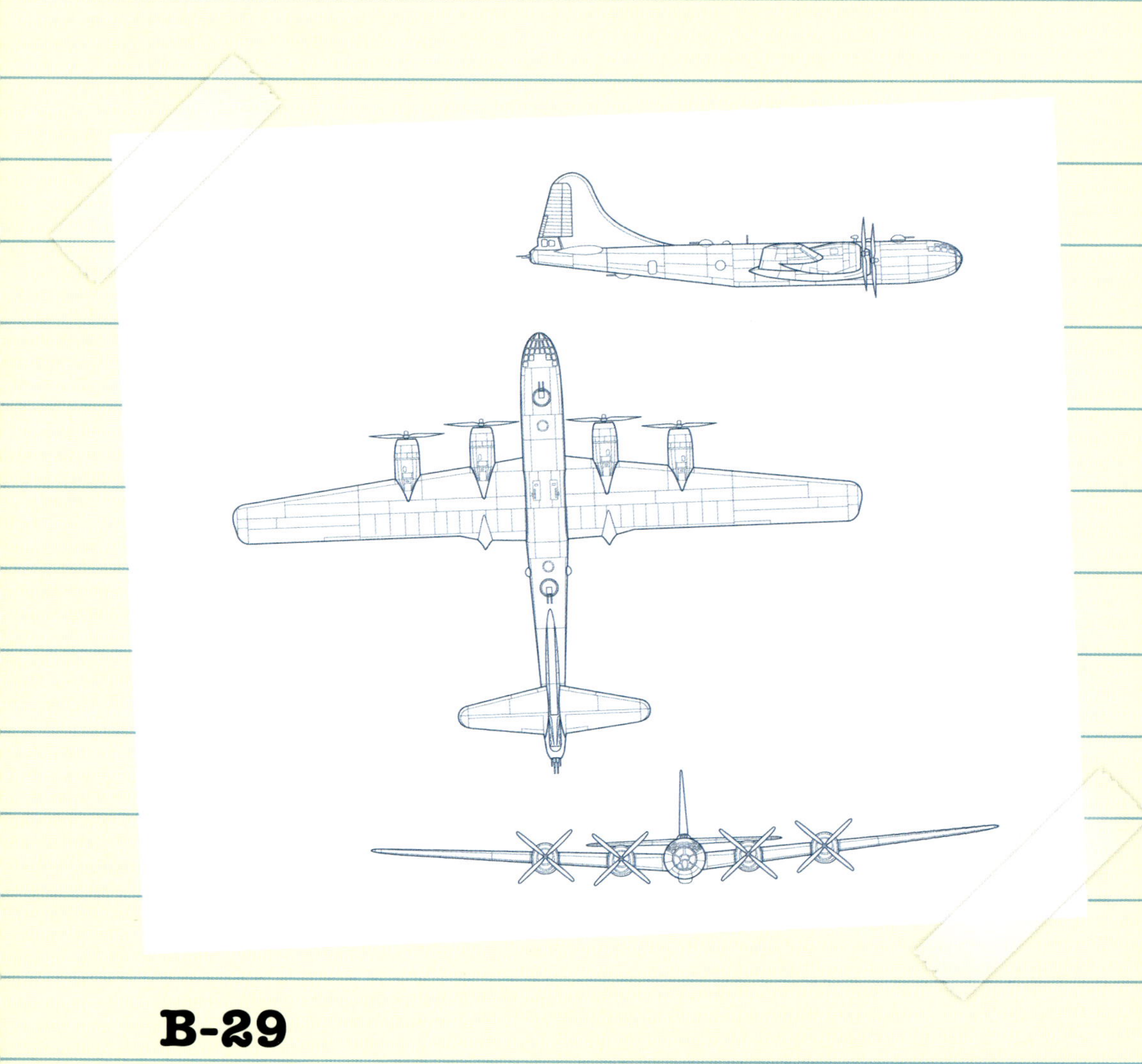

# B-29

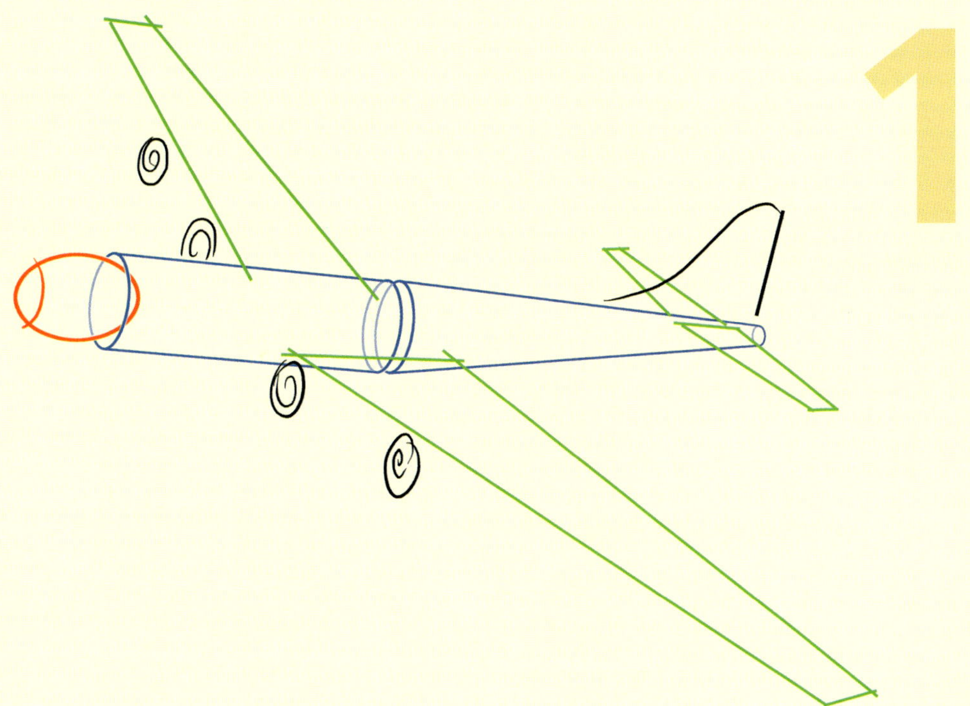


There is no exact number of elements needed for your outline to be correct. The most important thing is that you can understand and reproduce the plane's structure again and again. Making more effective outlines is matter of experience.

Il n'y a pas un nombre précis d'éléments à intégrer dans votre schéma pour que celui-ci soit correct. L'important est qu'il vous permette de comprendre et de reproduire à volonté la structure de l'avion. La réalisation de schémas plus efficaces vient avec l'expérience.

Es ist keine bestimmte Anzahl an Elementen erforderlich, damit das Grundschema korrekt ausfällt. Das Wichtigste ist, dass das Schema dazu beiträgt, die Struktur des Flugzeugs zu verstehen und in den einzelnen Arbeitsschritten wiederzugeben. Mit wachsender Erfahrung werden die Schemazeichnungen immer besser.

Er bestaat geen exact aantal elementen opdat ons schema juist is. Belangrijk is dat we de structuur van het vliegtuig begrijpen en kunnen reproduceren. Effectievere schema's maken is een kwestie van ervaring.

No hay un número de elementos exacto para que nuestro esquema sea correcto. Lo importante es que nos permita entender y reproducir, una y otra vez, la estructura del avión. Realizar esquemas más efectivos es cuestión de experiencia.

Non c'è un numero di elementi esatto da rispettare affinché lo schema sia corretto. L'importante è che esso ci permetta di capire e riprodurre, volta per volta, la struttura dell'aereo. Realizzare schemi sempre più efficaci è una questione di esperienza.

Não existe um número de elementos exacto para que o nosso esquema esteja correcto. O importante é que nos permita entender e reproduzir, uma e outra vez, a estrutura do avião. Realizar esquemas mais efectivos é uma questão de experiência.

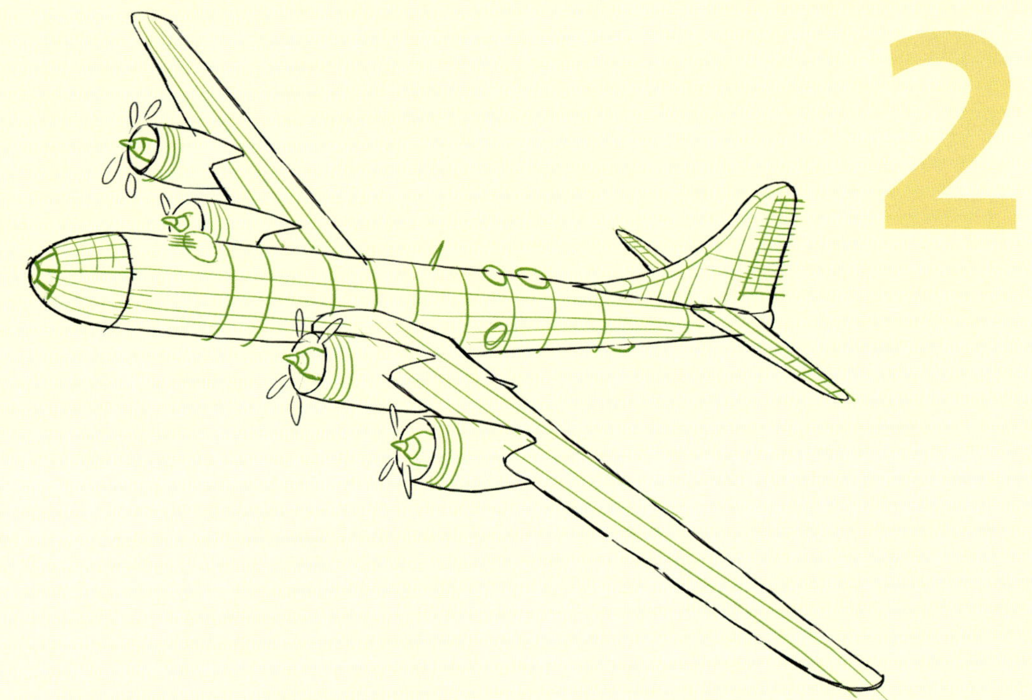

2

In addition to defining the volumes suggested by the outline, the sketch serves to make us ask questions and find the answers, as in: "Should I add more lines or will there be too many for the size of the drawing?"

L'ébauche, en plus de définir les volumes suggérés par le schéma, sert à se poser des questions et à obtenir des réponses. Ainsi dans cet exemple : « Est-il nécessaire de rajouter des lignes ou y en a-t-il suffisamment pour la taille du dessin ? »

Beim Zeichnen der Skizze wird den Elementen Volumen verliehen und der Zeichner hat Gelegenheit, sich Fragen zu stellen und diese entsprechend zu beantworten (in diesem Fall z.B.: „Soll ich weitere Linien hinzufügen oder wären das bei dieser Größe der Darstellung zu viele?").

Met de schets worden niet alleen de volumes die het schema suggereert verder uitgewerkt, maar hij dient er ook voor om ons dingen af te vragen en antwoorden te zoeken. Zoals in dit geval: "Voeg ik meer lijnen toe of worden het er dan te veel ten aanzien van de grootte van de tekening?"

El boceto, además de definir los volúmenes que sugiere el esquema, sirve para hacernos preguntas y obtener respuestas. En este caso: «¿Añado más líneas o serán demasiadas para el tamaño del dibujo?».

Il bozzetto, oltre a definire i volumi suggeriti dallo schema, serve per porci domande e ottenere risposte. In questo caso: "Aggiungo altre linee o saranno troppe per le dimensioni del disegno?"

O esboço, para além de definir os volumes que sugere o esquema, serve para fazer-nos perguntas e obter respostas. Neste caso: "Acrescento mais linhas ou serão demasiadas para o tamanho do desenho?"

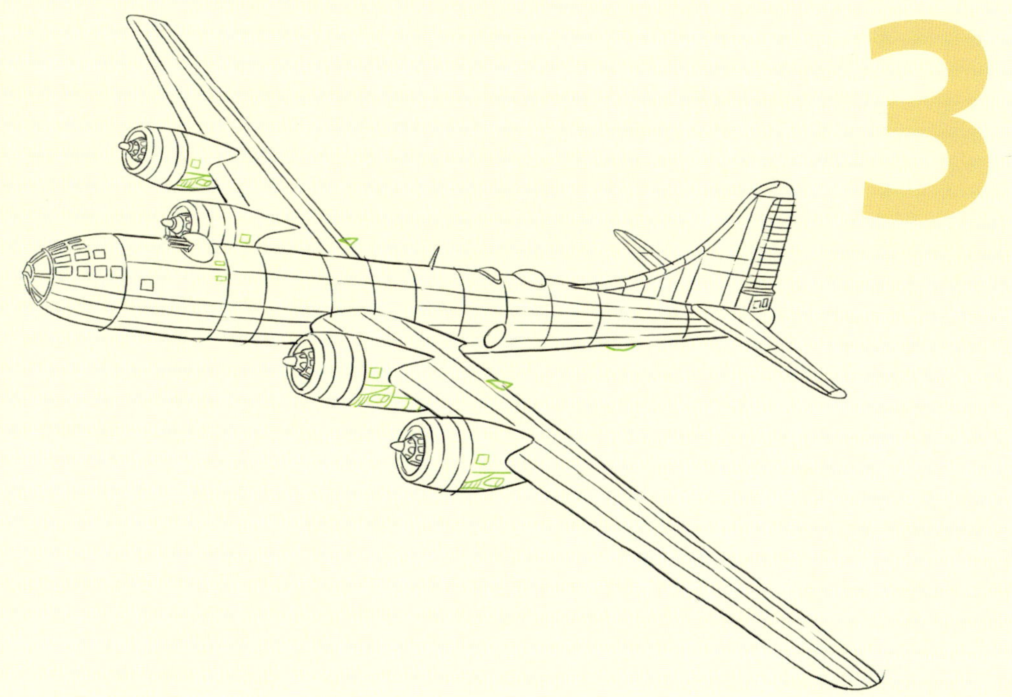

3

Admittedly, quite a few lines were erased from the sketch, but once you have made your decision, penciling lets you see whether you have made the right choice, and to draw a few details that you may have forgotten.

Vous avez effacé plusieurs lignes de l'ébauche mais, une fois la décision prise, le crayonné vous a permis de savoir si vous aviez raison de le faire et de rajouter quelques détails que vous aviez oubliés.

Wir müssen zugeben, dass einige zuvor hinzugefügte Linien wieder aus der Skizze gelöscht wurden. Nachdem diese Entscheidung getroffen wurde, hat man bei der Buntstiftzeichnung Gelegenheit, zu überprüfen, ob man richtig lag oder nicht. Außerdem werden einige Details hinzugefügt, die zuvor vergessen worden waren.

Ik moet toegeven dat in de schets een aantal lijnen zijn gewist, maar nadat een besluit is genomen, stelt de potloodtekening ons in staat om te constateren of we het bij het goede eind hebben gehad en kunnen we details tekenen die we waren vergeten.

Debo admitir que en el boceto se han borrado unas cuantas líneas, pero, una vez que nos hemos decidido, el lápiz nos permite comprobar si habíamos acertado, así como dibujar algunos detalles que se nos habían olvidado.

Devo ammettere che nel disegno sono state cancellate molte linee, ma una volta che ci siamo decisi, la matita ci permette di vedere se ci abbiamo azzeccato, oltre che disegnare alcuni dettagli che avevamo dimenticato.

Devo admitir que no esboço apagaram-se umas quantas linhas, mas uma vez que nos decidimos, o lápis permite-nos comprovar se acertámos, assim como desenhar certos detalhes que nos tínhamos esquecido.

4

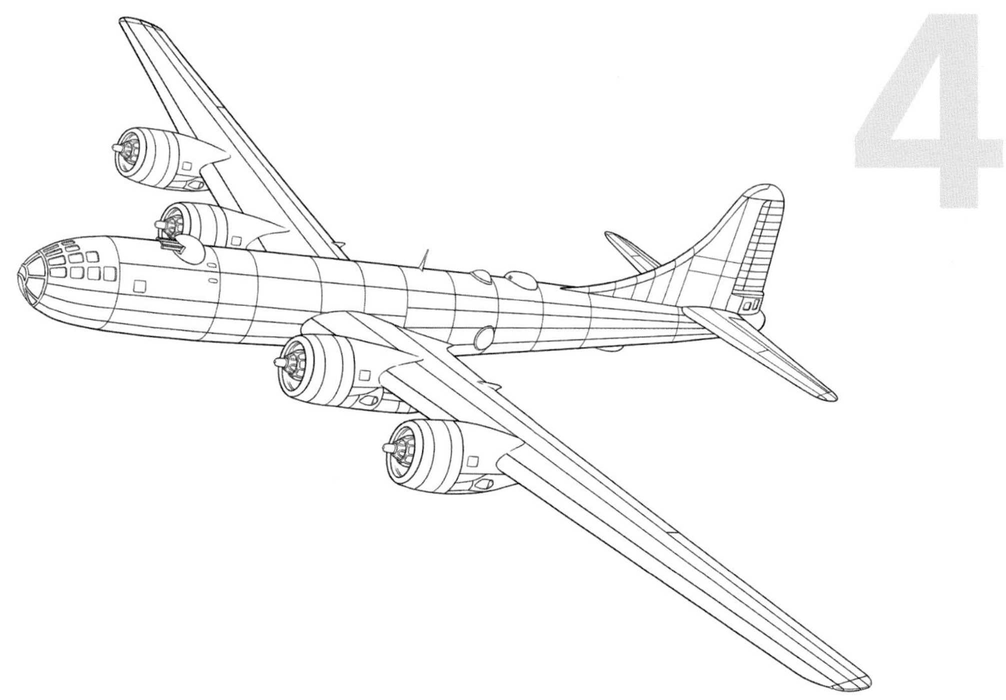

While penciling always gives you freedom and overlooks the inexactness of lines that happens when drawing freehand, inking requires neatness, for which the use of rulers or software line tools will be a great help.

Si le crayonné vous laisse une certaine liberté et autorise quelques lignes imprécises dues au dessin à main levée, l'encrage requiert quant à lui une plus grande rigueur. L'utilisation de règles ou d'outils de tracé informatiques pourra s'avérer d'une grande aide.

Der Bleistift ermöglicht eine freie Strichführung und nicht ganz genaue Linien, die beim Zeichnen frei Hand entstehen. Die Tuschezeichnung erfordert große Sorgfalt und wird durch die Verwendung von Linealen bzw. von Linien-Werkzeugen am Computer erheblich erleichtert.

De potloodtekening geeft ons altijd vrijheid en vergeeft ons onnauwkeurige lijnen die bij het uit de vrije hand tekenen ontstaan. De inkttekening vergt echter netheid. Daarom is het gebruik van linialen of hulpmiddelen voor het trekken van lijnen op de computer van grote hulp.

Si el lápiz nos da siempre libertad y nos perdona las líneas inexactas que surgen al dibujar a mano alzada, la tinta nos exige pulcritud, para lo que el uso de reglas o de herramientas de línea en el ordenador será de gran ayuda.

Se la matita dà sempre libertà e perdona le linee imprecise che sorgono durante il disegno a mano libera, il ripasso a china impone estrema pulizia. A questo scopo l'utilizzo di righelli o dello strumento linea sul computer sarà di grande aiuto.

Se o lápis nos dá sempre liberdade e nos perdoa as linhas inexactas que surgem ao desenhar à mão livre, a tinta exige-nos pulcritude, para a qual o uso de réguas ou de ferramentas geométricas no computador será de grande ajuda.

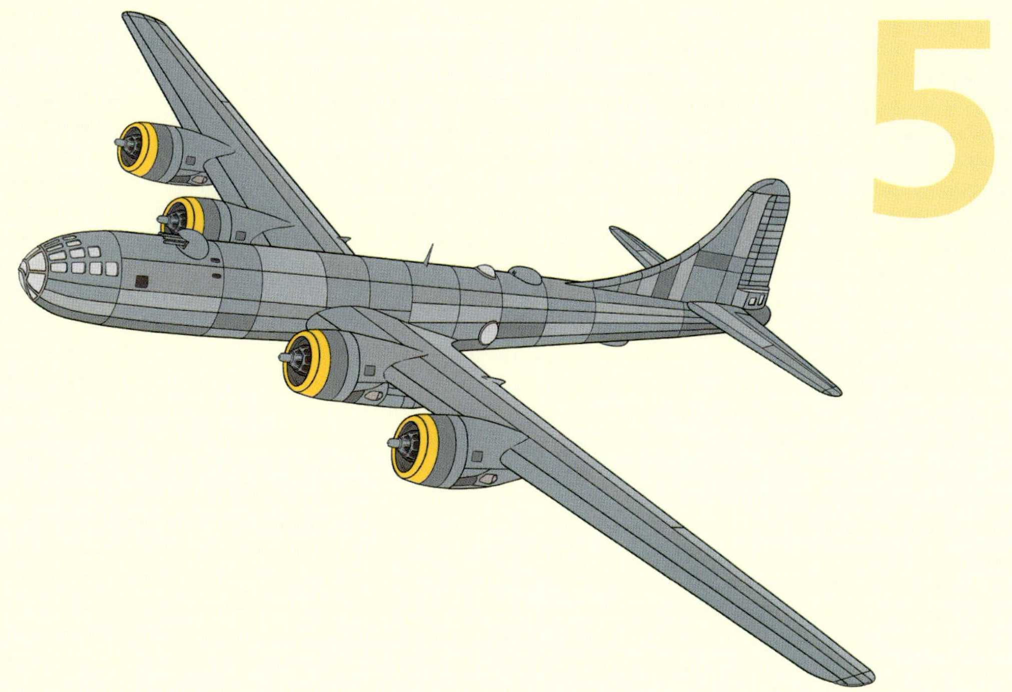

5

In order to make the metal plane not appear flat and boring, the different sections have been colored in different shades of gray, and creative licence means that the ends of the engines have been done in a yellow shade.

Pour que l'avion de couleur métallique ne paraisse pas trop plat ou monotone, colorez chacune de ses parties en différentes teintes de gris et dotez les extrémités des moteurs d'une couleur jaune.

Damit die Farbe des metallenen Flugzeugs nicht zu eintönig und langweilig wirkt, werden die einzelnen Bereich in unterschiedlichen Graunuancen gestaltet. Außerdem wird durch den gelben Rand an den Triebwerken ein Akzent gesetzt.

Opdat het metaliekkleurige vliegtuig niet vlak en saai lijkt, moeten de diverse secties in verschillende grijstinten worden gekleurd. Wij hebben de creatieve vrijheid genomen om een gele kleur voor de uiteinden van de motoren te gebruiken.

Para que el avión de color metálico no resulte plano y aburrido, hemos coloreado sus distintas secciones con diferentes tonos de gris y nos hemos tomado la licencia creativa de dar un tono amarillo a los extremos de los motores.

Affinché l'aereo di colore metallizzato non risulti piatto e noioso abbiamo colorato le diverse sezioni con tonalità distinte di grigio e ci siamo presi la licenza di aggiungere un tono giallo alle calotte dei motori.

Para que o avião de cor metálica não se torne plano e aborrecido pintámos as suas distintas secções com diferentes tons de cinzento e tomámos a liberdade criativa de dar um tom amarelo aos extremos dos motores.

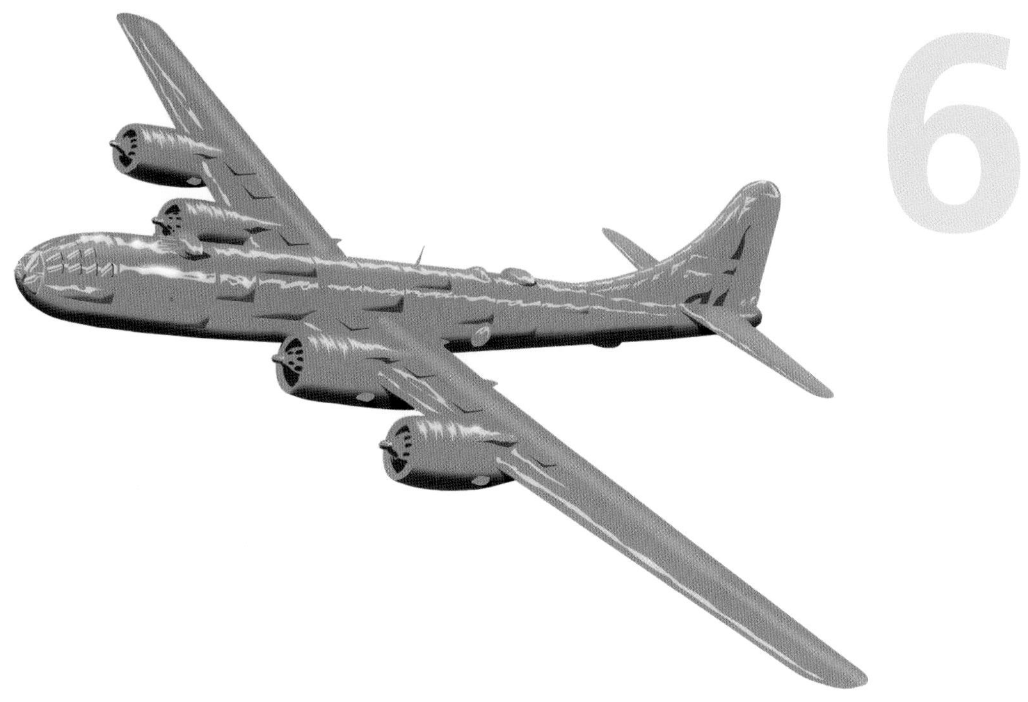

6

Lighting and shading on the B-29 is also highly contrasted. The shading has degradation, providing volume. The more specific lighting also helps to bring out the metal on the fuselage.

Les ombres et les lumières du B-29 sont également très contrastées. Les ombres sont dégradées et apportent du volume. Les lumières, plus concrètes, contribuent à rendre identifiable la nature métallique du fuselage.

Die Licht- und Schattenbereiche der B-29 sind recht kontrastreich. Die abgestuften Schatten verleihen der Zeichnung Tiefe. Die stärker abgegrenzten Lichtbereich unterstreichen die Wirkung des Metalls am Flugzeugrumpf.

Het licht en de schaduwen van de B-29 zijn eveneens zeer contrasterend. De schaduwen lopen af en zorgen voor volume. De concretere lichteffecten helpen bovendien om de metalen aard van de romp te herkennen.

Las luces y sombras del B-29 están también muy contrastadas. Las sombras están degradadas, aportando volumen. Las luces más concretas ayudan, además, a reconocer la naturaleza metálica del fuselaje.

Le luci e le ombre del B-29 sono molto contrastate. Le ombre sono state sfumate per aggiungere volume. Le luci più evidenti aiutano inoltre a riconoscere la natura metallica della fusoliera.

As luzes e sombras do B-29 estão também com muito contraste. As sombras estão esbatidas, concedendo volume. As luzes mais concretas ajudam, ainda, a reconhecer a natureza metálica da fuselagem.

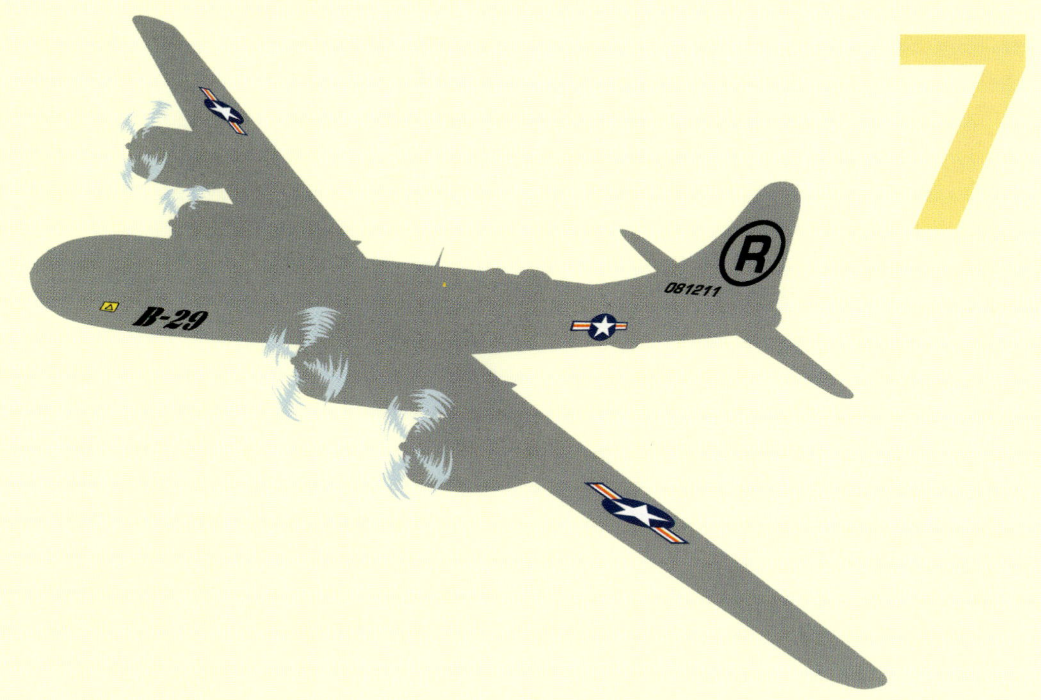


Aside from the necessary propellers, incorporating details like symbols and letters is always fun. In this case, given the large size of the plane, it is more believable if only the largest elements are visualized.

En plus des hélices, indispensables, il est toujours intéressant d'ajouter des détails tels que des symboles et des lettres. Ici, étant donné les dimensions importantes de l'avion, il semble plus réaliste de ne voir que les éléments les plus grands.

Neben den erforderlichen Propellern wird durch Hinzufügen einiger Details (wie z.B. von Symbolen und Buchstaben) eine besondere Wirkung erzielt. Aufgrund der großen Dimensionen des Flugzeugs erscheint die Darstellung in diesem Fall glaubhafter, wenn nur die größten Elemente zu sehen sind.

Naast de nodige propellers is het opnemen van details zoals symbolen en letters altijd erg leuk. In dit geval, vanwege de grote afmetingen van het vliegtuig, lijkt het geloofwaardiger om alleen de grotere elementen weer te geven.

Aparte de las necesarias hélices, incorporar detalles como símbolos y letras es siempre muy divertido. En este caso, dadas las grandes dimensiones del avión, parece más creíble visualizar sólo los elementos de mayor tamaño.

Oltre alle necessarie eliche, aggiungere dettagli come simboli e lettere è sempre molto divertente. In questo caso, data le grosse dimensioni dell'aereo, sembra più credibile mostrare solo gli elementi più evidenti.

À parte das necessárias hélices, incorporar detalhes como símbolos e letras é sempre muito divertido. Neste caso, dadas as grandes dimensões do avião, parece mais credível visualizar apenas os elementos de maior tamanho.

# 8

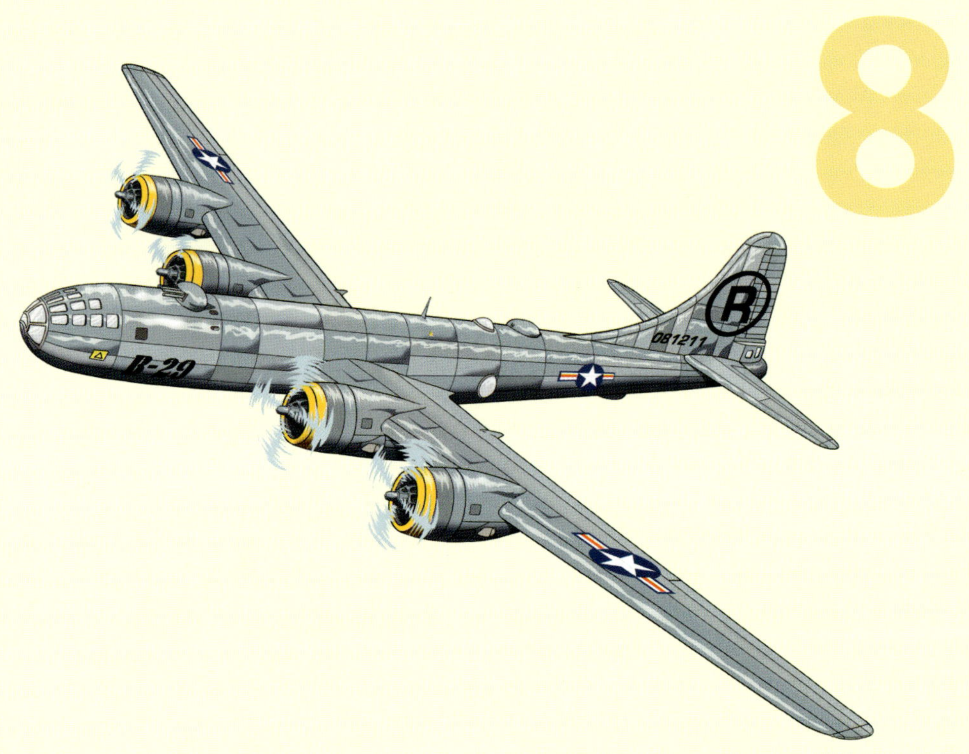


The finished drawing shows that the plane has been given a marked retro or even pulp aesthetic, which was very typical of the time.

Sur le dessin final, vous pouvez constater l'aspect rétro, voire pulp, de l'avion, caractéristique de l'époque.

In der fertigen Zeichnung sieht man, dass ein für die damalige Zeit typisches Flugzeug im Retro-Stil gelungen ist.

In de afgeronde tekening zien we dat een vliegtuig is getekend met een opmerkelijk retro en zelfs pulpeffect, dat zeer kenmerkend is voor die tijd.

En el dibujo acabado vemos que se ha conseguido un avión con un marcado aspecto retro e incluso pulp, muy característico de la época.

Nel disegno finito vediamo che si è ottenuto un aereo con un forte aspetto rétro, quasi pulp, molto caratteristico di quell'epoca.

No desenho acabado vemos que se conseguiu um avião com um marcado aspecto retro e inclusive vulgar, muito característico da época.

9

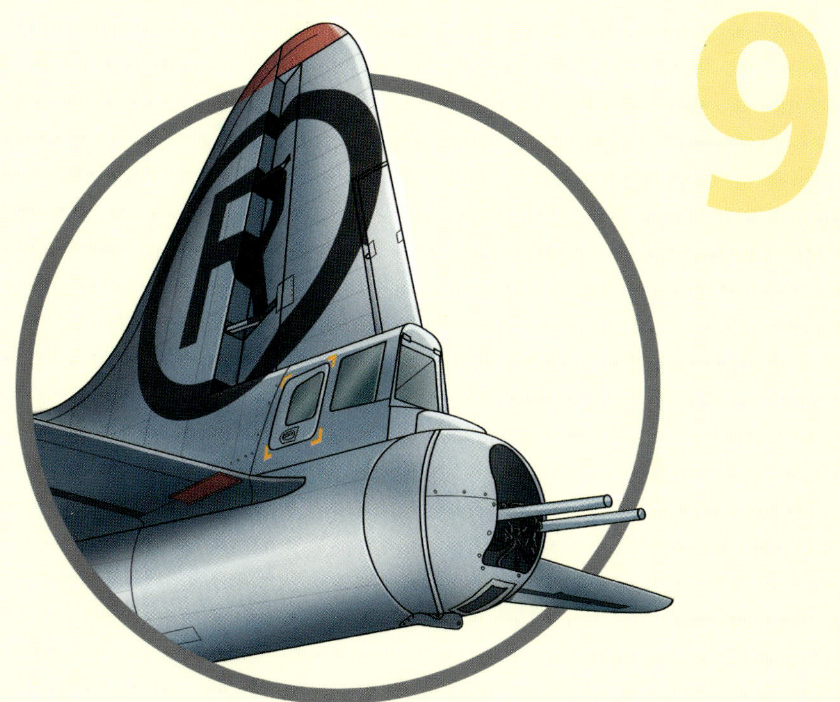

Pressurized cabins, advanced electronic systems, and remote control operated gun turrets were some of the technological innovations included in this plane. It was used to transmit television signals from the air.

Cabines pressurisées, systèmes électroniques de pointe et tourelles contrôlées à distance : voici quelques innovations technologiques intégrées à cet avion. Il a également été utilisé pour émettre des signaux TV depuis le ciel.

Druckkabinen, eine fortschrittliche Elektronik und fernbediente Türme für die Abwehrbewaffnung waren einige der technologischen Neuerungen, mit denen dieses Flugzeug aufwartete. Das Modell wurde auch für die Aussendung von Fernsehsignalen aus der Luft eingesetzt.

Cabines waarin de luchtdruk wordt geregeld, geavanceerde elektronische systemen en op afstand bediende geschuttorens waren enkele technologische innovaties waarmee dit vliegtuig was uitgerust. Het werd tevens gebruikt om vanuit de lucht televisiesignalen uit te zenden.

Cabinas presurizadas, avanzados sistemas electrónicos y torretas de tiro por control remoto fueron algunas de las innovaciones tecnológicas que incluía este avión. Llegó a ser utilizado para emitir señales de televisión desde el aire.

Cabine pressurizzate, avanzati sistemi elettronici e torrette armate telecomandate sono solo alcune delle innovazioni tecnologiche presenti su questo velivolo. Venne utilizzato persino per trasmettere segnali televisivi dal cielo.

Cabinas pressurizadas, avançados sistemas electrónicos e torretas de tiro por controlo remoto foram algumas das inovações tecnológicas que incluía este avião. Chegou a ser utilizado para emitir sinais de televisão a partir do ar.

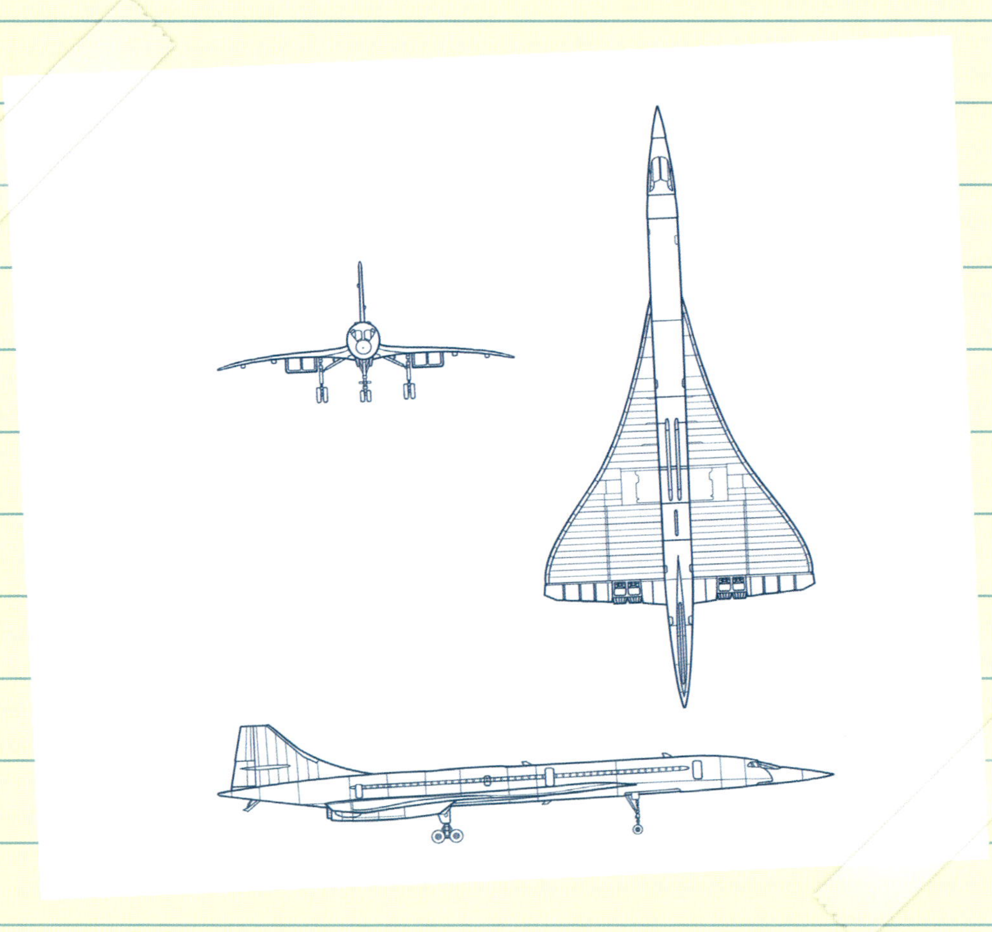

## Concorde

1

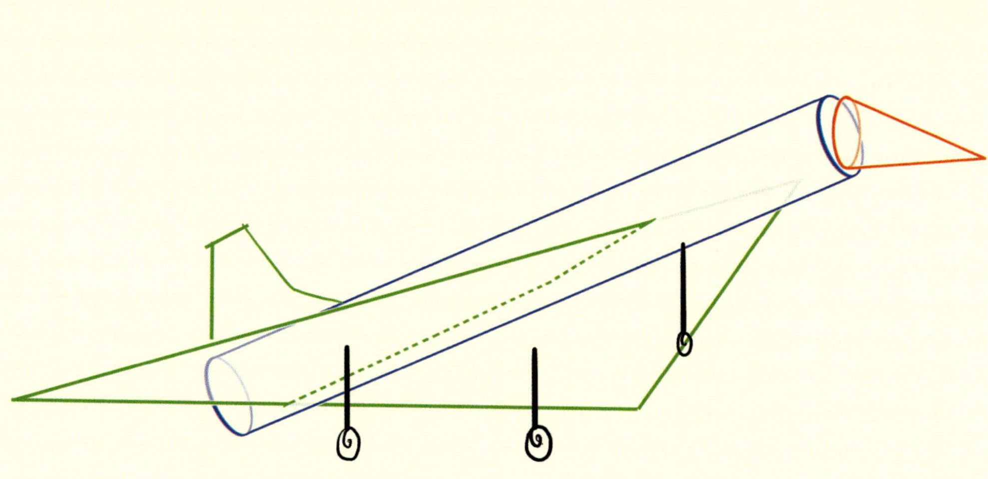

The simplest skeletons give shape to very beautiful aircraft. This is an important lesson to learn if you should ever design functional and believable airplanes of fiction.

Les squelettes les plus simples donnent des avions de grande beauté. C'est une leçon à retenir si l'on doit concevoir des avions fictifs qui soient fonctionnels et réalistes.

Die einfachsten Skelette verleihen außerordentlich schönen Flugzeugen ihre Form. Dies ist zu berücksichtigen, wenn funktionsfähige und glaubwürdige fiktive Flugmaschinen entworfen werden sollen.

Uit de eenvoudigste structuren ontstaan prachtige luchtschepen. Dit is een belangrijke les als we ooit denkbeeldige, functionele en geloofwaardige vliegtuigen moeten ontwerpen.

Los esqueletos más simples forman aeronaves de gran belleza. Es una lección importante si en alguna ocasión debemos diseñar aviones ficticios, funcionales y creíbles.

Dagli scheletri più semplici si creano aeroplani di grande bellezza. Questa è una lezione importante se ci capiterà di disegnare velivoli fittizi funzionali e credibili.

Os esqueletos mais simples formam aeronaves de grande beleza. Esta é uma lição importante se nalguma ocasião devemos desenhar aviões fictícios, funcionais e credíveis.

2

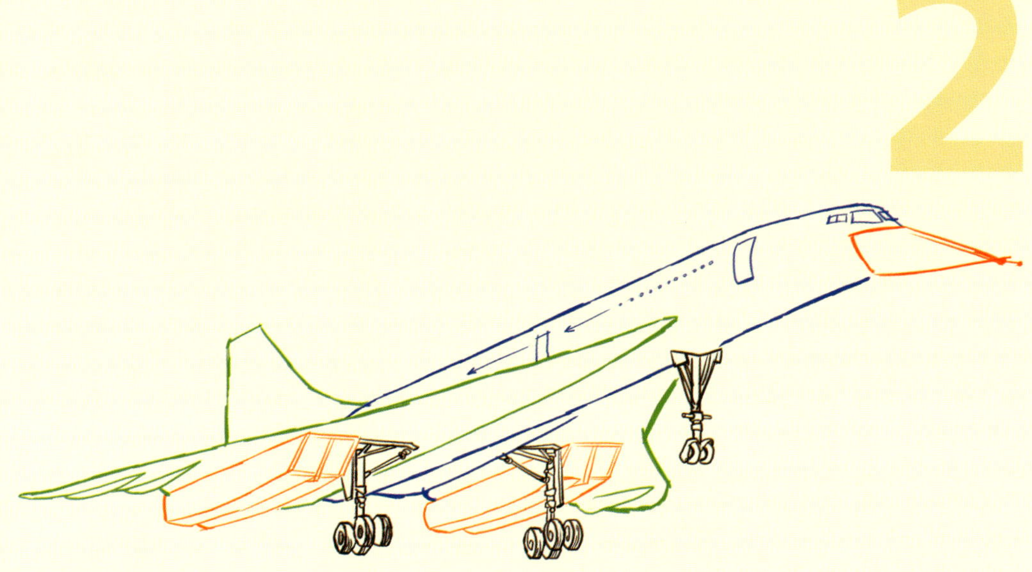

There was a trick used in making this computer sketch: for some reason I was not able to do the undercarriages, so I drew a large one on a separate layer and then shrank it until it fit in its place.

La réalisation de cette ébauche a nécessité quelques manipulations sur ordinateur : pour je ne sais quelle raison, je ne parvenais pas à dessiner le train d'atterrissage ; j'ai donc dessiné chaque train en grand sur des calques différents, puis je les ai réduits et placés correctement.

Bei dieser am Computer angefertigten Skizze wurde ein Trick angewandt: Da es sich als schwierig erwies, das Fahrwerk ordentlich zu zeichnen, wurden die einzelnen Elemente detailgenau und recht groß in einer separaten Ebene skizziert. Anschließend wurde die Größe reduziert, bis das Fahrwerk perfekt eingepasst werden konnte.

Er werd een truc gebruikt toen deze schets met de computer werd gemaakt: om de een of andere reden lukte het niet om het landingsgestel te maken, dus werd elk onderdeel op groot formaat in een aparte laag getekend en werden deze later gereduceerd om ze op hun plaats te brengen.

Hubo truco en la realización de este boceto con el ordenador: por alguna razón no conseguía hacer los trenes de aterrizaje, así que dibujé cada uno a gran tamaño en una capa aparte y después los reduje hasta encajarlo en su sitio.

Nella realizzazione di questo bozzetto con il computer ho usato un trucco: per qualche ragione non riuscivo a rendere correttamente il carrello di atterraggio, così l'ho disegnato a grande scala in un livello separato e poi l'ho ridotto inserendolo nella posizione esatta.

Houve truque na realização deste esboço com o computador: por qualquer razão não conseguia fazer os trens de aterragem, assim desenhei cada um em tamanho grande numa camada à parte e depois reduzi-os para encaixá-los no seu sítio.

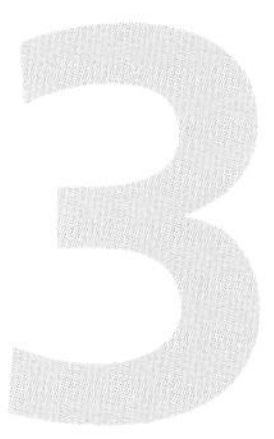

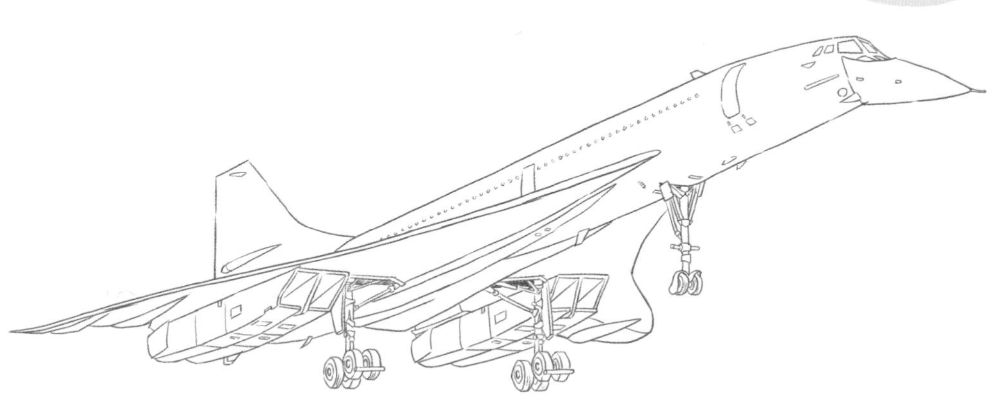

One trick for making a plane seem very large is to complete the penciling with small details, particularly those that serve as a reference for size, such as the passenger windows.

Une astuce pour que l'avion paraisse grand est de compléter le crayonné avec de petits détails qui vous serviront de référence de taille, comme par exemple les hublots.

Damit das Flugzeug den Eindruck einer besonders großen Maschine vermittelt, werden kleine Details in die Buntstiftzeichnung eingefügt (insbesondere Elemente, die den Größenunterschied verdeutlichen, wie z.B. die Fenster der Passagierkabine).

Een truc om de indruk te wekken dat het een groot vliegtuig is, is de potloodtekening af te ronden met kleine details, met name die details die als verwijzing naar de afmeting fungeren, zoals de raampjes van de passagiers.

Un truco para que el avión dé sensación de gran tamaño es completar el lápiz con detalles pequeños, sobre todo aquellos que nos sirven como referencia de tamaño, como las ventanillas de los pasajeros.

Un trucco per rendere le grandi dimensioni del velivolo è quello di completare le matite con alcuni piccoli dettagli, soprattutto quelli utili come riferimento per apprezzare le dimensioni, come i finestrini dei passeggeri.

Um truque para que o avião dê a sensação de grande tamanho é completar o lápis com detalhes pequenos, sobretudo aqueles que nos servem como referência de tamanho, como as janelas dos passageiros.

# 4

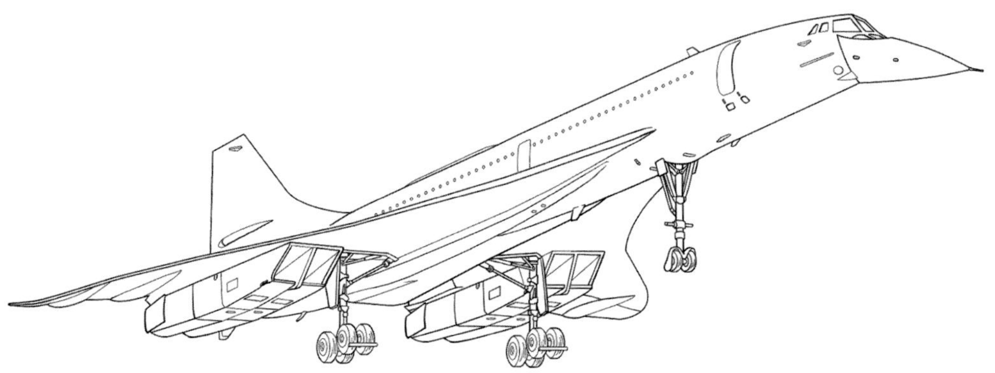

The inking done on the Concorde is like the aircraft itself, stylized and elegant. It is interesting to note that this aircraft has very few straight lines. Almost all of them are curved, even slightly.

Les tracés du Concorde sont élégants et stylisés, tout comme l'avion lui-même. Il est intéressant de noter que cet aéronef comporte très peu de lignes droites. Presque toutes les lignes sont courbes.

Die Tuschezeichnung der Concorde sollte genau wie das Flugzeug selbst fein und elegant ausfallen. Hier kann man unterstreichen, dass dieses Modell kaum gerade Linien aufweist. Fast alle Linien sind leicht gebogen.

De inktstrepen van de Concorde zijn, net als het vliegtuig zelf, gestyleerd en elegant. Het is interessant om erop te wijzen dat dit luchtschip maar heel weinig rechte lijnen heeft. Bijna alle lijnen zijn, hoewel soms minimaal, gebogen.

Las tintas del Concorde son, como el avión mismo, estilizadas y elegantes. Es interesante remarcar que esta aeronave contiene muy pocas líneas rectas. Casi todas las líneas están curvadas, aunque sea mínimamente.

Il tratto a china usato per il Concorde è, come l'aereo stesso, stilizzato ed elegante. È interessante notare che questo aereo contiene pochissime linee rette. Quasi tutte le linee sono curve, anche se in minima parte.

As tintas do Concorde são, como o próprio avião, estilizadas e elegantes. É interessante realçar que esta aeronave contém muito poucas linhas rectas. Quase todas as linhas são curvas, ainda que seja minimamente.

# 5

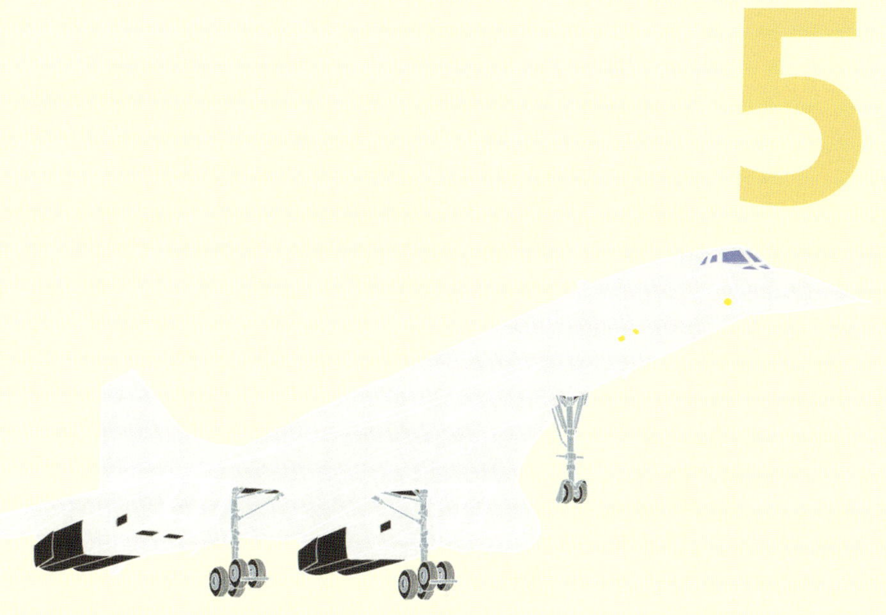

The gray or off white that predominates on the Concorde is only altered by the small windows of the cockpit, the undercarriage, and the black engines. They are the iconic and elegant colors of a tuxedo.

La prédominance du gris clair, presque blanc, du Concorde n'est altérée que par les vitres de la cabine, le train d'atterrissage et les moteurs noirs. Ce sont les couleurs élégantes et iconiques d'un frac.

Die hellgraue, fast weiße Farbe, die bei der Concorde vorherrscht, wird nur durch die kleinen Fenster, das Fahrwerk und die schwarzen Triebwerke unterbrochen – ein Flugzeug in den eleganten Farben eines Fracks.

De kleur grijs of praktisch wit die in de Concorde de overhand heeft, wordt alleen onderbroken door de kleine ramen van de cabine, het landingsgestel en de zwarte motoren: de iconische en elegante kleuren van een rokkostuum.

El color gris o prácticamente blanco que predomina en el Concorde sólo se ve alterado por los pequeños cristales de la cabina, el tren de aterrizaje y los negros motores: los icónicos y elegantes colores de un frac.

Il colore grigio o praticamente bianco che predomina nel Concorde è alterato soltanto dai piccoli cristalli della cabina, dal carrello e dai motori neri: i colori iconici ed eleganti di un frac.

A cor cinzenta ou praticamente branca que predomina no Concorde apenas se vê alterada pelos pequenos vidros da cabina, o trem de aterragem e os pretos motores: as icónicas e elegantes cores de um fraque.

# 6

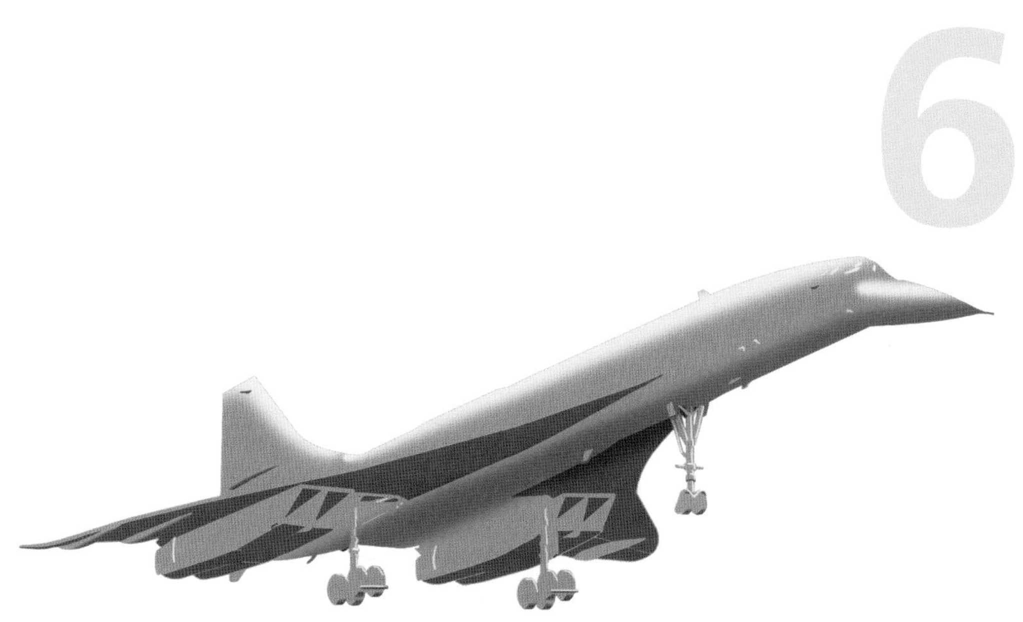

A single layer of diffuse light on the side of the plane places the sun as the light source and is a focal point for the white color of the Concorde. Volume is provided by two layers of shading, one dark and defined, and the other that is lighter and more diffuse.

Une seule couche de lumière diffuse sur le dos de l'avion place le soleil comme source lumineuse et met en évidence la couleur blanche du Concorde. Le volume est défini par deux couches d'ombres, l'une foncée et définie, l'autre plus claire et diffuse.

Ein sanfter Lichtschein auf der Oberseite des Flugzeugs ist das Resultat der Sonne, die in diesem Fall als Lichtquelle dient, und verstärkt die weiße Farbe der Concorde. Durch zwei Schattenebenen – eine dunkle, klar definierte und eine hellere, sanft verlaufende Abstufung – wird der Zeichnung Tiefe verliehen.

Eén enkele vage lichtlaag op de rug van het vliegtuig situeert de zon als lichtbron en zal de referentie van de witte kleur van de Concorde zijn. Het volume wordt verkregen met twee schaduwlagen, de ene donker en duidelijk omlijnd en de andere lichter en diffuus.

Una sola capa de luz difusa en el lomo del avión sitúa el sol como foco y será referencia del color blanco del Concorde. El volumen se consigue con dos capas de sombras, una oscura y definida y otra más clara y difusa.

Un singolo livello di luce diffusa sul dorso dell'aereo indica il sole come sorgente luminosa e definisce il colore bianco del Concorde. Il volume si ottiene con due livelli di ombreggiature, uno scuro e definito e un altro più chiaro e sfumato.

Uma só camada de luz difusa no corpo do avião coloca o sol como foco e será referência da cor branca do Concorde. O volume consegue-se com duas camadas de sombras, uma escura e definida e outra mais clara e difusa.

7

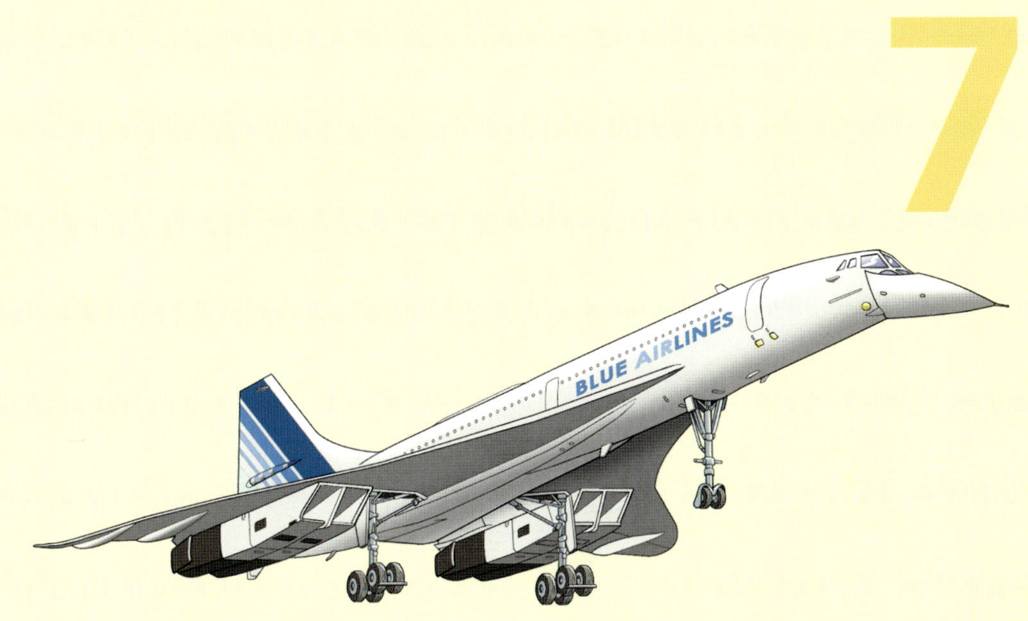


The harmonious image is completed with the logo and blue letters that confirm the nature of Concorde as a commercial and passenger aircraft. There will never be such an iconic and elegant plane as this.

L'ensemble harmonieux est complété par des logos et quelques lettres bleues qui mettent en avant la nature commerciale et civile du Concorde. Il n'existe pas d'avion aussi iconique et élégant que celui-ci.

Die harmonische Darstellung wird durch einige Logos und blaue Buchstaben vervollständigt, die für die Nutzung der Concorde als Passagierflugzeug stehen. Es wird wohl nie wieder ein derart besonderes und elegantes Flugzeug wie dieses geben.

Het harmonische geheel wordt afgerond met logo's en blauwe letters die de functie van de Concorde als commercieel en passagiersvliegtuig nog eens versterkt. Er zal nooit een dergelijk iconisch en elegant vliegtuig als dit bestaan.

El armónico conjunto se completa con unos logotipos y unas letras azules que reafirman la naturaleza de avión comercial y de pasajeros del Concorde. Jamás habrá otro avión tan icónico y elegante.

Questo insieme armonico è completato da alcuni stemmi e dalla scritta azzurra che conferma la natura di velivolo commerciale e passeggeri del Concorde. Non ci sarà mai un altro aereo così iconico ed elegante come questo.

O harmonioso conjunto completa-se com logótipos e umas letras azuis que reafirmam a natureza de avião comercial e de passageiros do Concorde. Jamais haverá outro avião tão icónico e elegante como este.

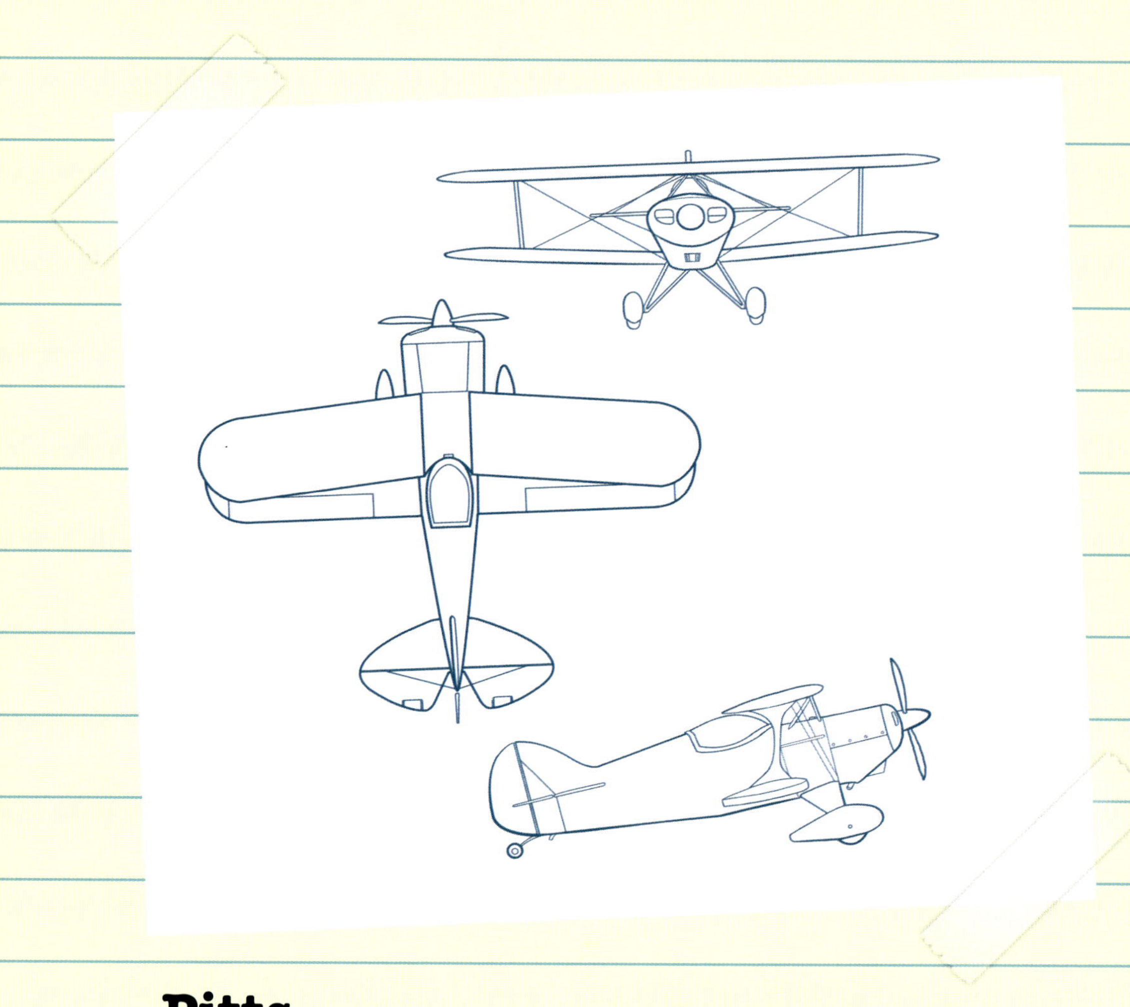

# Pitts

1

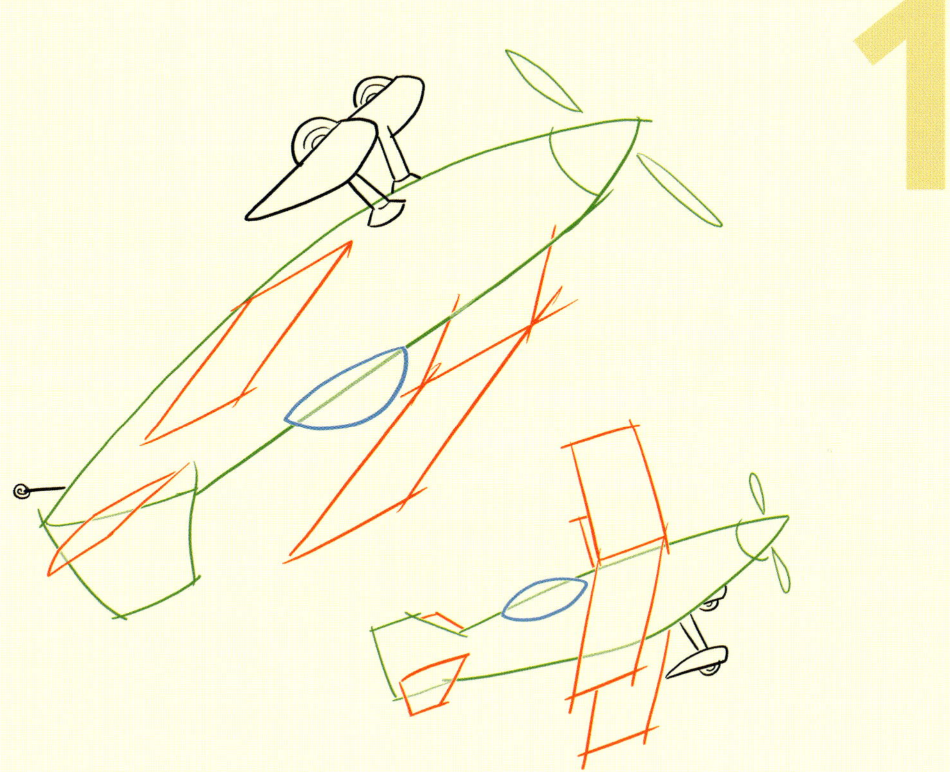

Drawing planes doing aerobatics or in aerial confrontations with similar aircraft is a good way of seeing whether your outline works from different angles.

Dessiner des acrobaties aériennes ou des affrontements d'aéronefs similaires est une bonne façon de voir si notre schéma fonctionne depuis différentes perspectives.

Beim Zeichnen von Flugzeugen, die Kunstflugfiguren ausführen oder sich entgegenfliegen, kann man leicht überprüfen, ob das Grundschema auch aus unterschiedlichen Winkeln anwendbar ist.

Het tekenen van vliegtuigen die stuntvluchten of soortgelijke confrontaties in de lucht tussen luchtschepen uitvoeren is een goede manier om na te gaan of ons schema vanuit diverse hoeken werkt.

Dibujar aviones realizando acrobacias o enfrentamientos aéreos de aeronaves similares es una buena manera de comprobar si nuestro esquema funciona desde varios ángulos.

Disegnare aeroplani che eseguono acrobazie oppure combattimenti fra aerei simili è un buon modo per verificare se il nostro schema funziona da varie angolazioni.

Desenhar aviões realizando acrobacias ou confrontos aéreos de aeronaves similares é uma boa maneira de comprovar se o nosso esquema funciona a partir de vários ângulos.

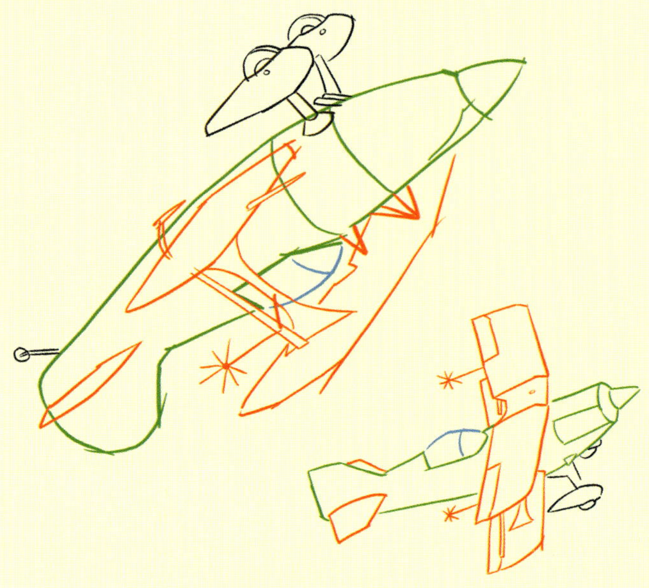

2

It can be a great help to make a sketch that continues with the colors of the outline, both for the first time you draw a model of an airplane and for when several elements are superimposed.

La réalisation d'une ébauche suivant les mêmes tonalités que le schéma peut être très utile, aussi bien lorsque vous dessinez pour la première fois un modèle d'avion que lorsque vous superposez différents éléments.

Das Anfertigen der Skizze unter Verwendung derselben Farben wie bei der Schemazeichnung ist äußerst hilfreich, sowohl bei den ersten Versuchen, ein bestimmtes Flugzeugmodell zu zeichnen, als auch für die korrekte Darstellung sich überlagernder Elemente.

Een schets in dezelfde kleurschakeringen als het schema maken helpt ons zowel de eerste keren dat we een vliegtuigmodel tekenen als wanneer we diverse elementen boven elkaar willen plaatsen.

Realizar un boceto siguiendo los mismos tonos de color que el esquema nos ayuda mucho, tanto en las primeras ocasiones en las que dibujamos un modelo de avión como cuando se superponen varios elementos.

Realizzare un bozzetto seguendo le stesse tonalità di colore dello schema ci aiuta molto, sia nei primi tempi quando disegniamo un modello di aereo, sia quando si sovrappongono più elementi.

Realizar um esboço continuando nos mesmos tons de cor que o esquema ajuda-nos muito, tanto nas primeiras ocasiões nas quais desenhamos um modelo de avião como quando se superpõem vários elementos.

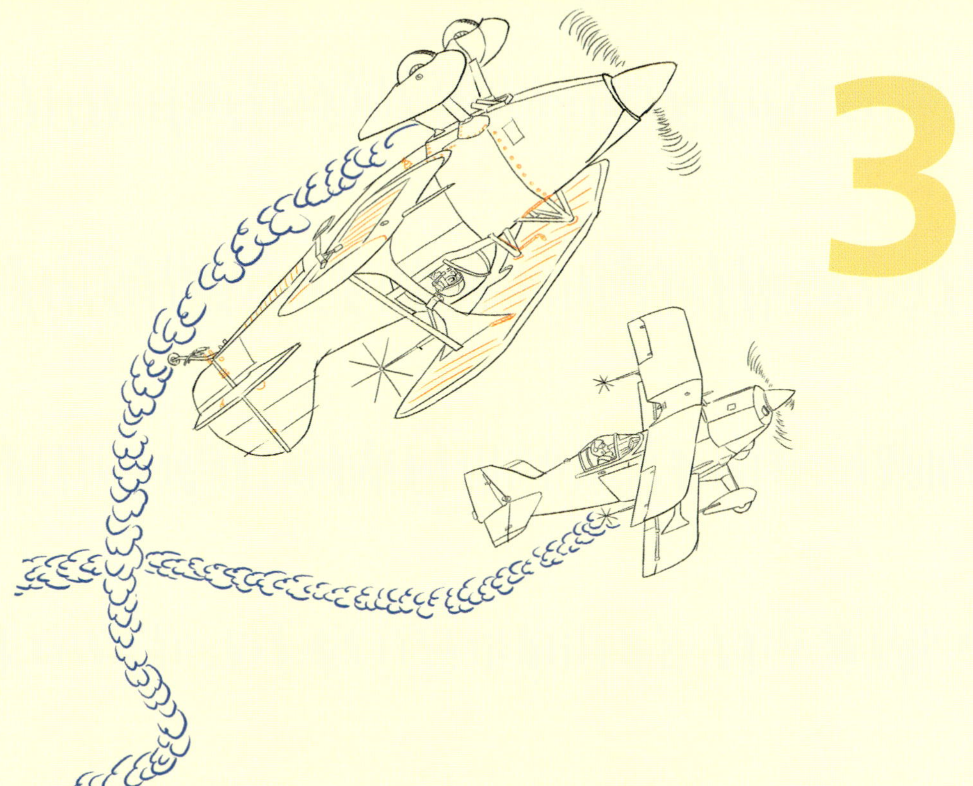


The pencil sketch of the more distant plane, although of a similar model, contains fewer details. Anything that is drawn to appear more distant needs to be less detailed, and vice versa.

Le crayonné du deuxième avion, bien que similaire au premier, comporte moins de détails. Plus une chose est éloignée, moins elle est détaillée, et vice-versa.

Die Zeichnung des weiter entfernten Flugzeugs, bei dem es sich um ein ähnliches Modell handelt, weist weniger Details auf. Je weiter entfernt sich die Bildelemente befinden, desto weniger Einzelheiten werden ausgearbeitet, und umgekehrt.

De potloodtekening van het verst afgelegen vliegtuig, ook al gaat het om een soortgelijk model, bevat minder details. Alles wat we tekenen maakt haar minder gedetailleerd naarmate we verderaf tekenen. En andersom.

El lápiz del avión más alejado, aunque es un modelo similar, contiene menos detalles. Cualquier cosa que dibujemos la haremos menos detallada a medida que la dibujemos más alejada, y viceversa.

Le matite dell'aereo più lontano, benché raffigurino un modello simile, contengono meno dettagli. Più un soggetto è distante, meno dettagliato bisogna disegnarlo. E viceversa.

O lápis do avião mais afastado, embora seja um modelo similar, contém menos detalhes. Qualquer coisa que desenhemos fazemo-la menos detalhada à medida que a desenhemos mais afastada e vice-versa.

# 4

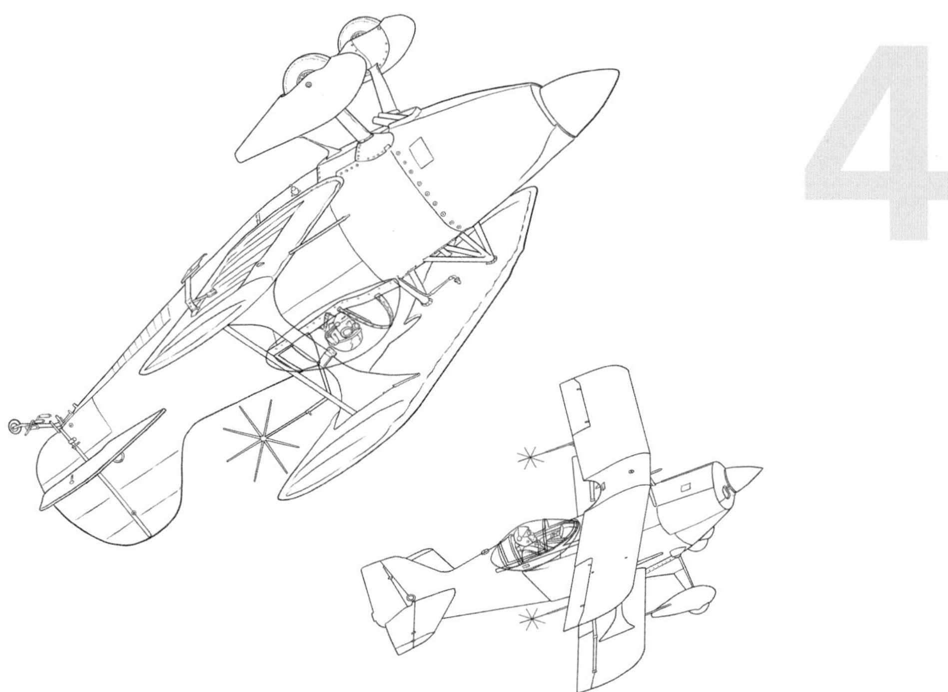

Another general rule for inking is that closer objects should be illustrated with thicker strokes and the more distant ones with finer strokes. If this is well done, your eye will correct the distances and let you believe that both planes have the correct inking.

Selon une autre règle générale d'encrage, les objets les plus proches sont dessinés avec des tracés plus épais tandis que les plus éloignés présentent des lignes plus fines. Si l'encrage est bien fait, l'œil corrigera les distances et il semblera que les deux avions ont des tracés de taille adéquate.

Bei der Tuschezeichnung ist zu beachten, dass näher liegende Elemente mit dickeren Strichen und weiter entfernte Objekte mit dünneren Linien zu versehen sind. Wird dieser Schritt korrekt ausgeführt, gleicht das Auge die Entfernung automatisch aus und es entsteht der Eindruck, dass beide Flugzeuge gleich groß sind.

Een andere algemene regel van het inkleuren is dat de dichtbij gelegen voorwerpen worden geïllustreerd met dikkere inktstrepen en de verderaf gelegen voorwerpen met dunnere inktstrepen. Als we het goed doen, dan corrigeert het oog de afstanden en laat het geloven dat beide vliegtuigen inktstrepen van de juiste grootte hebben.

Otra regla general del entintado es que los objetos cercanos se ilustran con tintas más gruesas y los lejanos con tintas más finas. Si lo hacemos bien, el ojo corregirá las distancias y hará creer que ambos aviones tienen tintas del tamaño correcto.

Un'altra regola generale del ripasso a china è che gli oggetti vicini vanno definiti con un tratto più spesso e quelli lontani con uno più sottile. Se lavoriamo nel modo giusto, l'occhio correggerà le distanze e ci farà credere che entrambi gli aerei abbiano le linee delle dimensioni corrette.

Outra regra geral da arte-final é que os objectos próximos ilustram-se com tintas mais espessas e os afastados com tintas mais finas. Se o fazemos bem, o olho corrigirá as distâncias e fará crer que ambos os aviões têm tintas do tamanho correcto.

5

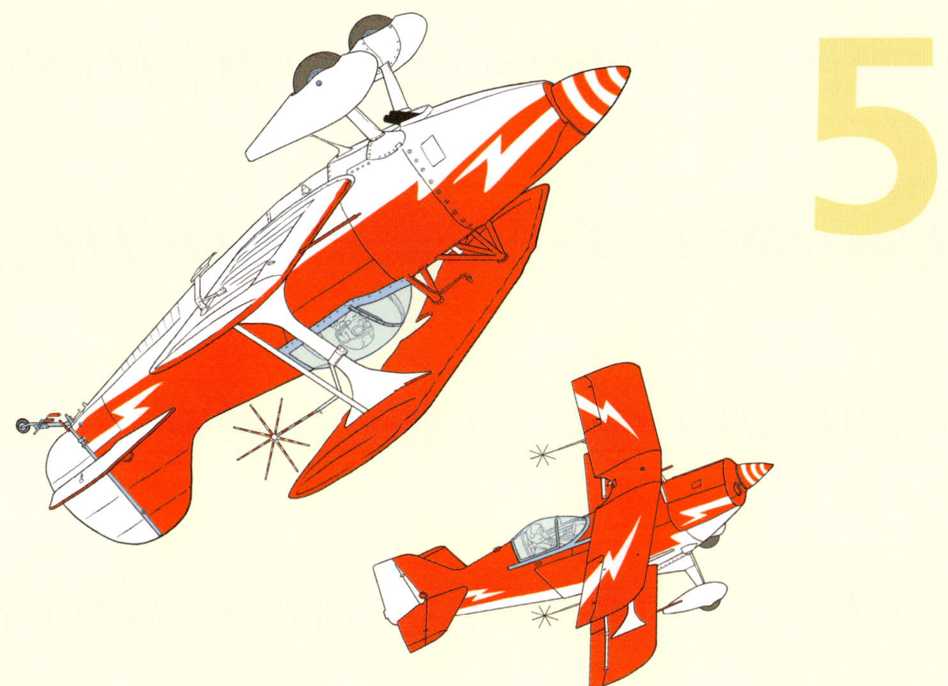

Red is a bold color and a highly visible one at great distance, making it ideal for aerobatic planes. The details of alternating lines on the propeller and the stripes on the fuselage and wings add a circus-like touch.

Le rouge est une couleur vive et bien visible à distance, idéale pour les avions d'acrobatie. Les rayures rouges et blanches sur les hélices et les éclairs sur le fuselage font penser aux décors d'un cirque.

Rot ist eine gewagte, auf weite Entfernung hin sichtbare Farbe und bietet sich daher für die Gestaltung von Kunstflugmaschinen an. Die abwechselnden Streifen am Propeller und die Blitze an Rumpf und Tragflächen verleihen dem Flugzeug einen Zirkus-Touch.

Rood is een gedurfde en op lange afstand goed zichtbare kleur, ideaal voor stuntvliegtuigen. De details van afwisselende strepen op de propeller en de bliksemstralen op de romp en vleugels zorgen voor iets circusachtigs.

El rojo es un color atrevido y bien visible a largas distancias, ideal para aviones acrobáticos. Los detalles de rayas alternas en la hélice y los rayos en el fuselaje y las alas aportan un toque circense.

Il rosso è un colore acceso e molto visibile a lunga distanza, ideale per gli aerei acrobatici. I dettagli a strisce alternate sull'elica e i lampi sulla fusoliera e sulle ali aggiungono un tocco circense.

O vermelho é uma cor atrevida e bem visível a longas distâncias, ideal para aviões acrobáticos. Os detalhes de riscas alternadas na hélice e os raios na fuselagem e as asas dão um toque circense.

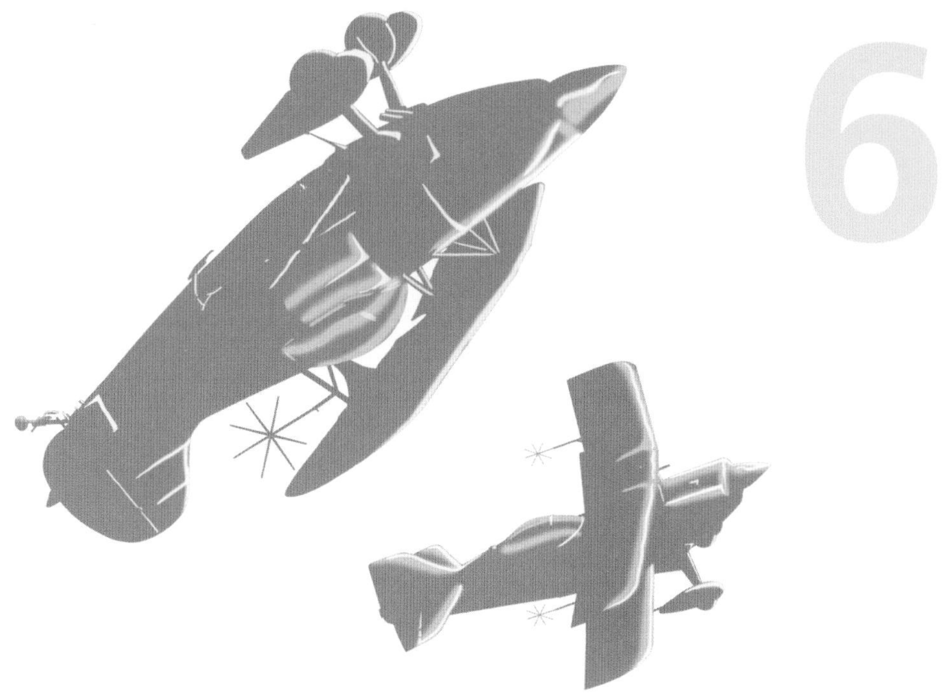


Separate the lighting and the shading for a better understanding of how they are done. You can see two layers of white light with different levels of opacity. Making separate layers enables you to adjust their opacity individually.

Les ombres et les lumières sont séparées pour une meilleure compréhension de leur réalisation. Vous pouvez observer deux couches de lumière blanche de différentes opacités. L'utilisation de couches distinctes permet de modifier les opacités séparément.

Die Licht- und Schattenbereiche werden in diesem Fall separat betrachtet, um ein besseres Verständnis zu ermöglichen. Im Bild sieht man zwei weiße Lichtebenen mit unterschiedlicher Transparenz. Durch die Einarbeitung in zwei Ebenen kann die Transparenz für jede einzelne Ebene separat abgeändert werden.

We scheiden de lichten van de schaduwen zodat het gemakkelijker is om te begrijpen hoe ze worden uitgewerkt. We kunnen twee witte lichtlagen van verschillende doorschijnendheid waarnemen. Door ze in gescheiden lagen uit te werken, kan de opaciteit ervan afzonderlijk worden gewijzigd.

Separamos las luces y las sombras para una mejor comprensión de cómo se realizan. Podemos observar dos capas de luz blanca a distinta opacidad. Hacerlas en capas separadas nos permite modificar su opacidad por separado.

Separiamo le luci e le ombre per capire meglio come vanno realizzate. Possiamo osservare due livelli di luce bianca dalla diversa opacità. Eseguirle su livelli separati ci consente di modificarne l'opacità individualmente.

Separamos as luzes e as sombras para uma melhor compreensão de como se realizam. Podemos observar duas camadas de luz branca com diferente opacidade. Fazê-las em camadas separadas permite-nos modificar a sua opacidade separadamente.

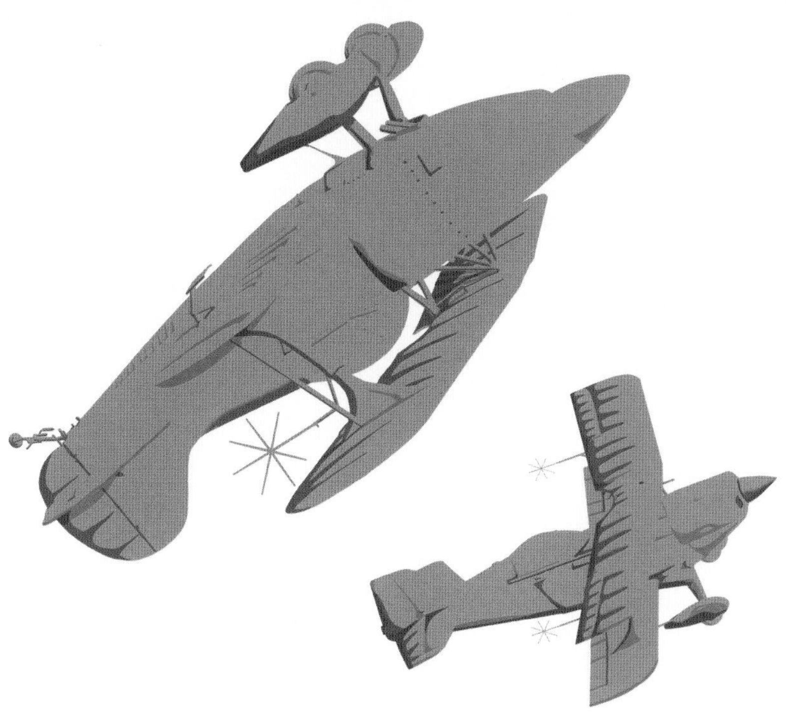

7

The two shading layers, following the inking lengthwise, add movement and speed. Their contribution to the volume and refinement of the final image is inherent to their existence and of a secondary nature.

Les deux couches d'ombres, suivant les tracés sur la longueur, confèrent aux appareils mouvement et vitesse. Leurs apports relatifs au volume et à la beauté de l'image finale sont secondaires.

Die zwei Schattenebenen, die in Längsrichtung über die Tuschezeichnung gelegt werden, sorgen für den Eindruck von Bewegung und Geschwindigkeit. Dass der Schatten der fertigen Zeichnung Tiefe verleiht und sie erheblich verschönert, ist selbstverständlich und hier zweitranging.

De twee schaduwlagen, die in de lengte aan de inktstrepen worden 'geplakt', zorgen voor beweging en snelheid. Wat betreft het volume en de precieuze stijl van de eindafbeelding is verbonden met het bestaan ervan en is secundair.

Las dos capas de sombras, adhiriéndose longitudinalmente a las tintas, dan movimiento y velocidad. Su aporte en cuanto al volumen y preciosismo de la imagen final es inherente a su existencia y secundario.

I due livelli di ombre, unendosi longitudinalmente alle chine, aggiungono movimento e velocità. Il loro contributo al volume e al preziosismo dell'immagine finale è inerente alla loro esistenza e secondario.

As duas camadas de sombras, aderindo longitudinalmente às tintas, dão movimento e velocidade. O seu contributo quanto ao volume e preciosismo da imagem final é inerente à sua existência e secundário.

## 8

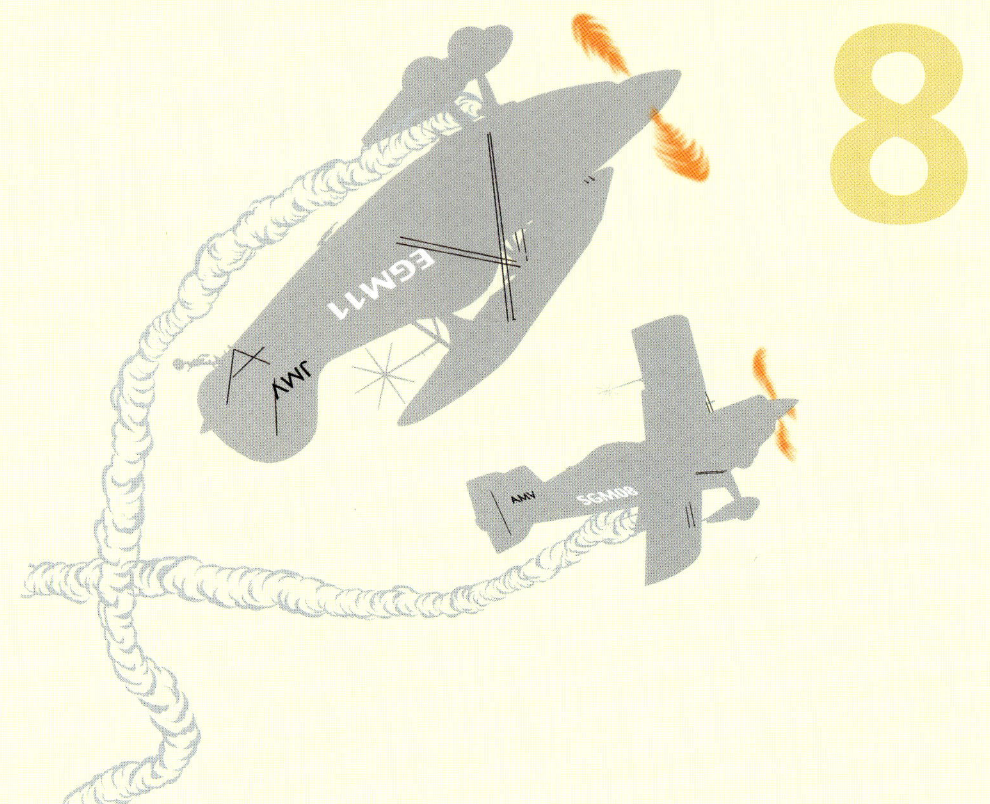


Here, except for a few letters and the braces on the fuselage, the details are the red propellers and the smoke trails, which are made by drawing groupings of small curved lines until they give the appearance of a large cloud.

Mis à part quelques lettres et câbles sur le fuselage, les détails sont principalement les hélices rouges et les traînées de fumée, que l'on obtient avec l'accumulation de petites lignes courbes qui finissent par donner cet aspect de long nuage.

In diesem Fall werden außer einigen Buchstaben und den Spannseilen am Rumpf rote Propellerflügel und Kondensstreifen eingefügt. Die Kondensstreifen bestehen aus zahlreichen kleinen Bögen, die den Eindruck einer langgestreckten Wolke erwecken.

In dit geval bestaan de details, naast wat letters en spanners op de romp, uit rode propellers en rooksporen, die worden verkregen door kleine kromme lijnen bij elkaar te tekenen totdat het aspect van een lange wolk wordt verkregen.

En este caso, los detalles, aparte de algunas letras y tensores sobre el fuselaje, son las hélices en rojo y las estelas de humo, que se consiguen acumulando pequeñas líneas curvas hasta dar ese aspecto de larga nube.

In questo caso i dettagli, a parte alcune lettere e i tiranti sulla fusoliera, sono le eliche rosse e le scie di fumo, che si ottengono accumulando piccole linee curve fino a raggiungere l'aspetto di una nube.

Neste caso, os detalhes, à parte dalgumas letras e tensores sobre a fuselagem, são as hélices em vermelho e os rastos de fumo, que se conseguem acumulando pequenas linhas curvas para dar esse aspecto de nuvem longa.

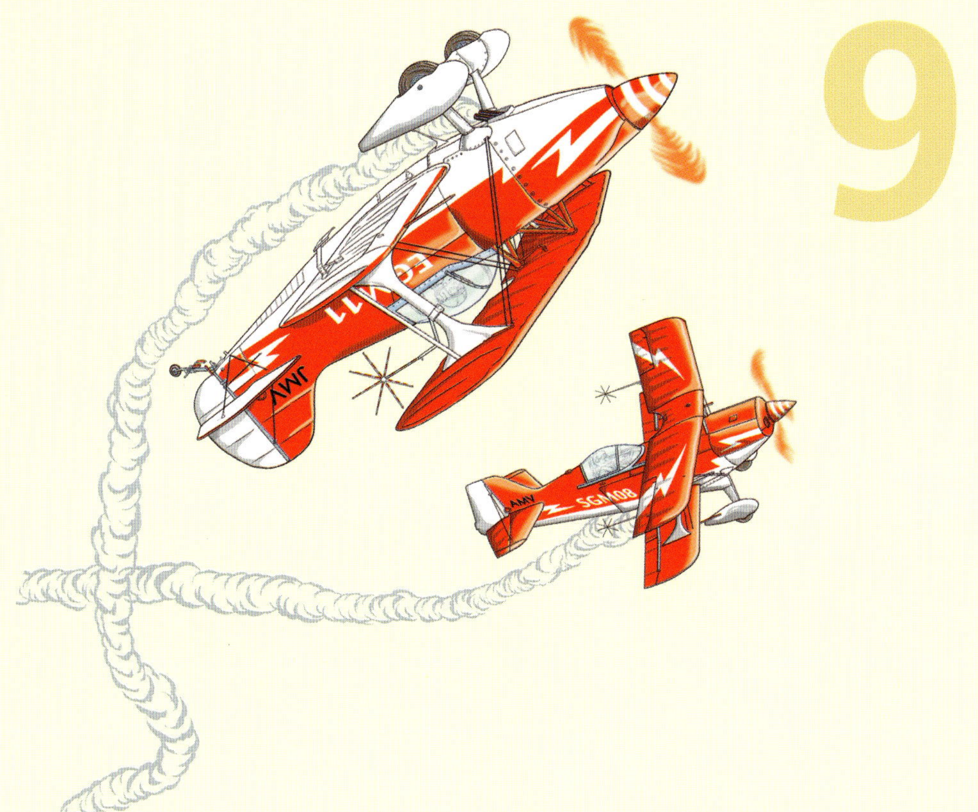


The finished drawing is dynamic and attractive, telling of two well-coordinated pilots on a bright and festive day.

Le dessin final est dynamique et esthétique ; il nous raconte l'histoire de deux pilotes extrêmement bien coordonnés, lors d'une journée ensoleillée et festive.

Die fertige Zeichnung wirkt dynamische und äußerst ansprechend. Sie zeigt dem Betrachter zwei Flugzeuge, die an einem sonnigen Festtag fliegen und deren Piloten sich hervorragend koordinieren.

De afgeronde tekening is dynamisch en aantrekkelijk en spreekt over twee zeer goed gecoördineerde piloten op een heldere, feestelijke dag.

El dibujo acabado es dinámico y atractivo y nos habla de dos pilotos muy bien coordinados en un día luminoso y festivo.

Il disegno finito è dinamico e attrattivo e mostra due piloti molto ben coordinati in una giornata luminosa e festiva.

O desenho acabado é dinâmico e atraente, fala-nos de dois pilotos muito bem coordenados num dia luminoso e festivo.

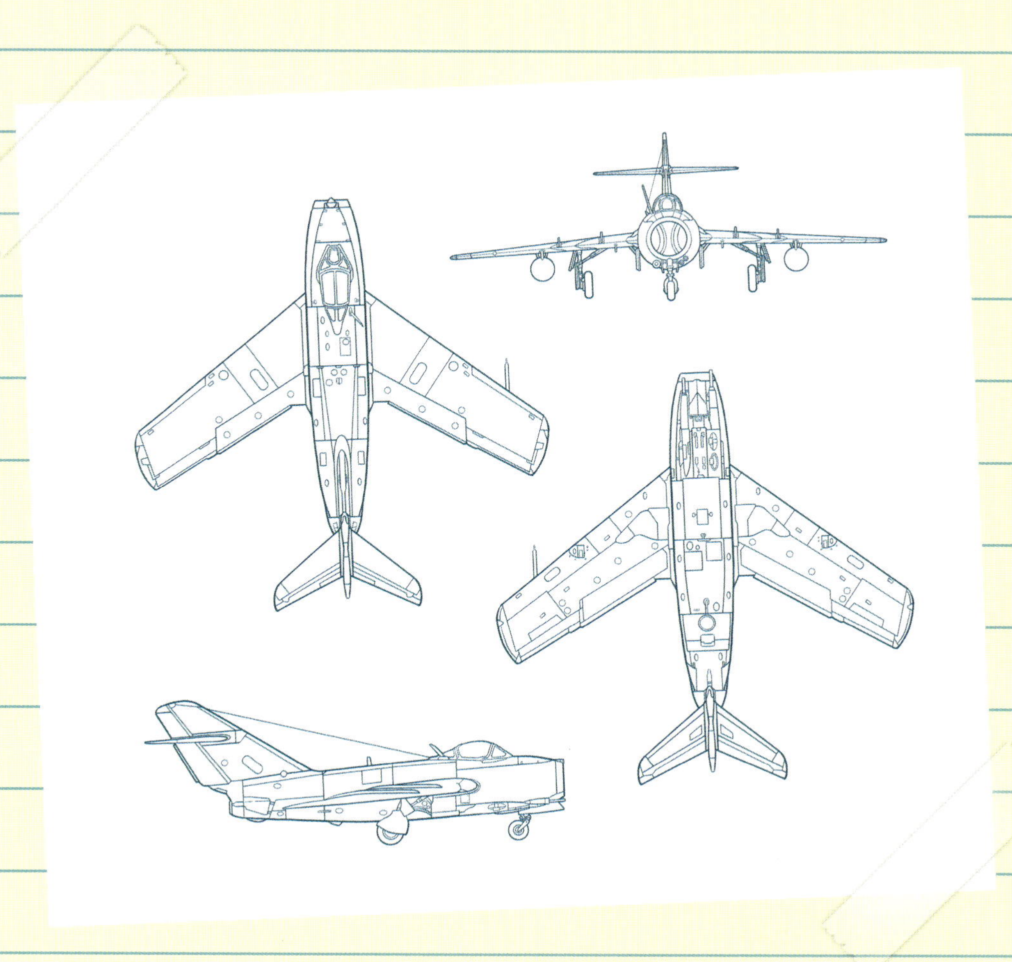

# MiG-15

## 1

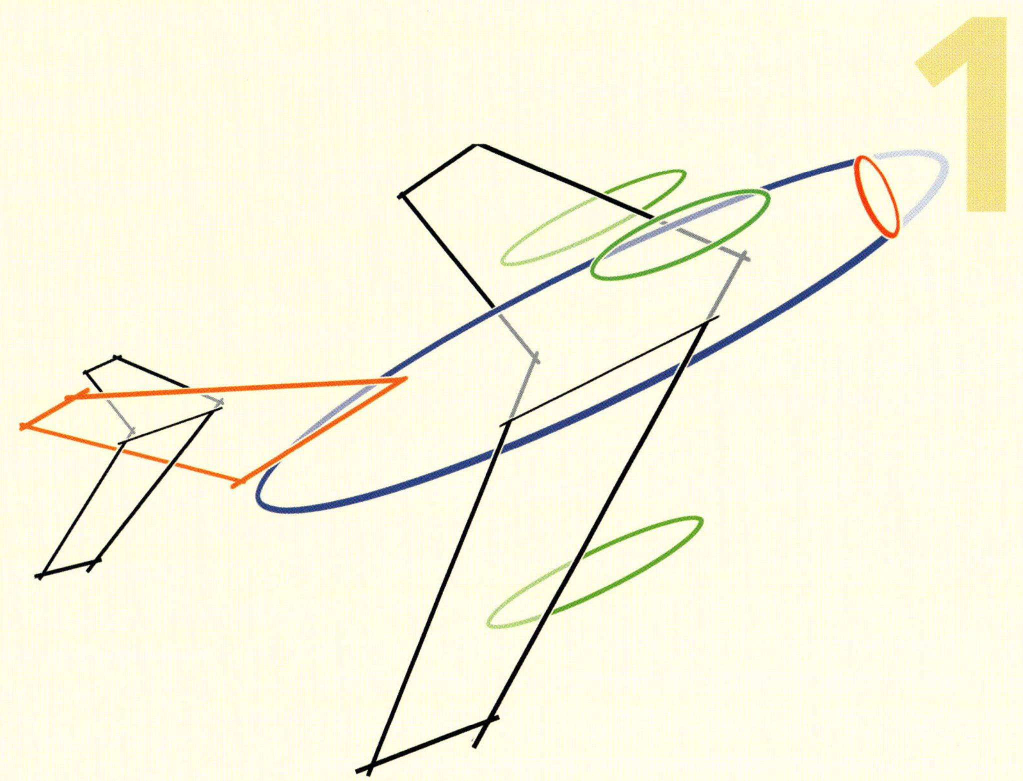

As the outline shows, the design of planes often follows similar geometries for large and small elements, as in this case with the ellipses and the wings with the tail flaps.

Comme le montre le schéma, le design des avions suit très souvent des formes géométriques similaires pour les petits et les grands éléments, comme c'est le cas ici avec les ellipses ou avec la forme des ailes et des ailerons de la queue.

Oftmals – wie auch bei dieser Schemazeichnung – bestehen die großen und kleinen Elemente von Flugzeugen im Grunde aus den gleichen geometrischen Formen: in diesem Fall handelt es sich um mehrere Ellipsen und gleiche Formen für Tragflächen und Ruder.

Zoals het schema blootlegt volgt het ontwerp van vliegtuigen vaak soortgelijke geometrische vormen voor de grote en kleine elementen, zoals in dit geval de ellipsen en vleugels met rolroeren.

Como desvela el esquema, en muchas ocasiones el diseño de los aviones sigue geometrías similares para los elementos de gran y pequeño tamaño, como en este caso las elipses y las alas con los alerones de cola.

Como rivela lo schema, in molte occasioni il design degli aerei segue geometrie simili negli elementi di dimensioni grandi e piccole, come in questo caso le ellissi e le ali rispetto agli alettoni di coda.

Como revela o esquema, em muitas ocasiões o desenho dos aviões segue geometrias similares para os elementos de grande e pequeno tamanho, como neste caso as elipses e as asas com os ailerons da empenagem.

2

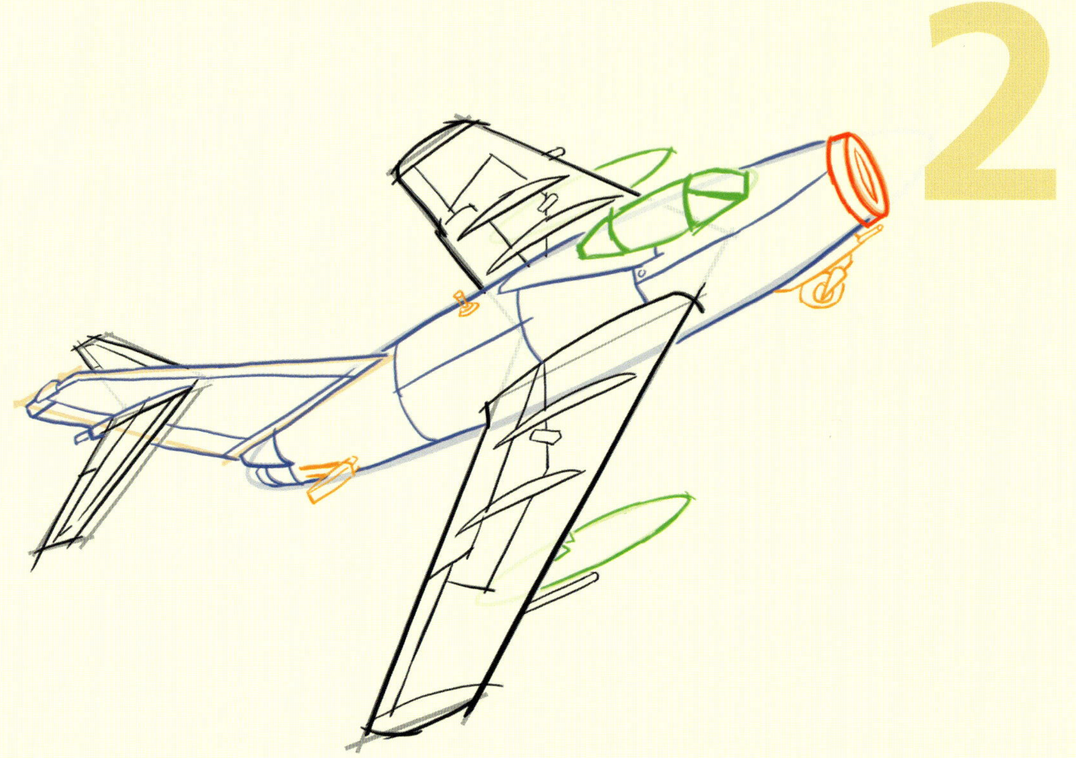

When things are flowing freely, you may find yourself making a sketch and thinking that you are not going to have to make a more detailed pencil drawing: you have enough to ink. Fantastic!

Parfois, lorsque les choses coulent de source, vous pouvez dessiner une ébauche si claire que la réalisation d'un crayonné plus détaillé est inutile : vous avez tout ce qu'il vous faut pour commencer l'encrage. Alors n'attendez pas !

Wenn man einen guten Lauf hat, kann es passieren, dass die Skizze so klar und deutlich ausfällt, dass keine detailliertere Buntstiftzeichnung mehr erforderlich ist. Hier kann direkt mit der Tuschezeichnung fortgefahren werden. Hervorragend!

Wanneer de dingen vloeiend verlopen, is het mogelijk dat je een schets maakt en zo duidelijk voor ogen hebt wat je wilt gaan tekenen, dat je geen gedetailleerde potloodtekening hoeft te maken: je hoeft de schets enkel in te kleuren. Voortreffelijk!

Cuando las cosas fluyen puedes encontrarte realizando un boceto y tenerlo tan claro que no vas a necesitar hacer un lápiz más detallado: tienes suficiente para entintar. ¡Estupendo!

Quando le cose scorrono puoi ritrovarti a realizzare un bozzetto con le idee così chiare che non è necessaria una fase a matita più dettagliata: si può passare direttamente al ripasso a china. Fantastico!

Quando as coisas fluem podes encontrar-te a realizar um esboço e tê-lo tão claro que não vais necessitar de fazer um lápis mais detalhado: tens o suficiente para a arte-final. Magnífico!

3

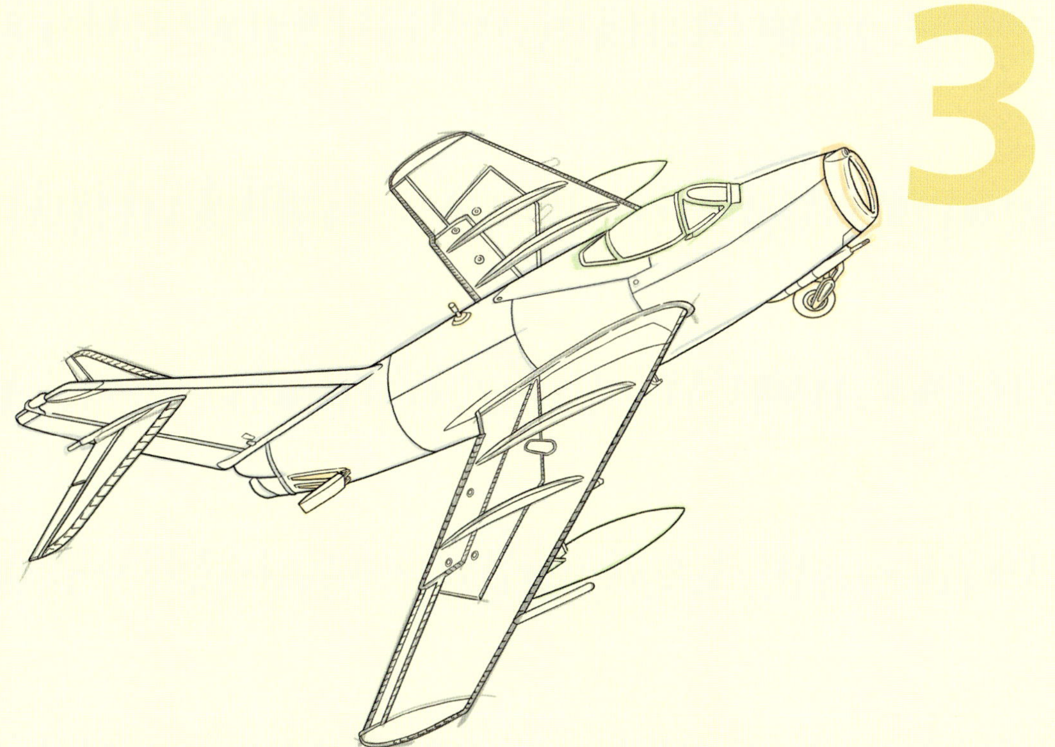

This is the opposite of the first exercises in this book. Almost all the inking is done with rulers or computer geometry tools. Only the small details like rivets and welds are done freehand.

Le procédé est ici à l'opposé de celui utilisé dans les premiers exercices. Presque tous les tracés sont réalisés avec des règles ou des outils informatiques de géométrie. Seuls les petits détails tels que les rivets et les soudures sont faits à main levée.

Dies ist der gegenteilige Fall zu den ersten Übungen in diesem Buch. Fast alle Tuschezeichnungen werden mithilfe von Linealen oder Geometrie-Werkzeugen am Computer erstellt. Nur kleine Details wie Nieten und Schweißnähte werden frei Hand eingezeichnet.

Dit in tegenstelling tot de eerste oefeningen van dit boek. Bijna alle inkttekeningen zijn gemaakt met linialen of geometrische hulpmiddelen van de computer. Alleen de kleine details zoals klinknagels en lasnaden worden uit de vrije hand getekend.

Este es el caso contrario al de los primeros ejercicios de este libro. Casi todas las tintas están realizadas con reglas o herramientas de geometría del ordenador. Sólo los pequeños detalles, como remaches y soldaduras, son a mano alzada.

Questo è il caso contrario a quello dei primi esercizi di questo libro. Quasi tutte le linee di ripasso sono realizzate con righelli o con gli strumenti geometrici del computer. Solo i piccoli dettagli come le rivettature e le saldature sono realizzati a mano libera.

Este é o caso contrário dos primeiros exercícios deste livro. Quase todas as tintas são realizadas com réguas ou ferramentas de geometria do computador. Apenas os pequenos detalhes como rebites e soldaduras são à mão livre.

# 4

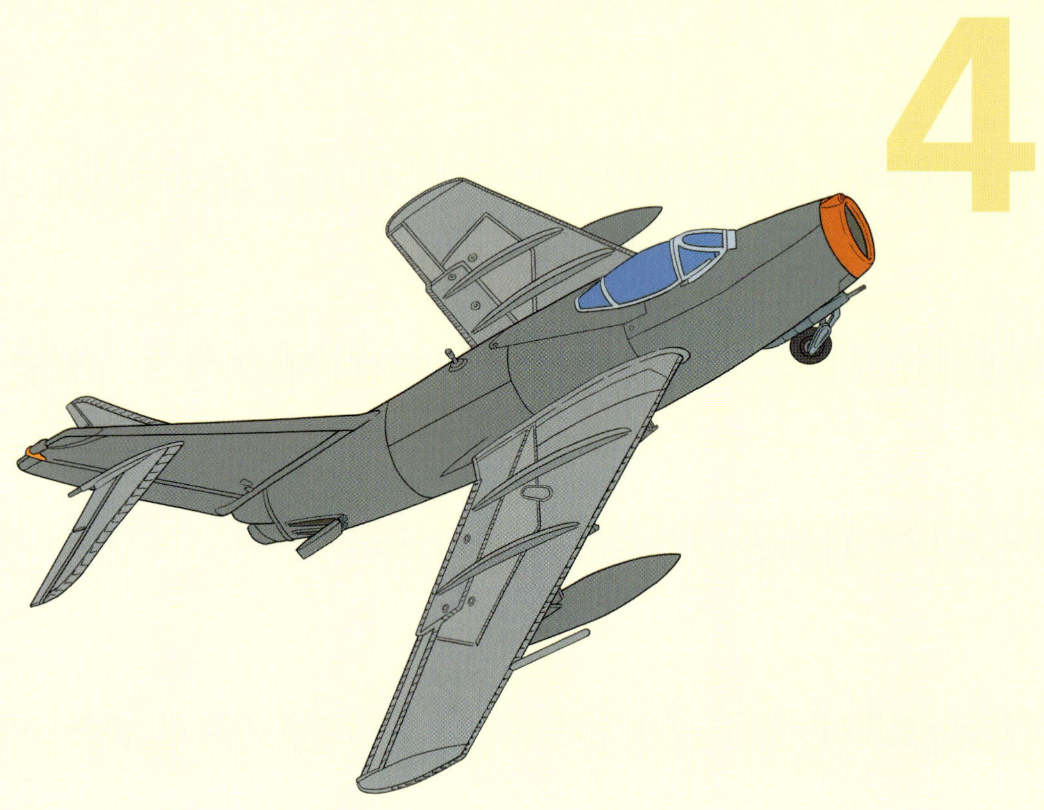

Gray metal, totally lacking in feeling and superfuous embellishment, like the MiG-15 itself. The red nose cone is artistic licence, a point of contrast to give your eyes a chromatic focal point.

La couleur de base est un gris métallique, dépourvu de nuances et décors superflus, comme celui du MiG-15. Le rouge du nez, en revanche, est une licence artistique, un point de contraste servant de référence chromatique.

Hier herrscht kaltes graues Metall vor, ohne überflüssige Zierelemente, genau wie bei der echten MiG-15. Die Schnauze wird rot gestaltet, um einen ansprechenden Kontrast zu schaffen.

Metallic grijs, gevoelloos en zonder overbodige versieringen, zoals de MiG-15 zelf. De rode kleur van de neus is een creatieve vrijheid, een contrastpunt zodat de blik een chromatisch referentiepunt heeft.

Metal gris, carente de sentimientos y adornos superfluos, como el mismo MiG-15. El rojo del morro es una licencia artística, un punto de contraste para que la vista tenga un punto de referencia cromática.

Metallo grigio, carente di sentimenti e di adorni superflui, come lo stesso MiG-15. Il rosso della punta è una licenza, un punto di contrasto per dare all'occhio un punto di riferimento cromatico.

Metal cinzento, carente de sentimentos e adornos supérfluos, como o próprio MiG-15. O vermelho do nariz é uma liberdade artística, um ponto de contraste para que a vista tenha um ponto de referência cromática.

# 5

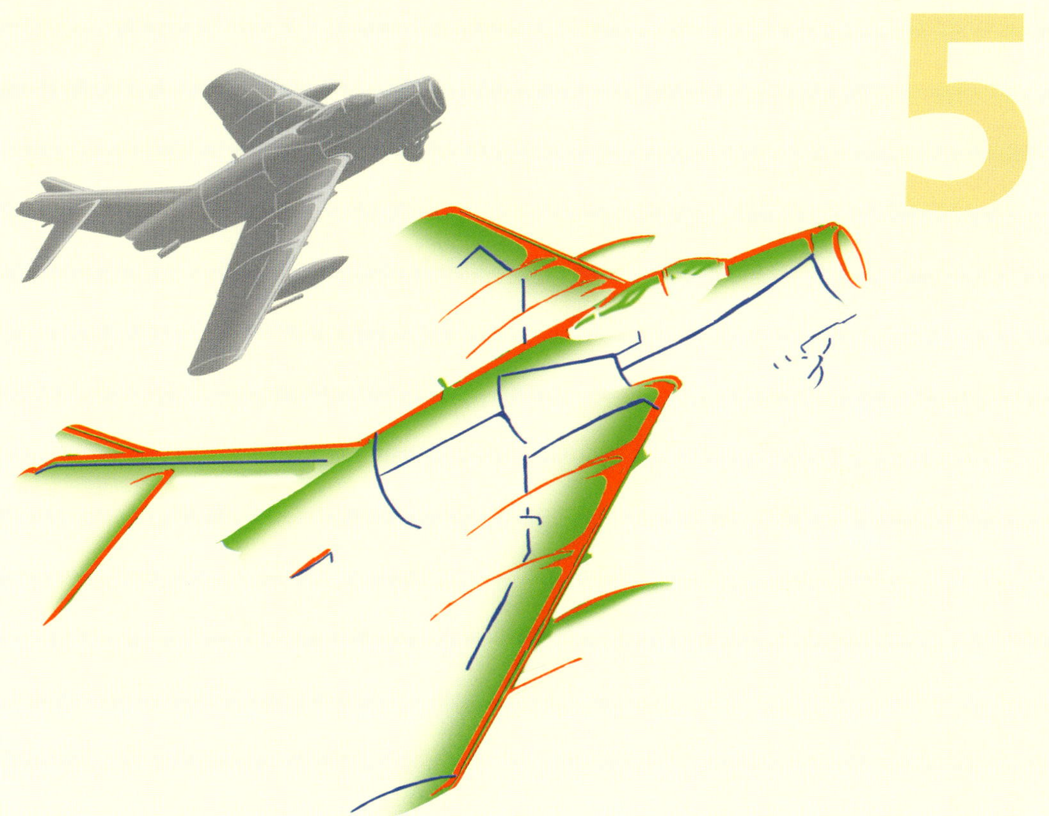

For better visualization of the three layers of lighting, they have been colored red, green, and blue. They will be turned white later, as observed at the top, and given different levels of opacity.

Pour une meilleure visualisation des trois couches de lumière, colorez-les en rouge, vert et bleu. Ensuite, passez-les en blanc et dotez-les d'opacités différentes comme montré ci-dessus.

Um die drei Lichtebenen besser zu verdeutlichen, wurden sie rot, grün und blau eingefärbt. Anschließend – wie oben im Bild zu sehen – wurden sie in Weiß konvertiert und mit unterschiedlicher Transparenz versehen.

Voor een betere weergave van de drie lichtlagen hebben we deze rood, groen en blauw gekleurd. Later, zoals aan de bovenkant te zien is, gaan we over op wit en geven we ze een verschillende opaciteit.

Para una mejor visualización de las tres capas de luces, las hemos coloreado en rojo, verde y azul. Posteriormente, tal como se observa en la parte superior, las pasaremos a blanco y les daremos distinta opacidad.

Per visualizzare meglio i tre livelli di luci, essi sono stati indicati in rosso, verde e blu. In seguito, come si osserva nella parte superiore, li metteremo in bianco e daremo loro distinta opacità.

Para uma melhor visualização das três camadas de luzes colorimo-las a vermelho, verde e azul. Posteriormente, tal como se observa na parte superior, passá-las-emos para branco e dar-lhe-emos diferente opacidade.

6

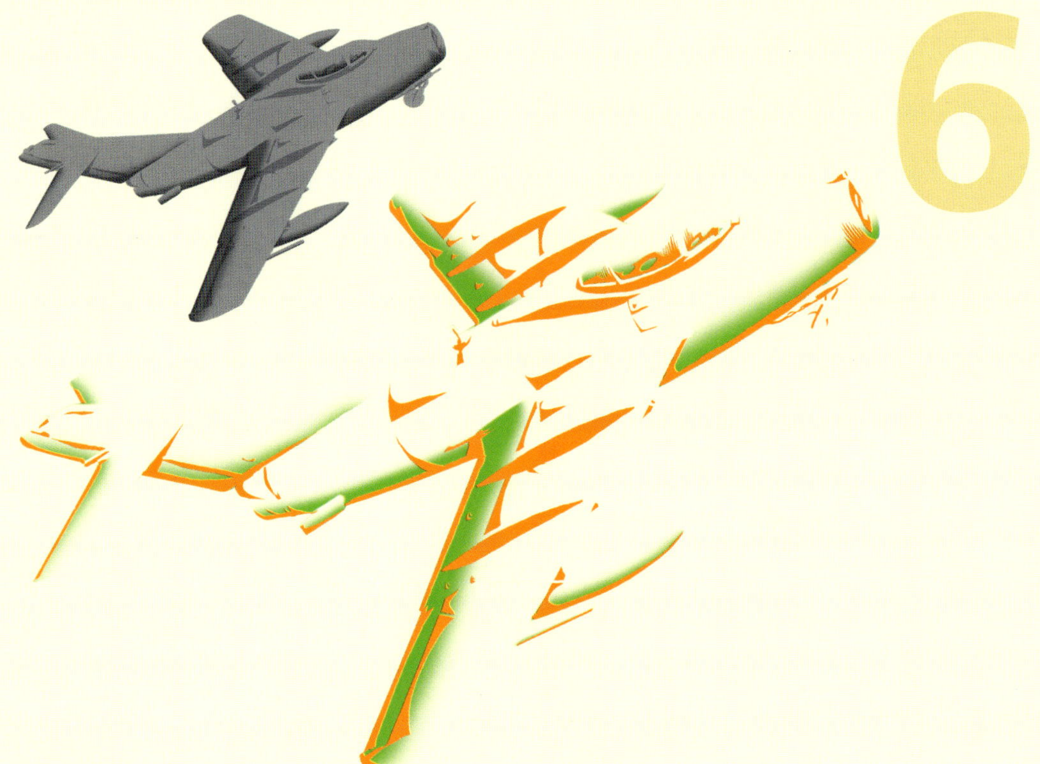

The two shading layers have also been colored. Both the lighting and shading show that it is not necessary to have a gray cover with which to distinguish the plane's shape. This shows that the work is well done.

Les deux couches d'ombre ont également été colorées. Tant avec les ombres qu'avec les lumières, vous pouvez constater que le fond gris n'est pas nécessaire pour distinguer la forme de l'avion. Cela montre que le travail a été bien fait.

Auch die beiden Schattenebenen wurden eingefärbt. Sowohl bei den Licht- als auch bei den Schattenbereichen ist zu sehen, dass keine graue Grundfarbe erforderlich ist, um die Form des Flugzeugs deutlich zu erkennen. Dies zeigt, dass unsere Arbeit gut ausgeführt wurde.

Ook zijn de twee schaduwlagen gekleurd. Zowel bij het licht als bij de schaduwen zien we dat er geen grijze laag nodig is om de vorm van het vliegtuig te onderscheiden. Dit duidt erop dat het werk goed gedaan is.

También las dos capas de sombras se han coloreado. Tanto en las luces como en las sombras, vemos que no es necesaria una tapa gris para distinguir la forma del avión. Esto indica que el trabajo está bien hecho.

Anche i due livelli di ombre sono stati colorati. Sia per le luci che per le ombre vediamo che non è necessaria una sagoma grigia per distinguere la forma dell'aereo. Ciò indica che il lavoro è ben fatto.

Também as duas camadas de sombras se coloriram. Tanto nas luzes como nas sombras vemos que não é necessária uma camada cinzenta para distinguir a forma do avião. Isto indica que o trabalho está bem feito.

# 7

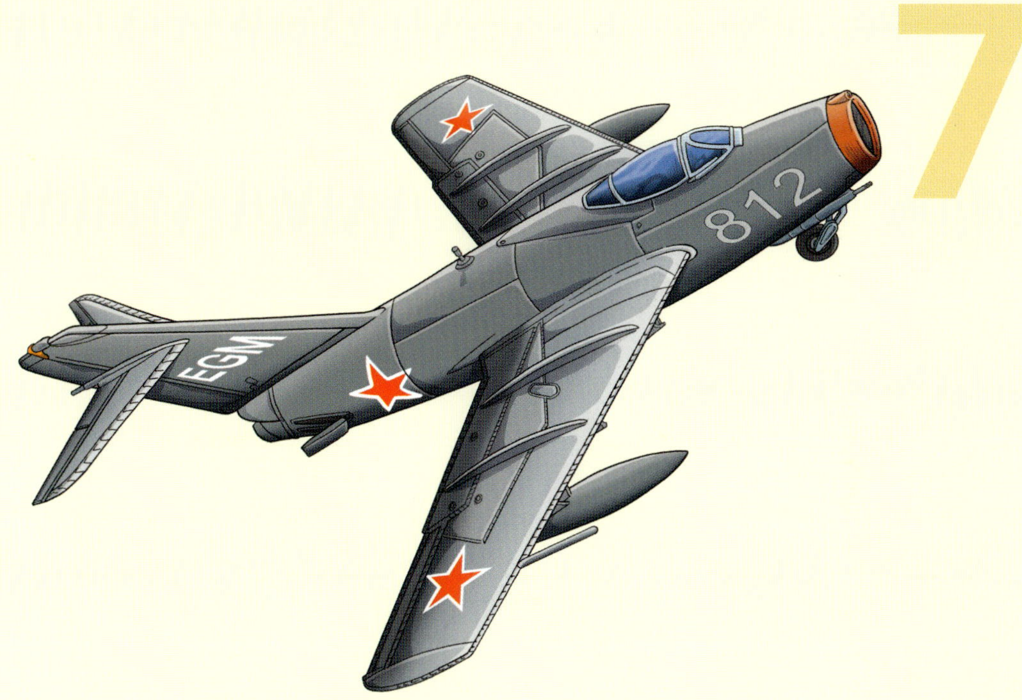


Some letters and red stars are added to the finished drawing to show the Soviet origin of the design, producing a believable and solid image.

Sur le dessin final, ajoutez quelques lettres et des étoiles rouges qui font référence à l'origine soviétique du design. Nous obtenons ainsi un ensemble réaliste et solide.

In die fertige Zeichnung werden einige Buchstaben und rote Sterne eingearbeitet, die auf den sowjetischen Ursprung dieses Modells anspielen. Auf diese Weise wird eine glaubhafte, solide Darstellung erzielt.

In de afgeronde tekening voegen we wat letters en een aantal rode sterren toe die op de Russische oorsprong van dit ontwerp wijzen en er een geloofwaardig en solide tekening van maken.

En el dibujo acabado añadimos algunas letras y unas estrellas rojas que muestran el origen soviético de este diseño, consiguiendo un conjunto creíble y sólido.

Nel disegno finito aggiungiamo alcune lettere e le stelle rosse che mostrano l'origine sovietica di questo disegno, ottenendo un insieme credibile e solido.

No desenho acabado acrescentamos algumas letras e umas estrelas vermelhas que mostram a origem soviética deste desenho, conseguindo um conjunto credível e sólido.

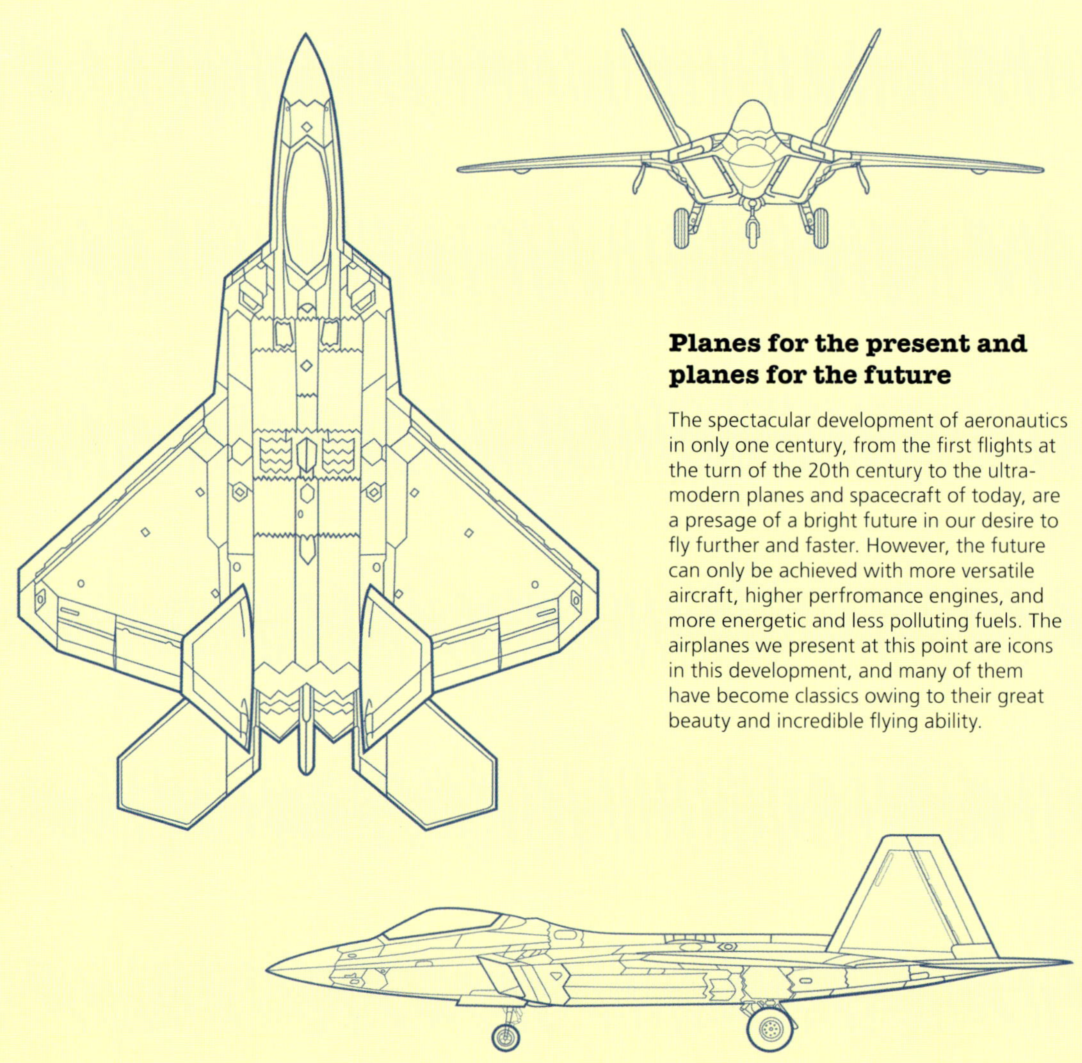

## Planes for the present and planes for the future

The spectacular development of aeronautics in only one century, from the first flights at the turn of the 20th century to the ultra-modern planes and spacecraft of today, are a presage of a bright future in our desire to fly further and faster. However, the future can only be achieved with more versatile aircraft, higher perfromance engines, and more energetic and less polluting fuels. The airplanes we present at this point are icons in this development, and many of them have become classics owing to their great beauty and incredible flying ability.

## Avions d'aujourd'hui et de demain

L'évolution spectaculaire de l'aéronautique en l'espace de seulement 100 ans, depuis les premiers vols du début du xxe siècle aux avions extrêmement modernes et vaisseaux spatiaux d'aujourd'hui, laisse présager un avenir brillant qui saura combler notre désir de voler toujours plus loin et toujours plus vite. Toutefois, ce futur doit nécessairement passer par la création d'aéronefs plus sophistiqués, de moteurs avec de meilleurs rendements ainsi que de combustibles plus énergétiques et moins polluants. Les avions présentés ici sont des icônes de cette évolution et bon nombre d'entre eux sont devenus de grands classiques grâce à leur beauté et à leur incroyable capacité de vol.

## Moderne Flugzeuge und Flugzeuge der Zukunft

Die atemberaubende Entwicklung der Luftfahrt in nur einem Jahrhundert – von den ersten Flugversuchen Anfang des 20. Jahrhunderts bis zu den modernen Flugzeugen und Raumschiffen der heutigen Zeit – sagt der Menschheit für ihr Bestreben, immer weiter und schneller zu fliegen, eine strahlende Zukunft voraus. Diese Zukunft muss jedoch unbedingt auch vielseitigere Flugzeuge, leistungsfähigere Triebwerke sowie effizientere und weniger umweltschädliche Treibstoffe hervorbringen. Die im Folgenden vorgestellten Flugzeuge sind echte Meilensteine dieser Entwicklung, und viele von ihnen sind aufgrund ihrer Schönheit und besonderen Flugeigenschaften bereits zu Klassikern geworden.

## Vliegtuigen van nu en vliegtuigen van de toekomst

De spectaculaire ontwikkeling van de luchtvaart in slechts een eeuw tijd, van de eerste vluchten aan het begin van de twintigste eeuw tot aan de ultramoderne vliegtuigen en ruimteschepen van tegenwoordig, voorspelt ons een glansrijke toekomst waarin wij ernaar streven om steeds verder weg en sneller te vliegen. Echter, in deze toekomst zijn veelzijdiger vliegtuigen, motoren met een beter rendement en krachtiger en minder verontreinigende brandstoffen een noodzaak. De vliegtuigen die wij je hier laten zien zijn iconen van deze ontwikkeling en vele ervan zijn om hun schoonheid en ongelofelijke vluchtvermogen klassiekers geworden.

## Aviones del presente y aviones para el futuro

La espectacular evolución de la aeronáutica en sólo un siglo, desde los primeros vuelos a inicios del siglo 20 hasta los modernísimos aviones y naves aeroespaciales de la actualidad, nos auguran un brillante futuro en nuestro afán por volar más lejos y más rápido. Sin embargo, ese futuro debe pasar obligatoriamente por la obtención de aeronaves más versátiles, motores con mejores rendimientos y combustibles más energéticos y menos contaminantes.
Los aviones que os presentamos a continuación son iconos en esa evolución y muchos de ellos se han convertido en clásicos por su gran belleza e increíble capacidad de vuelo.

## Aerei del presente e aerei per il futuro

La spettacolare evoluzione dell'aeronautica in soli cent'anni, dai primi voli agli inizi del XX secolo fino ai modernissimi aeroplani e navi aerospaziali dell'attualità, presagisce un brillante futuro per il nostro desiderio di volare sempre più lontano e sempre più veloce. Tuttavia, questo futuro deve fare i conti obbligatoriamente con la creazione di velivoli più versatili, motori con un miglior rendimento e carburanti più energetici e meno inquinanti. Gli aerei che vi presentiamo qui di seguito sono vere e proprie icone di questo sviluppo. Molti di loro sono diventati dei classici per la loro grande bellezza e la loro incredibile capacità di volo.

## Aviões do presente e aviões para o futuro

A espectacular evolução da aeronáutica em apenas um século, desde os primeiros voos no início do século 20 até os moderníssimos aviões e naves aeroespaciais da actualidade, auguram-nos um brilhante futuro no nosso afã por voar mais longe e mais rápido. Sem dúvida, esse futuro deve passar obrigatoriamente pela obtenção de aeronaves mais versáteis, motores com melhores rendimentos e combustíveis mais energéticos e menos contaminantes. Os aviões que apresentamos em seguida são ícones nessa evolução e muitos deles converteram-se em clássicos pela sua grande beleza e incrível capacidade de voo.

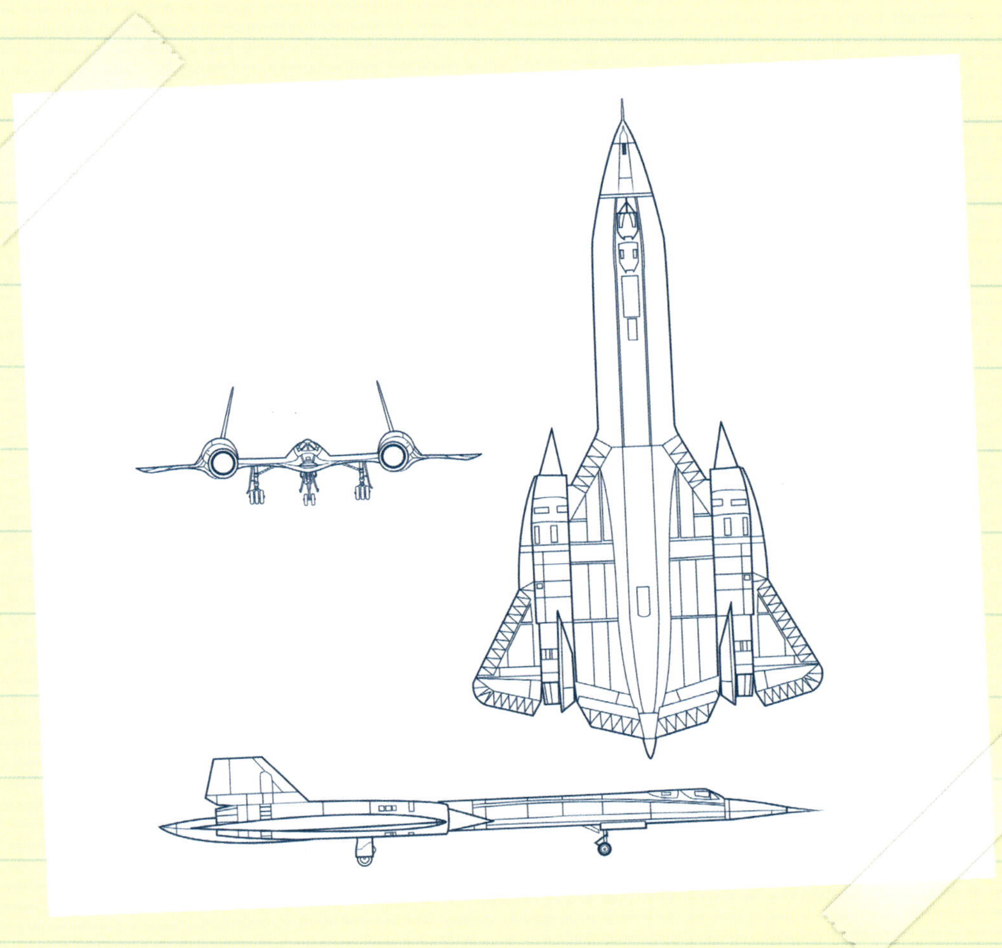

# Lockheed SR-71

1

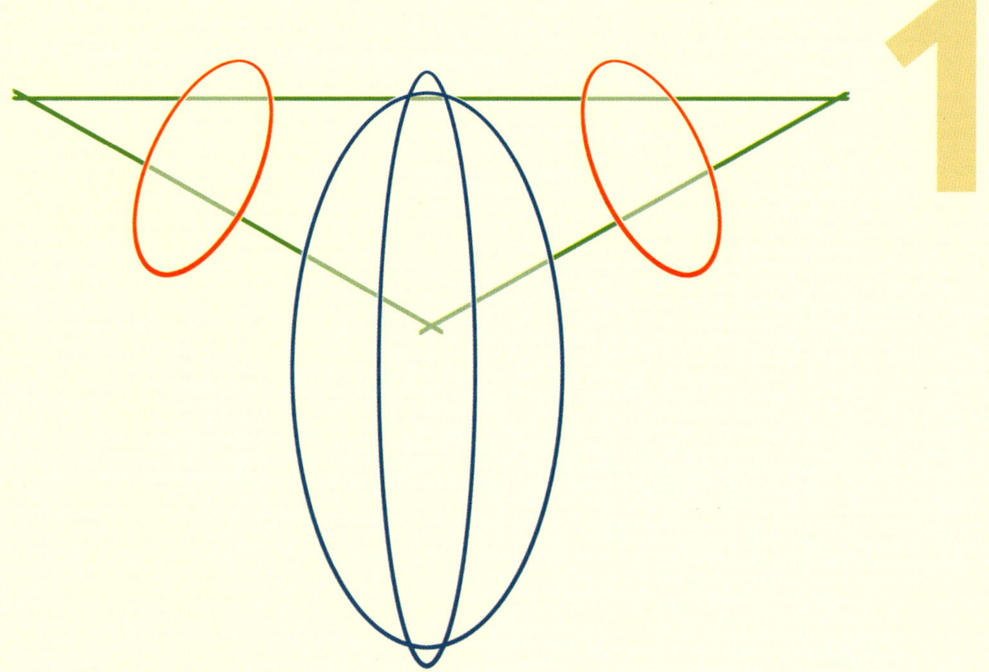

Drawing the simplest of skeletons helps to create the correct perspective, which we should follow in all the steps. This simple perspective is provided by the engines (red), which open to both sides.

Les squelettes extrêmement simples aident à réaliser une bonne perspective qu'il faudra ensuite suivre pour chaque étape. Cette perspective basique est donnée par les moteurs (en rouge) qui s'ouvrent vers l'extérieur.

Das Zeichnen besonders vereinfachter Skelette hilft dabei, die richtige Perspektive zu finden, die in den nachfolgenden Schritten einzuhalten ist. Diese einfache perspektivische Darstellung wird von den Triebwerken (rot) bestimmt, die sich etwas zur Seite neigen.

Uiterst simpele ontwerpen tekenen helpt bij het uitwerken van een juist perspectief dat we bij alle stappen moeten volgen. Dit eenvoudige perspectief wordt gegeven door de motoren (rood) die naar beide zijden geopend zijn.

Dibujar esqueletos de máxima simplicidad ayuda a realizar una correcta perspectiva, que deberemos seguir en todos los pasos. Esta sencilla perspectiva está dada por los motores (rojo) que se abren hacia ambos lados.

Disegnare scheletri estremamente semplici aiuta a realizzare una prospettiva corretta, che va poi seguita in tutte le fasi. Questa semplice prospettiva è data dai motori (rosso) che si aprono su entrambi i lati.

Desenhar esqueletos de máxima simplicidade ajuda a realizar uma correcta perspectiva, que deveremos seguir em todos os passos. Esta simples perspectiva é dada pelos motores (vermelho) que se abrem para ambos os lados.

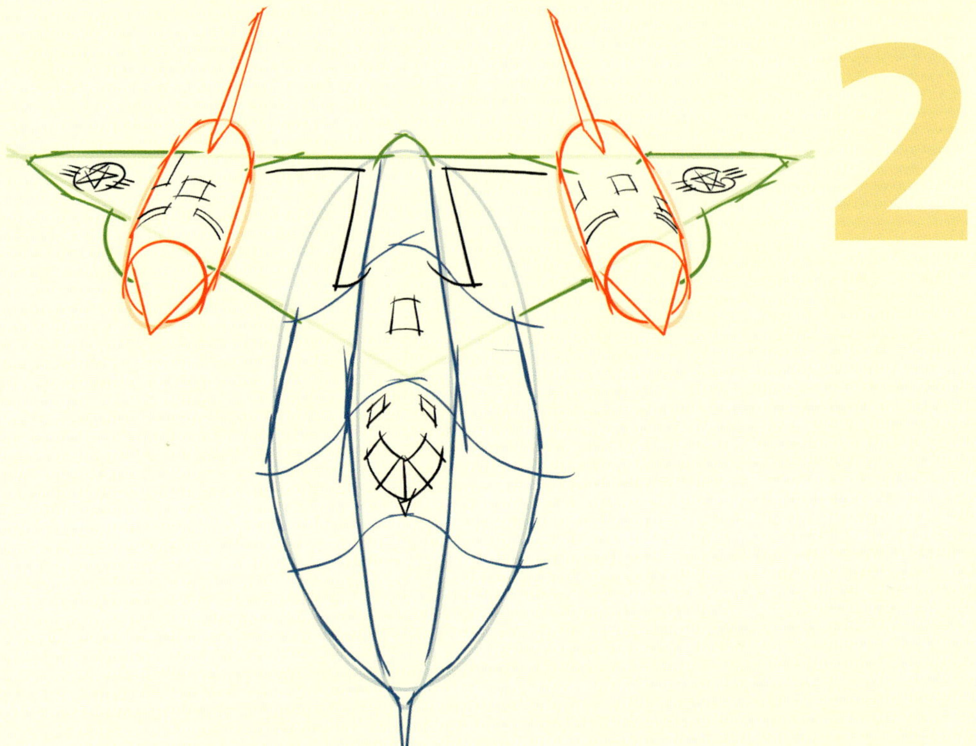


This sketch was made using a computer trick. Once the left half was done, it was turned around to serve as the base for the right half. If you are working with paper, you can trace from the back of the sheet.

Cette ébauche a été réalisée à l'aide de l'ordinateur. Une fois la moitié gauche réalisée, vous la renverserez afin qu'elle serve de base pour dessiner la moitié droite. Si vous travaillez sur papier, vous pouvez calquer le revers de la feuille.

Bei dieser am Computer angefertigten Skizze wurde ein Trick angewandt: Nach dem Zeichnen der linken Hälfte wurde diese gespiegelt und diente als Vorlage für die rechte Hälfte. Wenn Sie auf Papier arbeiten, können Sie das Blatt gespiegelt abpausen.

Voor deze schets werd een computertruc gebruikt. Eerst werd de linkerhelft getekend, die werd omgekeerd om als basis voor de rechterhelft te dienen. Als je op papier werkt kun je het blad omgekeerd overtrekken.

Este boceto se realizó con truco gracias a la ayuda del ordenador. Una vez realizada la mitad izquierda, la volteé para que me sirviera de base para la mitad derecha. Si trabajas con papel, puedes calcar la hoja del revés.

Questo bozzetto è stato realizzato con un trucco grazie all'ausilio del computer. Una volta realizzata la metà sinistra l'ho ribaltata per usarla come base per la metà destra. Se lavori su carta puoi ricalcare il foglio al contrario.

Este esboço realizou-se com truque graças à ajuda do computador. Uma vez realizada a metade esquerda virei-a para que me servisse de base para a metade direita. Se trabalhas com papel podes calcar o reverso da folha.

## 3

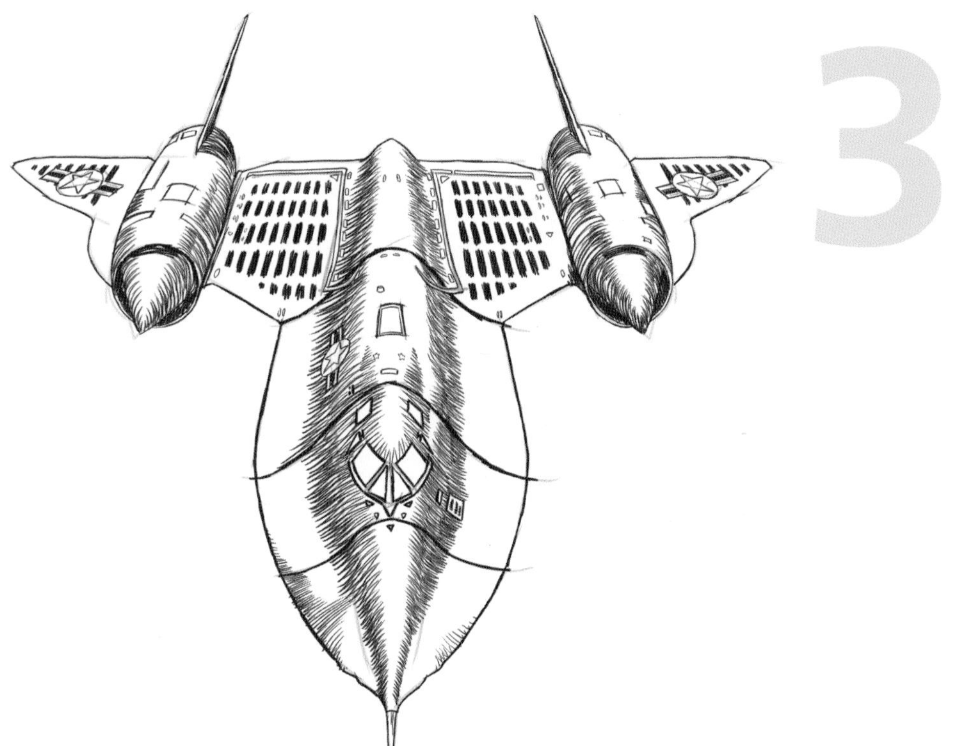

Here penciling is essential to give a clear impression before inking. Given the dark color of this plane, the volume of the middle area, and the engines, you are going to need a lot of black.

Ici, le crayonné est fondamental pour avoir les idées claires avant de commencer l'encrage car, étant donné la couleur foncée de cet avion, le volume de la zone centrale et les moteurs, il nous faudra utiliser beaucoup de noir.

In diesem Beispiel ist die Bunt- bzw. Bleistiftzeichnung von besonderer Wichtigkeit, um vor der Tuschezeichnung sämtliche Details zu klären. Aufgrund der dunklen Farbe dieses Flugzeugs sowie aufgrund des Volumens des mittleren Bereichs und der Triebwerke wird viel schwarze Farbe verwendet werden.

In dit geval is de potloodtekening van groot belang om een duidelijk idee te krijgen alvorens met het inkleuren te beginnen. Vanwege de donkere kleur van dit vliegtuig, het volume van het middendeel en de motoren gaan we namelijk veel zwart gebruiken.

En este caso, el lápiz es fundamental para tener las ideas claras antes de entintar, pues dado, el color oscuro de este avión, el volumen de la zona central y los motores, vamos a utilizar una gran cantidad de negro.

In questo caso le matite sono essenziali per avere le idee chiare prima del ripasso a china, dal momento che a causa del colore scuro di questo aereo, del volume della zona centrale e dei motori, useremo un'enorme quantità di nero.

Neste caso o lápis é fundamental para ter as ideias claras antes da arte-final, pois dada a cor escura deste avião, o volume da zona central e dos motores, vamos a utilizar uma grande quantidade de preto.

4

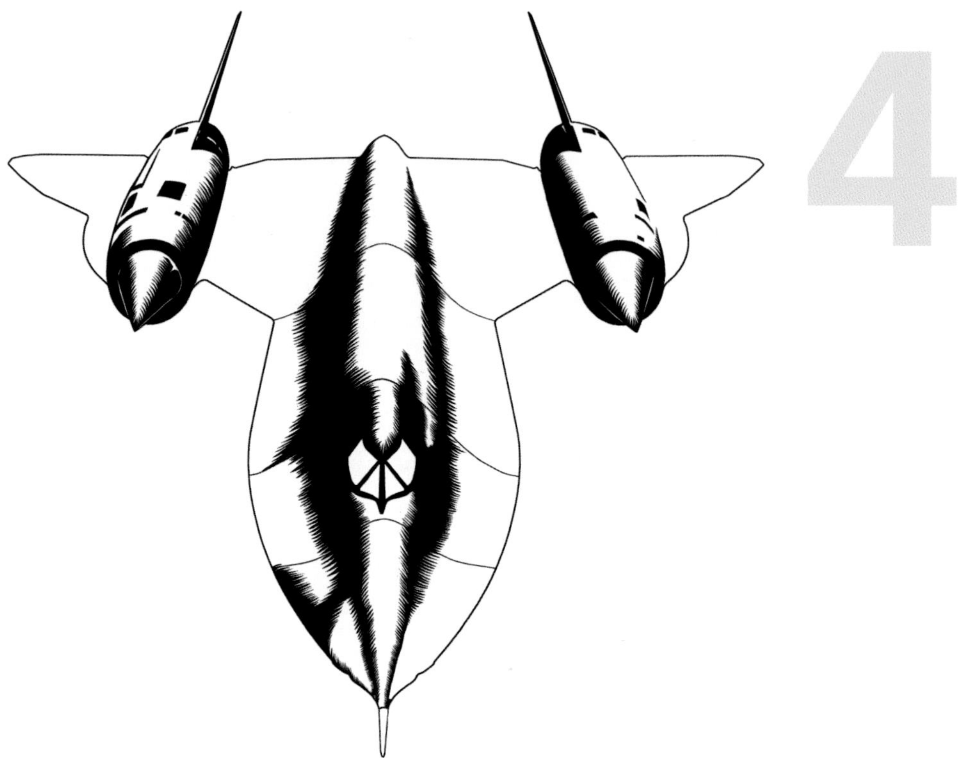

One way of representing graduated shading with defined inking is to make these kinds of spots that emerge from the black mass. Their curvature emphasizes the shape of the aircraft.

Pour représenter une ombre graduelle avec une tache d'encre définie, il est possible de réaliser des pointes jaillissant de la masse noire. Leur courbure contribue à faire ressortir la forme de l'aéronef.

Eine Möglichkeit, um einen auslaufenden Schatten mit klar definierten Tuschestrichen darzustellen, besteht darin, die hier gezeigten Spitzen auszuarbeiten, die sich aus der schwarzen Masse hervorheben. Die Krümmung trägt dazu bei, die Form des Flugzeugs zu unterstreichen.

Een manier om een graduele schaduw met een duidelijke inktvlek uit te beelden is het gebruik van dit soort puntjes die uit de zwarte massa ontstaan. De buiging helpt om de vorm van het luchtvaartuig uit te laten komen.

Una manera de representar una sombra gradual con una mancha de tinta definida es realizar este tipo de puntas que surgen de la masa negra. Su curvatura contribuye a resaltar la forma de la aeronave.

Un modo per rappresentare un'ombreggiatura graduale con una macchia di inchiostro definita è quello di aggiungere questo tipo di tratteggio che emerge dalla massa nera. La curvatura aiuta a enfatizzare la forma del velivolo.

Uma maneira de representar uma sombra gradual com uma mancha de tinta definida é realizar este tipo de pontas que surgem da massa preta. A sua curvatura contribui para realçar a forma da aeronave.

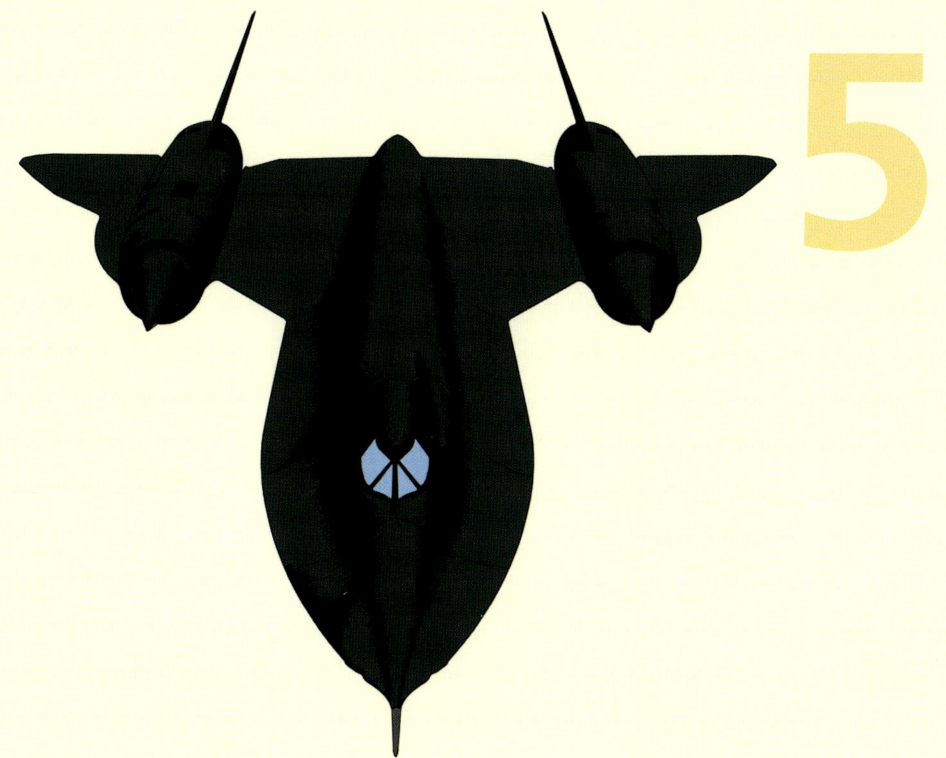

5

Playing on the name of this plane (Blackbird), the base blue has been adjusted to maximum darkness without concealing the inking. The light blue of the cockpit creates a cold and fearsome contrast.

Pour faire honneur au nom de l'avion, Blackbird (« merle »), la couleur de base bleue a été ajustée au maximum afin de la rendre aussi foncée que possible sans toutefois couvrir les tracés. Le bleu clair de la cabine crée un point de contraste froid et redoutable.

Um dem Beinamen („Blackbird", deutsch: „Amsel") des Flugzeugs Rechnung zu tragen, wird als Grundfarbe ein möglichst dunkles Blau gewählt, das die Tuschezeichnung nicht überdeckt. Das Hellblau des Cockpits sorgt für einen kalten, Furcht erregenden Kontrast.

Ter ere van de naam van het vliegtuig is de basiskleur blauw zoveel mogelijk aangepast en zo donker mogelijk gemaakt zonder de inktstrepen te verbergen. Het lichtblauw van de cabine zorgt voor een koud en geducht contrastpunt.

Haciendo honor al nombre por el que también es conocido el avión, Blackbird («mirlo»), se ha ajustado al máximo el color base azul para que sea lo más oscuro posible sin ocultar las tintas. El azul claro de la cabina crea un punto de contraste frío y temible.

Per rispettare il nome dell'aereo (Blackbird), abbiamo scurito il più possibile il colore blu di base, pur senza nascondere i tratti a china. L'azzurro chiaro della cabina crea un punto di contrasto freddo e temibile.

Dando honra ao nome do avião (Blackbird), ajustou-se ao máximo a cor base azul para que seja o mais escuro possível sem ocultar as tintas. O azul claro da cabina cria um ponto de contraste frio e temível.

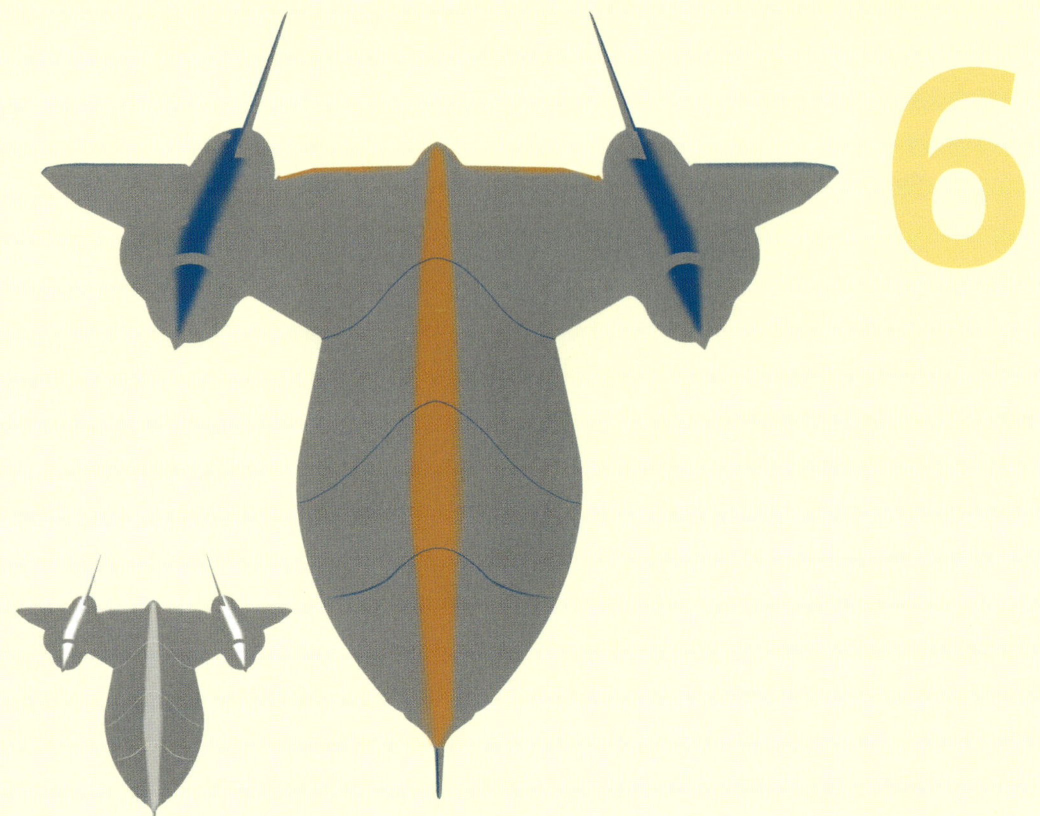

6

Only two layers of lighting are necessary for this illustration. They are located along the length of the top of the fuselage and engines. As the curve of the engines is more pronounces, greater opacity is given to their layer.

Pour cette illustration, seulement deux couches de lumières sont nécessaires. Elles sont situées sur la longueur supérieure du fuselage et des moteurs. Comme la courbe des moteurs est davantage prononcée, donnez à sa couche supérieure une opacité plus importante.

Für diese Darstellung sind zwei Lichtebenen erforderlich. Diese liegen auf den erhabenen Längsachsen von Rumpf und Motoren. Aufgrund der stärkeren Krümmung der Triebwerke ist die dortige Lichtebene weniger transparent.

Voor deze illustratie zijn alleen twee lichtlagen nodig. Zij bevinden zich over de zenitale lengte van de romp en de motoren. Aangezien de buiging van de motoren geprononceerder is, wordt deze laag ondoorzichtiger gemaakt.

Para esta ilustración sólo son necesarias dos capas de luces. Están situadas en las longitudinales cenitales del fuselaje y los motores. Dado que la curva en los motores es más pronunciada, daremos a su capa mayor opacidad.

Per questa illustrazione sono necessari solo due livelli di luci. Si trovano nel punto zenitale longitudinale della fusoliera e dei motori. Dal momento che la curva sui motori è più pronunciata, daremo a questo livello un'opacità maggiore.

Para esta ilustração só são necessárias duas camadas de luzes. Estão localizadas nas longitudinais zenitais da fuselagem e dos motores. Dado que a curva nos motores é mais pronunciada, daremos à sua camada maior opacidade.

# 7

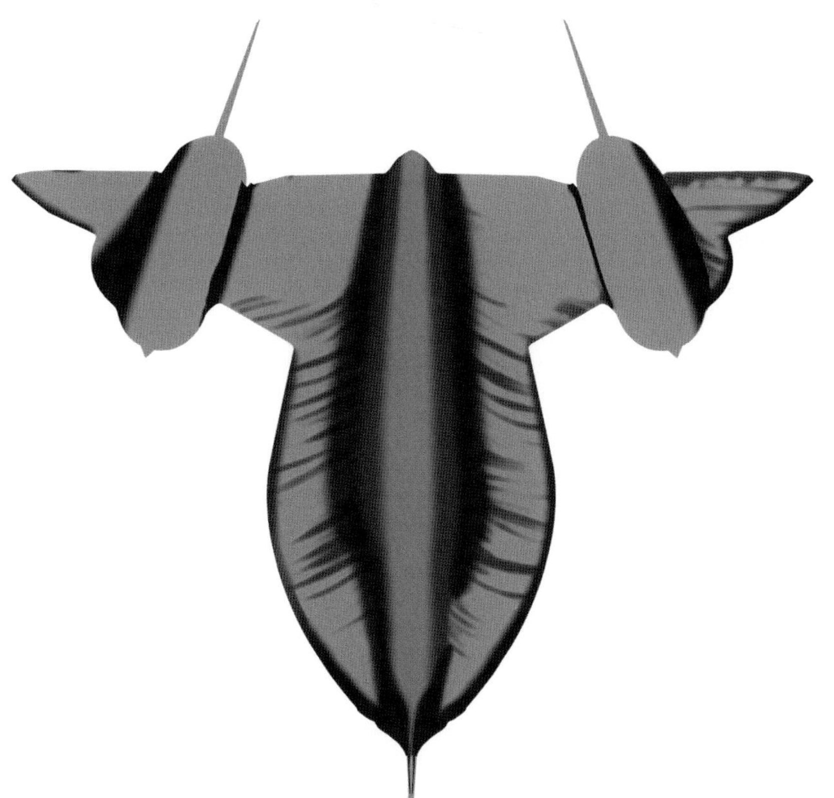

Shading is a mere accompaniment for the overpowering black ink. However it does provide a certain three-dimensional quality. It was drawn on two different layers: one for the lengthwise shadows and the other for the crosswise ones.

Les ombres ne sont là que pour accompagner les tracés puissants mais apportent tout de même une certaine tridimensionnalité. Elles ont été dessinées sur deux couches séparées : l'une pour les ombres longitudinales et l'autre pour les transversales.

Die Schatten dienen lediglich als Begleiter der kräftigen Tuschezeichnung und verleihen der Abbildung trotzdem eine gewisse Tiefe. Auch hier wurden zwei verschiedene Ebenen verwendet – eine für die Schatten in Längsrichtung und eine für die quer verlaufenden Schatten.

De schaduwen hebben een louter begeleidende functie van de krachtige zwarte inkt, maar desalniettemin geven ze enige driedimensionaliteit. Ze zijn in twee verschillende lagen getekend: de ene voor de schaduwen in de lengte en de andere voor de dwarsliggende schaduwen.

Las sombras son meras acompañantes de la poderosa tinta negra, pero, aun así, aportan cierta tridimensionalidad. Se han dibujado en dos capas distintas: una para las sombras longitudinales y otra para las transversales.

Le ombre fungono da mero accompagnamento della poderosa china nera, ma anche così aggiungono una certa tridimensionalità. Sono state disegnate su due livelli diversi: uno per le ombre longitudinali e un altro per quelle trasversali.

As sombras são meras acompanhantes da poderosa tinta preta, mas ainda assim concedem uma certa tridimensionalidade. Desenharam-se em duas camadas distintas: uma para as sombras longitudinais e outra para as transversais.

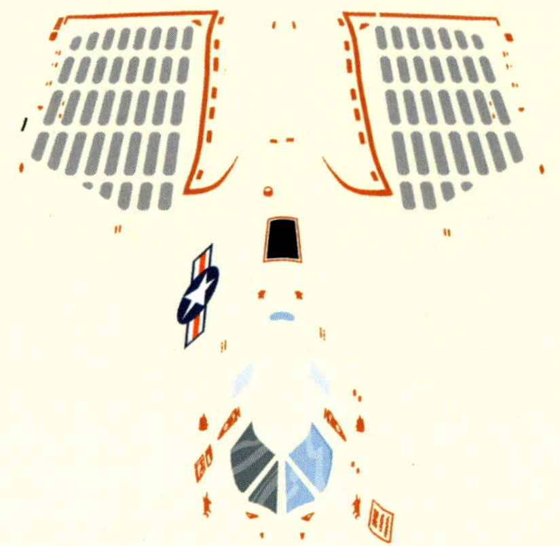

On such a dark aircraft, use should be made of the details, whether symbols or features of the plane structure, to provide points of light that enable the whole to be visualized better.

Sur un aéronef aussi sombre, les détails doivent être exploités au maximum, qu'il s'agisse de symboles ou d'éléments faisant partie de la structure même de l'avion, afin d'apporter quelques points de lumière permettant une meilleure visualisation de l'ensemble.

Bei einem derart dunklen Flugzeug müssen besonders die Details hervorgehoben werden. Durch Symbole und Elemente, die Bauteile des Flugzeugs darstellen, wird die Darstellung mit einigen Lichtpunkten versehen und dadurch besser erkennbar.

Bij een luchtvaartuig dat zo donker is moeten we gebruik maken van details, of het nu om symbolen of elementen die deel uitmaken van de vliegtuigstructuur gaat, om de tekening van lichtpuntjes te voorzien die het geheel beter doen uitkomen.

En una aeronave tan oscura debemos aprovechar los detalles, sean símbolos o elementos que formen parte de la estructura del avión, para dar puntos de luz que permitan visualizar mejor el conjunto.

In un aereo così scuro dobbiamo sfruttare i dettagli, i simboli o gli elementi che fanno parte della struttura, per creare punti di luce che consentono una migliore visualizzazione dell'insieme.

Numa aeronave tão escura devemos aproveitar os detalhes, quer sejam símbolos ou elementos que façam parte da estrutura do avião, para dar pontos de luz que permitam visualizar melhor o conjunto.

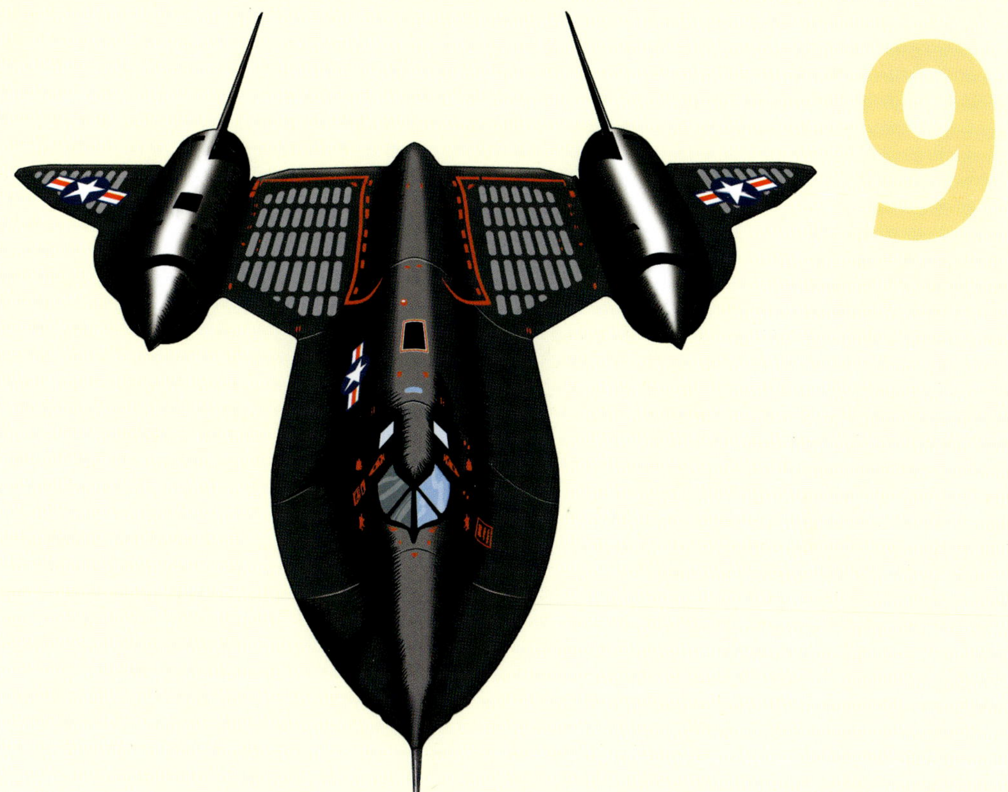

9

The series of different steps come together in the finished drawing, which is has amazing impact. This is a powerful and awe-inspiring aircraft.

L'assemblage des différentes phases donne un dessin final impressionnant. Il s'agit d'un appareil puissant et redoutable.

Durch Verbindung der einzelnen Arbeitsschritte entsteht eine äußerst beeindruckende Zeichnung. Der Betrachter blickt auf ein mächtiges, Angst einflößendes Aufklärungsflugzeug.

De som van de verschillende fases past in een enorm overweldigende afgeronde tekening. Het is een krachtig en afschrikwekkend luchtvaartuig.

El conjunto de las distintas fases cuaja en un dibujo acabado tremendamente impactante: es una aeronave potente y temible.

L'insieme delle distinte fasi si trasforma in un disegno finito dall'impatto straordinario. Si tratta di un velivolo potente y temibile.

O conjunto das distintas fases resulta num desenho acabado tremendamente impactante. Esta é uma aeronave potente e temível.

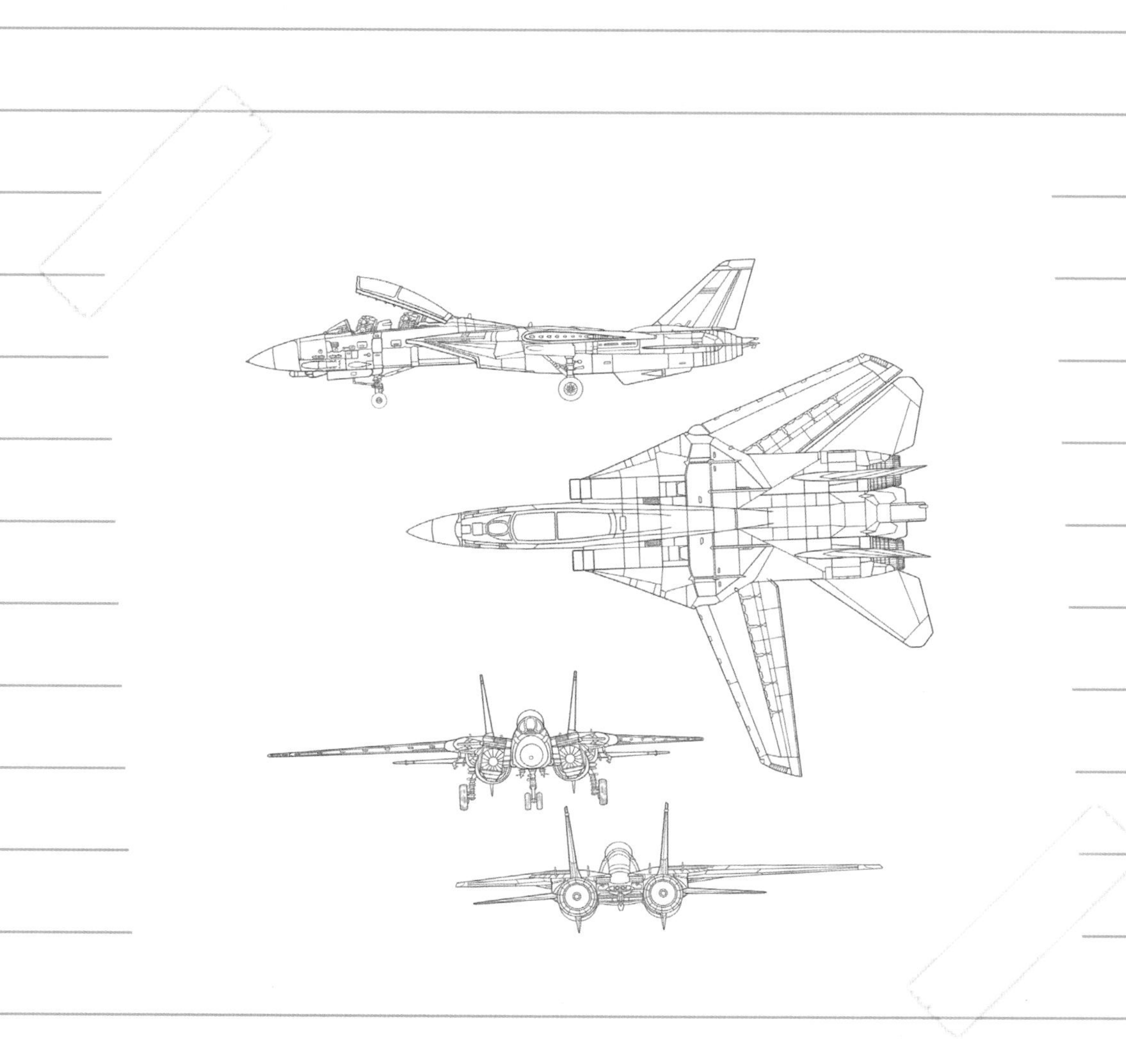

# F-14 Tomcat

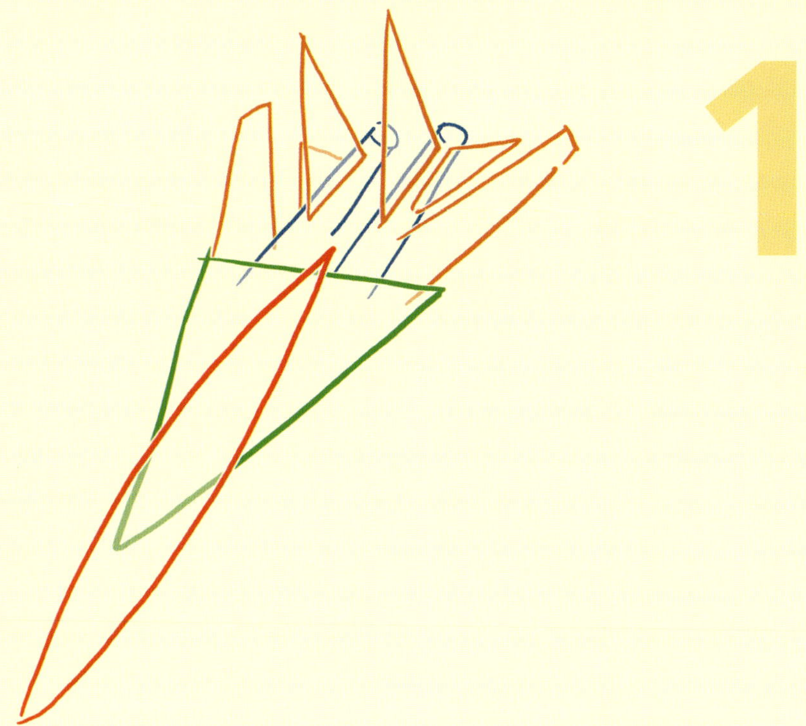

1

When drawing on paper, make several outlines on separate sheets until you are satisfied. When drawing on a computer, use a single layer for the outline, removing opacity from it so it can serve as a base.

Pour un dessin sur papier, vous réaliserez divers schémas sur des feuilles séparées jusqu'à trouver le bon. Pour un dessin sur ordinateur, utilisez une seule couche pour le schéma, dont vous pourrez ensuite supprimer l'opacité afin de vous en servir comme base.

Wird auf Papier gearbeitet, sind mehrere Schemazeichnungen anzufertigen, bis die Flugzeugstruktur zufrieden stellend wiedergegeben ist. Am Computer wird eine Bildebene nur für die Schemazeichnung verwendet. Diese kann anschließend transparenter gestaltet werden, um als Vorlage zu dienen.

Wordt op papier getekend, maak dan diverse schema's op afzonderlijke vellen papier totdat je het definitieve schema hebt gevonden. Bij een computertekening wordt voor het schema gebruik gemaakt van één laag, waarvan we de ondoorschijnendheid kunnen verwijderen om als basis te worden genomen.

Si dibujamos en papel, haremos varios esquemas en hojas aparte hasta dar con el definitivo. Si dibujamos mediante ordenador, utilizaremos una capa sólo para el esquema, al que podremos quitar opacidad para tomarlo como base.

Se disegniamo su carta, realizzeremo vari schemi su fogli separati prima di arrivare a quello definitivo. Se disegniamo al computer, utilizzeremo un livello solo per lo schema, a cui potremo togliere opacità per usarlo come base.

Se desenhamos em papel, faremos vários esquemas em folhas à parte até encontrar o definitivo. Se desenhamos no computador, utilizaremos uma camada só para o esquema, ao qual podemos tirar opacidade para tomá-lo como base.

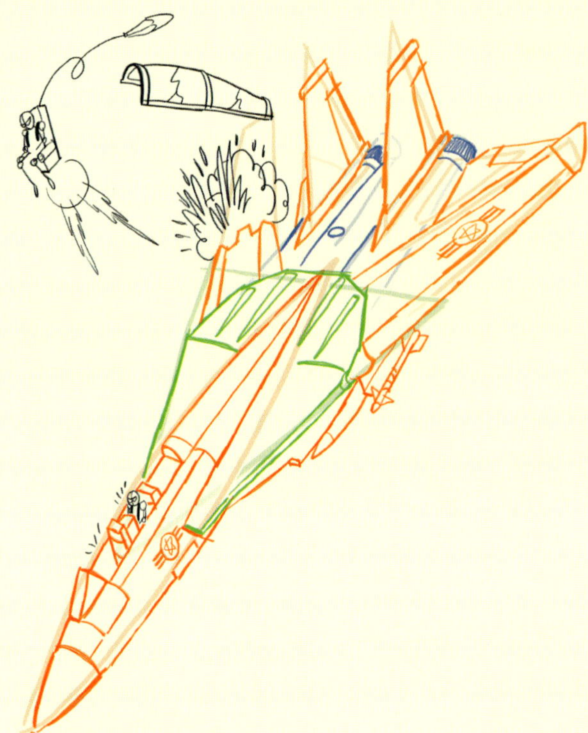

2

The roughness of the outline shows that the quality of the lines is not important in this step. This sketch needed several attempts until it was acceptable. The idea of an exploding wing and the ejecting pilot allowed me to turn the illustration into a mini-narrative.

La grossièreté du trait montre que la qualité de la ligne n'est pas importante dans cette étape. Cette ébauche a nécessité plusieurs essais. L'idée de l'aile qui explose et du pilote éjecté vous permet de transformer l'illustration en une petite histoire.

Die grobe Linienführung zeigt, dass die Qualität der Striche bei der Erarbeitung der Skizze nicht von Bedeutung ist. Diese Skizze erfordert mehrere Versuche. Durch den explodierenden Flügel und den Piloten, der sich mit dem Schleudersitz rettet, entsteht eine kleine Geschichte.

Het grove karakter van de schets toont dat de kwaliteit van de lijnen in deze fase niet belangrijk is. Voor deze schets waren diverse pogingen nodig. Het idee van de ontploffende vleugel en de piloot die uit het vliegtuig schiet stelde me in staat om de illustratie in een miniverhaaltje te veranderen.

La tosquedad del trazo demuestra que la calidad de la línea no es importante en esta fase. Este boceto requirió varios intentos. La idea del ala explotando y el piloto eyectado me permitió transformar la ilustración en una minihistoria.

La grossolanità del tratto dimostra che la qualità della linea in questa fase non è importante. Per realizzare questo bozzetto ci sono voluti diversi tentativi. L'idea dell'ala che scoppia e del pilota eiettato mi ha permesso di trasformare l'illustrazione in una ministoria.

A rudeza do traço demonstra que a qualidade da linha não é importante nesta fase. Este esboço requereu várias tentativas. A ideia da asa a explodir e o piloto ejectado permitiu-me transformar a ilustração numa mini história.

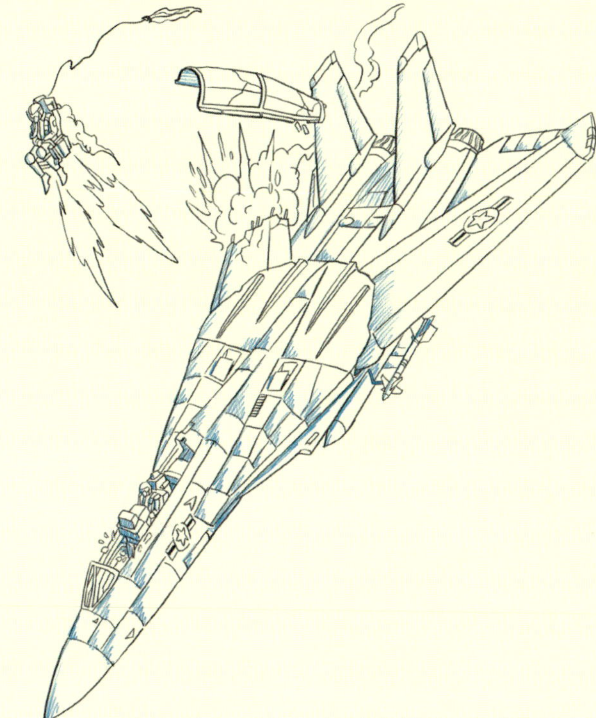

3

The pencil lines gives the elements a physical quality: straight lines for the plane, broken lines for the broken wing, and highly curved or pointed lines for the explosions. The raised cockpit increases the effect of volume.

Avec le crayonné, les éléments acquièrent une consistance physique : des lignes droites pour l'avion, des traits imprécis pour l'aile brisée et des lignes très courbes ou pointues pour les explosions. La cabine éjectée augmente l'effet de volume.

Die Strichführung des Buntstifts verleiht den einzelnen Elementen besondere Merkmale: Das Flugzeug weist gerade Linien auf, der zerstörte Flügel wird durch unregelmäßige Linien gekennzeichnet und die Explosion wird durch spitze Formen dargestellt. Die in die Luft geschleuderte Cockpitabdeckung verleiht der Abbildung mehr Tiefe.

De schets van de potloodtekening verstrekt de elementen een fysieke aard: rechtlijnige strepen voor het vliegtuig, streepjeslijnen voor de kapotte vleugel en zeer kromme of spitse lijnen voor de explosies. De gemonteerde cabine verhoogt het volume-effect.

El trazo del lápiz da naturaleza física a los elementos: rayas rectilíneas para el avión, líneas quebradas para el ala rota y líneas muy curvas o puntiagudas para las explosiones. La cabina montada aumenta el efecto de volumen.

Il tratto a matita dà una natura fisica agli elementi: linee rette per l'aereo, linee spezzate per l'ala rotta e linee molto curve o appuntite per le esplosioni. La cabina sovrapposta aumenta l'effetto complessivo, aggiungendo volume.

O traço do lápis dá natureza física aos elementos: riscas rectilíneas para o avião, linhas quebradas para a asa danificada e linhas muito curvas ou pontiagudas para as explosões. A cabina acabada aumenta o efeito de volume.

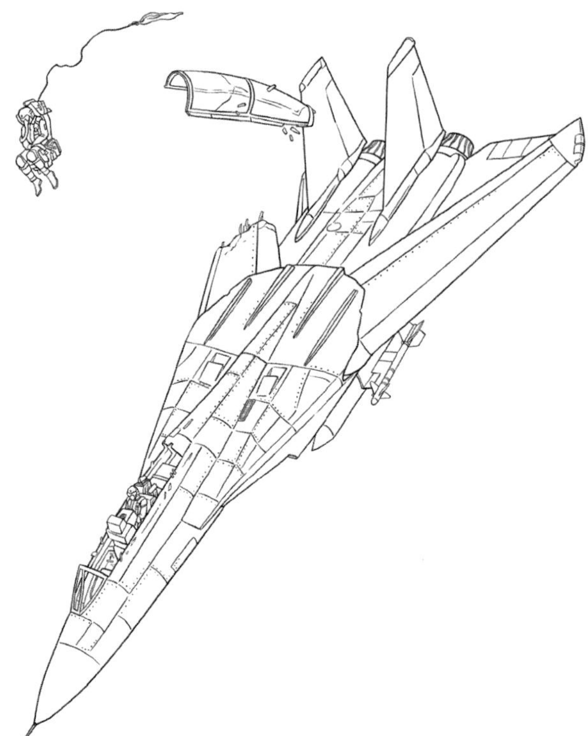

4

The style of inking also conveys emotion. Most of the inking in the illustration was done freehand to convey the vulnerability of the aircraft in this situation.

La nature de l'encrage transmet également certaines émotions. La majorité des tracés de l'illustration ont été réalisés à main levée pour transmettre à l'appareil un aspect vulnérable dans cette situation.

Auch die Tuschezeichnung kann Emotionen vermitteln. Die meisten Tuschelinien dieser Zeichnung wurden frei Hand gestaltet, um die Verwundbarkeit des Flugzeugs in dieser Situation zu verdeutlichen.

De aard van de inkttekening straalt ook emoties uit. De meeste inktstrepen van de illustratie zijn uit de vrije hand getekend om de kwetsbaarheid van het apparaat in deze situatie over te brengen.

La naturaleza de la tinta también transmite emociones. La mayoría de las tintas de la ilustración se han realizado a mano alzada para transmitir la vulnerabilidad del aparato en esta situación.

Anche la natura del ripasso a china trasmette emozioni. La maggior parte delle linee a china dell'illustrazione è stata realizzata a mano libera per trasmettere la vulnerabilità dell'apparecchio in questa situazione.

A natureza da tinta também transmite emoções. A maioria das tintas da ilustração realizaram-se à mão livre para transmitir a vulnerabilidade do aparelho nesta situação.

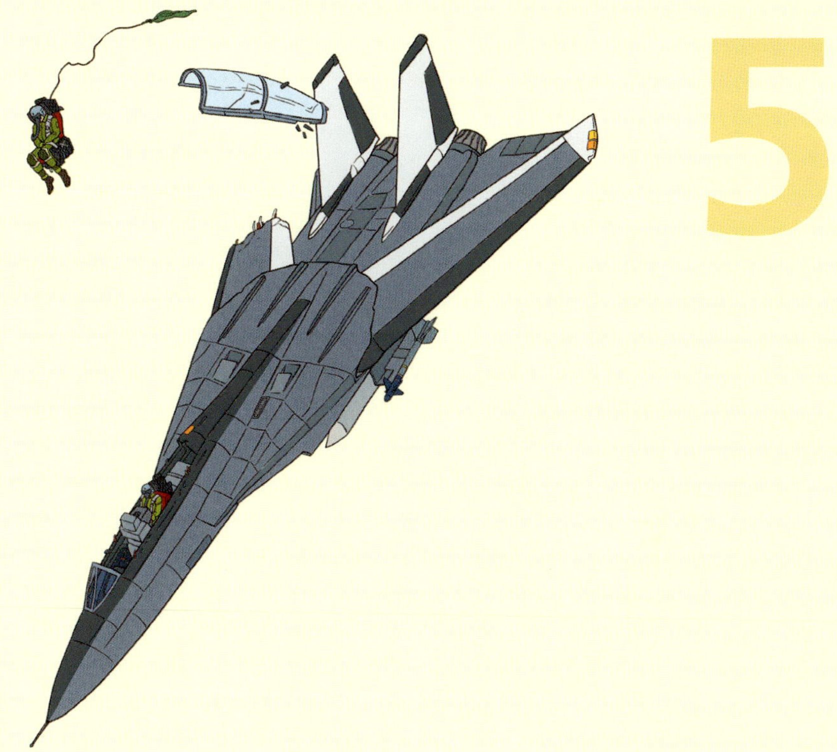

# 5

Although the base color is gray, the light and dark shades have been positioned to give the aircraft a bold and slightly sporting appearance. Contrast is provided by the pilots' green jumpsuits.

Avec le gris comme couleur de base, les tons clairs et obscurs ont été répartis de façon à donner à l'aéronef une allure audacieuse et légèrement sportive. Les contrastes sont apportés par les vêtements verts des pilotes.

Die Grundfarbe für dieses Bild ist Grau. Durch die Verwendung heller und dunkler Nuancen wirkt das Flugzeug verwegener und mutet sogar ein bisschen sportlich an. Die Grüntöne der Overalls der Piloten bilden einen erfrischenden Kontrast.

Hoewel de basiskleur grijs is, zijn de lichte en donkere kleuren zodanig aangebracht dat het luchtvaartuig er stoutmoedig en enigszins sportief uitziet. Het contrast ontstaat door de groene uniformen van de piloten.

Aunque el color base es el gris, se han situado los tonos claros y oscuros de manera que la aeronave tenga un aspecto atrevido y ligeramente deportivo. El contraste lo dan los trajes verdes de los pilotos.

Anche se il colore di base è grigio, sono stati collocati i toni chiari e quelli scuri in modo che il velivolo avesse un aspetto un po' audace e leggermente sportivo. Il contrasto è dato dalle tute verdi dei piloti.

Ainda que a cor base seja o cinzento, colocaram-se tons claros e escuros de maneira a que a aeronave tenha um aspecto atrevido e ligeiramente desportivo. O contraste é dado pelas roupas verdes dos pilotos.

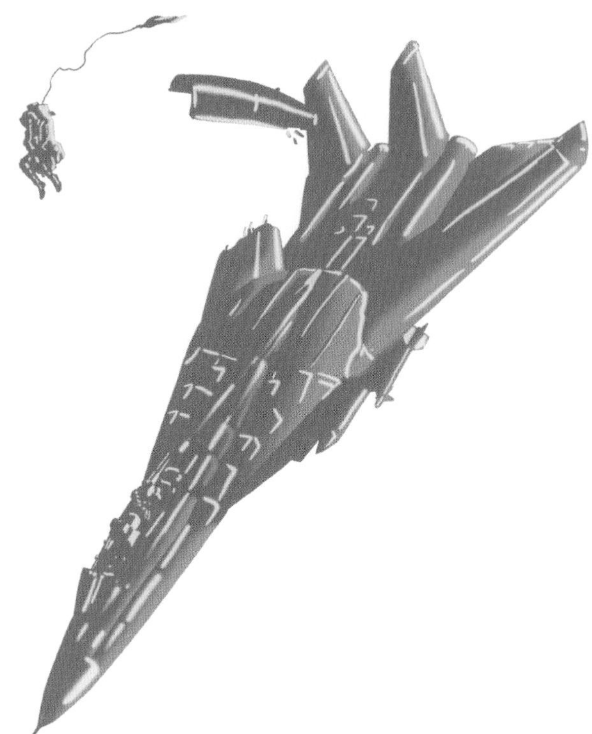

6

The light source has been placed at the rear because this is an unusual position that enhances the sensation of being in an emergency situation. Two layers with very different levels of opacity enhance the metal of the aircraft.

La source de lumière a été placée dans la partie arrière car il s'agit d'une position atypique qui accroît l'impression d'urgence. Les deux couches, d'opacité très différente, renforcent l'aspect métallique de l'appareil.

Die Lichtquelle befindet sich hinter dem Flugzeug (eine untypische Position, die das Gefühl einer Notsituation verstärkt). Die zwei unterschiedlich transparenten Lichtebenen unterstreichen das metallene Material des Kampfjets.

De lichtbron is aan de achterkant geplaatst, omdat het een atypische positie is die de indruk verhoogd dat we ons in een noodsituatie bevinden. De twee lagen met een zeer verschillende opaciteit versterken het metalen karakter van het vliegtuig.

Se ha situado el foco de luz en la parte de atrás porque es una posición atípica que aumenta la sensación de estar en una situación de emergencia. Las dos capas de muy distinta opacidad refuerzan el carácter metálico de la nave.

La sorgente luminosa è stata ubicata nella parte posteriore, perché è una posizione atipica che aumenta la sensazione di trovarsi in una situazione di emergenza. I due livelli, con opacità molto diversa, rafforzano il carattere metallico dell'aereo.

Colocou-se o foco de luz na parte de atrás porque é uma posição atípica que aumenta a sensação de estar numa situação de emergência. As duas camadas de muito distinta opacidade reforçam o carácter metálico da nave.

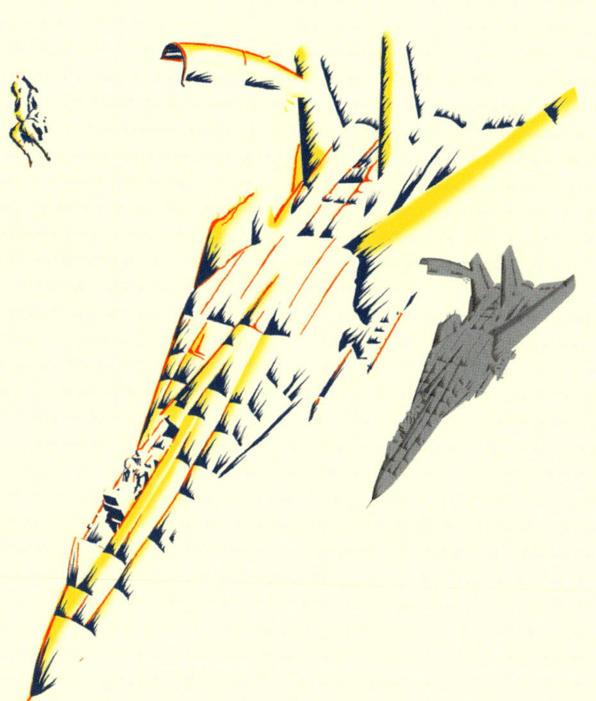

7

Shading was done using three layers of black with different levels of opacity. The shading represented in yellow marks the general volumes, but the blue and red, in dots, reveal segments of the fuselage and enhance the sensation of speed.

Les ombres ont été réalisées sur trois couches de noir de différentes opacités. Celle représentée en jaune définit les volumes généraux tandis que celles en bleu et rouge, en pointes, font ressortir les segments du fuselage et augmentent la sensation de vitesse.

Für die Schattenbereiche wurden drei schwarze Ebenen mit unterschiedlicher Transparenz erarbeitet. Die gelb dargestellte Ebene betont die allgemeine Form, die blaue und die rote Ebene mit spitz zulaufenden Schatten grenzen die einzelnen Abschnitte des Rumpfs ab und vermitteln das Gefühl von Schnelligkeit.

De schaduwen worden in drie lagen zwart met verschillende maten van opaciteit aangebracht. De gele schaduw markeert algemene volumes, maar de blauwe en rode, in puntjes, verraden segmenten van de romp en verhogen het gevoel van snelheid.

Las sombras se han dado en tres capas de negro de distintas opacidades. La representada en amarillo marca volúmenes generales, pero la azul y la roja, en puntas, delatan segmentos del fuselaje y aumentan la sensación de velocidad.

Le ombre sono state aggiunte mediante tre livelli di nero con diverse opacità. Quello rappresentato in giallo sottolinea i volumi generali, mentre quello blu e quello rosso, appuntiti, segnano i segmenti della fusoliera e aumentano la sensazione di velocità.

As sombras deram-se em três camadas de preto com diferentes opacidades. A representada em amarelo marca volumes gerais, mas a azul e a vermelha, em pontas, delatam segmentos da fuselagem e aumentam a sensação de velocidade.

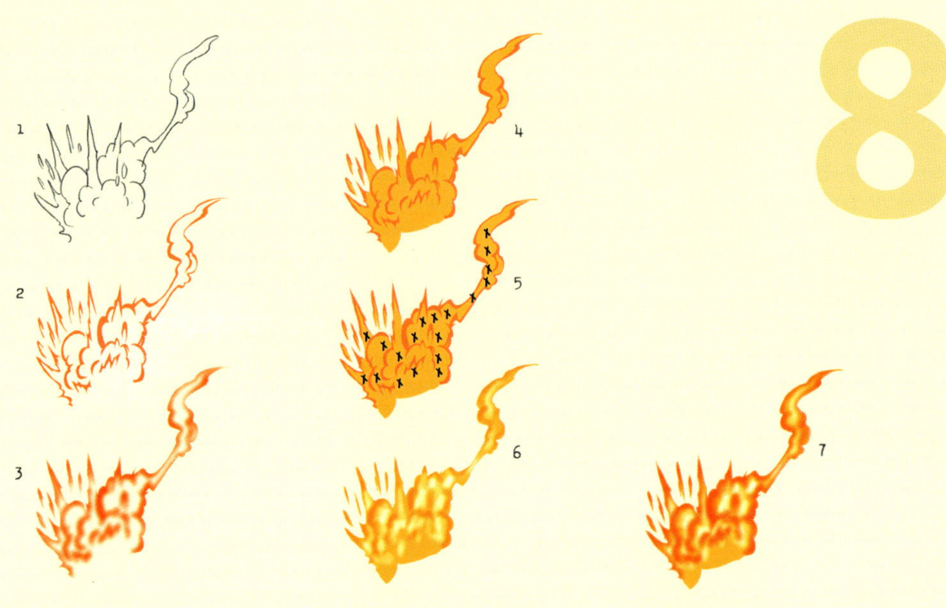


The explosion comes from inking (1) colored orange (2) and treated with a blurring filter (3). The interior of the explosion (4) is superimposed on key areas (5). The result of the overexposure (6) is merged with the layer (7).

L'explosion part d'un tracé (1) coloré en orange (2) et traité avec un filtre flou (3). L'intérieur de l'explosion (4) est surexposé à certains endroits clés (5). Le résultat de la surexposition (6) est associé à la couche (7).

Grundlage für das Element der Explosion ist eine Tuschezeichnung (1), die orange eingefärbt (2) und anschließend mit einem Gaußschen Weichzeichner (3) behandelt wird. Das Innere der Explosion (4) wird an wichtigen Stellen überbelichtet (5). Das Ergebnis dieser Überbelichtung (6) wird mit der ersten Ebene (7) verbunden.

De explosie gaat uit van een inktstreep (1) die oranje gekleurd (2) en met een onscherp filter behandeld (3) wordt. De binnenkant van de explosie (4) wordt op sleutelzones (5) overbelicht. Het resultaat van de overbelichting (6) wordt aan laag (7) gekoppeld.

La explosión parte de una tinta (1) coloreada en naranja (2) y tratada con un filtro de desenfoque (3). El interior de la explosión (4) se sobreexpone en zonas clave (5). El resultado de la sobreexposición (6) se une con la capa (7).

L'esplosione parte da una linea (1) colorata in arancione (2) e trattata con un filtro di sfocatura (3). L'interno dell'esplosione (4) viene sovraesposto nelle zone chiave (5). Il risultato della sovraesposizione (6) si unisce al livello (7).

A explosão parte de uma tinta (1) de cor-de-laranja (2) e tratada com um filtro de desfocagem (3). O interior da explosão (4) sobrepõe-se em zonas chave (5). O resultado da sobreexposição (6) une-se com a camada (7).

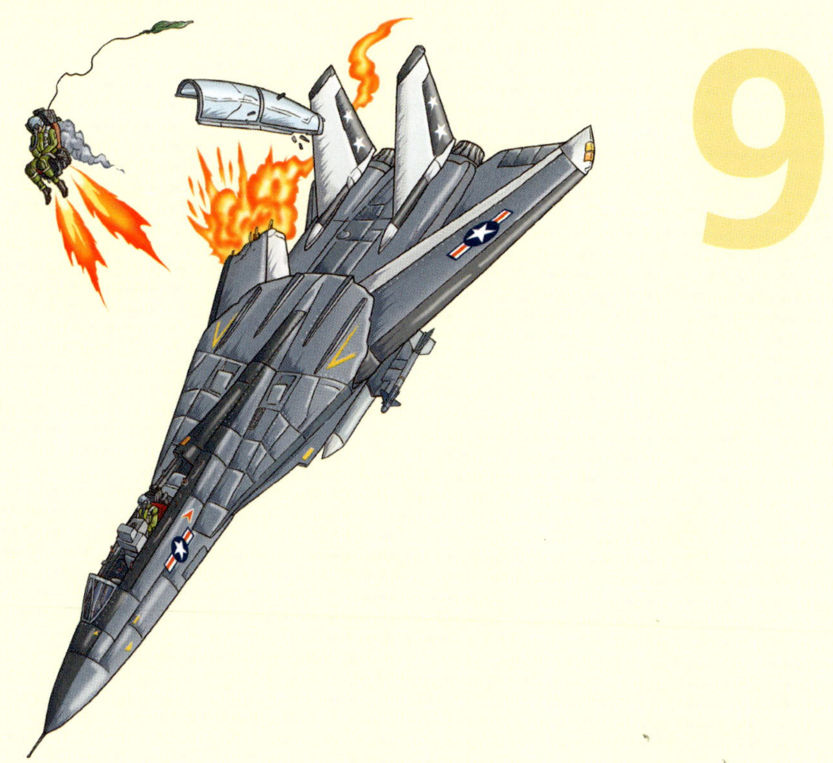

9

The result is quite dramatic. The red explosions contrast with the plane, to which several embellishments have been given, such as logos and indicative colors.

Le résultat obtenu est assez dramatique. Le rouge des explosions contraste avec l'avion, auquel divers éléments décoratifs ont été ajoutés, tels que des logos et couleurs caractéristiques.

Die fertige Zeichnung strahlt eine gewisse Dramatik aus. Das Rot der Explosionen kontrastiert mit dem Flugzeug, welches mit mehreren Zierelementen (Logos und farbigen Markierungen) versehen wurde.

Het resultaat heeft een nogal dramatisch karakter. Het rood van de explosies contrasteert met het vliegtuig, waaraan diverse versieringen zijn toegevoegd, zoals de logo's en onderscheidende kleuren.

El resultado es bastante dramático. El rojo de las explosiones contrasta con el avión, al que se han añadido diversos adornos, como logotipos y colores indicativos.

Il risultato è abbastanza drammatico. Il rosso delle esplosioni contrasta con l'aereo, a cui sono stati aggiunti diversi particolari, come i loghi e i colori indicativi.

O resultado é bastante dramático. O vermelho das explosões contrasta com o avião, ao qual se acrescentaram diversos adornos, como logótipos e cores indicativas.

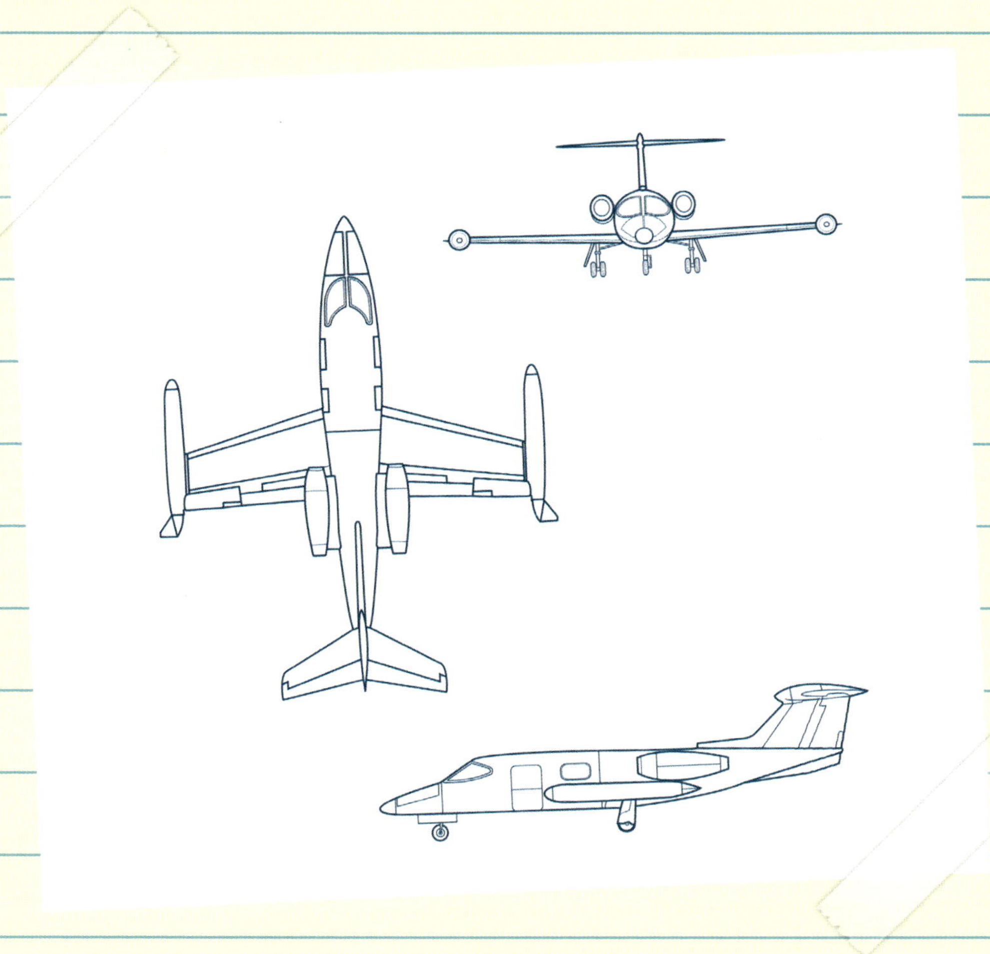

# Learjet 23

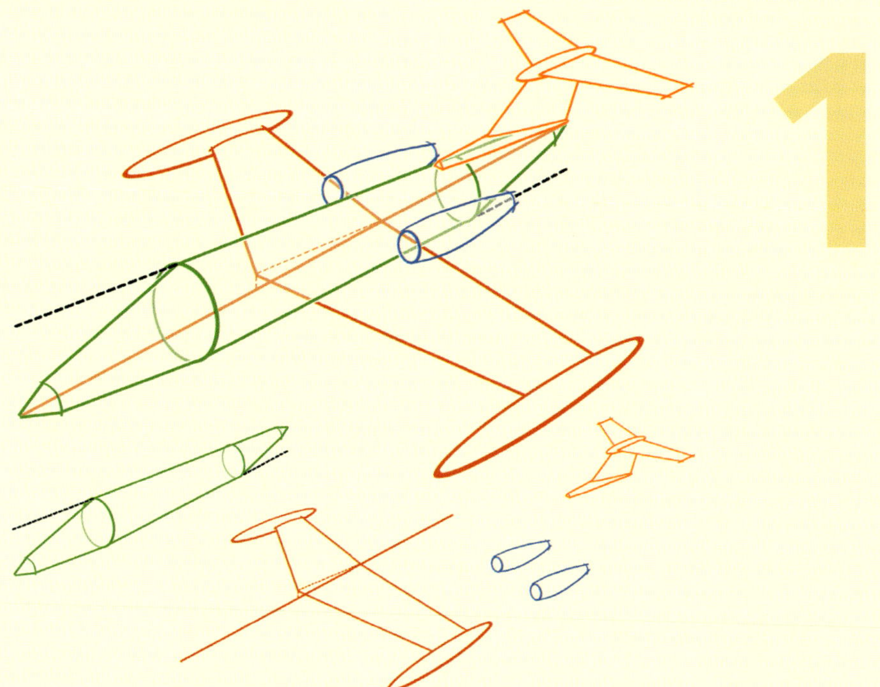


You should not be put off from making outlines of complex structures like those of planes. If you divide them in your head, you will see that they are actually made up of only a few simple elements. Dividing a whole into parts is a key strategy for illustrators.

Il ne faut pas avoir peur de réaliser des schémas de structures complexes telles que les avions. Si vous tentez de les démonter mentalement, vous vous apercevez qu'ils ne sont finalement composés que de quelques éléments simples. Il est donc indispensable pour les illustrateurs de séparer l'ensemble en plusieurs parties.

Das Anfertigen einer Schemazeichnung von Flugzeugen mit komplexen Strukturen sollte Sie nicht abschrecken. Wenn man die Grundstruktur im Kopf in einzelne Segmente aufteilt, wird deutlich, dass das Skelett im Grunde nur aus einigen einfachen Formen besteht. Das Zerlegen bestimmter Elemente in ihre Einzelteile gehört zu den grundlegenden Fertigkeiten eines Illustrators.

Laat je niet afschrikken door het maken van complexe vliegtuigstructuren zoals deze. Als we hem in gedachten in stukken verdelen dan zien we dat hij eigenlijk niet eens uit zoveel eenvoudige elementen bestaat. Het geheel in stukken verdelen is de sleutel voor illustrators.

No debe asustarte realizar esquemas de estructuras complejas como el de los aviones. Si dividimos mentalmente, veremos que no son tantos los elementos simples que los conforman. Dividir el todo en partes es clave para los ilustradores.

Realizzare schemi di strutture complesse come quelle degli aerei non deve spaventare. Se si suddivide mentalmente l'originale, vedremo che gli elementi semplici da cui è costituito non sono poi molti. Dividere il tutto in più parti è fondamentale per gli illustratori.

Não deve assustar-te realizar esquemas de estruturas complexas como a dos aviões. Se dividimos mentalmente, veremos que não são tantos os elementos simples que os formam. Dividir o todo em partes é chave para os ilustradores.

# 2

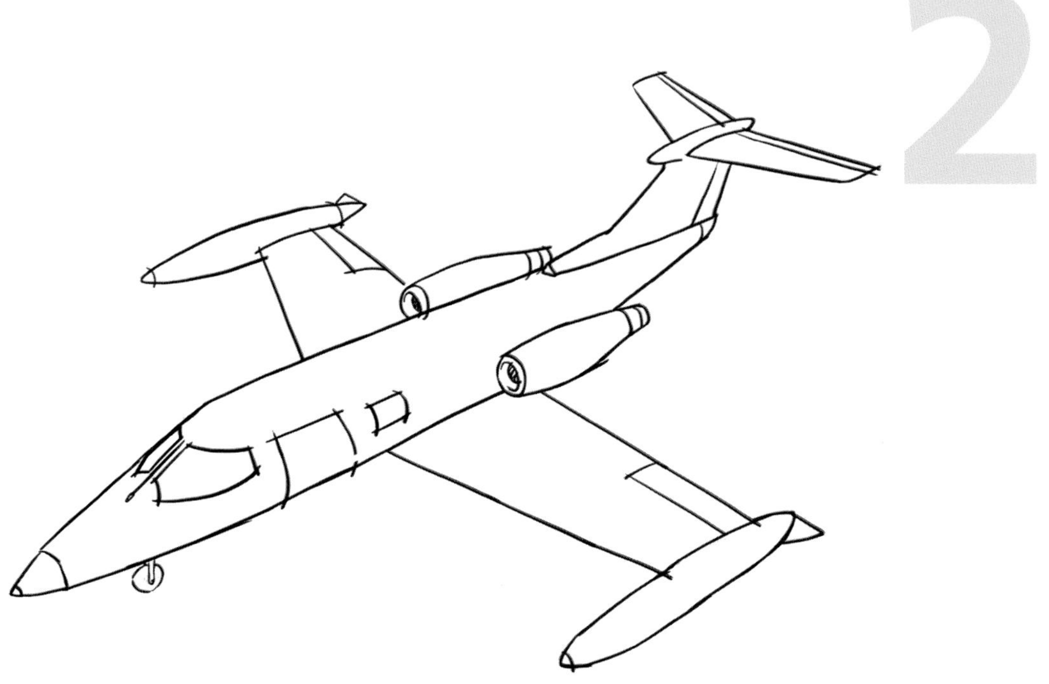

A simple and elegant design makes the illustrator's work easier. Capturing that elegance and transmitting it using only a few lines should be your main worry.

Un design simple et élégant facilite le travail du dessinateur. Votre préoccupation principale doit être de capter cette élégance et de la retransmettre.

Eine einfache, elegante Skizze erleichtert die Arbeit des Zeichners. Das Wichtigste bei diesem Arbeitsschritt ist es, die Eleganz des Flugzeugs zu erfassen und mit wenigen Strichen zu vermitteln.

Een eenvoudig en elegant ontwerp vereenvoudigt het werk van de tekenaar. Deze elegantie opvangen en met zo weinig mogelijk lijnen overbrengen moet onze voornaamste zorg zijn.

Un diseño simple y elegante facilita la labor del dibujante. Captar esa elegancia y transmitirla con tan pocas líneas debe ser nuestra preocupación principal.

Un design semplice ed elegante facilita il lavoro del disegnatore. Catturare questa eleganza e trasmetterla con così poche linee dovrebbe essere la nostra principale preoccupazione.

Um desenho simples e elegante facilita o trabalho do desenhador. Captar essa elegância e transmiti-la com tão poucas linhas deve ser a nossa preocupação principal.

## 3

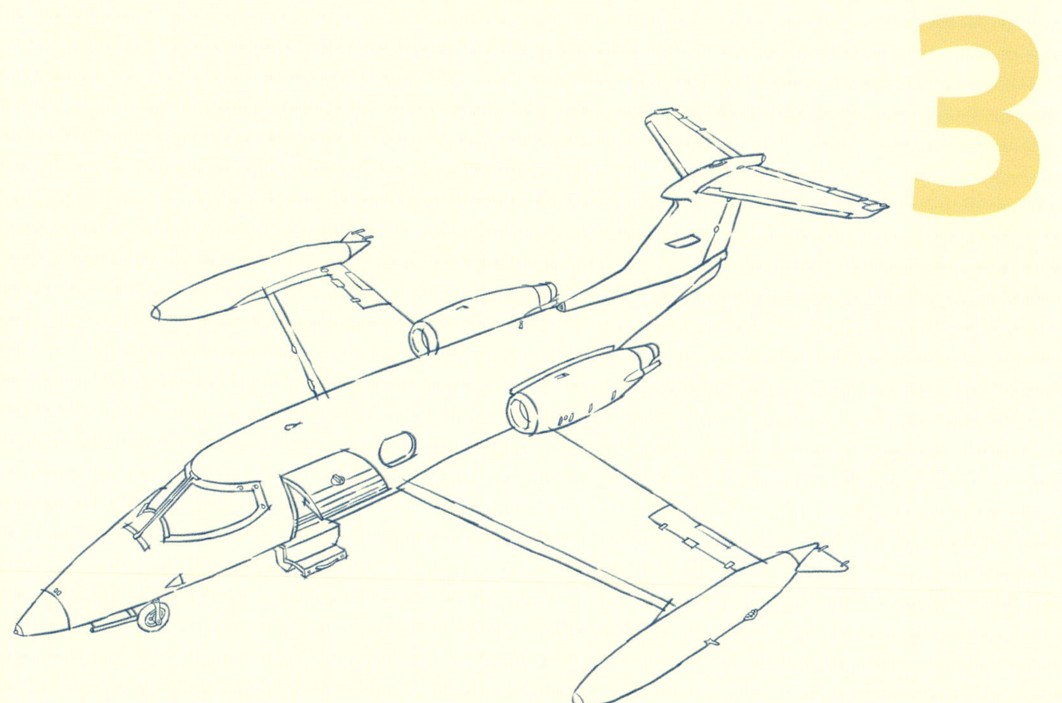

Adding small details along the fuselage during penciling stops the drawing from appearing empty and rough. The beauty is in the contrast: you have to combine spaces full of details with large empty spaces.

Ajouter sur le crayonné de petits détails le long du fuselage permet d'éviter que le dessin ne paraisse vide et peu travaillé. La grâce est dans le contraste : il faut combiner les espaces détaillés et les grands espaces vides.

Bei der Buntstiftzeichnung werden kleine Details am Rumpf hinzugefügt. Dadurch wird vermieden, dass dieser leer und zu wenig ausgearbeitet wirkt. Der besondere Kniff liegt im Kontrast: Bildsegmente mit Details müssen mit großen leeren Flächen kombiniert werden.

Door aan de potloodtekening kleine details langs de romp toe te voegen wordt voorkomen dat de tekening leeg en nauwelijks doorwrocht lijkt. Het leuke aan deze tekening is het contrast: er moeten ruimten met details worden gecombineerd met grote lege ruimten.

Añadir en el lápiz pequeños detalles a lo largo del fuselaje evita que el dibujo parezca vacío y poco trabajado. La gracia está en el contraste: hay que combinar espacios con detalles con grandes espacios vacíos.

Durante la fase a matita aggiungere piccoli dettagli lungo la fusoliera evita che il disegno appaia vuoto e poco elaborato. Il bello è ottenere un contrasto: bisogna combinare gli spazi pieni di dettagli con quelli ampi e vuoti.

Acrescentar no lápis pequenos detalhes ao longo da fuselagem evita que o desenho pareça vazio e pouco trabalhado. A graça está no contraste: há que combinar espaços com detalhes com grandes espaços vazios.

4

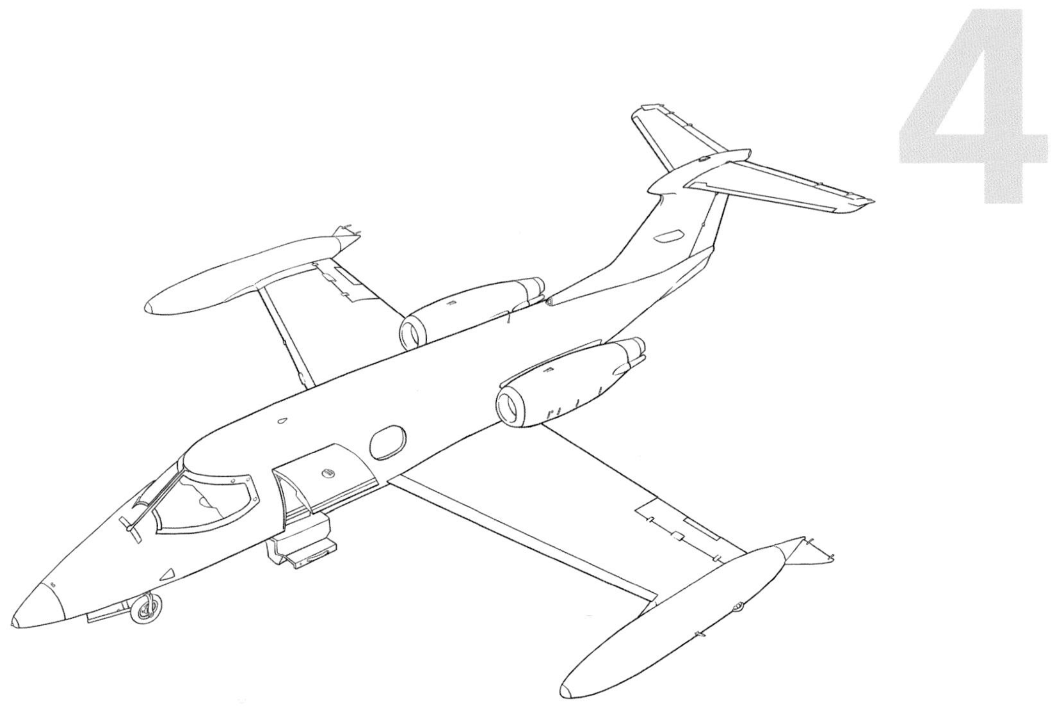

Use a ruler for inking large volumes, and freehand inking for small details. This will provide a balance between elegance and emotion for the plane.

Il convient ici d'associer des tracés effectués à la règle pour les grands volumes et des tracés réalisés à main levée pour les petits détails. Cela donnera à l'avion un équilibre, entre élégance et émotion.

Greifen Sie beim Anfertigen von Tuschezeichnungen auf Lineale zurück (für große Bildelemente) und zeichnen Sie kleine Details frei Hand. Dadurch wirkt das Flugzeug harmonisch und es herrscht ein Gleichgewicht zwischen Eleganz und Gefühl.

Trek inktlijnen met behulp van linialen voor de grote vlakken en teken de kleine details uit de vrije hand. Dit geeft het vliegtuig een evenwicht tussen elegantie en emotie.

Realiza tintas con la ayuda de reglas para los grandes volúmenes, junto a tintas a mano alzada para los pequeños detalles. Eso le dará al avión un equilibrio entre elegancia y emoción.

Traccia il disegno dei grandi volumi con l'aiuto di una riga, mentre ripassa a mano libera i piccoli dettagli. Ciò darà all'aereo un equilibrio tra eleganza ed emozione.

Realiza tintas com a ajuda de réguas para os grandes volumes, juntamente com tintas à mão livre para os pequenos detalhes. Isso dará ao avião um equilíbrio entre elegância e emoção.

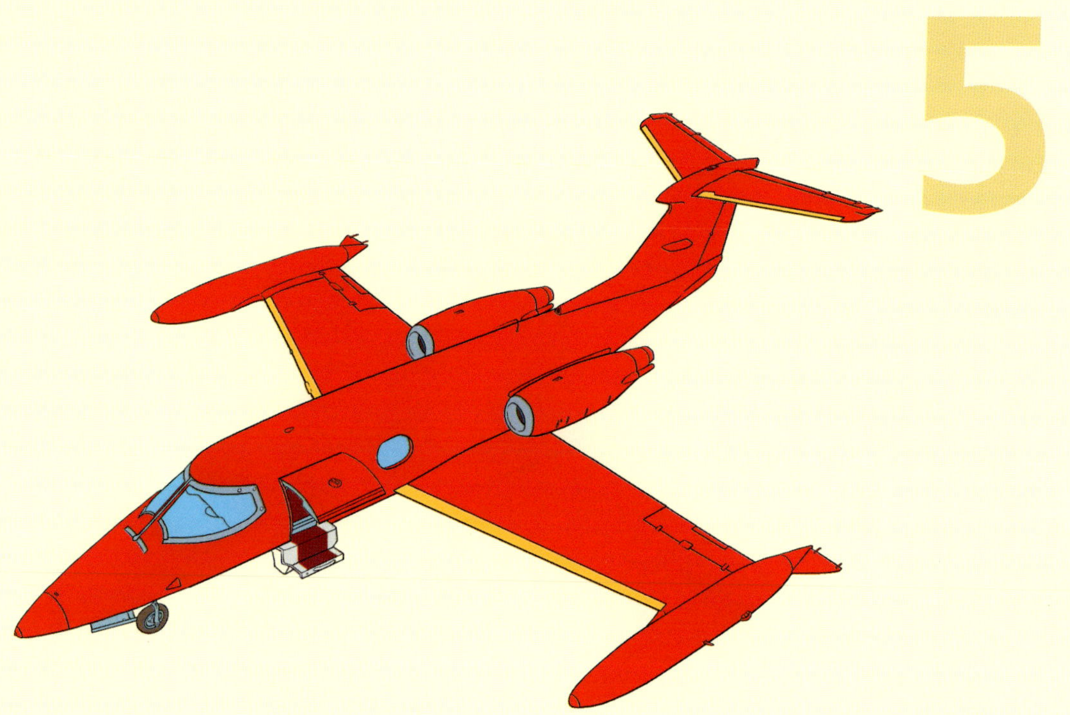

Is there anything sexier than a red sports car? This color was used on this plane with the same thing in mind. The yellow is for contrast. The blues and grays are mere tokens.

Existe-t-il plus sportif et attrayant qu'une voiture de sport rouge ? Cette couleur a été utilisée ici dans le but de produire le même effet. Le jaune sert de contraste. Les bleus et les gris font simplement office de figurants.

Gibt es etwas Sportlicheres und Anziehenderes als einen roten Sportwagen? Genau aus diesem Grund wurde für dieses Flugzeug die Farbe Rot gewählt. Die gelben Akzente bilden einen ansprechenden Kontrast, die Blau- und Grautöne spielen nur eine Nebenrolle.

Bestaat er iets sportievers en sexiers dan een rode sportwagen? Voor dit vliegtuig is deze kleur met dezelfde bedoeling gebruikt. Geel is het contrast. Blauw en grijs zijn enkel figuranten.

¿Hay algo más deportivo y sexy que un deportivo rojo? Para este avión se ha utilizado ese color con esa misma intención. El amarillo es el contraste. Los azules y grises son mera comparsa.

C'è qualcosa di più sportivo e sexy di una macchina sportiva rossa? Per questo aereo è stato utilizzato questo colore con la stessa intenzione. Il giallo serve da contrasto. I blu e i grigi sono mere comparse.

Há algo mais desportivo e sexy que um desportivo vermelho? Para este avião utilizou-se essa cor com essa mesma intenção. O amarelo é o contraste. Os azuis e cinzentos são meros comparsas.

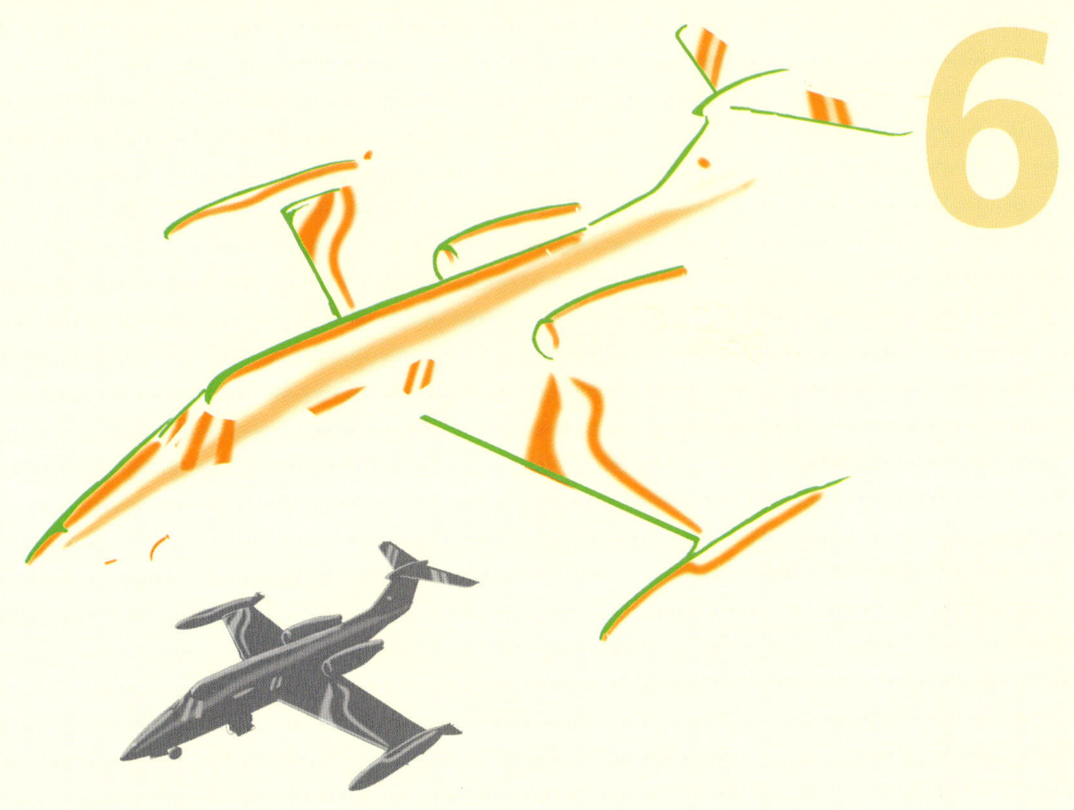


Lighting for the Learjet is divided into two longitudinal layers that provide a metallic sheen. The thumbnail shows how both layers are applied in white with different levels of opacity.

Les lumières du Learjet sont réparties sur deux couches longitudinales qui apportent cet éclat métallisé. Comme vous pouvez le voir sur la miniature, les deux couches ont été appliquées en blanc et avec différentes opacités.

Die Lichtbereiche des Learjet werden in zwei Ebenen aufgeteilt, die sich in Längsrichtung erstrecken und einen metallenen Glanz vermitteln. Die kleine Abbildung zeigt, dass beide Ebenen in Weiß und mit unterschiedlicher Transparenz in das Bild eingearbeitet werden.

De lichtvlakken van de Learjet worden verdeeld in twee lengtelagen die voor de gemetalliseerde glans zorgen. Zoals in de miniatuur te zien is, worden beide lagen in het wit en met een verschillende opaciteit aangebracht.

Las luces del Learjet se dividen en dos capas longitudinales que aportan el brillo metalizado. Como se observa en la miniatura, ambas capas se aplicarán en blanco y con diferente opacidad.

Le luci del Learjet sono divise in due livelli longitudinali che forniscono la lucentezza metallica. Come si osserva nella miniatura, entrambi i livelli verranno applicati in bianco con differenti opacità.

As luzes do Learjet dividem-se em duas camadas longitudinais que concedem o brilho metalizado. Como se observa na miniatura, ambas as camadas aplicar-se-ão em branco e com diferente opacidade.

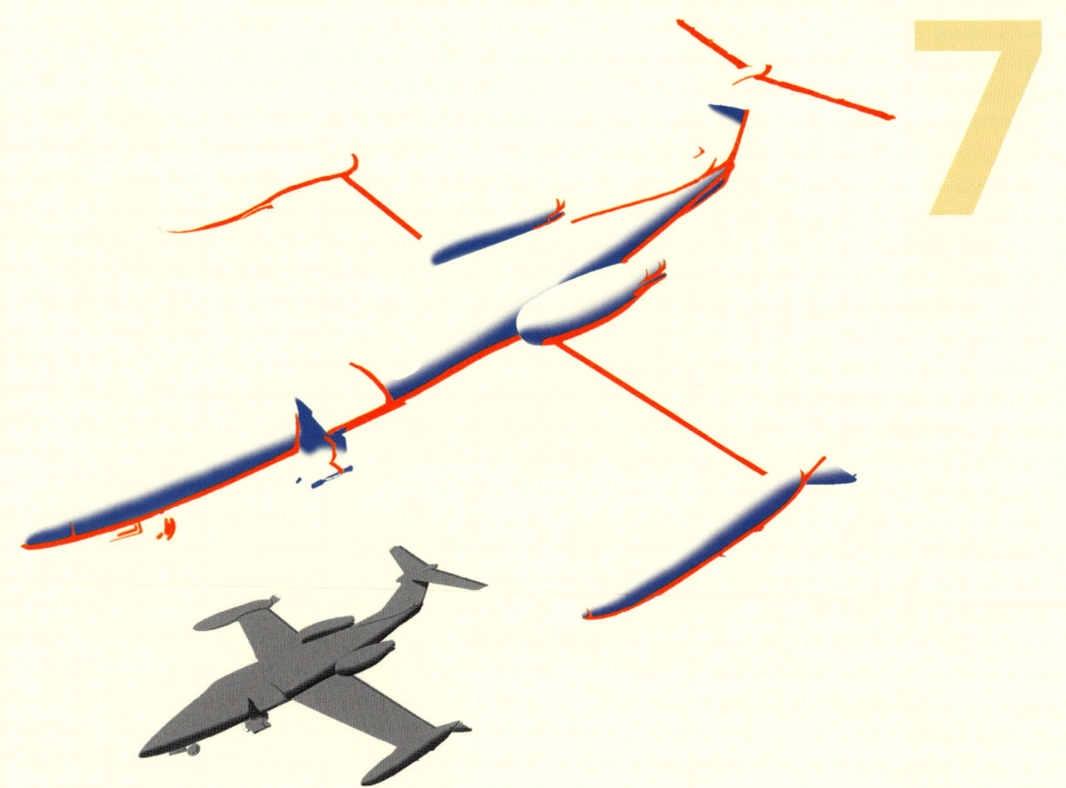


The two shading layers are to add volume and enhance the cylindrical shape of the aircraft. The thumbnail shows how both layers are applied in black with different levels of opacity.

Les deux couches d'ombres créent du volume et renforcent la forme cylindrique de l'aéronef. Comme vous pouvez le voir sur la miniature, toutes deux sont appliquées en noir avec des opacités différentes.

Die zwei Schattenebenen sorgen für mehr Tiefe und unterstreichen die zylindrische Form des Flugzeugs. In der kleinen Abbildung ist zu sehen, dass beide Ebenen in Schwarz und mit unterschiedlicher Transparenz eingesetzt werden.

De twee schaduwlagen proberen de cilindrische vorm van het vliegtuig volume te geven en te versterken. Zoals in de miniatuur te zien is, worden ze in het zwart met verschillende mates van opaciteit aangebracht.

Las dos capas de sombras buscan dar volumen y reforzar la forma cilíndrica de la aeronave. Como se observa en la miniatura, ambas se aplicarán en negro a diferentes opacidades.

I due livelli di ombre cercano di dare volume e di rafforzare la forma cilindrica del velivolo. Come si osserva nella miniatura, entrambi i livelli verranno applicati in nero con differenti opacità.

As duas camadas de sombras procuram dar volume e reforçar a forma cilíndrica da aeronave. Como se observa na miniatura, ambas aplicar-se-ão em preto com diferentes opacidades.

# 8

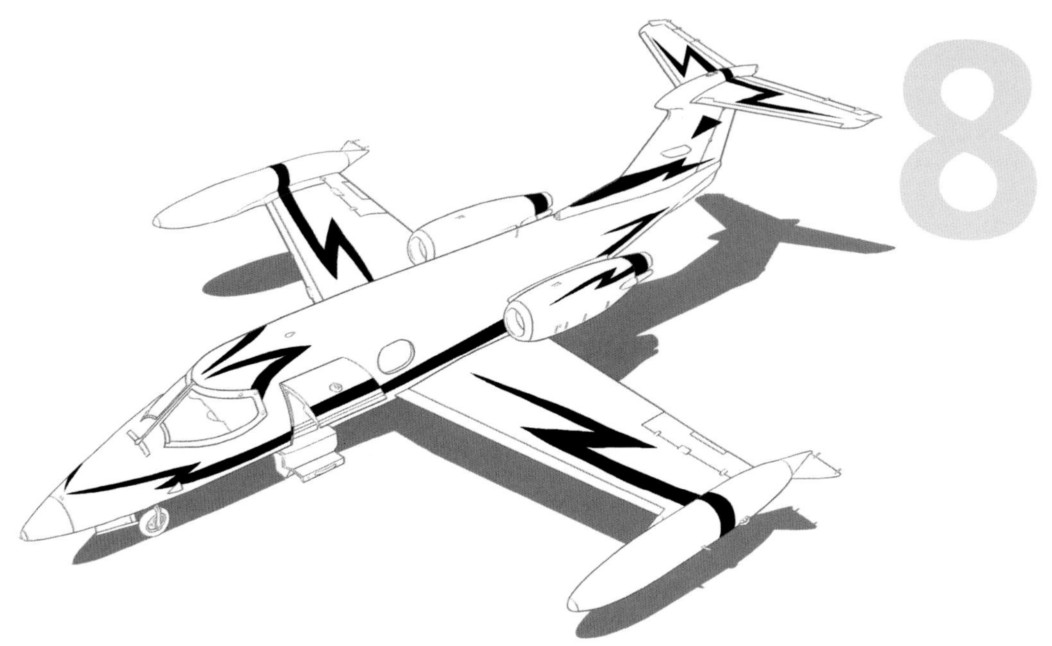

The bold decoration in the form of lightning bolts is applied here in black for better visualization, although it will be changed to white in the final drawing. The shading that links the aircraft to the ground is also shown.

Les décorations voyantes en forme d'éclairs sont ici appliquées en noir pour une meilleure visualisation, mais elles seront en blanc sur le dessin définitif. Reproduisez également l'ombre projetée sur le sol par l'appareil.

Die gewagten Zierelemente in Form von Blitzen werden hier zur besseren Darstellung in Schwarz eingefügt (in der fertigen Zeichnung erscheinen sie in Weiß). Außerdem wird der Schatten gezeichnet, den das Flugzeug auf den Boden wirft.

De gedurfde decoratie in de vorm van flitsen wordt hier in het zwart aangebracht voor een betere visualisatie, hoewel deze in de definitieve tekening wit zullen worden. Ook laten we de schaduw zien die het luchtvaartuig op de grond werpt.

La atrevida decoración en forma de rayos se aplica aquí en negro para una mejor visualización, aunque en el dibujo definitivo se cambiará a blanco. También mostramos la sombra que afianza la aeronave al suelo.

L'audace decorazione a forma di lampi viene applicata in nero per una migliore visualizzazione, anche se nel disegno definitivo verrà modificata in bianco. Mostriamo anche l'ombra proiettata dal velivolo sul terreno.

A atrevida decoração em forma de raios aplica-se aqui em preto para uma melhor visualização, embora no desenho definitivo se alterará para branco. Também mostramos a sombra que fixa a aeronave ao solo.

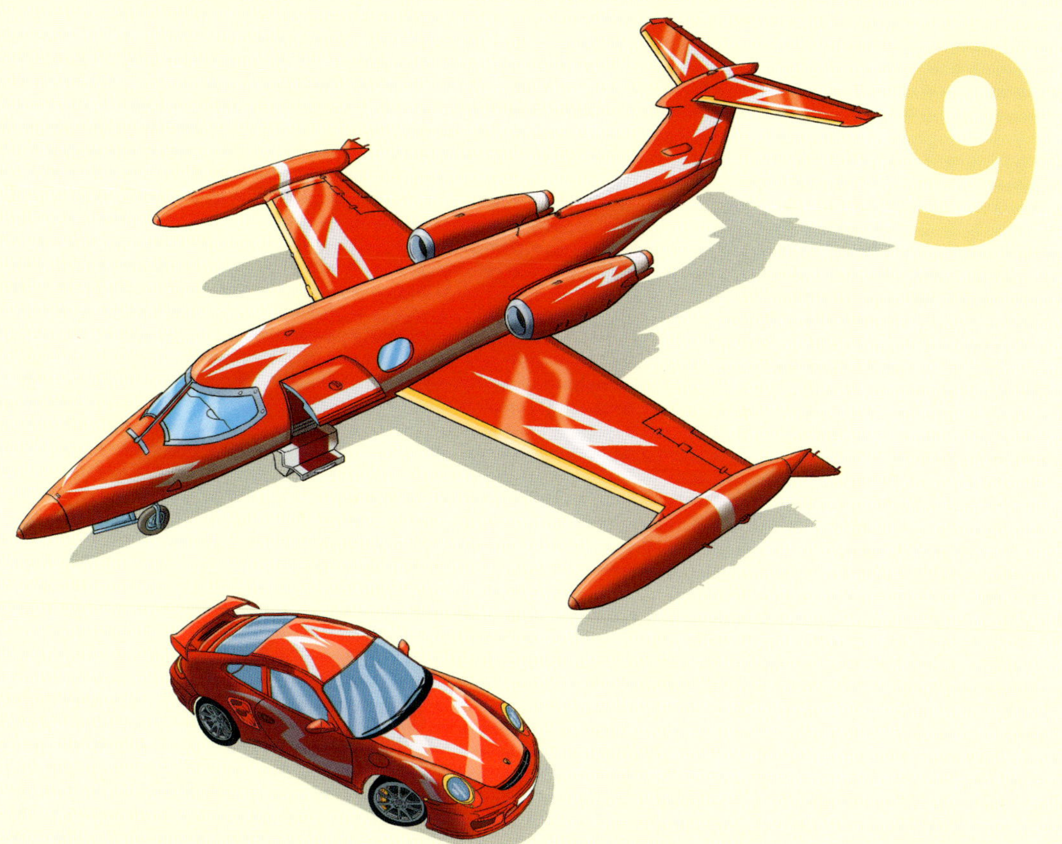

9

This attractive drawing also contains a surprise: the successful owner of this beautiful aircraft must have a matching sports car.

Le dessin final est très esthétique et comporte également une surprise : le riche propriétaire de ce bel avion doit également posséder la voiture assortie.

Die ansprechende fertige Zeichnung wartet mit einer Überraschung auf: Der erfolgreiche Eigentümer dieser schönen Maschine besitzt einen Sportwagen im gleichen Stil.

De aantrekkelijke afgeronde tekening bevat bovendien een verrassing: de succesvolle eigenaar van dit mooie vliegtuig moet een bijpassende sportwagen hebben.

El atractivo dibujo acabado contiene además una sorpresa: el exitoso propietario de este bello avión debe poseer un deportivo a juego.

L'attrattivo disegno finito contiene una sorpresa: il proprietario di questo bel velivolo deve possedere anche un'auto sportiva coordinata, a dimostrazione del suo successo.

O atraente desenho acabado contém ainda uma surpresa: o bem-sucedido dono deste belo avião deve possuir um carro desportivo a condizer.

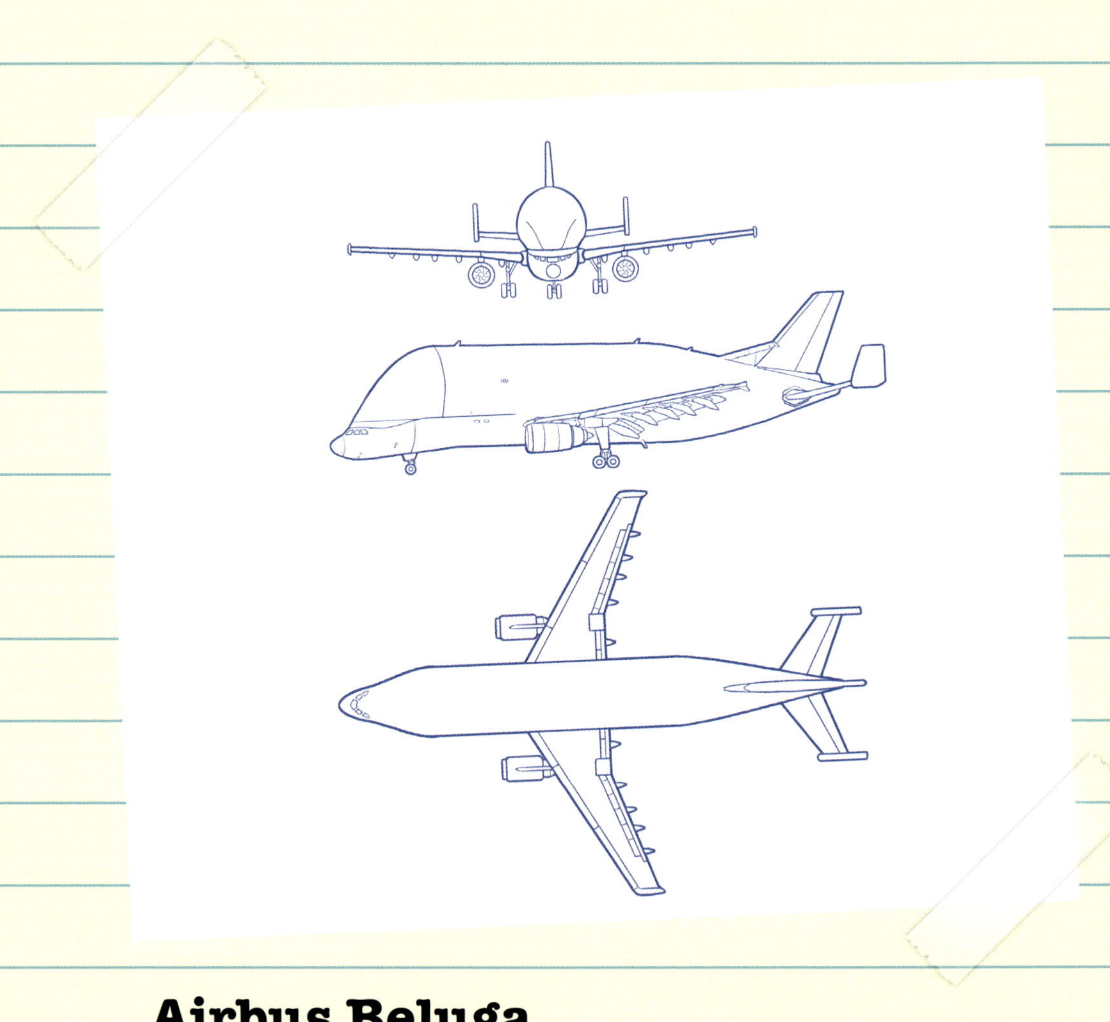

# Airbus Beluga

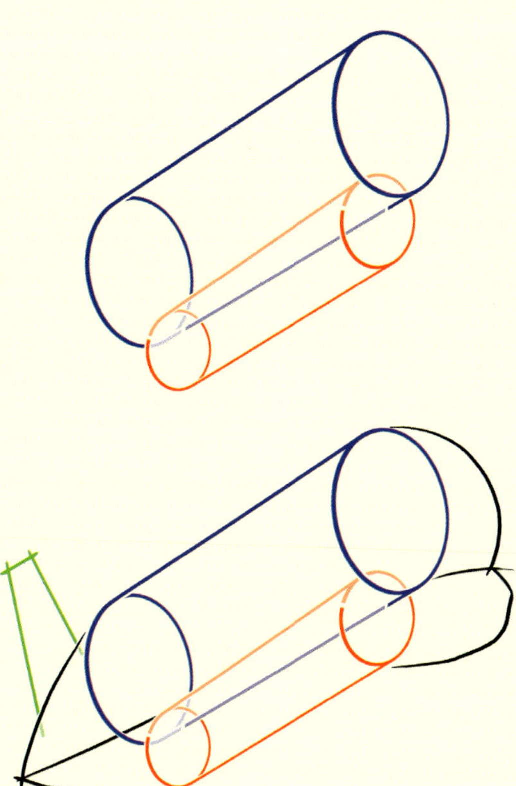

1

There are often basic elements that alone make up the skeleton and are the concept of the plane. The rest of the outline seems to lack importance.

Il existe bien souvent des éléments basiques qui forment à eux seuls le squelette et représentent tout le concept de l'avion. Le reste du schéma semble donc dérisoire.

Oftmals bilden schon einige grundlegenden Elemente das gesamten Skelett eines Flugzeugs. Der Rest der Schemazeichnung scheint nur von unwesentlicher Bedeutung zu sein.

Er zijn vaak basiselementen die op zichzelf de vorm bepalen en het hele vliegtuigconcept zijn. De rest van het schema lijkt onbelangrijk.

En muchas ocasiones existen elementos básicos que conforman por sí mismo el esqueleto y que son todo el concepto del avión. El resto del esquema parece carecer de importancia.

In molti casi esistono elementi di base che compongono lo scheletro e che racchiudono tutto il concetto dell'aereo. Il resto dello schema sembra non avere molta importanza.

Em muitas ocasiões existem elementos básicos que formam por si mesmo o esqueleto e que são todo o conceito do avião. O resto do esquema parece carecer de importância.

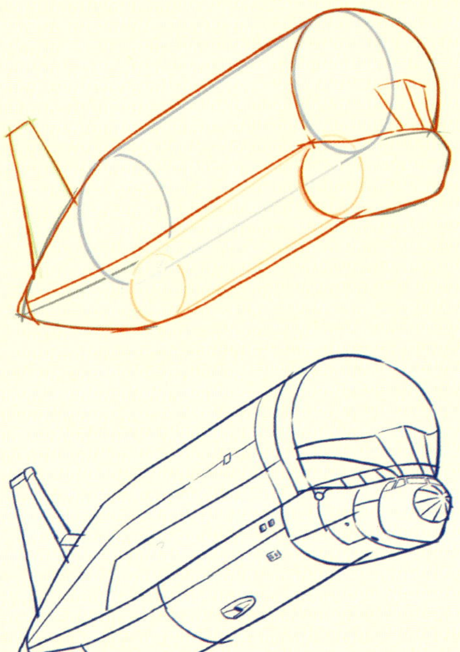

2

The lines that reveal the outline disappear in the sketch. If the volume works in this perspective, you can pencil in details in different sizes that give an idea of the huge dimensions of this aircraft.

Les lignes du schéma disparaissent dans l'ébauche. Si le volume fonctionne dans cette perspective, vous pouvez ajouter sur le crayonné des détails de différentes tailles afin de donner une idée de l'immensité de l'aéronef.

Die Hilfslinien der Schemazeichnung sind in der Skizze nicht mehr vorhanden. Gelingt die perspektivische Darstellung des Volumens, können bei der Buntstiftzeichnung einzelne Details unterschiedlicher Größe hinzugefügt werden, die die riesigen Ausmaße des Flugzeugs unterstreichen.

De lijnen die het schema verklappen verdwijnen in de schets. Als het volume in dit perspectief functioneert, dan kunnen we in de potloodtekening details van verschillende grootte toevoegen die de indruk wekken dat het om een enorm vliegtuig gaat.

Las líneas que delatan el esquema desaparecen en el boceto. Si el volumen funciona en esta perspectiva, podemos añadir en el lápiz detalles de varios tamaños que den idea de la enormidad de la aeronave.

Le linee che rivelano lo schema spariscono nel bozzetto. Se il volume funziona in questa prospettiva, possiamo aggiungere a matita dettagli di varie dimensioni che rendono l'idea dell'enormità di questo aeroplano.

As linhas que revelam o esquema desaparecem no esboço. Se o volume funciona nesta perspectiva, podemos acrescentar no lápis detalhes de vários tamanhos que dêem ideia da enormidade da aeronave.

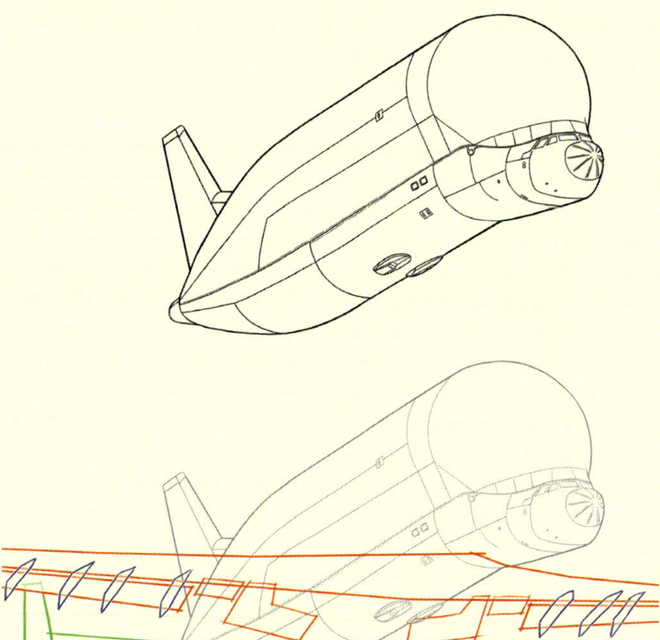

3

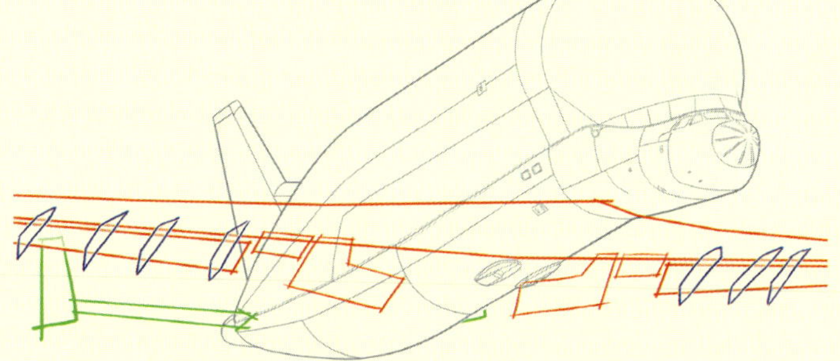

Inking for the fuselage is done with three brush sizes: exterior (thickest), interior (normal), and details (finer). The process starts again with a basic outline of the wings. By drawing through the plane, mistakes in perspective can be avoided.

L'encrage du fuselage de l'avion comporte trois tailles différentes de tracés : les contours extérieurs (plus épais), les lignes intérieures (normales) et les détails (plus fins). Recommencez le processus avec un schéma basique des ailes. En traversant l'avion, faites bien attention à la perspective.

Der Flugzeugrumpf wird mit drei verschieden starken Linien gestaltet: Die Umrisse werden mit einer breiteren Spitze gezeichnet, die inneren Linien mit einer normalen Spitze und die Details mit einer feinen Spitze. Nun wird der gesamte Zeichenvorgang mit einem Grundschema der Tragflächen erneut begonnen. Indem die Tragflächen den Rumpf durchtrennen, wird eine falsche perspektivische Darstellung vermieden.

Kleur de romp van het vliegtuig met drie inktstreepdikten in: buitenkant (dikker), binnenkant (normaal) en detail (dunner). Begin het proces opnieuw met een basisschema van de vleugels. Door ze dwars door het vliegtuig te tekenen vermijden we perspectieffouten.

Entintamos el fuselaje del avión con tres tamaños de tinta: exterior (más gruesa), interior (normal) y detalle (más fina). Recomenzamos el proceso con un esquema básico de las alas. Atravesando el avión evitamos fallos de perspectiva.

Ripassiamo a china la fusoliera dell'aereo con tre tratti di spessore differente: esterno (più spesso), interno (normale) e dettaglio (più sottile). Ricominciamo il procedimento con uno schema di base delle ali. Incrociando l'aereo evitiamo errori di prospettiva.

Fazemos a arte-final da fuselagem do avião com três tamanhos de tinta: exterior (mais espessas), interior (normal) e detalhe (mais fina). Recomeçamos o processo com um esquema básico das asas. Atravessando o avião evitamos falhas de perspectiva.

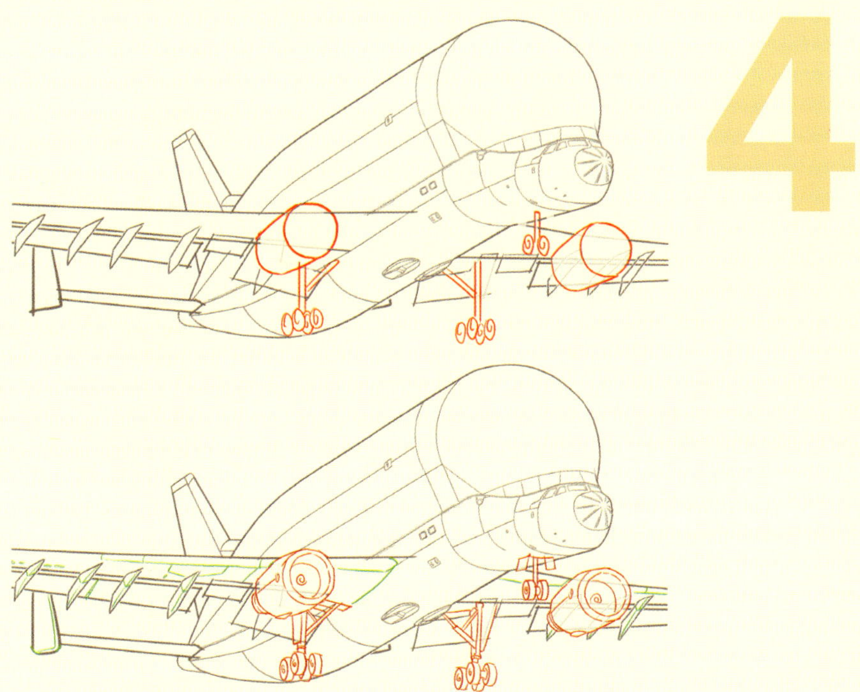

4

When an illustration is complex, a solution can be found by drawing outlines and sketches of each part of the plane separately, as here with the engines and undercarriage. Divide and you will conquer.

Lorsque l'illustration est un peu complexe, il est possible de réaliser des schémas et ébauches séparés pour chaque partie de l'avion, comme ici avec les moteurs et le train d'atterrissage. Diviser pour mieux régner.

Wenn eine Abbildung sehr komplex ist, können Schemazeichnungen und Skizzen für einzelne Teile des Flugzeugs erarbeitet werden, wie in diesem Fall für Triebwerke und Fahrwerk. „Zerlegen" lautet das Geheimnis!

Wanneer een illustratie ons complex lijkt kunnen we dit probleem oplossen door schema's en schetsen voor elk onderdeel van het vliegtuig afzonderlijk te tekenen, zoals hier met de motoren en het landingsgestel is gedaan. Verdeel in stukken en je zult zien dat het je zal lukken.

Cuando una ilustración nos resulta compleja podemos solucionarla realizando esquemas y bocetos para cada parte del avión independientemente, como ahora con los motores y el tren de aterrizaje. Divide y vencerás.

Quando un'illustrazione ci risulta troppo complessa possiamo affrontarla realizzando schemi e bozzetti indipendenti per ogni parte dell'aereo, come abbiamo fatto qui con i motori e il carrello di atterraggio. Divide et impera.

Quando uma ilustração nos parece complexa podemos solucioná-la realizando esquemas e esboços para cada parte do avião independentemente, como agora com os motores e o trem de aterragem. Divide e vencerás.

## 5

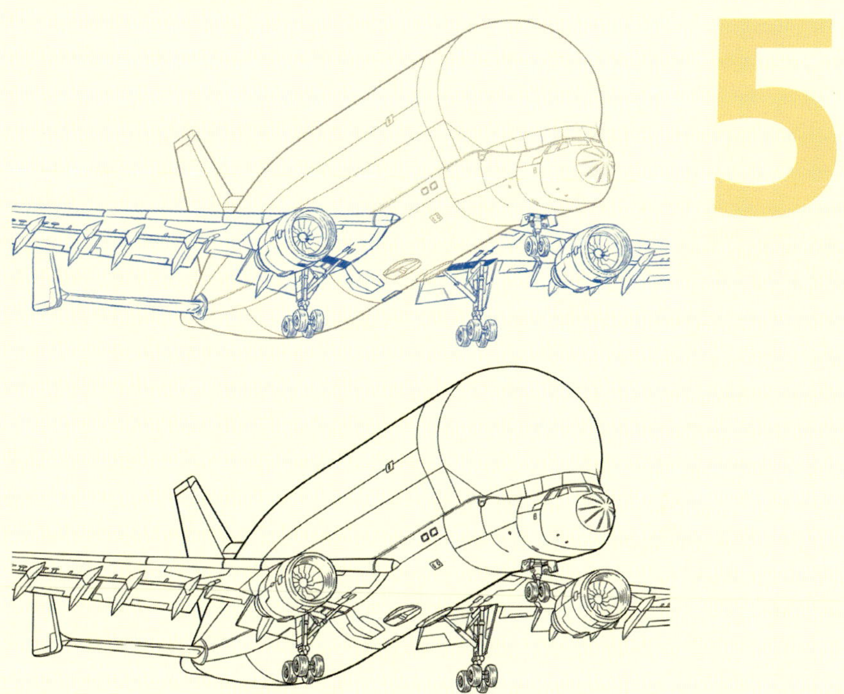

Now a detailed pencil drawing can be made of the wings. At first I thought the plane was complex, but if I center my attention on the wings, I feel I can do a better job. The inking corroborates this.

Vous pouvez maintenant passer au crayonné détaillé des ailes. Au départ, l'avion semblait complexe mais, maintenant que votre attention n'est centrée que sur les ailes, il devrait être plus facile de réaliser un bon travail. L'encrage vous le dira.

Nun folgt die detaillierte Buntstiftzeichnung der Tragflächen. Zu Beginn erschien das Flugzeug sehr komplex, doch jetzt, da die gesamte Aufmerksamkeit des Zeichner ausschließlich auf den Flügeln liegt, ist klar, dass auf diese Weise ein besseres Ergebnis erzielt wird. Die Tuschezeichnung ist der Beweis dafür.

Je kunt nu een gedetailleerde tekening van de vleugels maken. In het begin leek het vliegtuig complex, maar nu ik enkel mijn aandacht op de vleugels hoef te richten heb ik het gevoel dat ik beter werk kan leveren. De inkttekening bevestigt dit.

Ahora podré realizar un lápiz detallado de las alas. Al principio, el avión me parecía complejo, pero ahora que sólo debo centrar mi atención en las alas siento que puedo hacer un mejor trabajo. La tinta lo corrobora.

Ora potrò realizzare le matite dettagliate delle ali. All'inizio l'aereo mi sembrava complesso, ma ora che devo concentrarmi solo sulle ali mi sento di poter fare un lavoro migliore. Il ripasso a china lo conferma.

Agora poderei realizar um lápis detalhado das asas. Ao princípio, o avião parecia-me complexo, mas agora que só devo centrar a minha atenção nas asas, sinto que posso fazer um melhor trabalho. A tinta confirma-o.

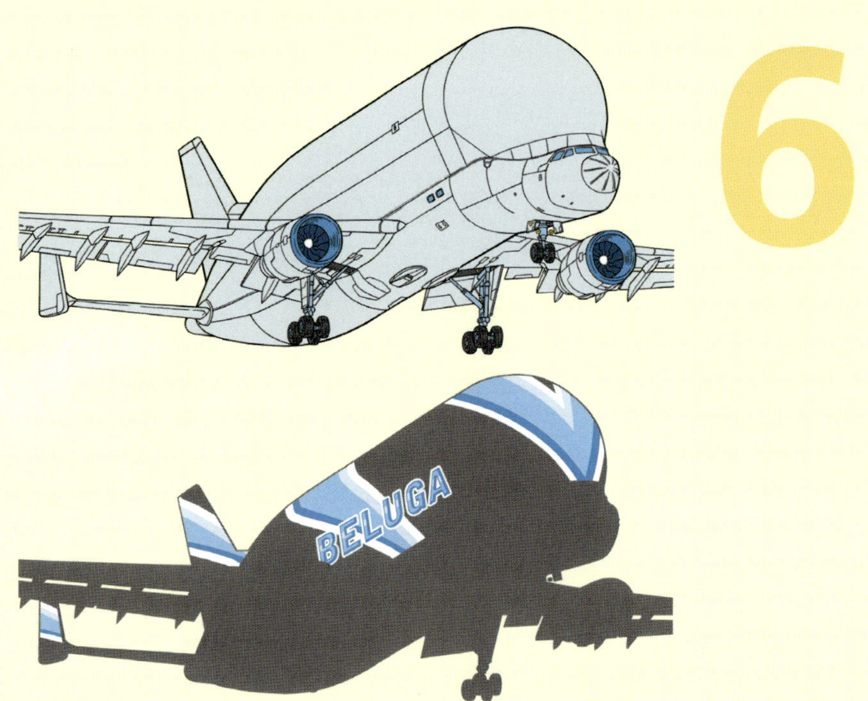


6

The base colors, different shades of blue, represent the nature of the setting and the animal after which the plane is named, which in the case of the details are located in a more iconic order that is more in the style of commercial designs.

Les couleurs de base, à savoir les différentes nuances de bleu, font référence à l'environnement naturel et à l'animal qui donne son nom à l'avion. La disposition des détails est plus symbolique, propre aux designs commerciaux.

Die Grundfarben – unterschiedliche Blautöne – stehen für die Natur und für das Tier (den Belugawal), dem das Flugzeug seinen Namen verdankt. Die farbigen Details wurden so angeordnet, dass sie die gewerbliche Nutzung dieser Maschine verdeutlichen.

De basiskleuren, in dit geval verschillende blauwtinten, beelden de aard van de natuurlijke omgeving en van het dier waarnaar het vliegtuig is vernoemd uit. Deze zijn bij de details in een iconischer volgorde geplaatst, wat typisch is voor commerciële ontwerpen.

Los colores base, que son los distintos tonos de azul, representan la naturaleza del entorno natural y del animal que da nombre al avión, situados en el caso de los detalles en un orden más icónico, propio de los diseños comerciales.

I colori di base, che sono le diverse tonalità di blu, rappresentano la natura dell'ambiente e l'animale che dà il nome all'aereo, situati come dettagli in un ordine schematico tipico dei design commerciali.

As cores base, que são os distintos tons de azul, representam a natureza da envolvente natural e do animal que dá nome ao avião, colocados no caso dos detalhes numa ordem mais icónica, próprio dos desenhos comerciais.

7

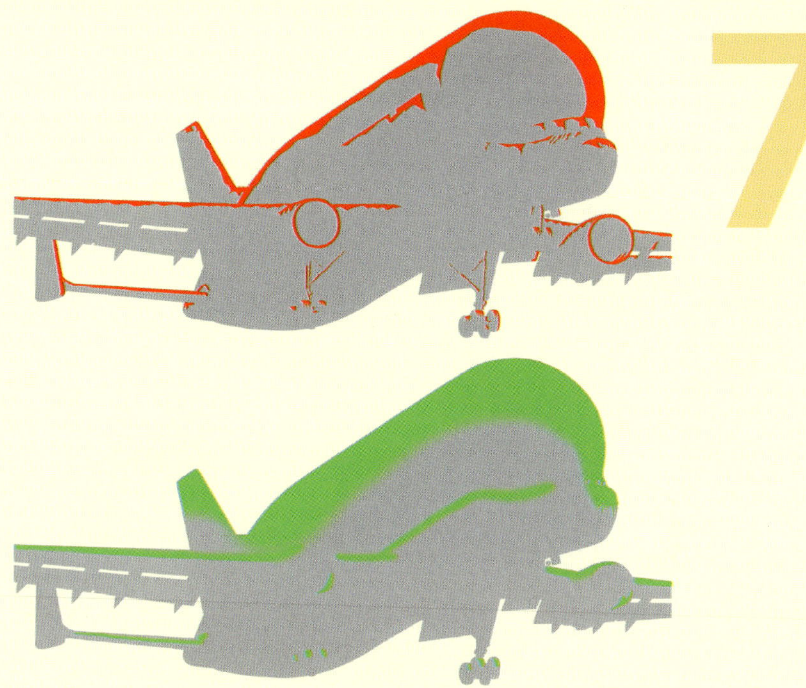

The two lighting layers have been separated on two gray backgrounds for better visualization and understanding. You can see how the smaller one is more defined, while the larger one is more diffuse.

Pour une meilleure visualisation et compréhension, les deux couches de lumière ont été séparées sur deux fonds gris. Comme vous pouvez le voir, la plus petite est plus définie tandis que la plus grande est plus diffuse.

Für mehr Sichtbarkeit und ein besseres Verständnis werden die zwei Lichtebenen auf zwei grauen Grundformen dargestellt. Die kleineren Lichtbereiche sind klar abgegrenzt, während der große Lichtbereich sanft verläuft.

Voor een betere visualisatie en een beter begrip zijn de twee lichtlagen gescheiden op twee grijze achtergronden. Zoals men kan zien is de kleinste laag duidelijker, terwijl de grotere vager is.

Para una mejor visualización y comprensión, las dos capas de luces se han separado sobre dos fondos grises. Como se puede observar, la más pequeña está más definida, mientras que la más grande es más difusa.

Per una migliore visualizzazione e comprensione, i due livelli di luce sono stati separati su due sfondi grigi. Come si può notare, quello più piccolo è più definito, mentre in quello più grande la luce è più sfumata.

Para uma melhor visualização e compreensão, as duas camadas de luzes separaram-se sobre dois fundos cinzentos. Como se pode observar, a mais pequena está mais definida, enquanto que a maior é mais difusa.

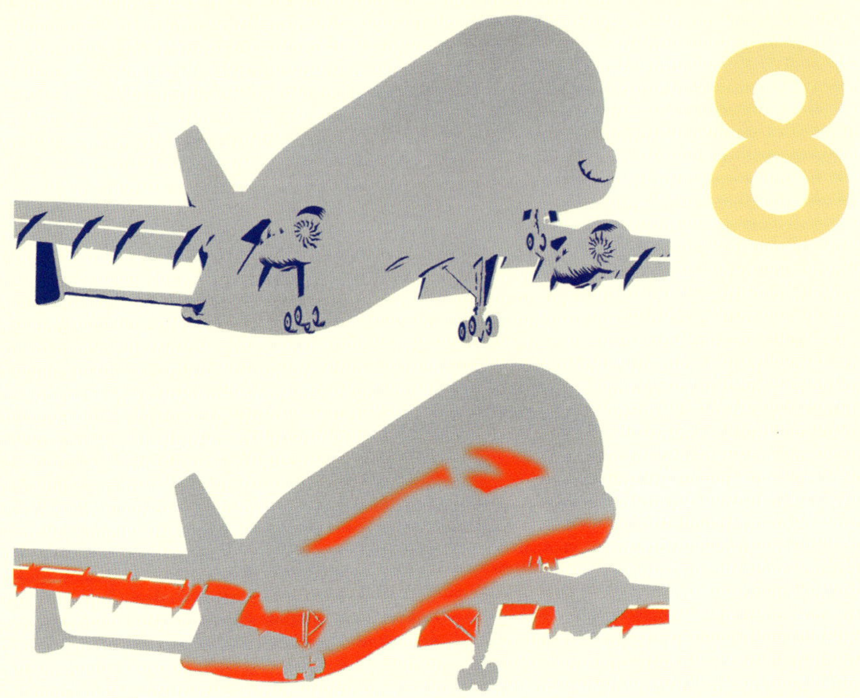


The two shading layers have also been separated on two gray backgrounds. You can see how the more defined layer adds shade to specific details, while the larger one covers larger areas.

Les deux couches d'ombres ont également été séparées sur deux fonds gris. La plus définie se concentre sur des détails spécifiques tandis que la plus grande englobe des zones plus importantes.

Auch die beiden Schattenebenen werden über zwei graue Grundformen gelegt. Hier ist zu sehen, dass die scharf abgegrenzten Schattenbereiche kleinere Details kennzeichnen, während der große Schatten größere Bereiche des Flugzeugs verdunkelt.

De twee schaduwlagen zijn ook gescheiden op twee grijze achtergronden. Zoals te zien is werpt de duidelijkste schaduw op specifieke details, terwijl de grootste laag grotere zones behelst.

Las dos capas de sombras también se han separado sobre dos fondos grises. Como se puede observar, la más definida sombrea detalles específicos, mientras que la más grande abarca zonas mayores.

Anche i due livelli delle ombre sono stati separati su due sfondi grigi. Come si può osservare, in quello più definito si ombreggiano dettagli specifici, mentre il livello più esteso copre zone più grandi.

As duas camadas de sombras também se separaram sobre dois fundos cinzentos. Como se pode observar, a mais definida sombreia detalhes específicos, enquanto que a maior abarca zonas maiores.

9

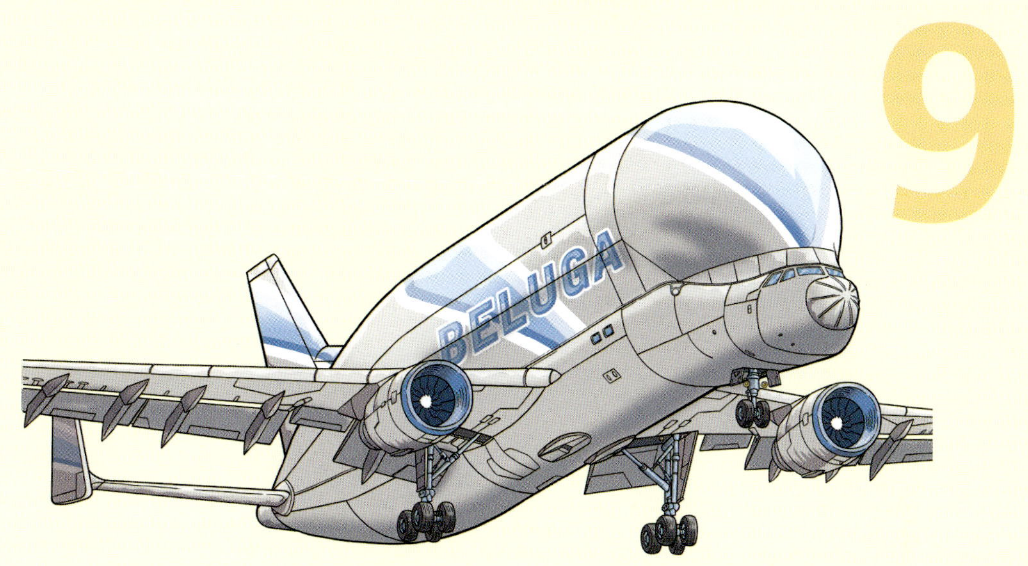


The finished drawing shows the Airbus Beluga to be solid and robust, with enough power to lift its huge mass. The colors are reconciled with the lighting and shading, giving a harmonious appearance.

Sur le dessin final, l'Airbus Beluga apparaît comme solide et robuste, doté d'une puissance suffisante pour soulever une masse impressionnante. Les couleurs se mêlent aux ombres et aux lumières pour donner à l'ensemble un aspect harmonieux.

In der fertigen Zeichnung erscheint der Airbus Beluga solide und robust und ausreichend stark, um sein unglaubliches Gewicht durch die Lüfte zu tragen. Die Farben werden auf die Licht- und Schattenbereiche abgestimmt, wodurch ein harmonisches Ganzes entsteht.

In de afgeronde tekening ziet de Airbus Beluga er solide en stevig uit met voldoende kracht om zijn enorme massa op te tillen. De kleuren passen bij het licht en de schaduwen en zorgen voor een harmonisch aspect.

En el dibujo acabado, el Airbus Beluga se muestra sólido y robusto, con potencia suficiente para elevar su tremenda masa. Los colores se acoplan a las luces y sombras, dando un aspecto armónico.

Nel disegno finito, l'Airbus Beluga appare solido e robusto, con una potenza sufficiente a sollevare la sua enorme massa. I colori si uniscono alle luci e alle ombre, dando un aspetto armonico.

No desenho acabado, o Airbus Beluga mostra-se sólido e robusto, com potência suficiente para elevar a sua tremenda massa. As cores acoplam-se às luzes e às sombras, dando um aspecto harmonioso.

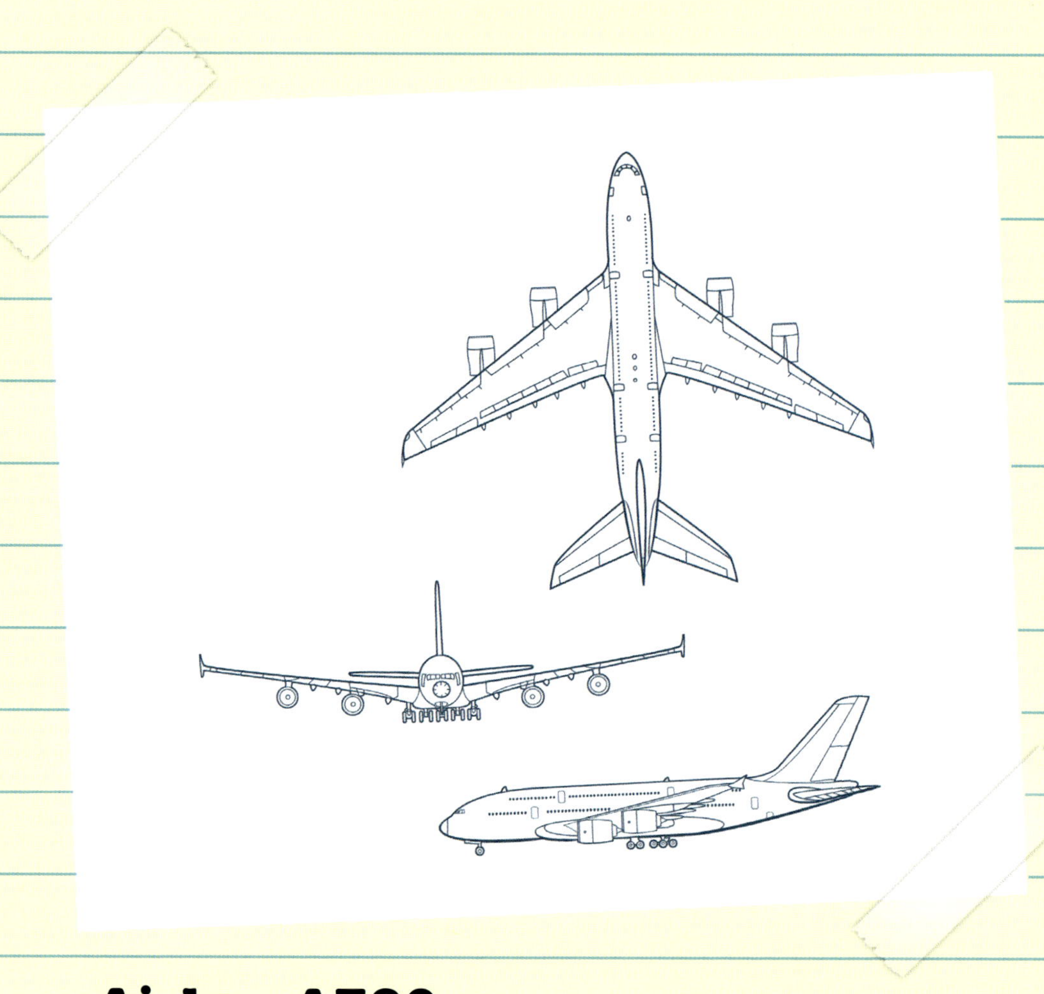

# Airbus A380

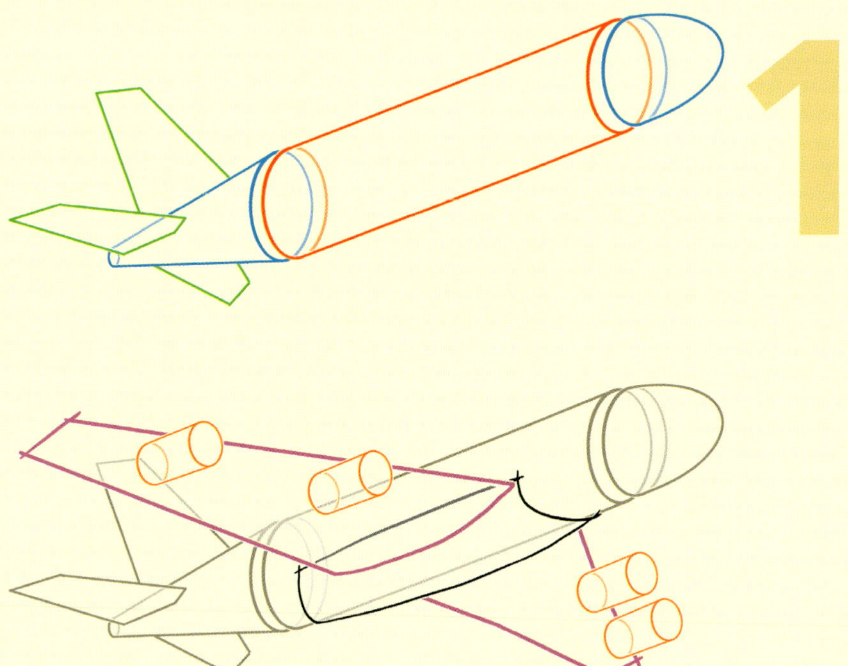


If you cannot see a simple skeleton, it means that you are doing something wrong. But once you understand what you are doing, you can unify its color and, using a second sheet of paper or layer, complete an outline that seemed complex beforehand.

La visualisation d'un squelette simple est indispensable. Une fois que vous aurez bien compris la structure, il sera possible d'unifier sa couleur et d'achever, sur une seconde feuille ou couche, un schéma qui semblait à priori complexe.

Wenn ein Flugzeugskelett nicht wirklich vereinfacht dargestellt wird, dann hat der Zeichner etwas falsch gemacht. Sobald der grundlegende Aufbau verstanden wurde, können die verschiedenen Teile allesamt in einer Farbe gestaltet werden, und auf einem zweiten Blatt (bzw. in einer zweiten Ebene) kann eine Schemazeichnung erarbeitet werden, die zunächst äußerst komplex erschien.

Als we geen eenvoudige vorm kunnen zien doen we iets niet goed, maar zodra we het door hebben, kan de kleur worden geünificeerd en kan op een tweede vel of laag een schema bepaald worden dat a priori complex lijkt.

Si no vemos un esqueleto sencillo es que hay algo que no estamos haciendo bien, pero, una vez comprendido, podemos unificar su color y, en una segunda hoja o capa, terminar un esquema que a priori parecía complejo.

Se non vediamo uno scheletro semplice è segno che non stiamo facendo bene qualcosa. Tuttavia, una volta capito cosa, siamo in grado di unificare il colore e, in un secondo foglio o in un altro livello, possiamo terminare uno schema che a priori ci sembrava complesso.

Se não vemos um esqueleto simples é que há algo que não estamos a fazer bem, mas, uma vez compreendido, podemos unificar a sua cor e, numa segunda folha ou camada, terminar um esquema que a priori parecia complexo.

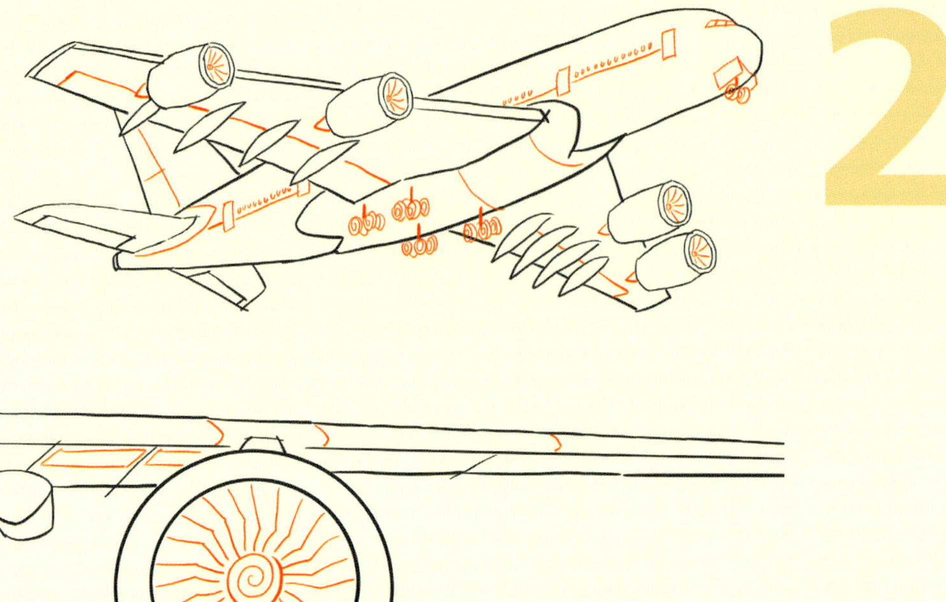


It is essential to adjust the details in the sketch step in order for your plane to reflect reality as faithfully as possible. The key to this lies in the bulging underbelly and engines, of which you can make a close up.

Il est fondamental d'ajuster les détails durant la phase d'ébauche afin que votre avion soit une représentation fidèle de la réalité. La clé est ici de bien bomber le ventre et les moteurs de l'avion, également montrés en gros plan.

Bei der Skizze geht es darum, Einzelheiten einzuarbeiten, damit das Flugzeug möglichst wirklichkeitsgetreu dargestellt wird. Der Schlüssel dafür ist in diesem Fall die Ausbauchung des Flugzeugrumpfs und der Triebwerke, die in einer separaten Ebene im Detail gezeichnet werden.

De details in de fase van de schets aanpassen is belangrijk opdat ons vliegtuig getrouw de werkelijkheid weerspiegelt. In dit geval ligt de verklaring in het welven van de buik en de motoren, waarvan we een detailtekening verschaffen.

Ajustar los detalles en la fase del boceto es fundamental para que nuestro avión refleje fielmente la realidad. La clave en este caso reside en el abombamiento de la panza y los motores, del que damos un plano detalle.

Sistemare i dettagli nella fase del bozzetto è essenziale affinché il nostro aereo rispecchi fedelmente la realtà. La chiave in questo caso sta nel rigonfiamento della fusoliera e nei motori, di cui offriamo un dettaglio.

Ajustar os detalhes na fase do esboço é fundamental para que o nosso avião reflicta fielmente a realidade. A chave neste caso reside no abaulamento da barriga e dos motores, do qual mostramos um plano detalhe.

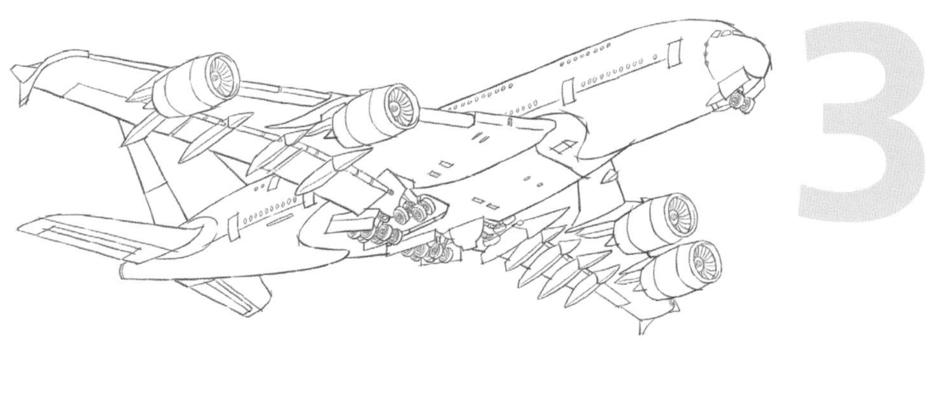

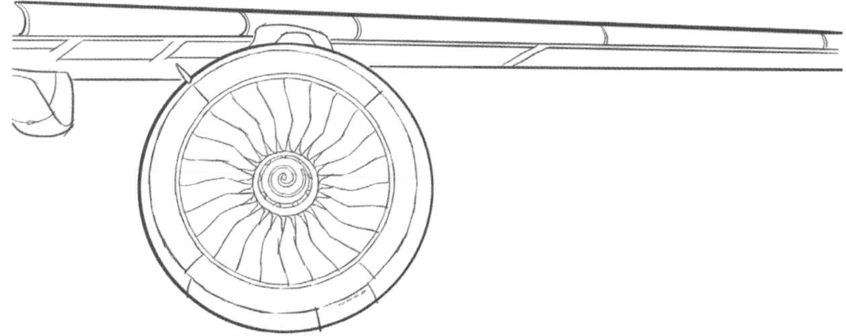

You gain experience each time you draw a plane. The understanding of the wings gained with the Airbus Beluga makes it easier to do this penciling, adding all the details in a single layer.

Chaque dessin d'avion contribue à étendre votre expérience. Grâce à la compréhension des ailes acquise avec l'Airbus Beluga, il est désormais plus facile de réaliser ce crayonné, en ajoutant tous les détails sur une seule couche.

Mit jedem gezeichneten Flugzeug erweitern Sie Ihre Erfahrung. Durch das zuvor beim Modell Airbus Beluga erlangte Verständnis der Tragflächen gestaltet sich die Buntstiftzeichnung erheblich einfacher. So können alle Details in einer einzigen Ebene dargestellt werden.

Elk vliegtuig dat we tekenen breidt onze ervaring uit. Dankzij het inzicht dat we bij het model Airbus Beluga in de vleugels hebben verkregen is het gemakkelijker om deze potloodtekening te maken en alle details in één laag toe te voegen.

Cada avión dibujado amplía nuestra experiencia. Gracias a la comprensión de las alas adquirida en el modelo Airbus Beluga, nos es más sencillo realizar este lápiz, añadiendo todos los detalles en una sola capa.

Ogni aereo che disegniamo espande la nostra esperienza. Grazie alla comprensione delle ali acquisita nel modello Airbus Beluga ci risulta più semplice realizzare le matite di questo aereo, aggiungendo tutti i dettagli in un solo livello.

Cada avião desenhado amplia a nossa experiência. Graças à compreensão das asas adquirida no modelo Airbus Beluga, é nos mais simples realizar este lápis, acrescentando todos os detalhes numa só camada.

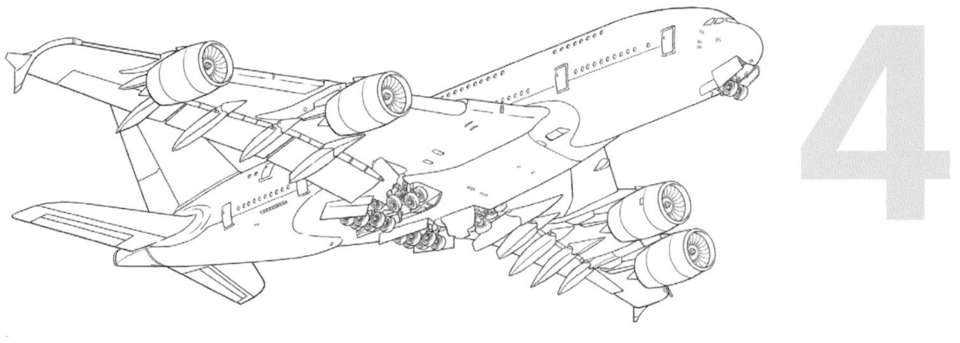

4

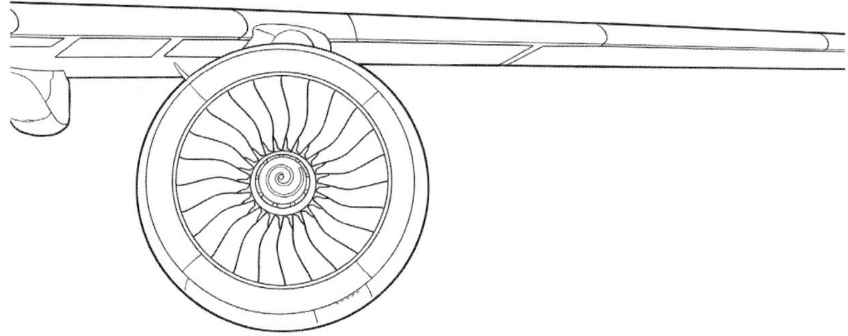

Given the plane's large size and the distance from which it is observed, you should not ink using different brush sizes. The thickness of the ink lines, however, is much more variable in the engine detail.

Étant donné la taille imposante de l'avion et la distance à laquelle vous l'observez, l'épaisseur des tracés doit être relativement régulière. Sur le détail du moteur, toutefois, l'épaisseur des tracés est beaucoup plus variable.

Aufgrund der enormen Größe und der Entfernung, aus der das Flugzeug betrachtet wird, sollten keine sehr unterschiedlich dicken Zeichenspitzen verwendet werden. Bei der Detailansicht des Triebwerks kann die Linienführung jedoch weitaus vielfältiger ausfallen.

Gezien de grootte en de afstand van waaraf we het vliegtuig zien, hoeven we geen dikke, afwijkende inktstrepen te gebruiken. In de detailtekening van de motor is de dikte van de inktstrepen echter erg afwisselend.

Dado el gran tamaño y la distancia a la que observamos el avión, no debemos utilizar tintas de grosores muy dispares. En el detalle del motor, sin embargo, el grosor de las tintas es mucho más variable.

Date le grandi dimensioni dell'aereo e la distanza dalla quale lo osserviamo, non dovremmo usare tratti dagli spessori molto diversi. Nel dettaglio del motore, tuttavia, lo spessore dei tratti è molto più variabile.

Dado o grande tamanho e a distância à qual observamos o avião, não devemos utilizar tintas de espessura muito díspares. No detalhe do motor, sem dúvida, a espessura das tintas é muito mais variável.

# 5

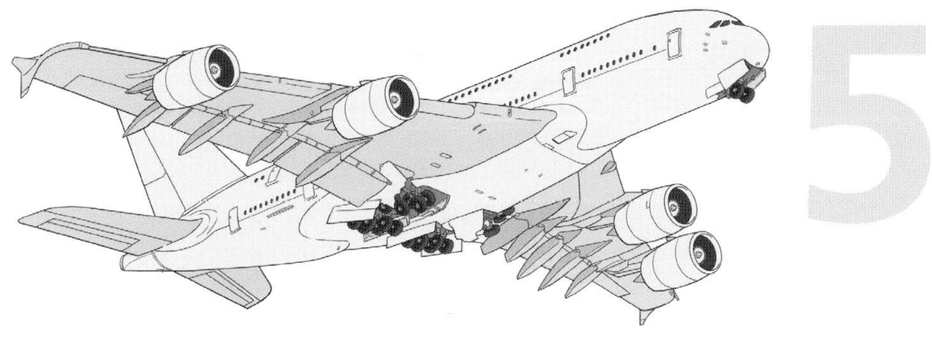

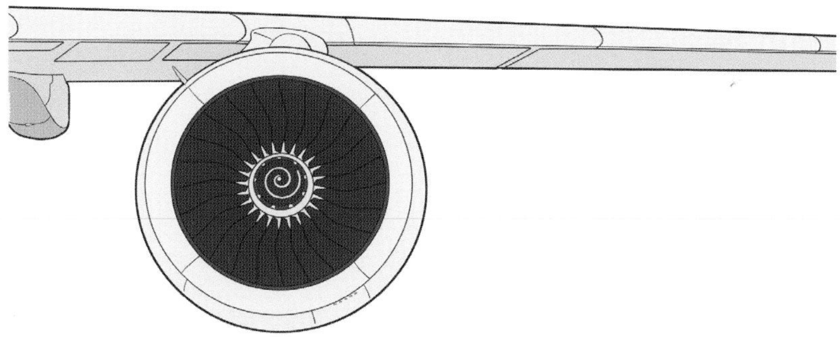

When representing the colors of a totally white plane, use an off white base color and darken the areas in the shade. Lighting and shading will do the rest.

Lorsque vous souhaitez reproduire les couleurs d'un avion entièrement blanc, il convient de lui donner une couleur de base presque blanche pour ensuite obscurcir les zones à l'ombre. Les ombres et les lumières feront le reste.

Um die Farben eines vollständig weißen Flugzeugs wiederzugeben, wird eine fast weiße Grundfarbe gewählt und die im Schatten liegenden Bauteile werden verdunkelt. Die Licht- und Schattenbereiche erledigen den Rest.

Wanneer we de kleuren van een geheel wit vliegtuig willen afbeelden, wordt een vrijwel witte basiskleur gebruikt en worden de schaduwzones donkerder gemaakt. Het licht en de schaduwen doen de rest.

Cuando deseamos representar los colores de un avión totalmente blanco, damos un color base casi blanco y oscurecemos las zonas en sombra. Las luces y sombras harán el resto.

Quando vogliamo rappresentare i colori di un aereo completamente bianco, stendiamo un colore di base quasi bianco e scuriamo le zone in ombra. Le luci e le ombre faranno il resto.

Quando desejamos representar as cores de um avião totalmente branco, damos uma cor base quase branca e escurecemos as zonas de sombra. As luzes e as sombras farão o resto.

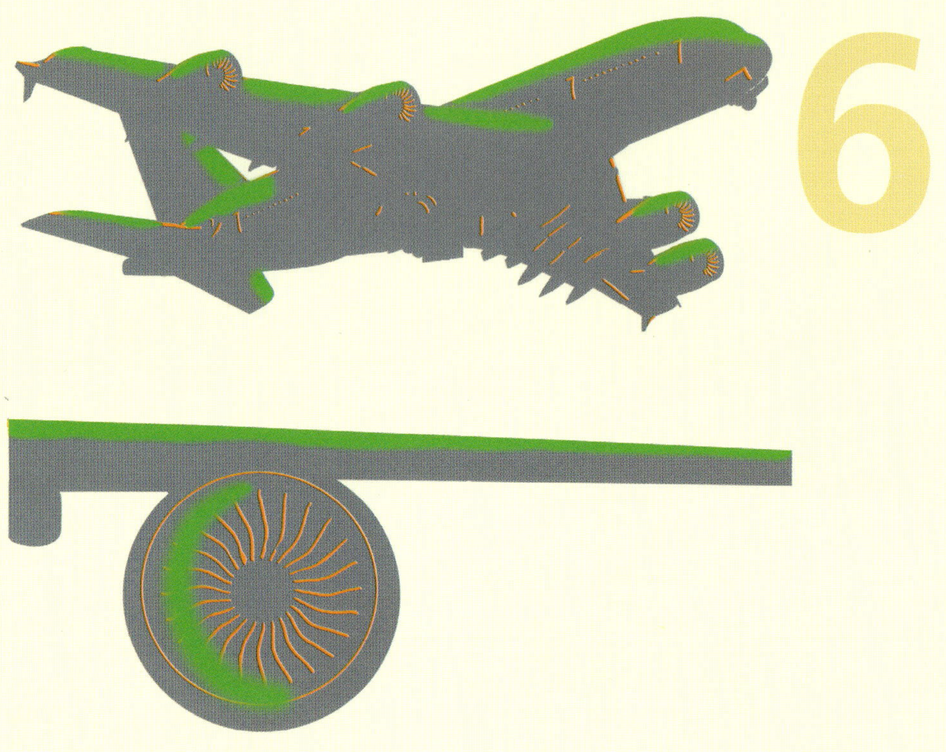

Given the large surface area of the Airbus A380, two very different lighting layers have been applied. The one shown in green is very extensive and general, while the orange one is applied to small, specific points.

Étant donné la surface importante de l'Airbus A380, deux couches de lumières très différentes ont été utilisées. Celle qui apparaît en vert est très étendue et générale tandis que celle qui apparaît en orange est appliquée à des points plus spécifiques.

Aufgrund der großen Oberfläche des Airbus A380 werden zwei sehr unterschiedliche Lichtebenen eingefügt. Die grüne Ebene ist recht groß und allgemein gehalten, während die orange eingefärbte Ebene kleinere, klar abgegrenzte Lichtbereiche beschreibt.

Vanwege het grote oppervlak van de Airbus A380 zijn twee zeer verschillende lichtlagen toegepast. De in groen weergegeven laag is zeer uitgestrekt en algemeen, terwijl oranje wordt aangebracht op kleine specifieke punten.

Debido a la gran superficie del Airbus A380, se han aplicado dos capas de luces muy diferentes. La que se muestra en verde es muy extensa y general, mientras que la naranja se aplica a pequeños puntos específicos.

Dato che la superficie dell'Airbus A380 è molto estesa, sono stati applicati due livelli di luci molto differenti. Quello mostrato in verde è molto ampio e generale, mentre quello arancione si applica ai piccoli punti specifici.

Devido à grande superfície do Airbus A380, aplicaram-se duas camadas de luzes muito diferentes. A que se mostra a verde é muito extensa e geral, enquanto que a laranja se aplica a pequenos pontos específicos.

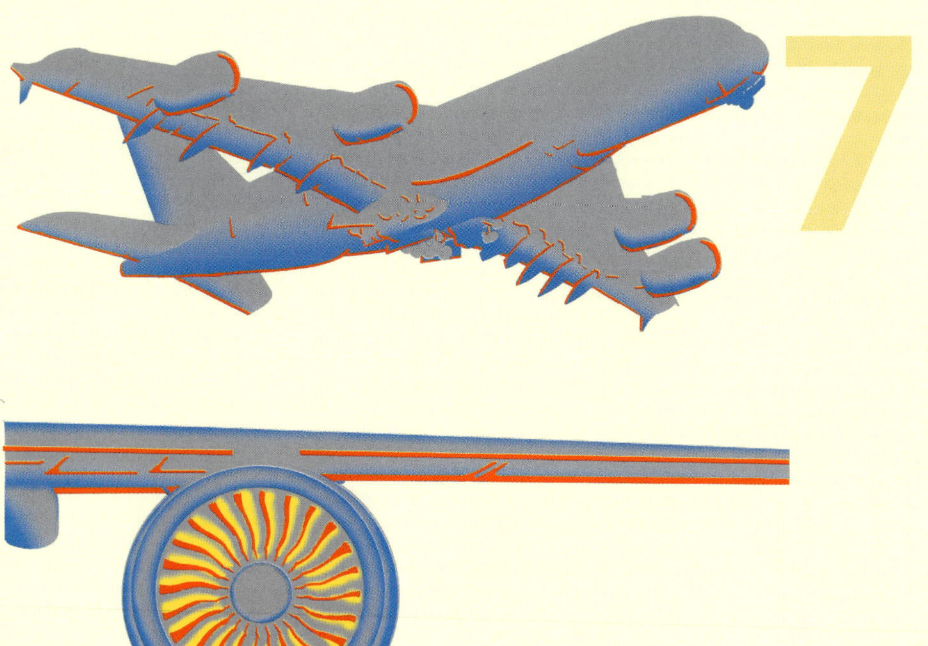


The same principle that served for lighting is applied to shading, although a third shading layer will be used to provide more detail and volume for the detailed close up of the engine.

Appliquez le même principe aux ombres puis aux lumières. Toutefois, pour le gros plan du moteur, utilisez une troisième couche d'ombres qui apportera plus de détails et de volume.

Bei den Schatten wird genauso vorgegangen wie bei den Lichtbereichen. Außerdem wird für die Detailansicht des Triebwerks eine dritte Ebene hinzugefügt, die der Abbildung mehr Tiefe verleiht.

Op de schaduwen wordt hetzelfde principe als bij het licht toegepast. Voor de eerste detailtekening van de motor wordt een derde schaduwlaag gebruikt die voor meer details en volume zorgt.

El mismo principio que ha servido para las luces se aplica a las sombras, si bien para el primer plano detalle del motor utilizaremos una tercera capa de sombras que aportará más detalle y volumen.

Lo stesso principio seguito per le luci si applica anche alle ombre, anche se per il dettaglio in primo piano del motore useremo un terzo livello di ombre che darà maggior dettaglio e volume.

O mesmo princípio que serviu para as luzes aplica-se às sombras, se bem que para o primeiro plano detalhe do motor utilizaremos uma terceira camada de sombras que concederá mais detalhe e volume.

# 8

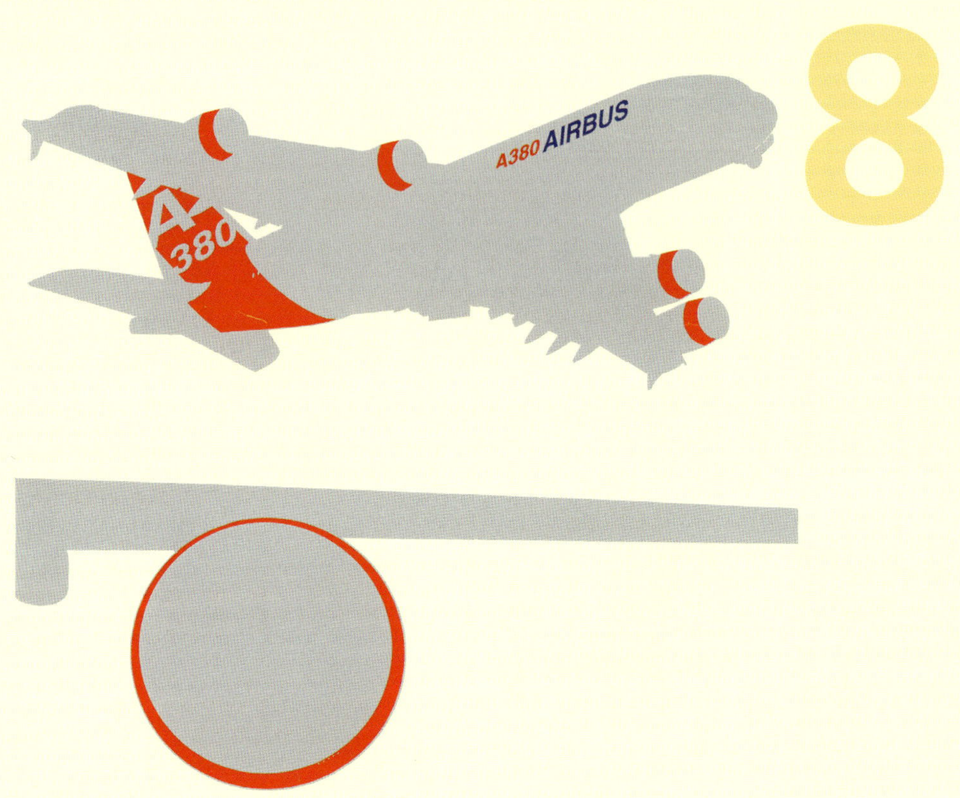


The details basically serve to give the plane a commercial image, taking advantage of the same opportunity to achieve elements of contrast that make the finished drawing more appealing.

Les détails consistent principalement à donner une allure commerciale à l'avion, tout en cherchant à obtenir des éléments de contraste qui rendront le dessin final plus esthétique.

Die hinzugefügten Details basieren im Wesentlichen auf einer gewerblichen Abbildung des Flugzeugs und sorgen für einen ansprechenden Kontrast, der die fertige Zeichnung weiter verschönert.

De details hebben als voornaamste doel het vliegtuig van een commercieel uiterlijk te voorzien. Tevens worden ze gebruikt voor contrastelementen die de afgeronde tekening aantrekkelijker maken.

Los detalles se basan principalmente en dar una imagen comercial al avión, aprovechando a su vez para conseguir elementos de contraste que den mayor atractivo al dibujo acabado.

I dettagli mirano principalmente a dare un'immagine commerciale all'aereo, e al tempo stesso ottenere elementi contrastanti che rendano il disegno finito più attrattivo.

Os detalhes baseiam-se principalmente em dar uma imagem comercial ao avião, aproveitando por sua vez para conseguir elementos de contraste que dêem maior beleza ao desenho acabado.

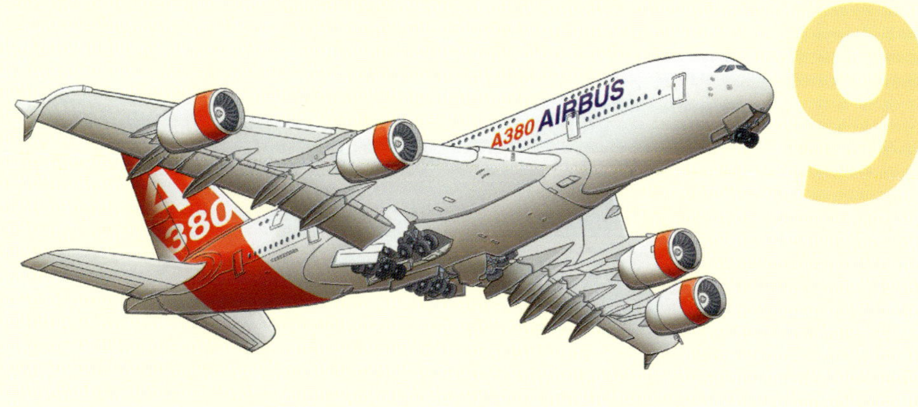


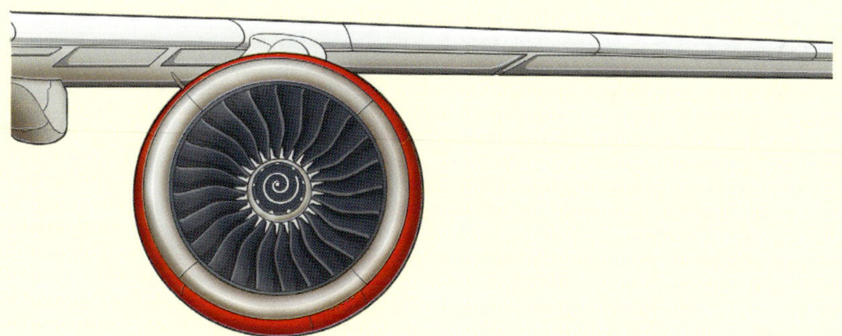

The finished drawing is surprising owing to how well the combination of the layers created during the different steps works. The result is solid and attractive.

Il est surprenant d'observer sur le dessin final l'union harmonieuse des couches créées durant les différentes étapes de cet exercice. Le résultat est solide et élégant.

Die fertige Zeichnung überrascht durch die harmonische Verbindung der einzelnen Ebenen, die in den vorhergehenden Arbeitsschritten entstanden sind. Der Airbus strahlt Robustheit aus und wirkt äußerst attraktiv.

De afgeronde tekening verrast vanwege het feit dat de bijeenvoeging van de lagen die we in de verschillende fases van de oefening hebben gemaakt zo goed functioneren. Het resultaat is solide en aantrekkelijk.

El dibujo acabado sorprende por lo bien que funciona la unión de las capas que hemos generado en las diferentes fases del ejercicio. El resultado es sólido y atractivo.

Nel disegno finito sorprende la perfetta sintonia dei livelli creati nelle varie fasi dell'esercizio. Il risultato è solido e attraente.

O desenho acabado surpreende pelo bem que funciona a união das camadas que geramos nas diferentes fases do exercício. O resultado é sólido e atraente.

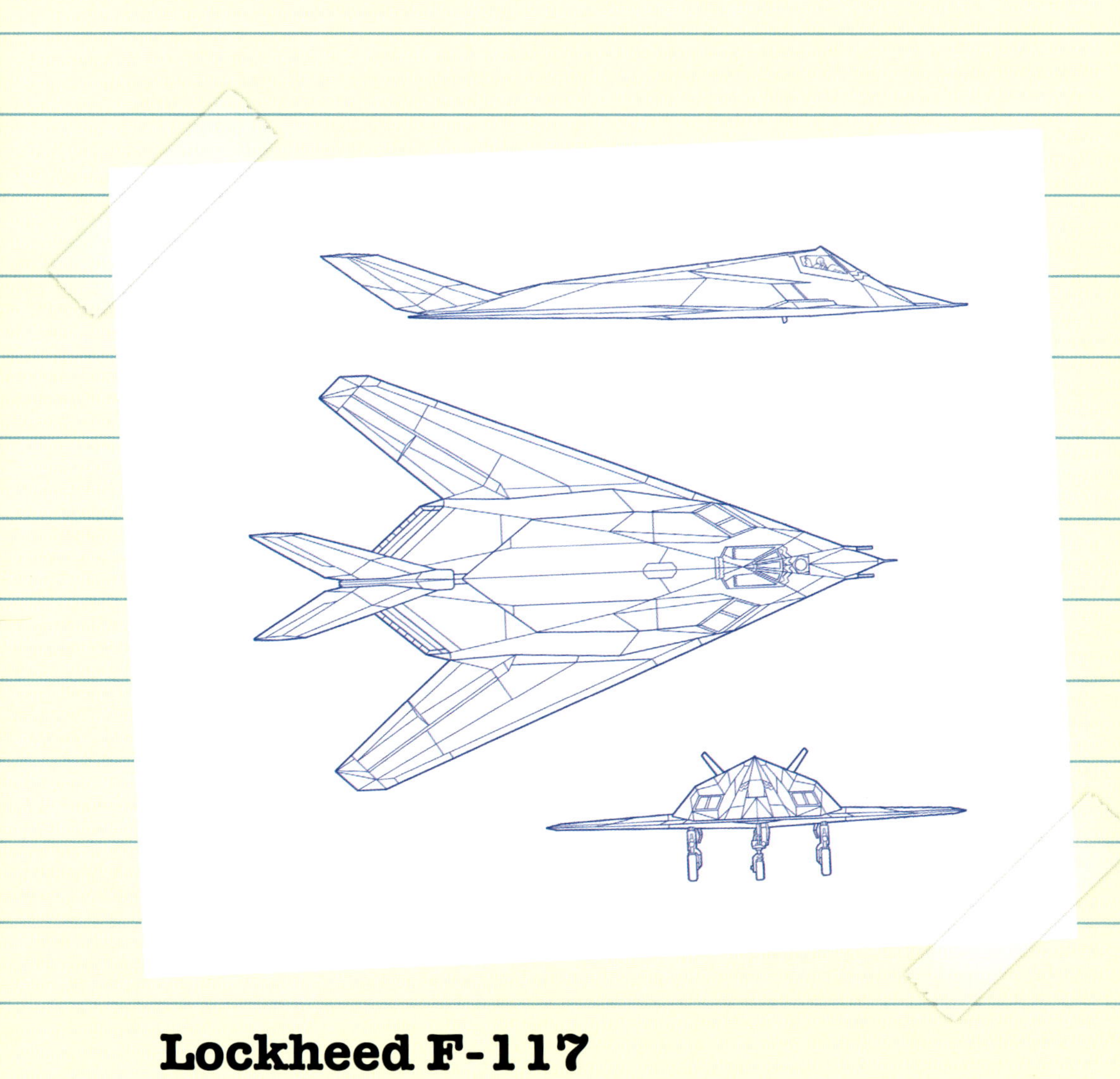

# Lockheed F-117

# 1

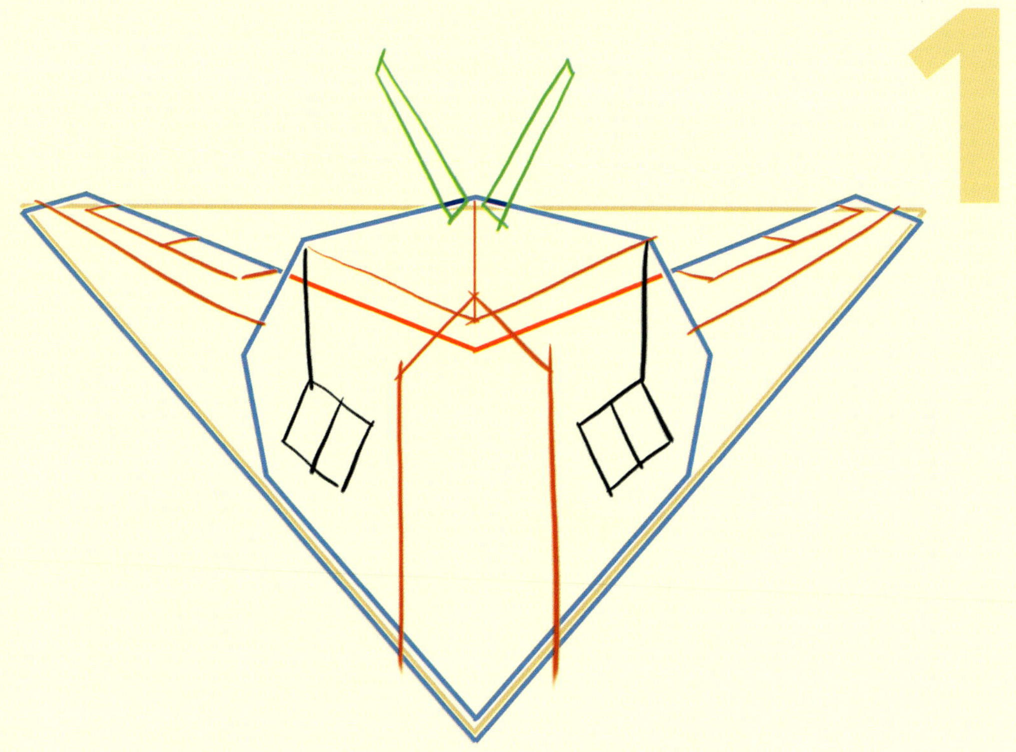

When an aircraft is very complex, it is better to start with simple views, such as this front view from above. Over a skeleton that is nothing more than a triangle (yellow), draw an outline of the main volumes.

Lorsqu'un avion est très complexe, il vaut mieux commencer par des vues simples telles que cette plongée frontale. Sur ce squelette composé d'un simple triangle (en jaune), dessinez un schéma des principaux volumes.

Bei einem sehr komplexen Flugzeug sollte man mit einer einfachen Ansicht wie z.B. dieser Vorderansicht aus der Vogelperspektive beginnen. Über dem einfachen Skelett aus einem Dreieck (gelb) werden die wesentlichen Formen des Flugzeugs eingezeichnet.

Wanneer een vliegtuig erg complex is, is het beter om te beginnen met eenvoudige aanzichten, zoals dit frontaal vogelperspectief. Over de vormtekening van een simpele driehoek (geel) wordt een schema met de voornaamste delen getekend.

Cuando un avión es muy complejo, es mejor empezar con las vistas sencillas, como este frontal picado. Sobre un esqueleto que es un simple triángulo (amarillo) dibujaremos un esquema de los volúmenes principales.

Quando un aereo è molto complesso, è meglio iniziare con viste semplici, come questa inquadratura frontale dall'alto. Su uno scheletro che è un semplice triangolo (giallo) disegniamo uno schema dei volumi principali.

Quando um avião é muito complexo, é melhor começar com as vistas simples, como este frontal picado. Sobre um esqueleto que é um simples triângulo (amarelo) desenharemos um esquema dos volumes principais.

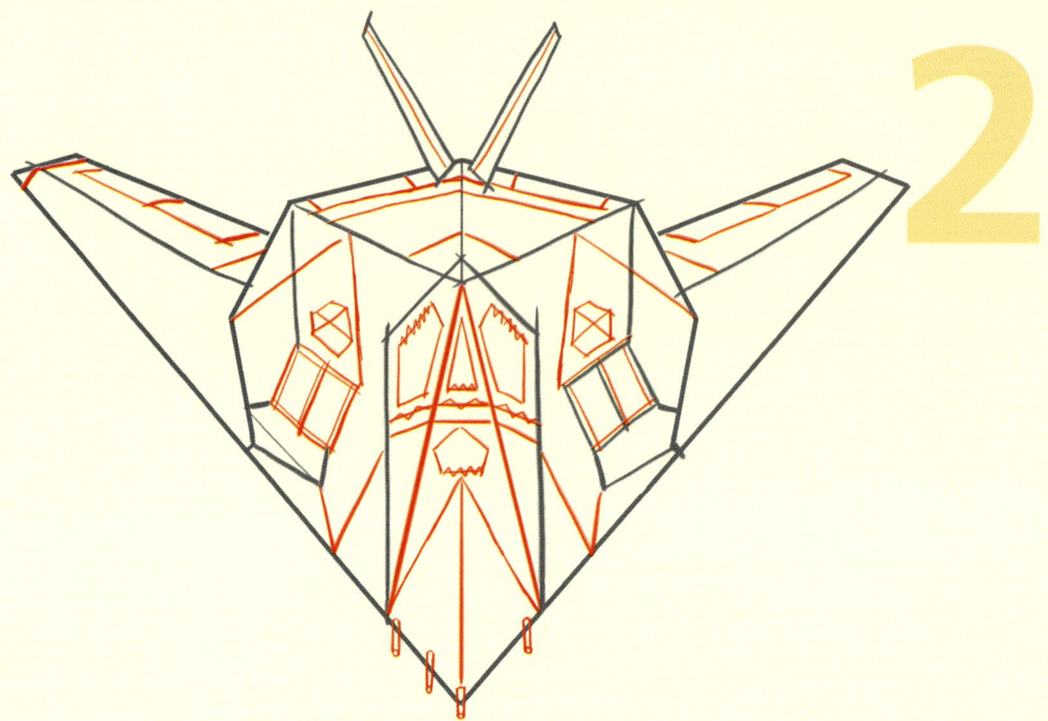

2

Given the geometric structure of the plane, the sketch (red) is made directly over the outline, to which one color (gray) has been applied using a drawing program.

Étant donné la structure géométrique de l'avion, vous ferez l'ébauche (en rouge) directement sur le schéma, préalablement doté d'une seule couleur (gris) à l'aide de l'ordinateur.

Aufgrund des geometrischen Aufbaus des Flugzeugs wird die Skizze (rot) direkt über die Schemazeichnung gelegt, welche mithilfe des Computers in die Farbe Grau konvertiert wurde.

Uitgaand van de geometrische structuur van het vliegtuig, maken we de schets (rood) rechtstreeks op het schema, dat we met behulp van de computer één kleur (grijs) hebben gegeven.

Dada la estructura geométrica del avión, hacemos el boceto (rojo) directamente sobre el esquema, al que le hemos dado un solo color (gris) con la ayuda del ordenador.

Data la struttura geometrica del velivolo, realizziamo il bozzetto (rosso) direttamente sullo schema, a cui abbiamo dato un solo colore (grigio) con l'aiuto del computer.

Dada a estrutura geométrica do avião, fazemos o esboço (vermelho) directamente sobre o esquema, ao qual demos uma só cor (cinzenta) com a ajuda do computador.

# 3

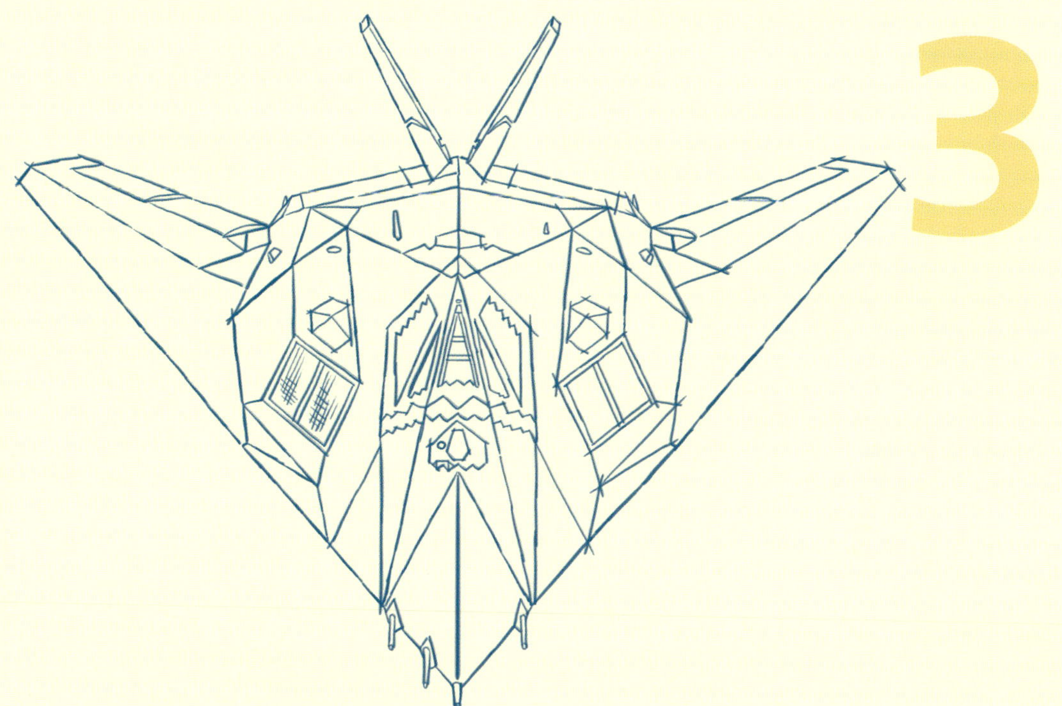

While the geometry of the aircraft may encourage you to ink directly over the sketch, it is better to do things well. Penciling enables you to check that the structure works, and to add many small details.

Bien que la géométrie de l'avion vous invite à passer directement à l'encrage, il vaut mieux faire les choses correctement. Le crayonné permet de vérifier le fonctionnement de votre structure et d'y ajouter une multitude de petits détails.

Auch wenn die Geometrie des Flugzeugs dazu verleitet, direkt zur Tuschezeichnung überzugehen, sollte man ordnungsgemäß Schritt für Schritt vorgehen. Anhand der Buntstiftzeichnung kann sichergestellt werden, dass die entworfene Struktur umsetzbar ist, und es können zahlreiche kleine Details hinzugefügt werden.

Hoewel de geometrie van het vliegtuig aanzet tot het direct inkleuren, is het beter om de dingen goed uit te werken. Dankzij de potloodtekening is het mogelijk om na te gaan of onze structuur functioneert en kunnen vele kleine details worden toegevoegd.

Aunque la geometría del avión induce a entintar directamente, es mejor hacer las cosas bien. El lápiz permite comprobar que nuestra estructura funciona, y añadir multitud de pequeños detalles.

Anche se la geometria dell'aereo induce a ripassare a china direttamente, è meglio fare le cose per bene. La fase a matita ci permette di verificare che la nostra struttura funziona e di aggiungere una moltitudine di piccoli dettagli.

Ainda que a geometria do avião induza a fazer a arte-final directamente, é melhor fazer as coisas bem-feitas. O lápis permite comprovar que nossa estrutura funciona, e acrescentar uma multiplicidade de pequenos detalhes.

4

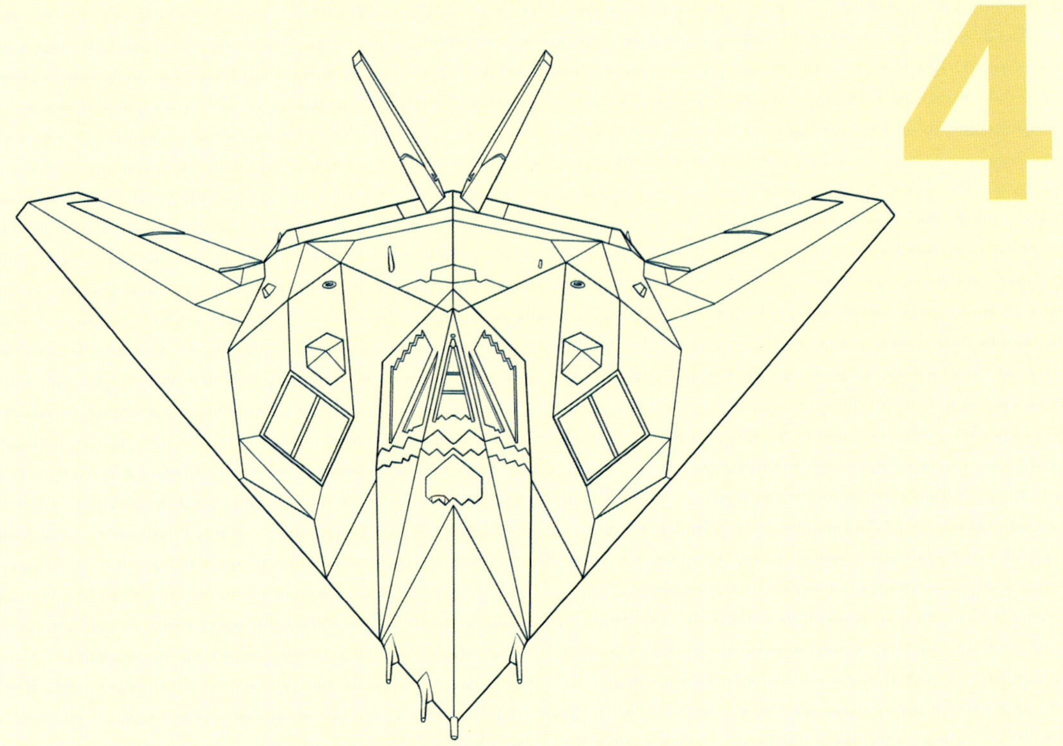

The use of rulers or line tools is essential when inking this aircraft. Avoiding freehand lines enhances the cold, technological aspect and dehumanizes the plane.

L'utilisation de règles ou d'outils de tracé est fondamentale pour l'encrage de cet aéronef. En évitant les tracés à main levée, l'aspect froid et déshumanisé de l'appareil est renforcé.

Bei diesem Flugzeug ist für die Tuschezeichnung die Verwendung von Linealen oder Linien-Werkzeugen unabdingbar. Indem frei Hand gezeichnete Linien vermieden werden, wird die kalte, technologische und entmenschlichte Wirkung der Abbildung verstärkt.

Het gebruik van linialen en andere hulpmiddelen is essentieel voor het inkleuren van dit luchtschip. Door geen lijnen uit de vrije hand te tekenen wordt het kille, technologische en ontmenselijkte aspect van het luchtschip versterkt.

El uso de reglas o herramientas de línea es fundamental para entintar esta aeronave. Evitando las líneas a mano alzada potenciamos el aspecto frío, tecnológico y deshumanizado de la aeronave.

L'uso di righelli o strumenti linea è essenziale per ripassare a china questo aereo. Evitando le linee a mano libera mettiamo in rilievo l'aspetto freddo, tecnologico e disumanizzato del velivolo.

O uso de réguas ou ferramentas geométricas é fundamental para fazer a arte-final desta aeronave. Evitando as linhas à mão livre potenciamos o aspecto frio, tecnológico e desumanizado da aeronave.

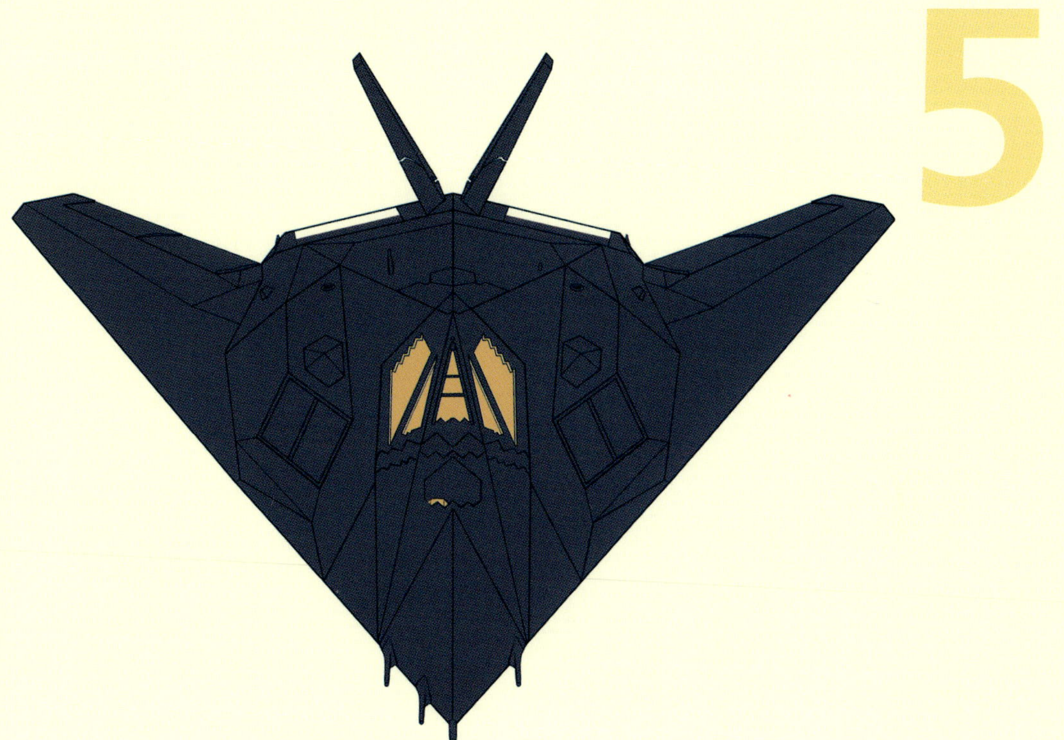


As with the Blackbird, the base color for this plane is practically black. Only the contrast provided by the yellow cockpit and the white engines breaks the uniformity of the aircraft.

De même que pour le Blackbird, la couleur de base de cet avion est presque noire. Seul le contraste de la cabine jaune et des moteurs blancs brise l'uniformité de l'aéronef.

Genau wie beim Blackbird ist die Grundfarbe dieses Flugzeugs nahezu schwarz. Nur der Kontrast des gelben Cockpits und die weißen Triebwerke unterbrechen das gleichförmige Aussehen des Tarnkappenbombers.

Net als het geval is bij de Blackbird is de basiskleur van dit vliegtuig vrijwel zwart. Alleen het contrast van de gele cabine en de witte motoren onderbreken de uniformiteit van het luchtschip.

Al igual que en el caso del Blackbird, el color base de este avión es prácticamente negro. Sólo el contraste de la cabina amarilla y los motores blancos rompen la uniformidad de la aeronave.

Come nel caso del Blackbird, il colore di base di questo aereo è praticamente nero. Solo il contrasto della cabina gialla e dei motori bianchi rompe l'uniformità del velivolo.

Tal como no caso do Blackbird, a cor base deste avião é praticamente preta. Só o contraste da cabina amarela e os motores brancos rompem a uniformidade da aeronave.

# 6

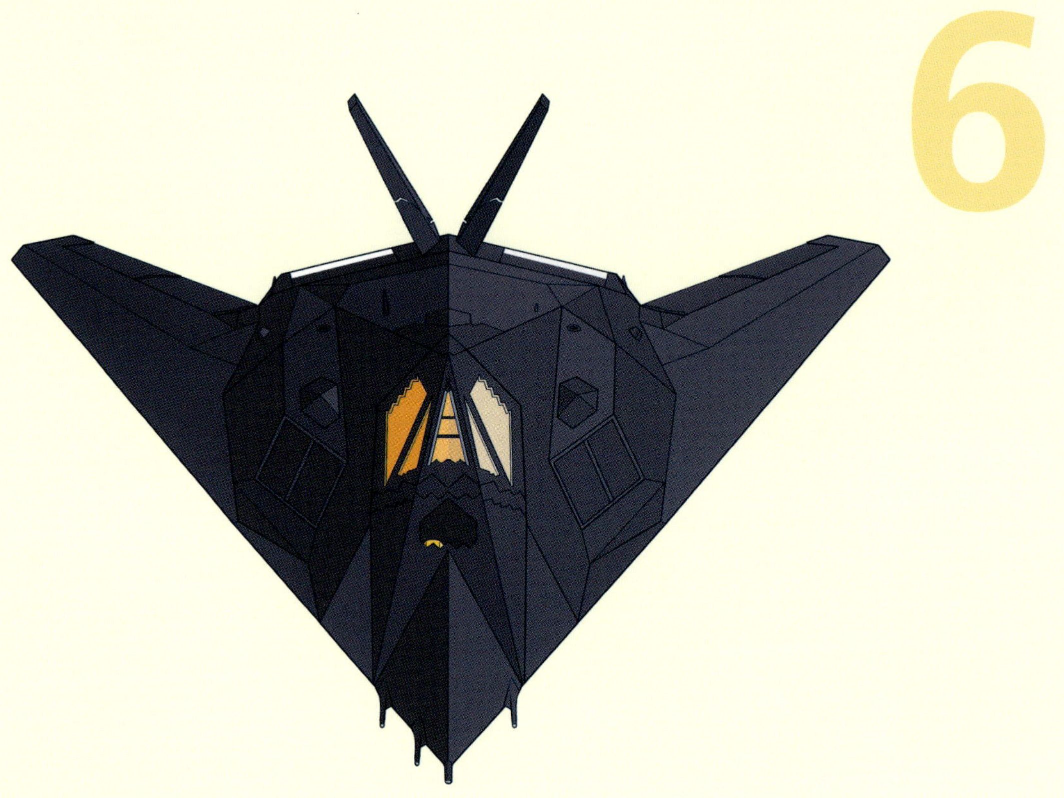

As we saw in earlier exercises, you can use the base color to add volume to the drawing, varying the hues and always taking the same light source into account.

Comme vous l'avez vu dans les exercices précédents, vous pouvez utiliser la couleur de base pour donner du volume au dessin en variant la gamme de couleur et en tenant toujours compte de la source de lumière.

Genau wie bei den vorhergehenden Übungen kann die Grundfarbe verwendet werden, um der Zeichnung Tiefe zu verleihen, und zwar durch den Einsatz verschiedener Farbabstufungen (unter Berücksichtigung der stets gleichen Lichtquelle).

Net als we in de voorgaande oefeningen hebben gezien, kunnen we de basiskleur gebruiken om de tekening volume te geven door de kleurengamma af te wisselen en altijd rekening te houden met dezelfde lichtbron.

Al igual que vimos en ejercicios anteriores, podemos utilizar el color base para dar volumen al dibujo, variando la gama de color y teniendo siempre en cuenta un mismo foco de luz.

Come abbiamo già visto negli esercizi precedenti, possiamo utilizzare il colore di base per dare volume al disegno, variandone la gamma e tenendo sempre presente la stessa sorgente luminosa.

Tal como vimos em exercícios anteriores, podemos utilizar a cor base para dar volume ao desenho, variando a gama de cor e tendo sempre em conta um mesmo foco de luz.

7

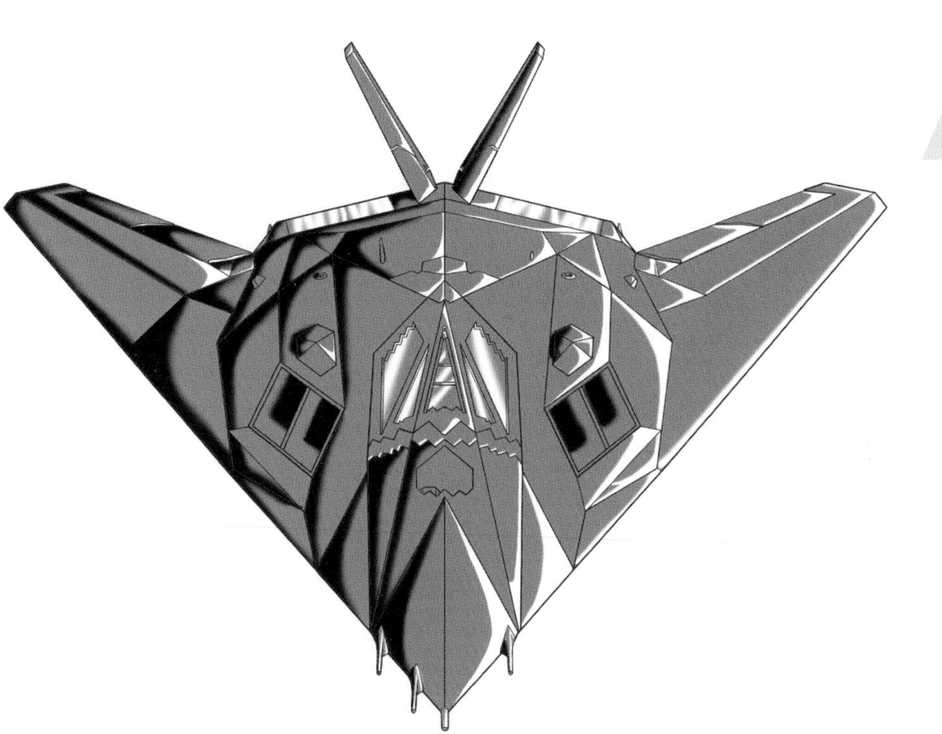

As the lighting and shading are not needed to give volume, they can be used to embellish the image and add specific details.

Comme les ombres et lumières ne sont pas nécessaires pour donner du volume, vous pouvez les utiliser pour embellir l'image en apportant des détails spécifiques.

Da die Licht- und Schattenbereiche dem Flugzeug nicht noch mehr Tiefe verleihen müssen, können diese Akzente dazu dienen, die Zeichnung zu verschönern und noch detaillierter zu gestalten.

Aangezien het licht en de schaduwen het geheel geen volume hoeven te geven, kunnen we ze gebruiken om de afbeelding mooier te maken en van specifieke details te voorzien.

Ya que las luces y las sombras no necesitan dar volumen al conjunto, podemos utilizarlas para embellecer la imagen, aportando detalles específicos.

Dal momento che le luci e le ombre non devono dare volume all'insieme, possiamo usarle per abbellire l'immagine, aggiungendo dettagli specifici.

Já que as luzes e as sombras não necessitam de dar volume ao conjunto, podemos utilizá-las para embelezar a imagem, fornecendo-lhe detalhes específicos.

# 8

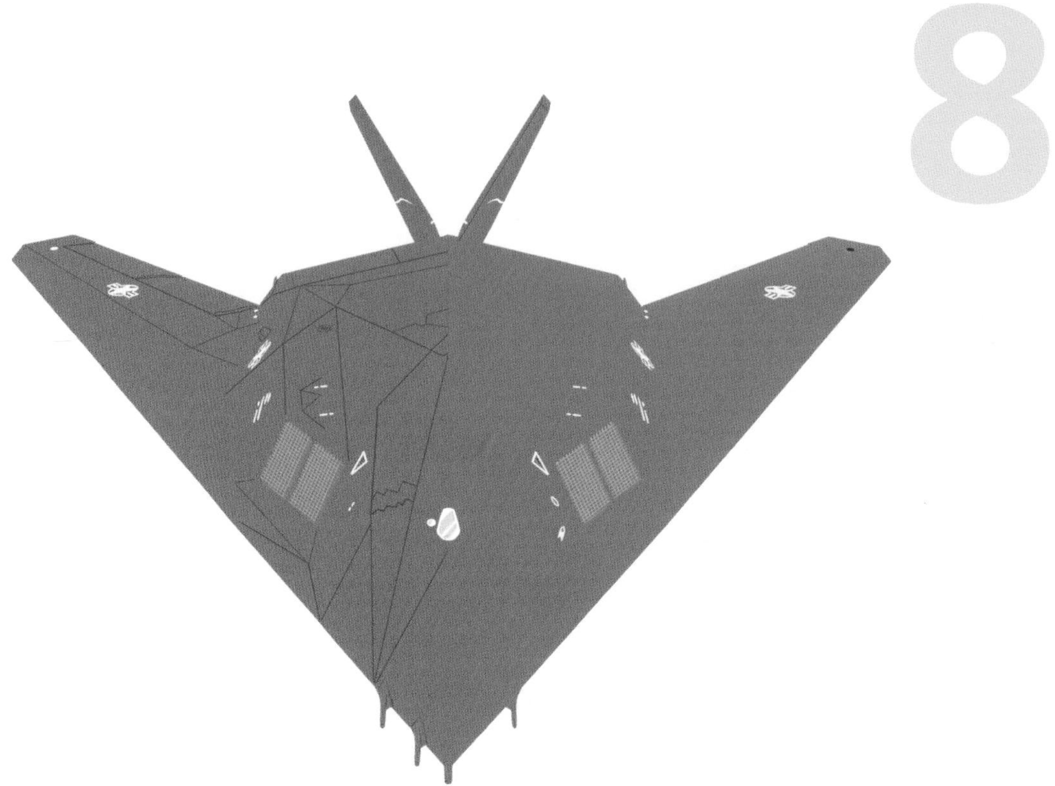

In addition to the small details like grilles, icons, and markings on the fuselage, touching up the inking of the part of the plane in shade makes it more visible.

En plus des petits détails tels que les quadrillages, les symboles et les marques sur le fuselage, il faudra arranger les tracés de la partie ombragée de l'avion pour les rendre plus visibles.

Nun werden Einzelheiten wie Schutzgitter, Symbole und Markierungen am Rumpf eingearbeitet und die in den Schattenbereichen liegenden Tuschelinien werden hervorgehoben.

Naast de kleine details zoals de roosters, iconen en merktekens op de romp, gaan we de inktstrepen aan de schaduwzijde van het vliegtuig opvoeren zodat ze duidelijker zichtbaar zijn.

Además de los pequeños detalles, como rejillas, iconos y marcas en el fuselaje, vamos a trucar las tintas que están en la parte en sombra del avión para que sean más visibles.

Oltre ai piccoli dettagli, come griglie, icone e marchi sulla fusoliera, sottolineiamo le linee della parte in ombra dell'aereo per renderle più visibili.

Para além dos pequenos detalhes como grelhas, ícones e marcas na fuselagem, vamos trocar as tintas que estão na parte de sombra do avião para que sejam mais visíveis.

9

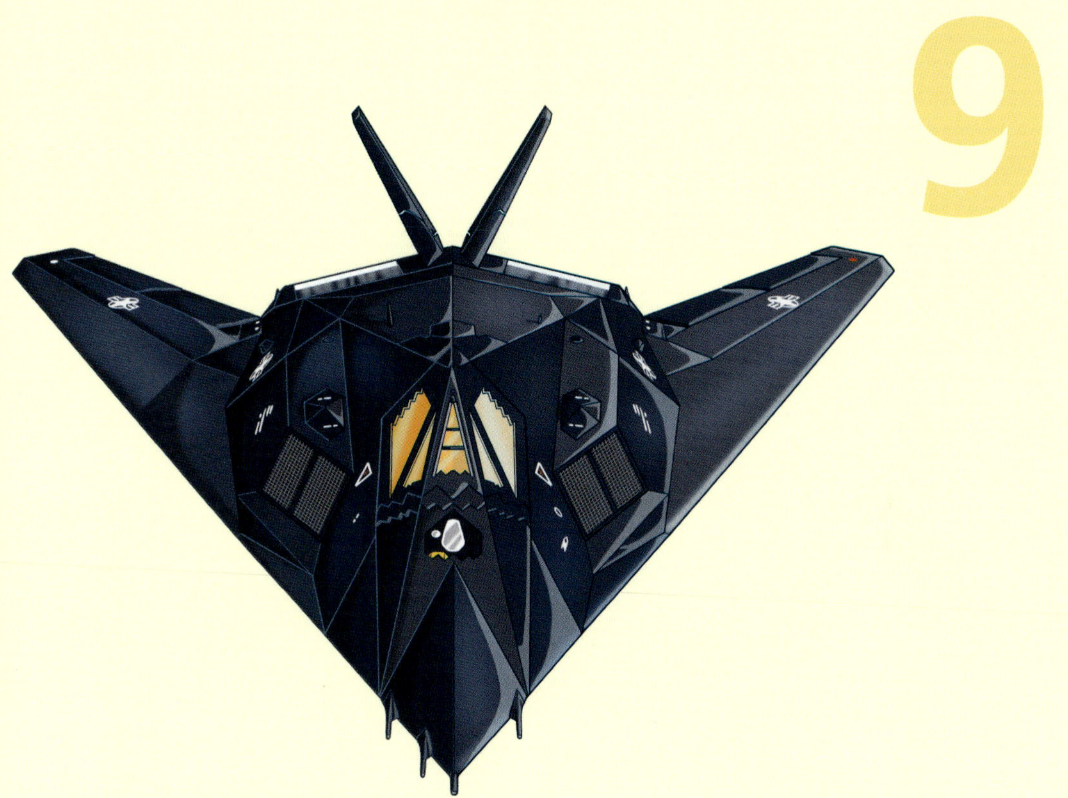

The finished drawing shows that touching up the inking works well, as it enables the facets on both sides of the plane to be distinguished. The result is a detailed and attractive image.

Sur le dessin final, on peut voir que la manipulation des tracés fonctionne bien et permet de distinguer les deux côtés de l'avion. L'ensemble donne un dessin très travaillé et esthétique.

In der fertigen Zeichnung wird deutlich, dass der Trick mit der Tuschezeichnung gut funktioniert und dadurch die einzelnen Facetten auf beiden Seiten des Flugzeugs gut erkennbar sind. Das Ergebnis ist eine detailgenaue, sehr ansprechende Abbildung.

In de afgeronde tekening is te zien dat het opvoeren van de inktstrepen goed werkt en de facetten aan weerszijden van het vliegtuig kunnen worden onderscheiden. Het resultaat is een nauwkeurig uitgewerkte en aantrekkelijke tekening.

En el dibujo acabado se observa que el trucaje de las tintas funciona bien, permitiendo distinguir las facetas a ambos lados del avión. El conjunto es un dibujo muy trabajado y atractivo.

Nel disegno finito si osserva che la sottolineatura delle linee funziona bene, facendo distinguere le sfaccettature su entrambi i lati dell'aereo. Nel complesso è un disegno molto elaborato e attrattivo.

No desenho acabado observa-se que a alteração das tintas funciona bem, permitindo distinguir as facetas de ambos os lados do avião. O conjunto é um desenho muito trabalhado e apelativo.

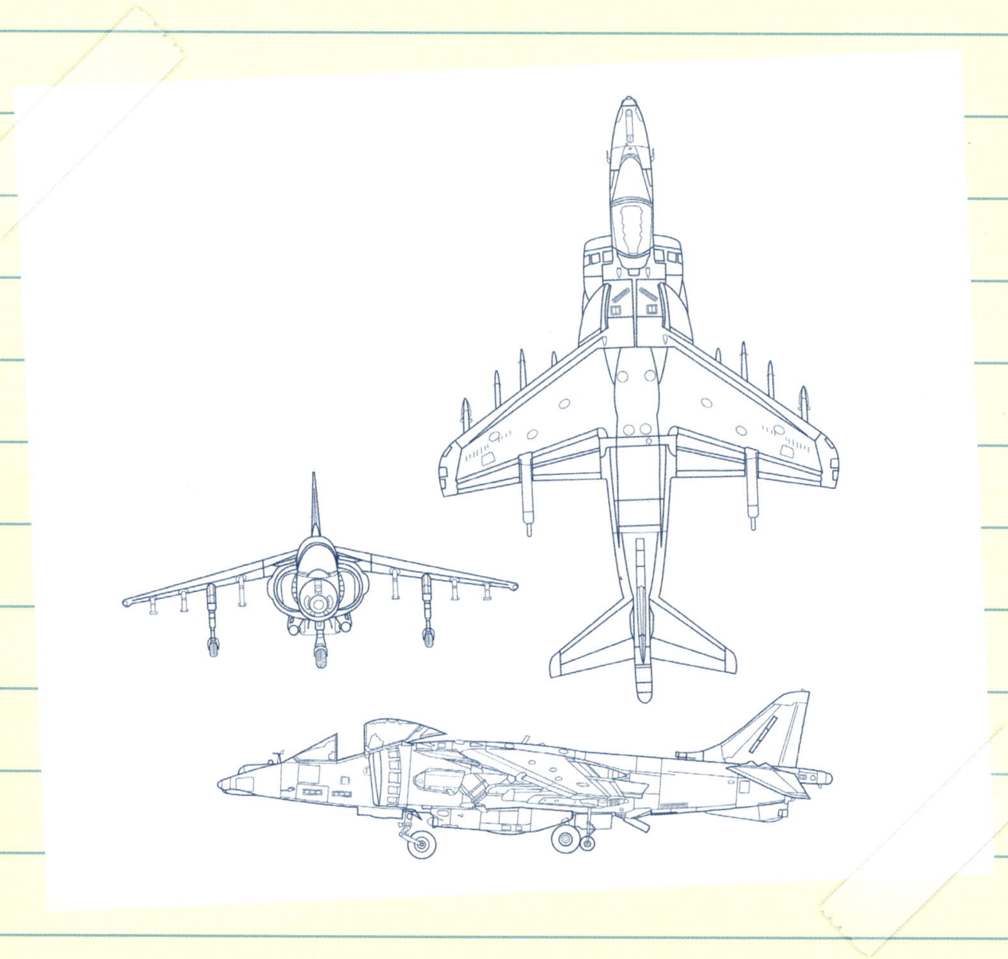

# Harrier

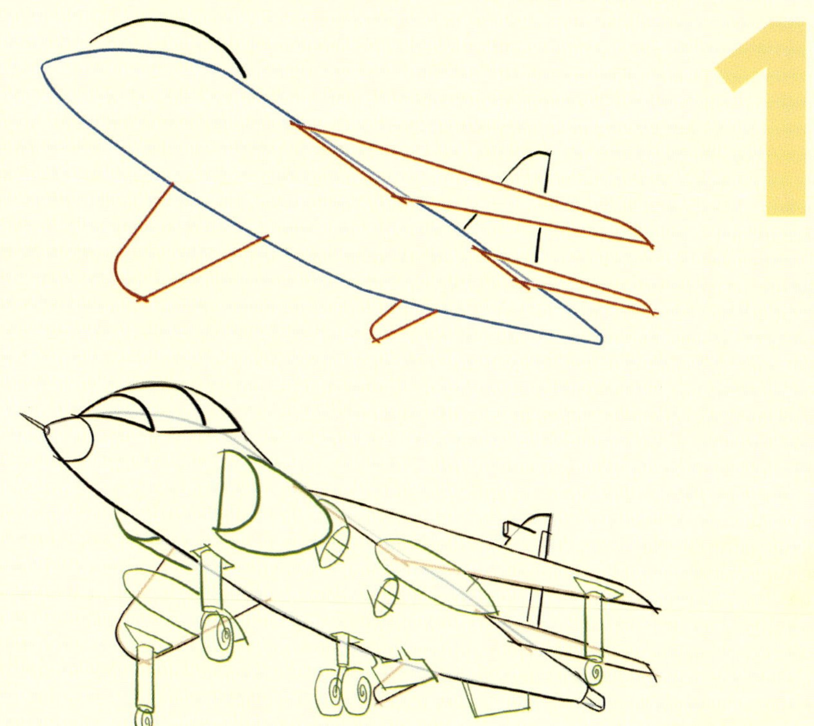


Moving from the outline step to a sketch is like dressing a naked figure that needs garments and accessories. If you think of it as a single task, it seems difficult, but it can be a lot more fun doing it one part at a time.

Passer d'un schéma à une ébauche revient à habiller une silhouette à laquelle vous ajoutez des vêtements et accessoires. Si vous partez d'une vision globale, la tâche semble complexe mais, si vous la travaillez partie par partie, l'exercice peut s'avérer très divertissant.

Der Übertrag des Grundschema in eine Skizze ist so ähnlich wie das Anziehen einer nackten Figur mit diversen Kleidungsstücken und Accessoires. Wenn man vom Gesamtbild ausgeht, gestaltet sich die Arbeit sehr schwierig, doch wenn man Schritt für Schritt vorgeht, wird vieles einfacher.

Van een schema overgaan op een schets is als een naakt figuur aankleden en van steeds meer kledingstukken en accessoires voorzien. Als we globaal denken lijkt het ingewikkeld, maar als we in delen denken dan kan het zeer vermakelijk zijn.

Pasar de un esquema a un boceto es como vestir una figura desnuda a la que vamos añadiendo prendas y complementos. Si lo pensamos globalmente resulta complicado, pero si lo hacemos por partes, puede resultar muy entretenido.

Passare da uno schema a un bozzetto è come vestire una figura nuda a cui si aggiungono abiti e accessori. Se lo pensiamo a livello globale sembra difficile, ma se lo facciamo separatamente può risultare molto divertente.

Passar de um esquema para um esboço é como vestir uma figura despida à qual vamos acrescentando roupas e acessórios. Se pensarmos globalmente torna-se complicado, mas se o fizermos por partes pode tornar-se muito divertido.

# 2

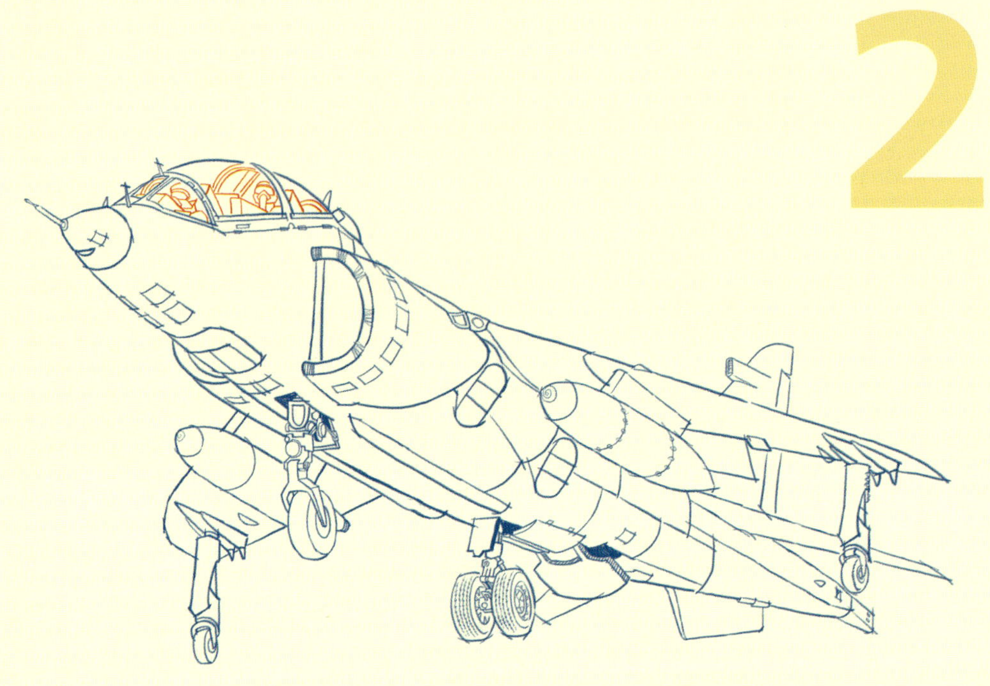

Once again, we insist on the importance of dividing the task and treating each part of the drawing as if it were separate. Proceeding with penciling after the sketch is like dressing one of the bare parts of the plane.

Là encore, il faut insister sur l'importance de diviser l'ensemble et de traiter chaque partie du dessin comme s'il s'agissait d'une illustration indépendante. Passer de l'ébauche au crayonné revient à vêtir chaque partie encore dénudée de l'avion.

Auch hier ist es erneut sehr wichtig, die Abbildung in Einzelteile zu zerlegen und vorzugehen, als ob es sich um mehrere Zeichnungen handelte. Der Schritt von der Skizze zur Buntstiftzeichnung entspricht dem Ankleiden der einzelnen Bestandteile des Flugzeugs.

We dringen er opnieuw op aan dat het belangrijk is om de tekening in stukken te verdelen en elk deel van de tekening als een afzonderlijke tekening te behandelen. Van een schets overgaan op een potloodtekening is als het aankleden van elk naakt vliegtuigonderdeel.

De nuevo insistimos en la importancia de dividir y de tratar cada parte del dibujo como si fuese un dibujo independiente. Pasar de un boceto a un lápiz es como vestir cada una de las partes desnudas del avión.

Ancora una volta insistiamo sull'importanza di dividere e trattare ogni parte del disegno come se fosse un disegno a sé stante. Passare da un bozzetto alle matite è come vestire ciascuna delle parti nude dell'aereo.

De novo insistimos na importância de dividir e de tratar cada parte do desenho como se fosse um desenho independente. Passar de um esboço a um lápis é como vestir cada uma das partes despidas do avião.

# 3

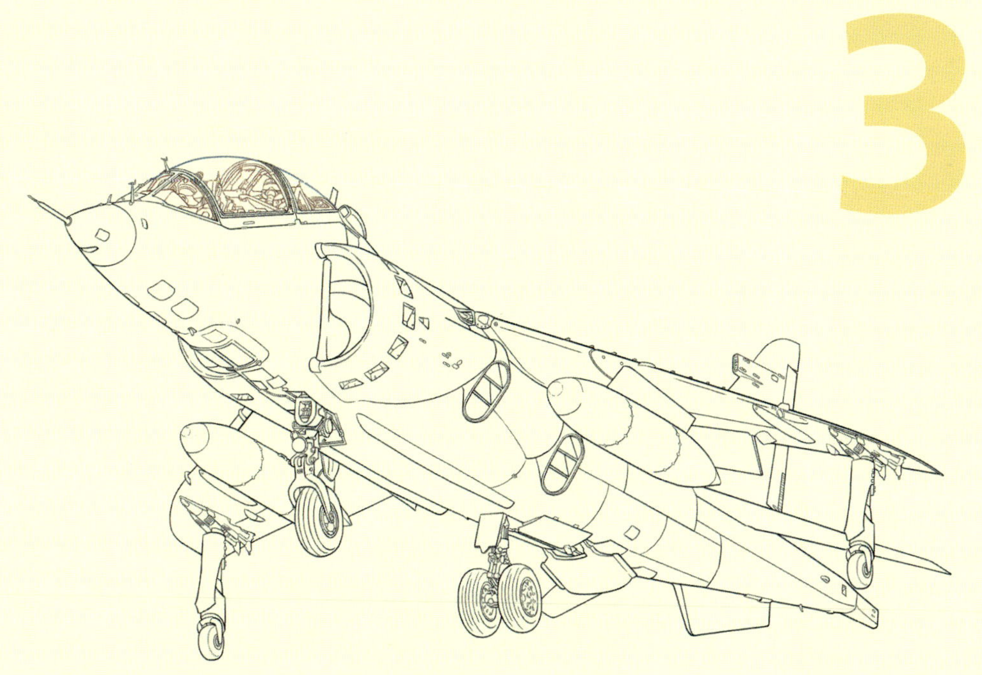

There is a trick to the inking of this plane: the interior of the cockpit and the pilots (red) were done on a separate layer. In fact, they are behind a semi-transparent blue layer to give the effect of glass.

L'encrage de cet avion comporte une astuce : l'intérieur de la cabine et les pilotes (en rouge) sont réalisés sur une couche séparée. En effet, ils sont placés derrière une couche bleue semi-transparente afin de reproduire l'aspect du verre.

Das Besondere an der Tuschezeichnung dieser Maschine ist, dass das Innere des Cockpits und die Piloten (rot) in einer separaten Ebene gezeichnet wurden. Diese Ebene liegt hinter einer halbtransparenten blauen Ebene, die das Glas des Cockpits darstellt.

Het inkleuren van dit vliegtuig heeft een truc. De binnenkant van de cabine en de piloten (rood) zijn namelijk in een aparte laag getekend. Feitelijk bevinden ze zich achter een halfdoorzichtig blauwe laag waarmee een glaseffect wordt verkregen.

El entintado de este avión tiene truco, pues el interior de la cabina y los pilotos (rojo) están realizados en una capa aparte. De hecho, están detrás de una capa de azul semitransparente para dar efecto de cristal.

Per il ripasso a china di questo aereo c'è un trucco: l'interno della cabina e i piloti (rosso) sono stati realizzati in un livello a parte. Di fatto, si trovano dietro un livello blu semitrasparente che rende l'effetto del vetro.

A arte-final deste avião tem truque, pois o interior da cabina e os pilotos (vermelha) são realizados numa camada à parte. De facto, estão por trás de uma camada de azul semitransparente para dar efeito de vidro.

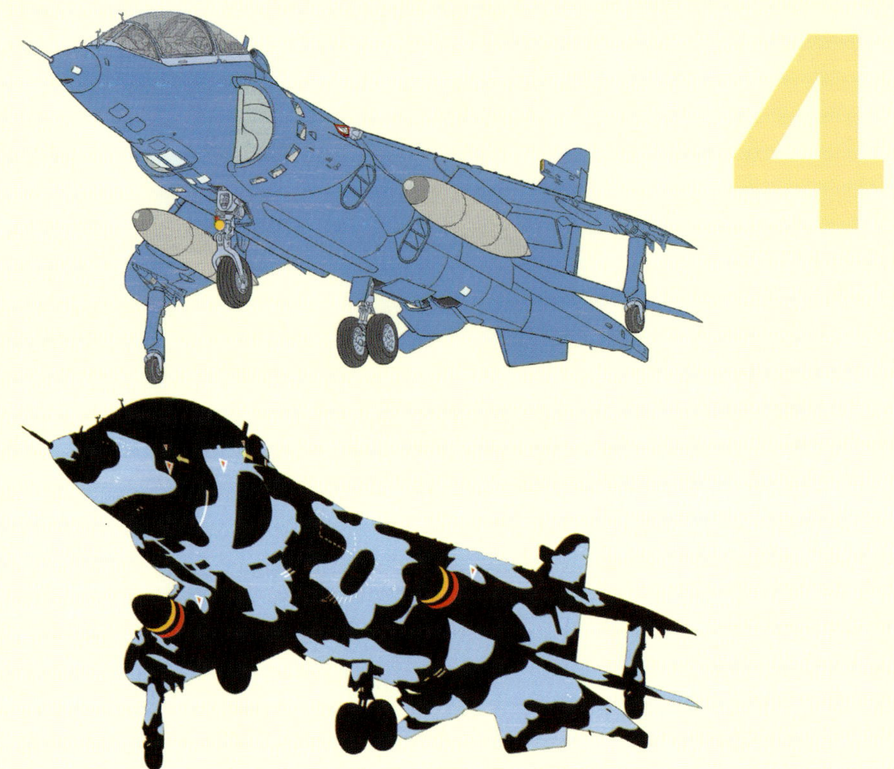

4

Add the base color in two layers. The first is predominantly blue, while the second has clear areas and small decorative elements. The black on the bottom does not really exist and only helps you to visualize this image.

Les couleurs de base sont réalisées sur deux couches. Le bleu prédomine dans la première tandis que la seconde comporte des taches claires et de petits éléments décoratifs. Le noir de la partie inférieure n'existe pas en réalité, il sert uniquement à visualiser cette image.

Die Grundfarben werden in zwei Ebenen aufgetragen. In der ersten herrscht Blau vor, die zweite weist helle Flecken und kleinere Zierelemente auf. Die schwarze Farbe in der unteren Abbildung dient lediglich der Veranschaulichung.

De basiskleuren worden in twee lagen aangebracht. De eerste is overwegend blauw en de tweede heeft lichte vlekken en kleine decoratieve elementen. Het zwart van de onderkant bestaat in werkelijkheid niet en fungeert enkel om deze afbeelding te visualiseren.

Damos colores base en dos capas. La primera con predominio de azul y la segunda, con manchas claras y pequeños elementos decorativos. El negro de la parte inferior no existe en realidad y sirve sólo para visualizar esta imagen.

Diamo i colori di base in due livelli. Nel primo prevale il blu, mentre nel secondo le macchie chiare e i piccoli oggetti decorativi. Il nero della parte inferiore in realtà non esiste e serve soltanto per visualizzare questa immagine.

Damos cores base em duas camadas. A primeira com predomínio de azul e a segunda, com manchas claras e pequenos elementos decorativos. O preto da parte inferior não existe na realidade e serve apenas para visualizar esta imagem.

5

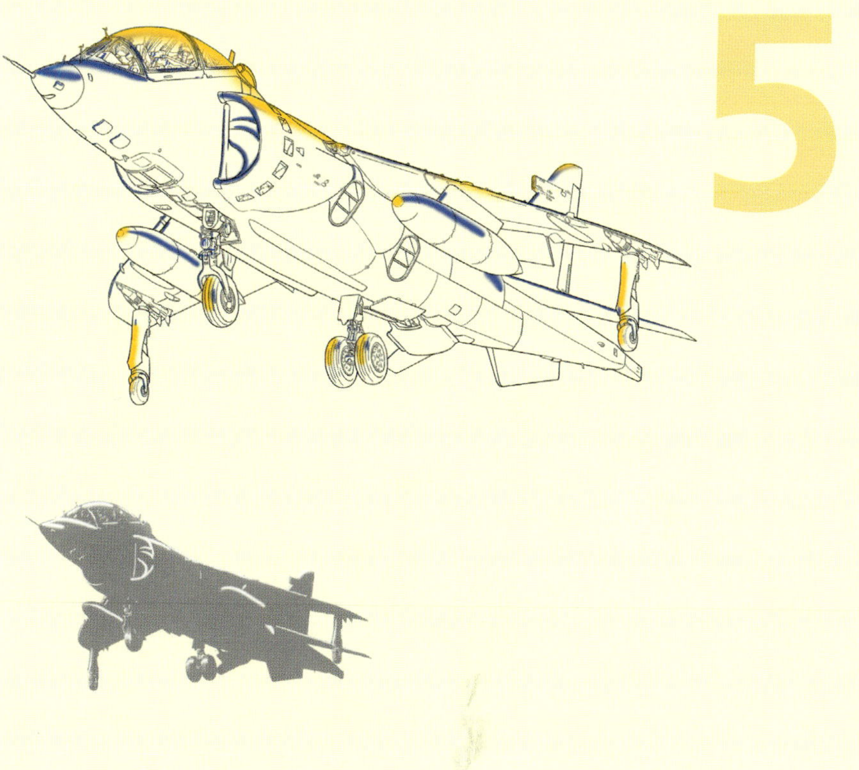

Given that the Harrier has very few flat surfaces on top, a choice was made in this exercise to apply two very fine lighting layers that emphasize the tops of the curved features.

Comme le Harrier présente très peu de surfaces planes sur sa partie supérieure, nous avons choisi pour cet exercice d'appliquer deux couches de lumières très fines en faisant ressortir les zones zénithales des éléments arrondis.

Da die Harrier an ihrer Oberseite über wenige ebene Flächen verfügt, werden zwei sehr kleine Lichtebenen eingefügt, welche die höchsten und seitlichsten Bereiche der gekrümmten Bauteile hervorheben.

Aangezien de Harrier heel weinig vlakke oppervlakken aan de bovenkant heeft, is er in deze oefening voor gekozen om twee hele dunne lichtlagen aan te brengen en de zenitale zones van de gebogen elementen te doen uitkomen.

Puesto que el Harrier tiene muy pocas superficies planas en la parte superior, en este ejercicio se ha optado por aplicar dos capas de luces muy finas, remarcando las zonas cenitales de los elementos curvos.

Dato che l'Harrier ha pochissime superfici piatte nella parte superiore, in questo esercizio si è deciso di applicare due livelli di luci molto sottili, evidenziando le zone zenitali degli elementi curvi.

Uma vez que o Harrier tem muito poucas superfícies planas na parte superior, neste exercício optou-se por aplicar duas camadas de luzes muito finas, sinalizando as zonas zenitais dos elementos curvos.

6

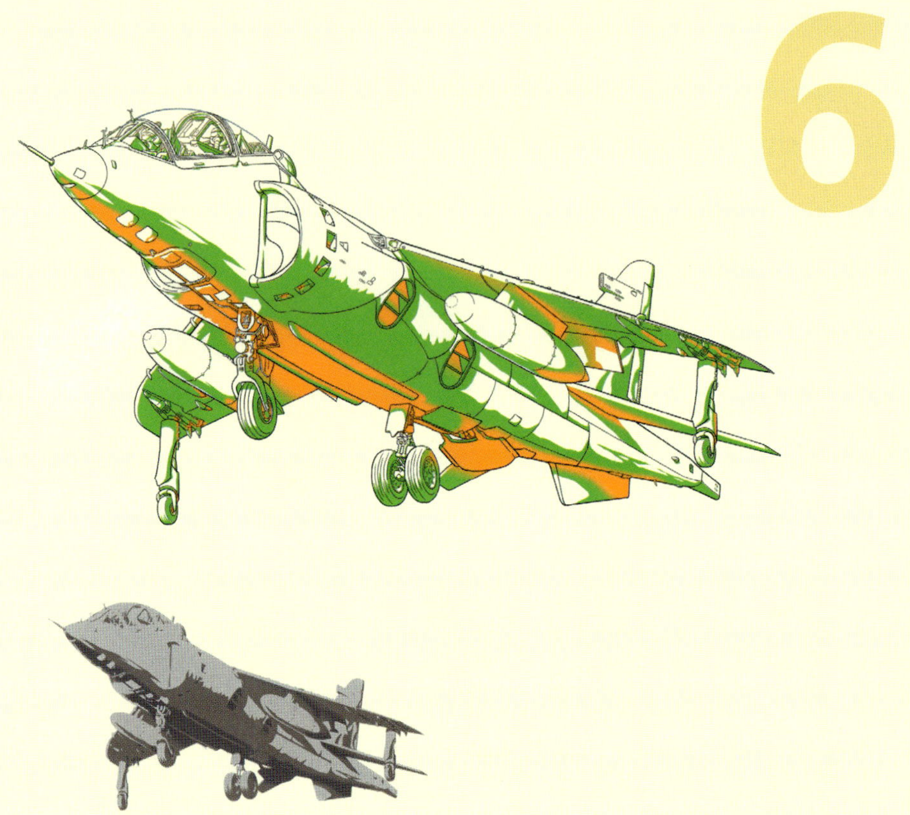

The shading, however, takes up a large surface area, given that the Harrier is flatter on the underside. These large shaded areas add solidity to the image.

Les ombres, à l'inverse, occupent une grande surface car le Harrier est plus plat sur sa partie inférieure. Ces ombres si étendues apporteront de la solidité à l'ensemble.

Die Schatten nehmen hingegen viel Raum ein, da die Harrier im unteren Bereich flacher ist. Die ausgedehnten Schatten verleihen der Abbildung eine besonders robuste Ausstrahlung.

De schaduwen nemen daarentegen een groot oppervlak in beslag, aangezien de Harrier aan de onderkant platter is. Deze grote schaduwvlekken geven het geheel meer soliditeit.

La sombras, por el contrario, ocupan una gran superficie, puesto que el Harrier es más plano por la parte inferior. Estas sombras tan extensas aportarán gran solidez al conjunto.

Al contrario, le ombre occupano una superficie estesa, dal momento che l'Harrier è più piatto nella parte inferiore. Queste ombre così estese daranno grande solidità al disegno.

As sombras, pelo contrário, ocupam uma grande superfície, uma vez que o Harrier é mais plano na parte inferior. Estas sombras tão extensas conferem grande solidez ao conjunto.

# 7

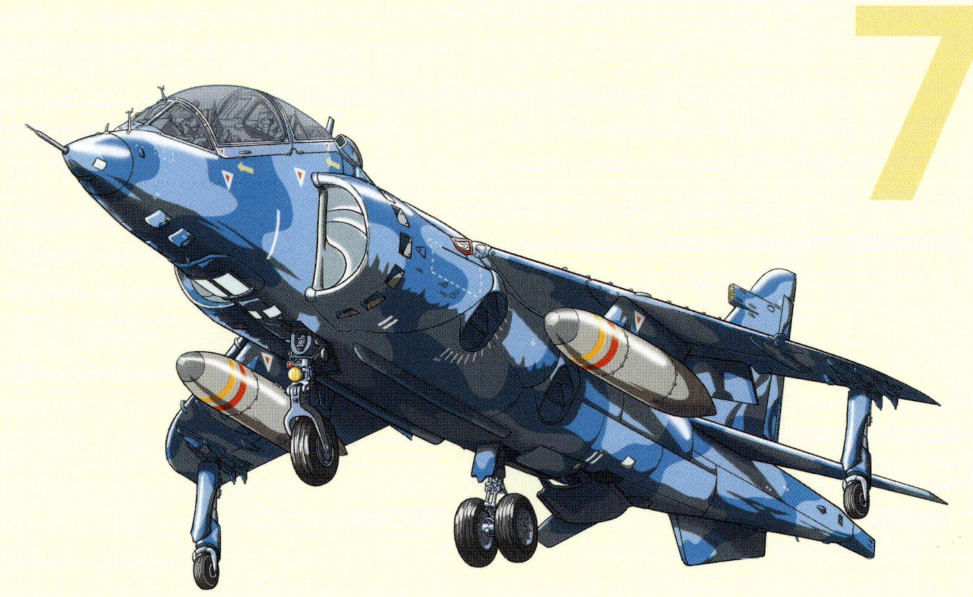

Although choosing the base colors and the clear zones involve some risk, the combination of steps fits together very well. The aircraft is a robust steel beast ready for action.

Bien que les couleurs de base et les taches claires constituent un choix risqué, l'ensemble est très harmonieux. L'avion ressemble à un monstre d'acier robuste prêt à bondir.

Obwohl die Auswahl der Grundfarben und der hellen Flecken recht gewagt ist, wirkt die Kombination aller Arbeitsschritte sehr gelungen. Das Kampfflugzeug ist eine widerstandfähige Bestie aus Stahl, die bereit für den Einsatz ist.

Hoewel de selectie van basiskleuren en lichte vlekken een gewaagde keuze is, passen de verschillende fases goed bij elkaar. Het vliegtuig is een robuust stuk staal, klaar voor de actie.

Aunque la selección de colores base y las manchas claras son una elección arriesgada, el conjunto de las fases se acopla muy bien. El avión es una robusta bestia de acero lista para la acción.

Sebbene i colori di base e le macchie chiare sono una scelta rischiosa, l'insieme di tutte le fasi dà un ottimo risultato. L'aereo è una robusta bestia di acciaio pronta per l'azione.

Ainda que a selecção de cores base e as manchas claras sejam uma eleição arriscada, o conjunto das fases liga muito bem. O avião é uma robusta besta de aço pronta para a acção.

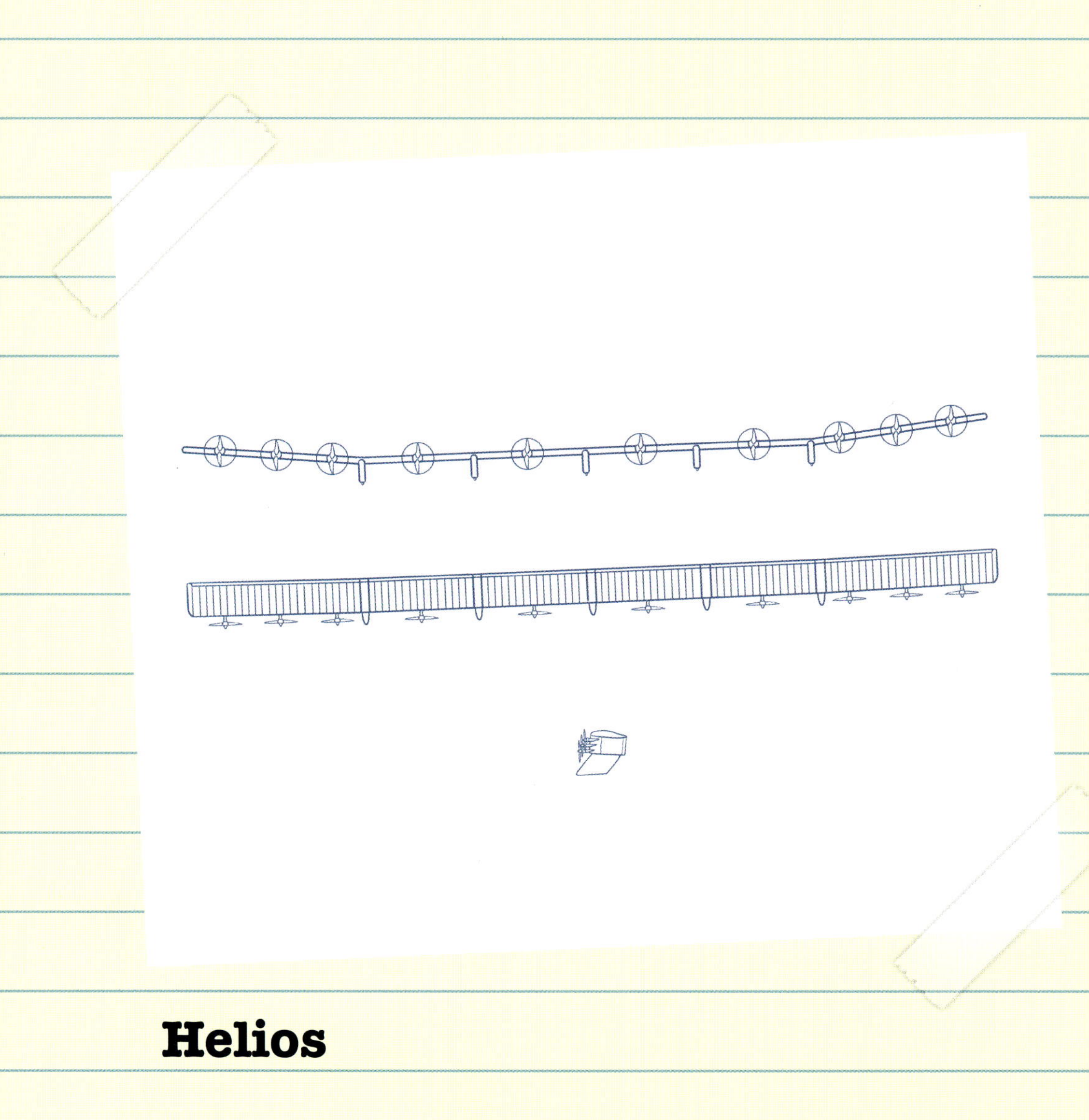

# Helios

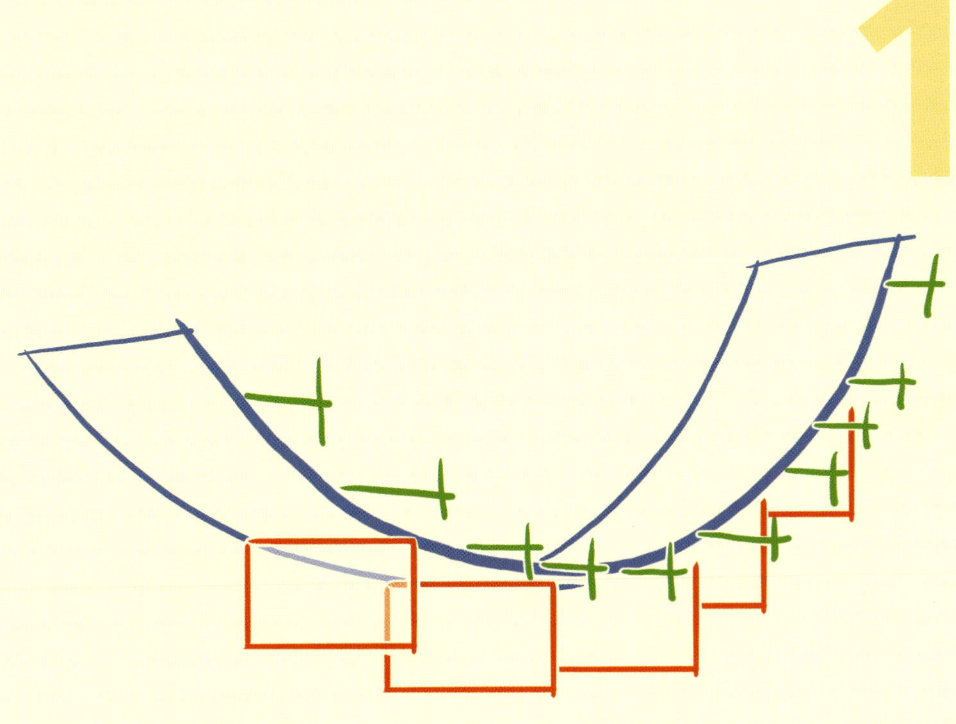

This outline reflects the power of repetition. This may make this plane appear complex but, as the colors reveal, it is only made up of three different elements.

Ce schéma démontre la force de la répétition. Cette technique permet de donner à un avion un aspect complexe alors que, comme le dévoile l'utilisation des couleurs, sa structure ne comporte que trois éléments différents.

Die Schemazeichnung zeigt insbesondere sich wiederholende Elemente. Aus diesem Grund kann ein Flugzeug, das – wie die Verwendung der Farben veranschaulicht – lediglich aus drei verschiedenen Elementen besteht, recht komplex erscheinen.

Dit schema weerspiegelt de kracht van de herhaling. Deze kan een vliegtuig, dat uit slechts drie verschillende elementen bestaat, zoals bij het gebruik van kleuren naar voren komt, complex doen lijken.

Este esquema refleja la fuerza de la repetición, que puede hacer parecer complejo un avión que, tal como se revela al utilizar colores, está compuesto por sólo tres elementos diferentes.

Questo schema riflette la forza della ripetizione. Essa può far sembrare complesso un aereo che, come rivelato dai colori, è composto da tre soli elementi diversi.

Este esquema reflecte a força da repetição. Esta pode fazer parecer complexo um avião que, tal como se revela ao utilizar cores, é composto apenas por três elementos diferentes.

# 2

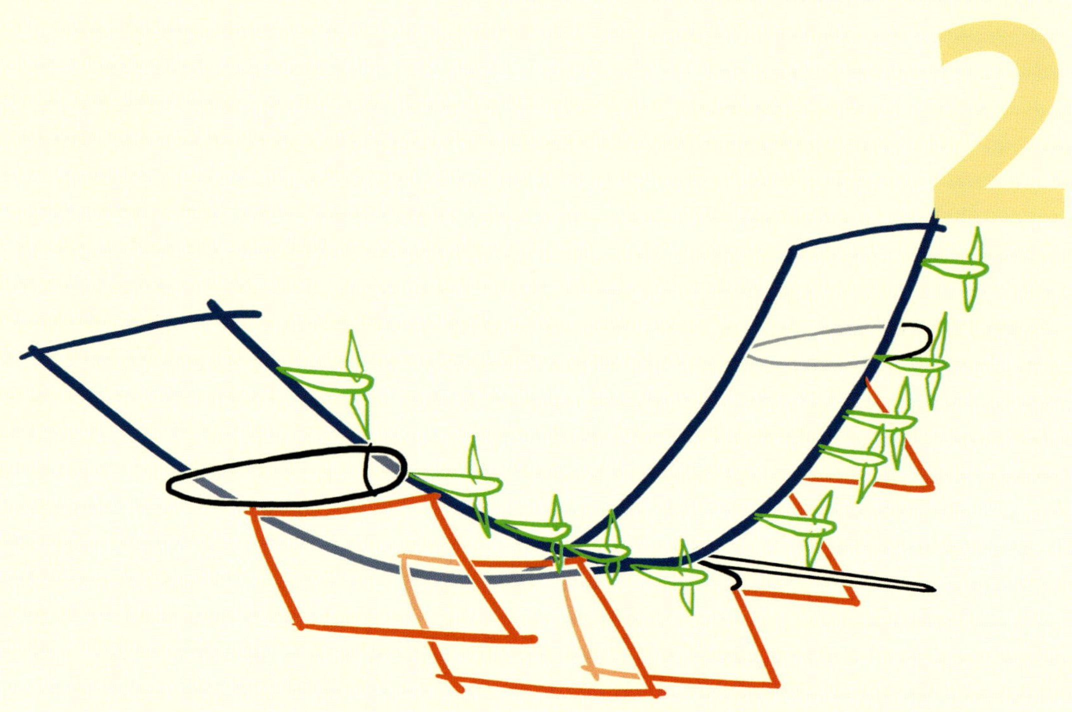

The sketch is nothing more than a correction of the outline, adding volume to the propellers (green) and their angle to the hydrogen containers (red). We added the fuel tanks and the central rib (black).

L'ébauche n'est rien de plus qu'une correction du schéma visant à donner du volume aux hélices (en vert) et à ajuster l'angle des containers d'hydrogène (en rouge). Nous avons également ajouté les réservoirs de combustible et la barre centrale (en noir).

Bei der Skizze handelt es sich in diesem Fall um eine Korrektur des Grundschemas, bei der die Propeller (grün) und die Wasserstoffbehälter (rot) Volumen erhalten. Außerdem werden die Treibstofftanks und die Mittelstange (schwarz) hinzugefügt.

De schets is niets meer of minder dan een verbetering van het schema, die de propellers (groen) volume en een hoek aan de waterstofreservoirs (rood) geeft. We hebben de brandstoftanks en de middenstaaf (zwart) toegevoegd.

El boceto no es más que una corrección del esquema, que da volumen a las hélices (verde) y su ángulo a los contenedores de hidrógeno (rojo). Hemos añadido los tanques de combustible y la varilla central (negro).

Il bozzetto non è altro che una correzione dello schema, che aggiunge volume alle eliche (verde) e la giusta angolazione ai contenitori di idrogeno (rosso). Abbiamo aggiunto i serbatoi del carburante e l'asta centrale (nero).

O esboço não é mais que uma correcção do esquema, que dá volume às hélices (verde) e o seu ângulo aos contentores de hidrogénio (vermelhos). Acrescentámos os tanques de combustível e a vareta central (preta).

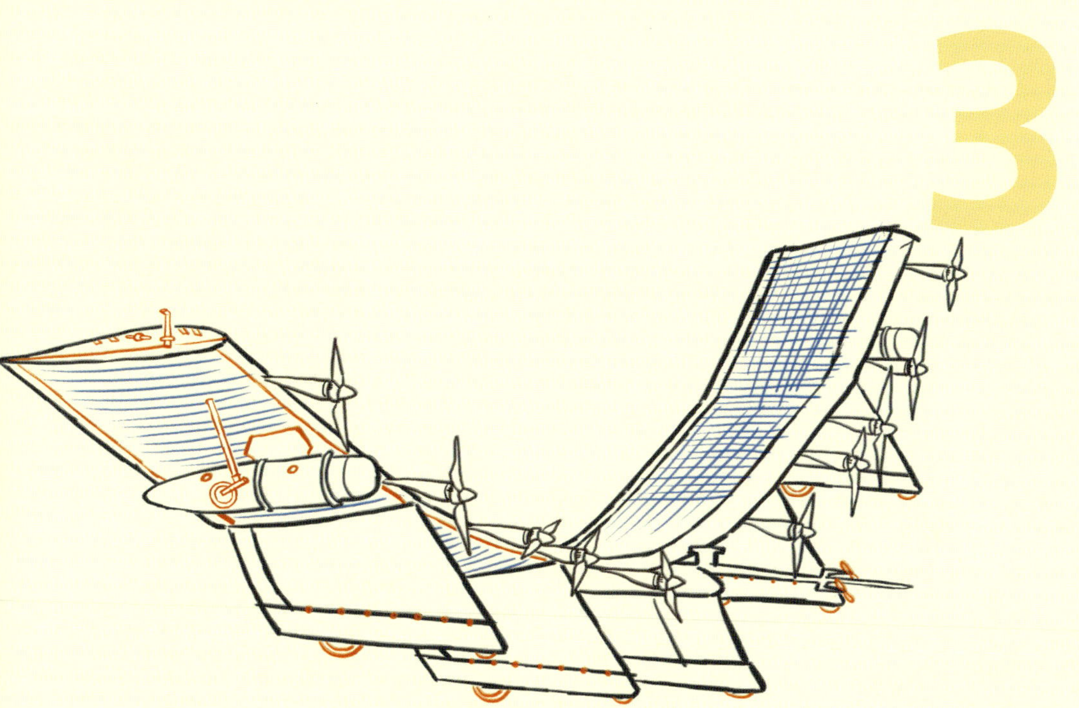


A quick pencil drawing (black) can be made from the simple sketch so you can focus on the details that give the image its appeal. The penciling of the solar panels gives you an idea of the cell size that is suitable to illustrate.

À partir de cette simple ébauche, vous pouvez réaliser un crayonné rapide (en noir) et vous concentrer sur les détails qui apportent à la structure un aspect esthétique. Le crayonné des panneaux solaires vous donne une idée de la taille de la cellule appropriée pour l'illustration.

Ausgehend von der einfachen Skizze wird eine schnelle Buntstift-zeichnung (schwarz) angefertigt, bei der insbesondere auf die Details Wert gelegt wird, welche die Abbildung attraktiver machen.
Bei der Gestaltung der Solarzellen bekommt man ein Gefühl dafür, in welcher Größe diese am besten dargestellt werden sollten.

Vanaf de eenvoudige schets kunnen we een snelle potloodtekening (zwart) maken en ons richten op de details die de tekening aantrekkelijk maken. De potloodtekening van de zonnepanelen geeft ons een idee van de juiste te illustreren celgrootte.

A partir del sencillo boceto podemos hacer un lápiz rápido (negro) y centrarnos en los detalles que aportan atractivo a la figura. El lápiz de las placas solares nos da una idea del tamaño de celda que resulta adecuado ilustrar.

Dal semplice bozzetto possiamo realizzare delle matite rapide (nero) e concentrarci sui dettagli che aggiungono fascino al soggetto. Il disegno a matita dei pannelli solari ci dà un'idea delle dimensioni adeguate per rappresentare le celle.

A partir do simples esboço podemos fazer um lápis rápido (preto) e centrar-nos nos detalhes que fornecem beleza à figura. O lápis das placas solares dá-nos uma ideia do tamanho da célula que é adequada ilustrar.

# 4

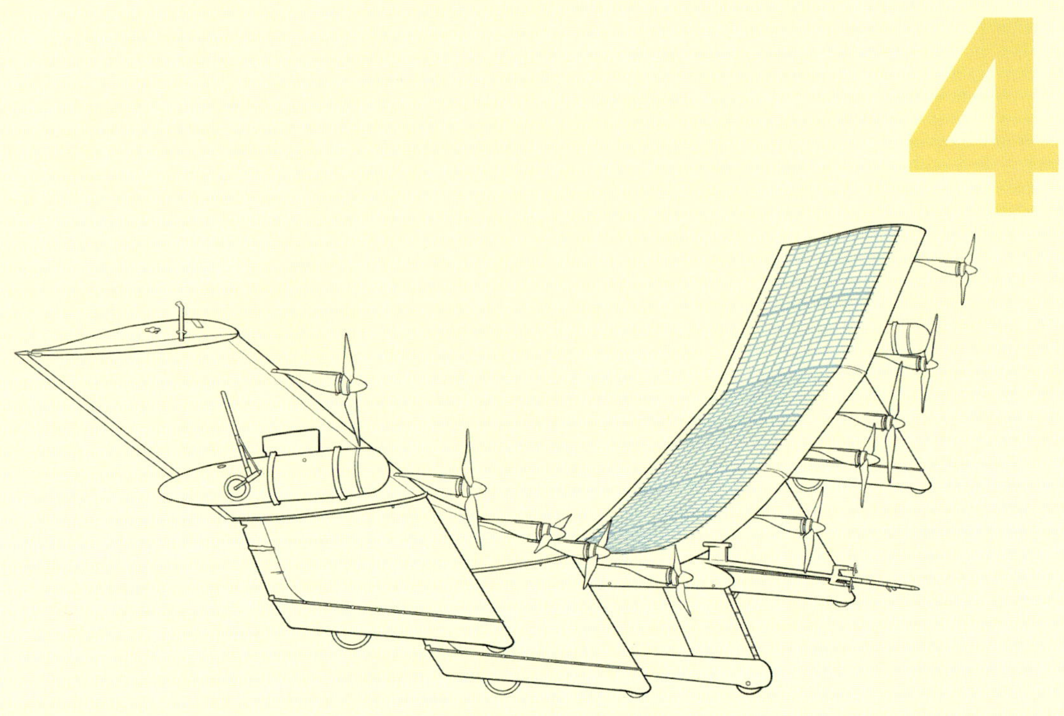

Thinking ahead is important if you want the effects to be good. The inking of the solar panels is done on a separate layer, which will be turned to white later. If you are working on paper, you need to do this last and in opaque white.

Il est important d'être prévoyant pour obtenir de bons effets. L'encrage des panneaux solaires est réalisé sur une couche séparée afin de pouvoir par la suite colorer les tracés en blanc. Pour un travail sur papier, il faudra le réaliser en dernier avec un blanc opaque.

Um die gewünschte Wirkung zu erzielen, sollte man stets vorausschauend arbeiten. Die Tuschezeichnung der Solarzellen wird in einer separaten Ebene angefertigt, um sie später in Weiß zu konvertieren. Wer auf Papier arbeitet, fügt die Solarzellen ganz am Schluss in Opakweiß hinzu.

Het is belangrijk om vooruit te zien om goede effecten te bereiken. De inkttekening van de zonnepanelen is gemaakt in een aparte laag om later wit te maken. Als we op papier werken moeten we deze in de laatste plaats met ondoorzichtig wit uitwerken.

Ser previsor es importante para conseguir buenos efectos. La tinta de las placas solares está hecha en una capa aparte para más tarde pasarla a blanco. Si trabajamos en papel, deberemos realizarla en último lugar con blanco opaco.

Essere previdenti è importante per ottenere buoni effetti. Il ripasso a china dei pannelli solari è stato realizzato in un livello separato, per poterlo colorare di bianco successivamente. Se lavoriamo sulla carta dobbiamo realizzarlo per ultimo con del bianco opaco.

Ser precavido é importante para conseguir bons efeitos. A tinta das placas solares é feita numa camada à parte para mais tarde passá-la para branco. Se trabalhamos em papel deveremos realizá-la em último lugar com branco opaco.

5

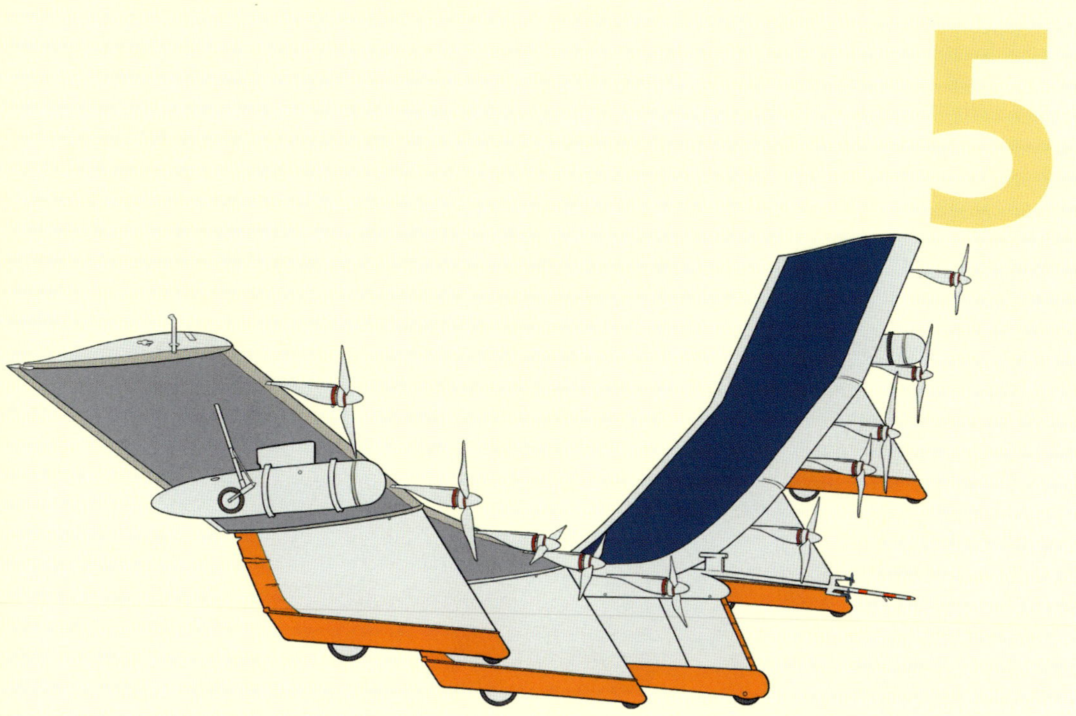

The (off) white and orange colors of the plane give the impression that the design is more commercial than functional. Dark blue is the base color used to represent believable solar panels.

Les couleurs (presque) blanches et orangées de l'avion lui confèrent un aspect plus commercial que fonctionnel. Le bleu foncé sert de base pour la reproduction d'un panneau solaire réaliste.

Die (fast) weiße Farbe und der Orangeton des Flugzeugs erwecken den Eindruck eines eher gewerblichen anstatt funktionellen Designs. Die dunkelblaue Farbe bildet die Grundlage für eine glaubwürdige Darstellung der Solarzellen.

De (vrijwel) witte en oranje kleuren van het vliegtuig geven het gevoel dat het eerder een commercieel dan een functioneel ontwerp is. Donkerblauw is de basis om geloofwaardige zonnepanelen af te beelden.

Los colores (casi) blancos y naranjas del avión dan sensación de diseño comercial más que funcional. El azul oscuro es la base para representar unas placas solares creíbles.

I colori (quasi) bianchi e arancioni dell'aereo danno la sensazione di un design commerciale piuttosto che funzionale. Il blu scuro è la base per rappresentare dei pannelli solari credibili.

As cores (quase) brancas e laranjas do avião dão sensação de desenho comercial mais do que funcional. O azul-escuro é a base para representar umas placas solares credíveis.

# 6

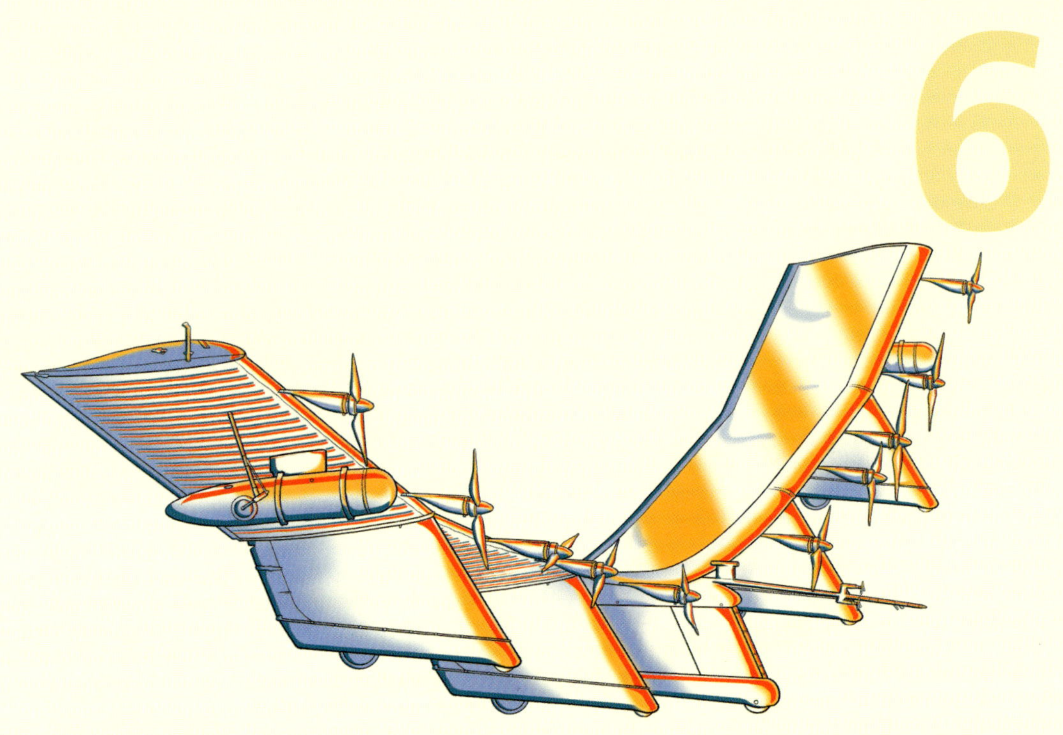

The two lighting layers (red and orange) are token on the underside, but gain in importance on the solar panels. The two layers of shading (blue) give volume to the image.

Les deux couches de lumière (en rouge et orange) font seulement acte de présence sur la partie inférieure mais revêtent une importance capitale sur les panneaux solaires. Les deux couches d'ombre (en bleu) apportent du volume à la structure.

Die zwei Lichtebenen (rot und orange) spielen auf der Unterseite des Flugzeugs nur eine untergeordnete Rolle, sind auf den Solarzellen jedoch von besonderer Bedeutung. Die zwei Schattenebenen (blau) verleihen der Abbildung Tiefe.

De twee lichtlagen (rood en oranje) geven aan de onderkant enkel acte de présence, maar krijgen een voorname rol op de zonnepanelen. De twee schaduwlagen (blauw) geven de figuur volume.

Las dos capas de luces (rojo y naranja) hacen simple acto de presencia en la parte inferior, pero cobran protagonismo sobre las placas solares. Las dos capas de sombras (azules) aportan volumen a la figura.

I due livelli di luce (rosso e arancione) sono solo accennati nella parte inferiore, ma diventano i protagonisti sui pannelli solari. I due livelli di ombre (blu) aggiungono volume al soggetto.

As duas camadas de luzes (vermelha e laranja) apenas estão presentes na parte inferior, mas ganham protagonismo sobre as placas solares. As duas camadas de sombras (azuis) concedem volume à figura.

7

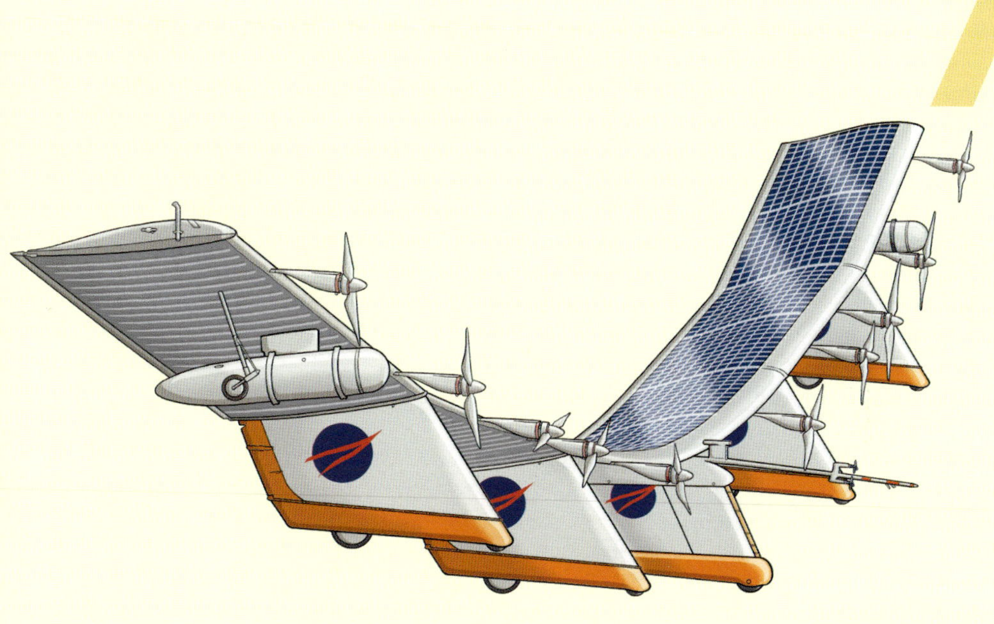

The finished drawing makes sense when the grid form of the solar panels is applied in white. Helios conveys a sensation of the peacefulness offered by an aircraft powered by renewable resources.

Le dessin final prend tout son sens avec l'application du quadrillage blanc pour les panneaux solaires. L'Helios transmet une sensation de paix en accord avec les énergies renouvelables qu'il utilise.

Die fertige Zeichnung wird durch das Hinzufügen des weißen Gittermusters der Solarzellen vervollständigt. Das Solarflugzeug Helios vermittelt Ruhe und Frieden, da es sich um eine Maschine handelt, die durch erneuerbare Energien angetrieben wird.

De afgeronde tekening krijgt inhoud wanneer het rooster voor de zonnepanelen wit wordt gemaakt. De Helios wekt de vredige indruk die wordt verwacht van een luchtschip die wordt gevoed met hernieuwbare energie.

El dibujo acabado cobra sentido cuando se le aplica la rejilla para las placas solares en blanco. El Helios transmite la sensación pacífica que se le supone a una nave que se alimenta de energías renovables.

Il disegno finito acquista significato se si applica la griglia per i pannelli solari in bianco. L'Helios trasmette il senso di pace insito in un velivolo alimentato da energie rinnovabili.

O desenho acabado ganha sentido quando se aplica a grelha para as placas solares em branco. O Helios transmite a sensação pacífica que se pressupõe numa nave que se alimenta de energias renováveis.

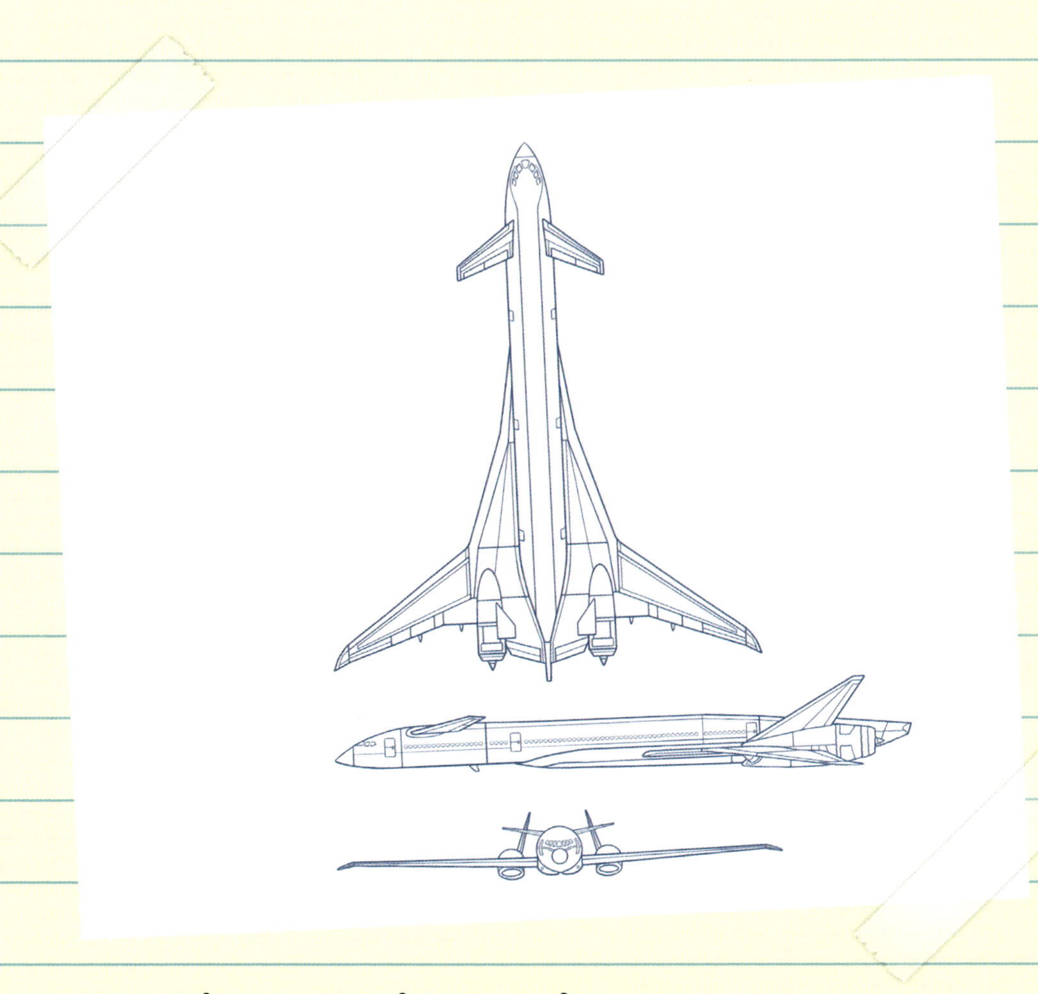

## Boeing Sonic Cruiser

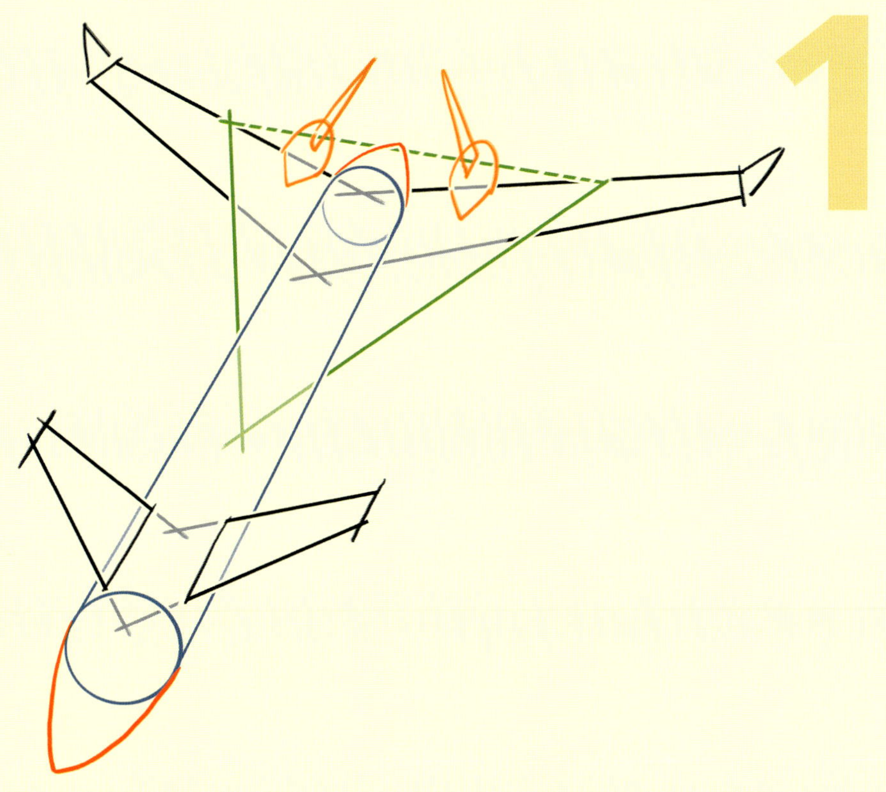


This is basic but sufficient. Add features in freehand, such as the engines (orange), the tips (red), and the bent wings.

Basique mais efficace. Ajoutez quelques éléments à main levée tels que les moteurs (en orange), les extrémités (en rouge) et les ailes doubles.

In diesem Fall ist ein sehr vereinfachtes Schema ausreichend. Elemente wie die Triebwerke (orange), die Nase (rot) und die angewinkelten Spitzen der Deltaflügel werden frei Hand eingezeichnet.

Essentieel maar voldoende. Teken uit de vrije mand elementen zoals de motoren (oranje), de uiteinden (rood) en de dubbele vleugels.

Básico pero suficiente. Añade elementos a mano alzada, como los motores (naranja), los extremos (rojo) y las alas dobladas.

Semplice ma adeguato. Si aggiungono elementi a mano libera, come i motori (arancione), le estremità (rosso) e le ali inclinate.

Básico mas suficiente. Acrescenta elementos à mão livre como os motores (laranja), os extremos (vermelha) e as asas dobradas.

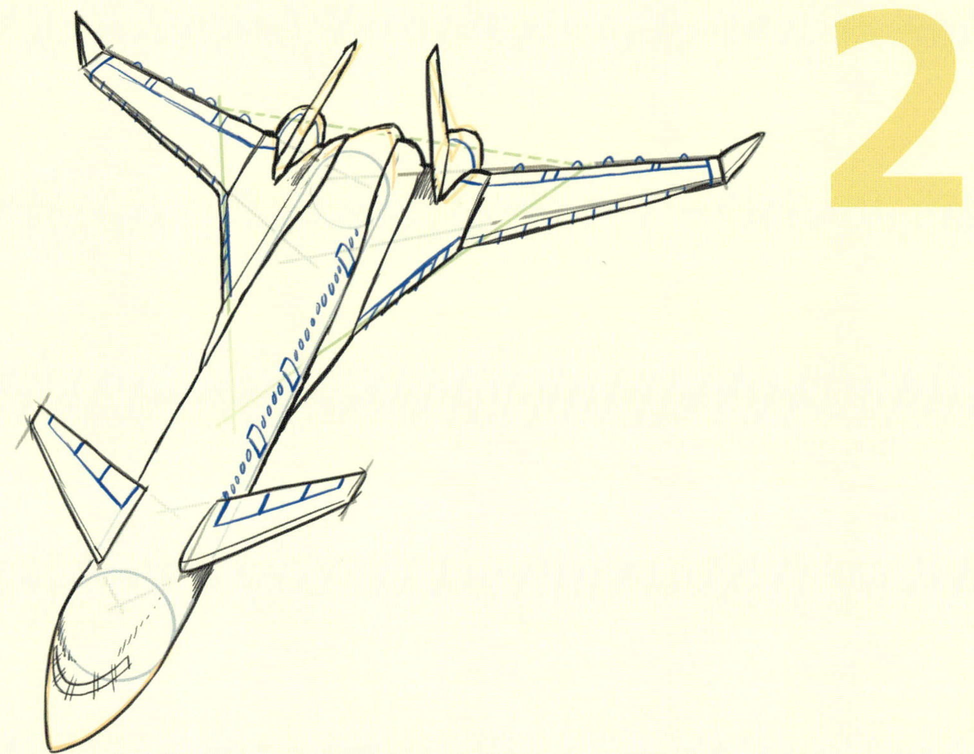

2

Because the surface of the aircraft is polished, penciling is done directly over the sketch. You should check that it works when details (blue) are added. There is no need to complicate matters if nothing more has to be done.

Étant donné l'aspect lisse de la surface de cet aéronef, réalisez directement le crayonné (en noir) sur le schéma. L'ajout de détails (en bleu) vous permettra de juger le résultat. Il est inutile de compliquer les choses si ce n'est pas nécessaire.

Dank der glatten Oberfläche des Flugzeugs wird die Buntstiftzeichnung (schwarz) direkt über das Schema gelegt. Beim Hinzufügen von Details (blau) wird deutlich, dass die vorherigen Schritte korrekt ausgeführt wurden. Warum komplizierter vorgehen als nötig?

Dankzij het verzorgde oppervlak van het luchtschip kunnen we de potloodtekening (zwart) rechtstreeks bovenop het schema uitwerken. Door details (blauw) toe te voegen, kunnen we nagaan of het werkt. We hoeven het ons niet onnodig moeilijk te maken.

Gracias a la pulida superficie de la aeronave, pasamos a realizar el lápiz (negro) directamente sobre el esquema. Al añadir detalles (azul) comprobamos que funciona. No hay que complicarse si no hace falta más.

Grazie alla superficie lineare del velivolo passiamo alla fase delle matite (nera) direttamente dallo schema. Aggiungendo i dettagli (blu) verifichiamo che tutto funziona. Non è necessario complicarsi la vita quando non serve altro.

Graças à polida superfície da aeronave passamos a realizar o lápis (preto) directamente sobre o esquema. Ao acrescentar detalhes (azul) comprovamos que funciona. Não há que complicar se não faz falta mais.

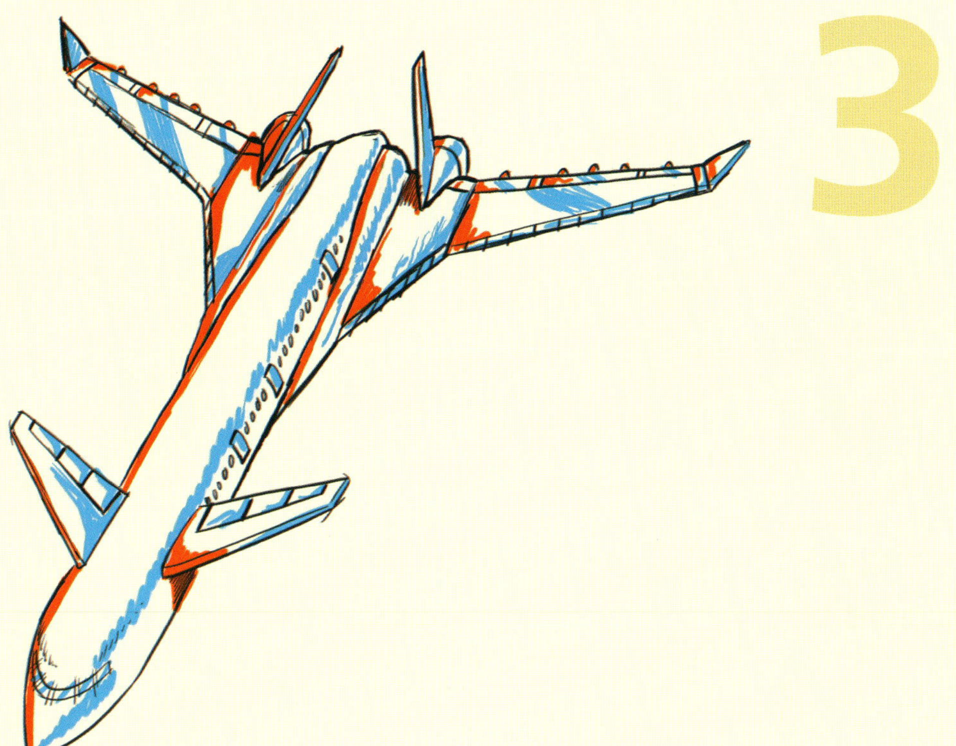

3

Although it was not mentioned in the previous step, it is interesting to make sketches of the positioning of lighting (blue) and shading (red) by placing the light source on different sides until you are happy with the result.

Nous ne l'avons pas évoqué jusque là mais il est intéressant de réaliser des ébauches de l'emplacement des lumières (en bleu) et des ombres (en rouge) avec différentes sources de lumières jusqu'à trouver le meilleur résultat.

Zwar wurde dies zuvor nicht angesprochen, doch es ist äußerst nützlich, Skizzen von der Anordnung der Licht- (blau) und Schattenbereiche (rot) anzufertigen und die Lichtquelle dabei unterschiedlich zu positionieren, bis das gewünschte Ergebnis erzielt wurde.

Hoewel dit reeds eerder is opgemerkt is het interessant om schetsen van de plaats van de lichten (blauw) en de schaduwen (rood) te maken en de lichtbron in verschillende hoeken te situeren totdat het gewenste resultaat wordt bereikt.

Aunque no se ha comentado anteriormente, es interesante realizar bocetos de la situación de las luces (azul) y las sombras (rojo) situando el foco de luz en lados distintos hasta dar con un resultado satisfactorio.

Sebbene non sia stato discusso in precedenza, è interessante realizzare bozzetti della posizione delle luci (blu) e delle ombre (rosso) situando la sorgente luminosa su vari lati, fino a quando si ottiene un risultato soddisfacente.

Ainda que não se tenha comentado anteriormente, é interessante realizar esboços da situação das luzes (azul) e das sombras (vermelha) colocando o foco de luz em lados distintos até encontrar um resultado satisfatório.

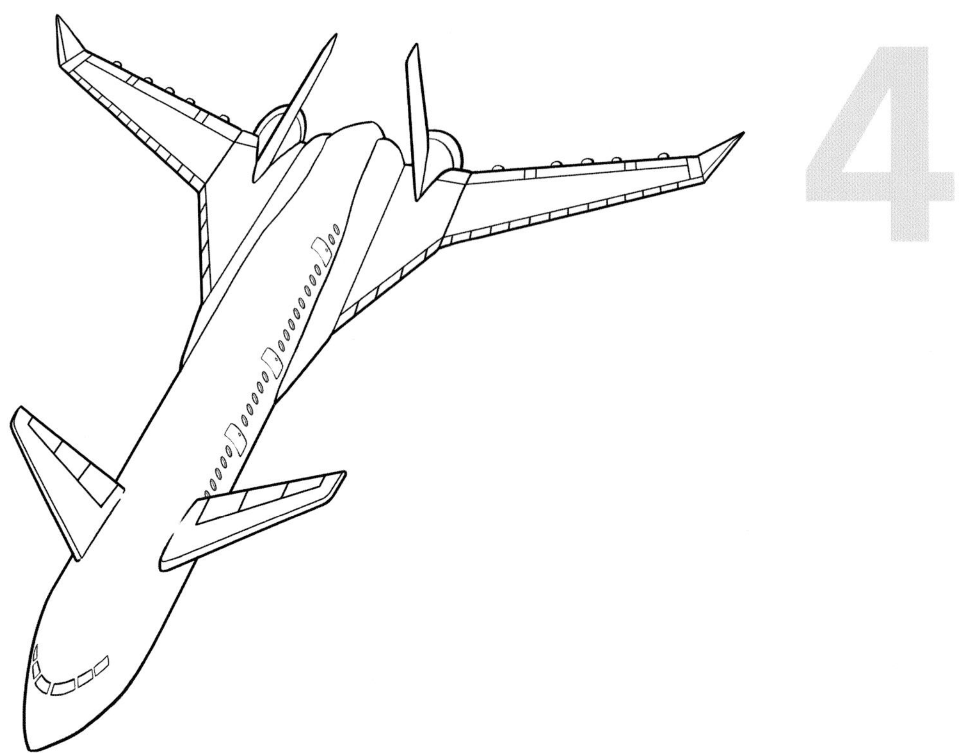

4

As it was necessary to use rulers or line tools to give the plane its missile-like appearance, the use of thicker strokes when inking helps to counter the absence of details.

Pour conserver l'allure de missile de cet avion, il était nécessaire d'utiliser pour l'encrage des règles ou des outils de tracés ; nous avons donc réalisé des lignes plus épaisses afin de compenser l'absence de détails.

Um das raketenähnliche Aussehen des Flugzeugs aufrechtzuerhalten, sollten die Tuschelinien mithilfe von Linealen oder Linien-Werkzeugen eingearbeitet werden. In dieser Abbildung wurden dickere Striche verwendet, um den Mangel an Details zu überspielen.

Om hem er als een raket te laten uitzien, moeten linialen of andere hulpmiddelen worden gebruikt voor de inktstrepen van dit vliegtuig. Er is gebruik gemaakt van dikkere strepen om de afwezigheid van details te verdoezelen.

Puesto que para mantener su aspecto de misil era necesario utilizar reglas o herramientas de línea en las tintas de este avión, se han utilizado unas tintas más gruesas para disimular la gran ausencia de detalles.

Dato che per mantenere l'aspetto da missile era necessario utilizzare righelli o strumenti linea per il ripasso a china di questo aereo, abbiamo usato tratti più spessi per nascondere la grande mancanza di dettagli.

Uma vez que para manter o seu aspecto de míssil era necessário utilizar réguas ou ferramentas geométricas nas tintas deste avião, utilizaram-se tintas mais espessas para dissimular a grande ausência de detalhes.

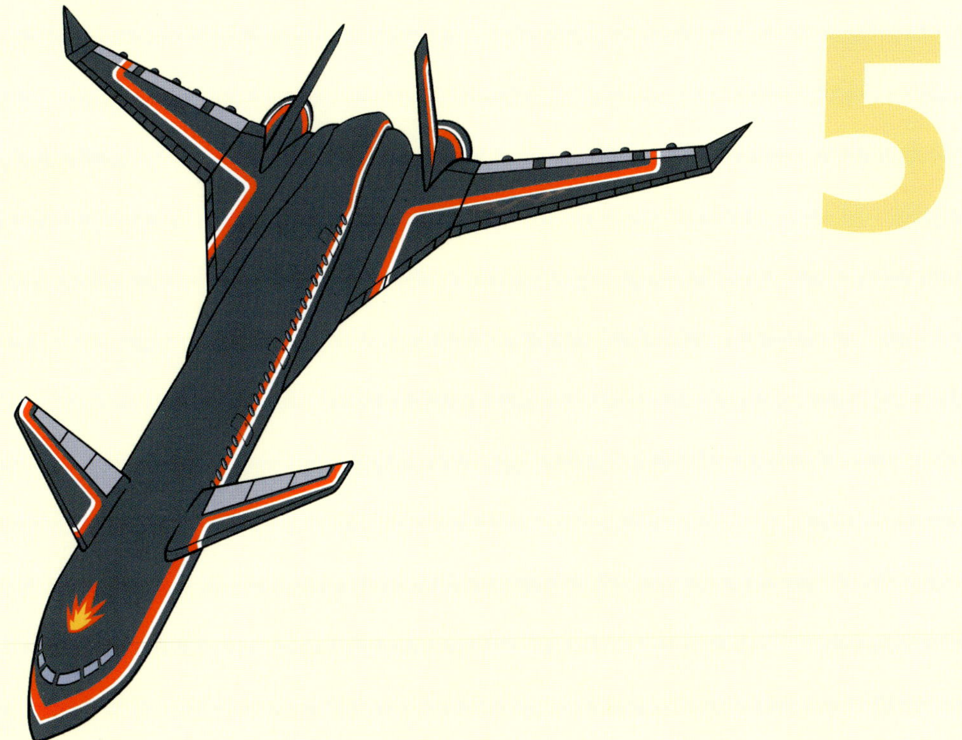

5

The dark base color and the strong contrast with the red and white lines makes the design sharp, sporting, and slightly futuristic. The flame icon is a bold focus of contrast.

La base de couleurs foncée et le contraste puissant généré par les lignes rouges et blanches donne naissance à un design d'aspect incisif, sportif et légèrement futuriste. Le symbole en forme de flamme constitue un point de contraste très vif.

Die dunkle Grundfarbe und der deutliche Kontrast der roten und weißen Linien sorgen für ein schnittiges, sportliches und leicht futuristisch anmutendes Design. Die Flamme auf der Oberseite stellt einen gewagten Akzent dar.

De donkere basiskleur en het enorme contrast van de rode en witte lijnen zijn aanleiding tot een ontwerp dat er scherp, sportief en ietwat futuristisch uitziet. De vlamvormige icoon is een gewaagd contrastpunt.

El color base oscuro y el alto contraste de las líneas roja y blanca dan pie a un diseño de aspecto incisivo, deportivo y ligeramente futurista. El icono en forma de llama es un atrevido punto de contraste.

Il colore di base scuro e l'alto contrasto della linea rossa e di quella bianca danno luogo ad un design con un aspetto incisivo, sportivo e leggermente futuristico. L'icona a forma di fiamma è un azzardato punto di contrasto.

A cor base escura e o alto contraste das linhas, vermelha e branca, dão azo a um desenho de aspecto incisivo, desportivo e ligeiramente futurista. O ícone em forma de chama é um atrevido ponto de contraste.

# 6

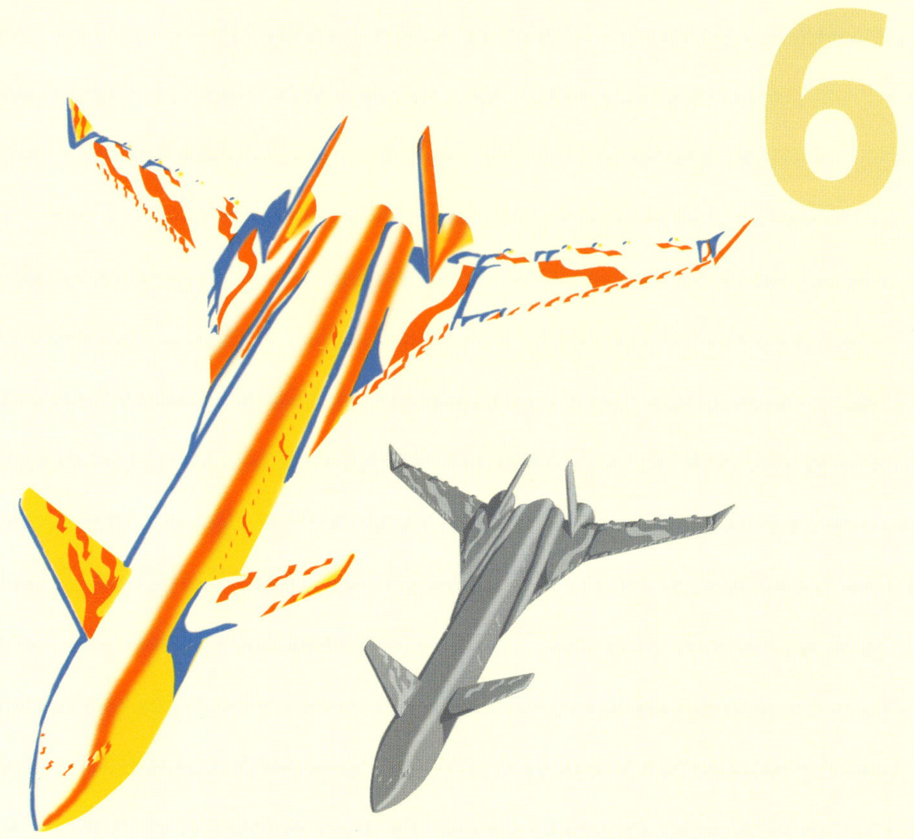

Based on the lighting and shading sketch, two lighting layers (orange and yellow) and one shading layer (blue) are applied to give volume and appeal to the aircraft.

En vous basant sur l'ébauche des ombres et lumières, appliquez deux couches de lumière (en orange et jaune) et une couche d'ombre (en bleu) qui apporteront du volume et de l'élégance à l'avion.

Ausgehend von der Licht- und Schatten-Skizze werden zwei Lichtebenen (orange und gelb) und eine Schattenebene (blau) eingearbeitet, die dem Flugzeug Tiefe verleihen und sein Aussehen weiter verschönern.

We baseren ons op de licht- en schaduwschets en brengen twee lichtlagen (oranje en geel) aan en een schaduwlaag (blauw) die het vliegtuig volume geven en aantrekkelijk maken.

Basándonos en el boceto de luces y sombras, aplicamos dos capas de luces (naranja y amarillo) y una capa de sombras (azul), que darán volumen y atractivo al avión.

Basandoci sul bozzetto delle luci e delle ombre, applichiamo due livelli di luci (arancio e giallo) e uno di ombre (blu), che daranno volume e fascino all'aereo.

Baseando-nos no esboço de luzes e sombras, aplicamos duas camadas de luzes (laranja e amarela) e uma camada de sombras (azul) que darão volume e beleza ao avião.

7

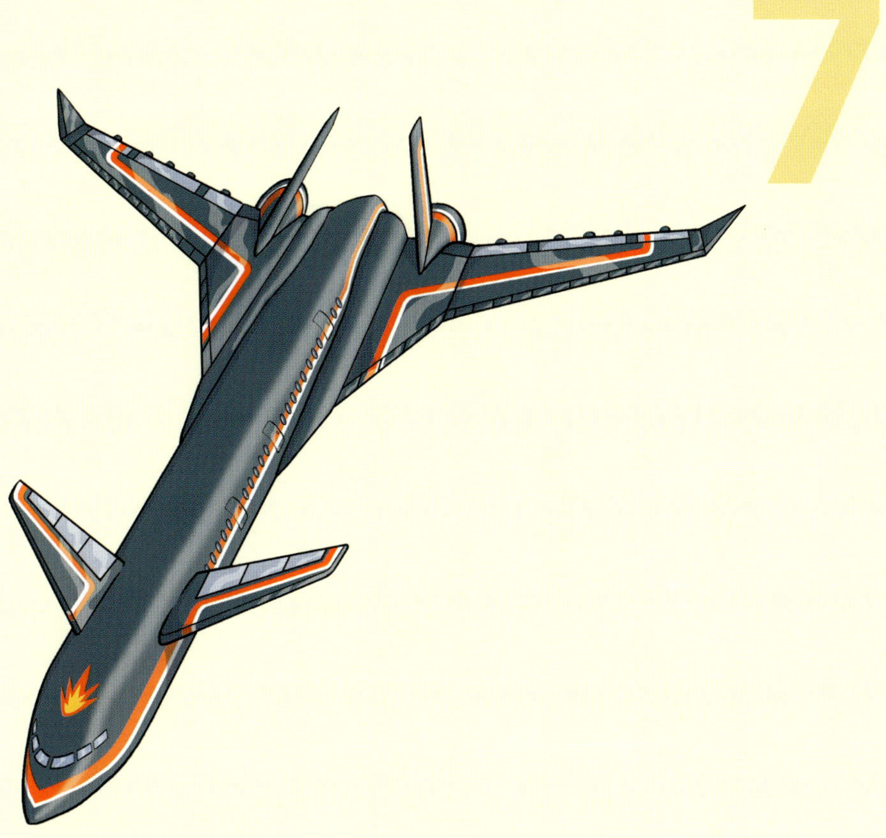

The finished drawing is one of a futuristic missile. You need to look twice to notice, by way of the side row of windows, that it was designed to carry passengers.

Le dessin final est un missile du futur. Il faut le regarder attentivement pour constater, grâce aux hublots, qu'il a été conçu pour transporter des passagers.

In der fertigen Zeichnung ist eine Rakete der Zukunft zu sehen. Man muss eigentlich zwei Mal hinsehen, um anhand der Fenster festzustellen, dass die Maschine für den Passagierverkehr entworfen wurde.

De afgeronde tekening is een raket van de toekomst. Je moet twee keer kijken om, dankzij de zijraampjes, te zien dat het is ontworpen om passagiers te vervoeren.

El dibujo acabado es un misil del futuro. Hay que mirar dos veces para confirmar, gracias a sus ventanillas laterales, que está diseñado para transportar pasajeros.

Il disegno finito è un missile del futuro. Bisogna guardarlo due volte per confermare, per via dei finestrini laterali, che è stato progettato per il trasporto di passeggeri.

O desenho acabado é um míssil do futuro. Há que olhar duas vezes para confirmar, graças às suas janelas laterais, que está desenhado para transportar passageiros.

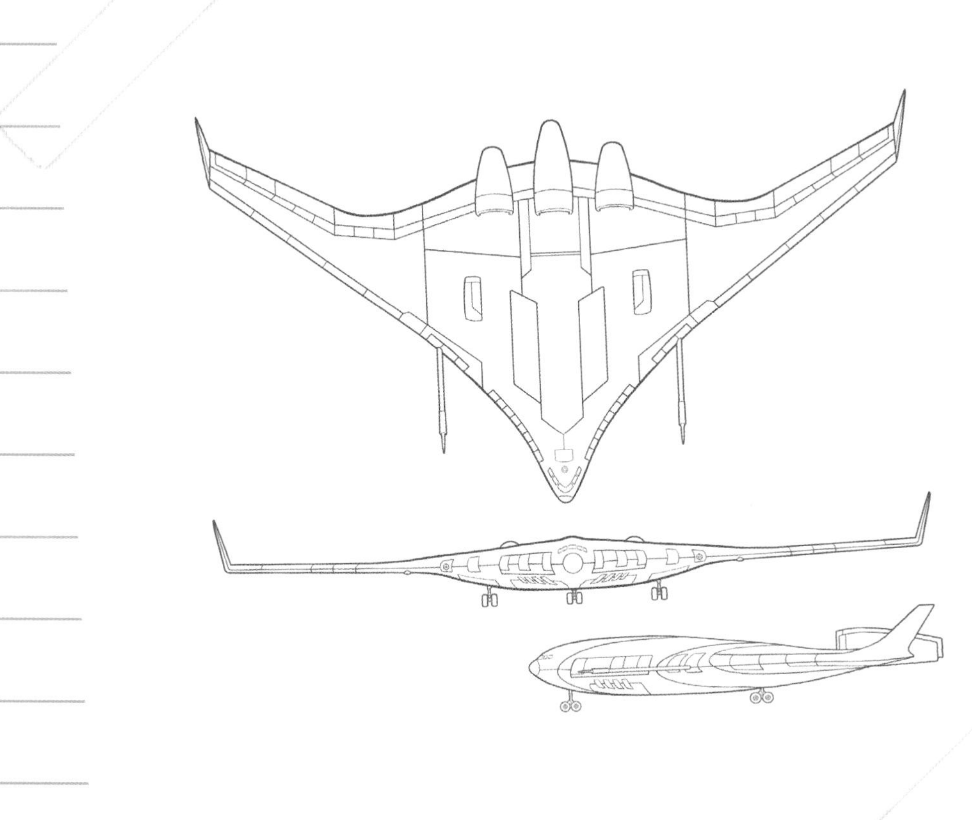

# X-48B

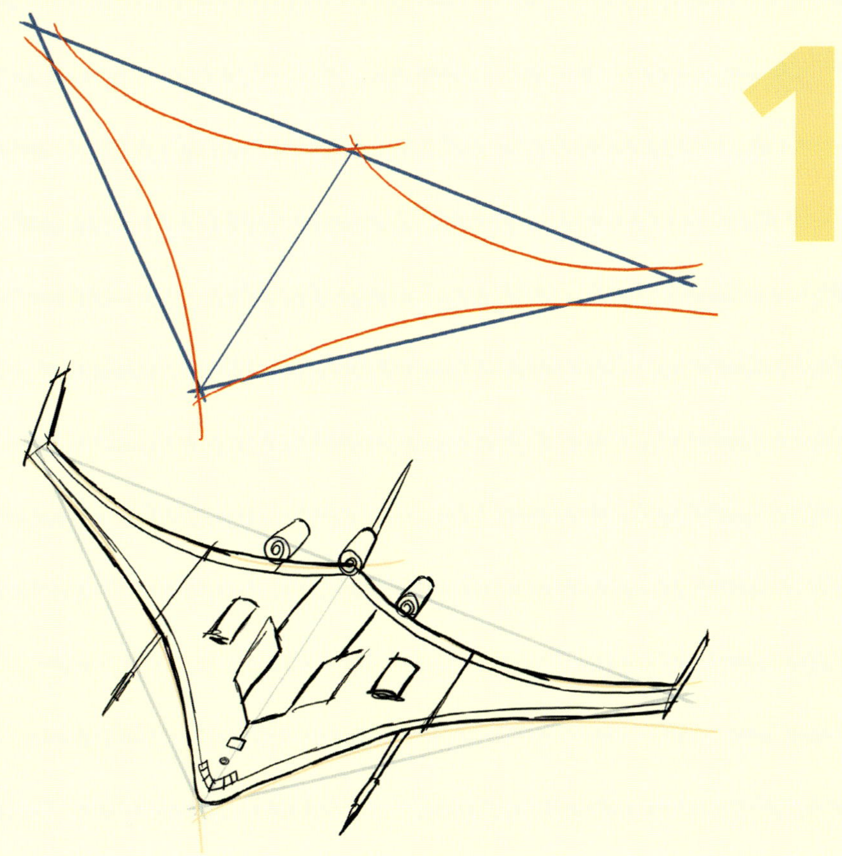

Sometimes the skeleton can appear to be anything but that of an airplane. At the same time, starting with such a basic, elegant, and brilliant idea allows you to proceed directly with the sketch.

Parfois, le squelette peut ressembler à tout sauf à un avion mais reposer néanmoins sur une idée si essentielle, élégante et brillante qu'elle vous permet de passer directement à l'ébauche.

Manchmal erscheint das Skelett ganz und gar nicht wie ein Flugzeug, doch dann entsteht aus einer so einfachen, eleganten und besonderen Form direkt und ohne weiteren Zwischenschritt die Skizze.

Soms lijkt de vormtekening helemaal niet op een vliegtuig en gaat deze uit van een elegant en briljant basisidee dat ons in staat stelt om direct aan de schets te beginnen.

En ocasiones, el esqueleto puede parecer cualquier cosa menos un avión y, a la vez, partir de una idea tan básica, elegante y brillante que nos permite saltar directamente al boceto.

A volte lo scheletro può sembrare tutt'altro fuorché un aereo ma, al tempo stesso, può essere un'idea così basilare, elegante e brillante che ci permette di saltare direttamente al bozzetto.

Em certas ocasiões, o esqueleto pode parecer qualquer coisa menos um avião e, ao mesmo tempo, partir de uma ideia tão básica, elegante e brilhante que nos permite saltar directamente para o esboço.

## 2

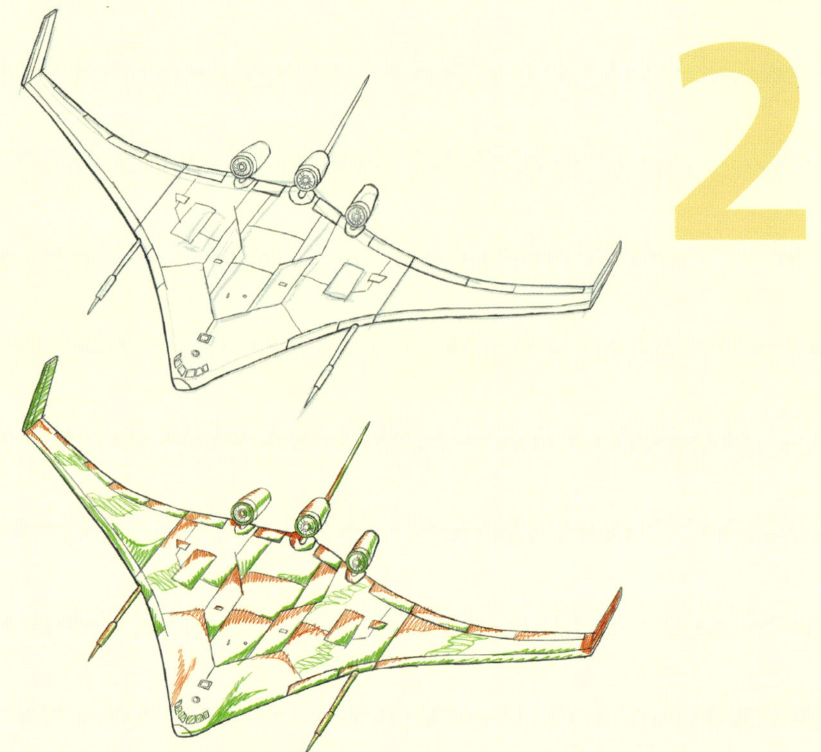

With such a spectacularly simple plane, penciling is practically the same as inking. It is almost a case of inventing details so that the drawing does not look empty. Once again, you can play with the positioning of the lighting (green) and shading (red).

Pour un avion si simple, le crayonné s'apparente presque à un travail d'encrage et il est même nécessaire d'inventer des détails pour que le dessin ne semble pas trop vide. Là encore, recherchez le meilleur emplacement des lumières (en vert) et des ombres (en rouge).

Bei einem so außergewöhnlich einfach strukturierten Flugzeug kommt die Buntstiftzeichnung schon beinahe einer Tuschezeichnung gleich. Fast muss man sich zusätzliche Details ausdenken, damit die Abbildung nicht z u leer erscheint. Auch hier wird die Position der Licht- (grün) und Schattenbereiche (rot) untersucht.

In een dergelijk spectaculair eenvoudig vliegtuig is de potloodtekening bijna een inkttekening en moeten we bijna details verzinnen opdat de tekening niet leeg lijkt. We onderzoeken opnieuw de plaats van de lichten (groen) en de schaduwen (rood).

En un avión tan espectacularmente sencillo, el lápiz es prácticamente una tinta, y casi debemos inventarnos detalles para que el dibujo no parezca vacío. De nuevo, investigamos la situación de las luces (verde) y las sombras (rojo).

In un aereo così straordinariamente semplice, le matite corrispondono al ripasso a china. Dobbiamo quasi inventarci dei dettagli per fare in modo che il disegno non sembri vuoto. Ancora una volta, studiamo la posizione delle luci (verde) e delle ombre (rosso).

Num avião tão espectacularmente simples, o lápis é praticamente uma tinta, e quase devemos inventar detalhes para que o desenho não pareça vazio. De novo, investigamos a colocação das luzes (verde) e das sombras (vermelha).

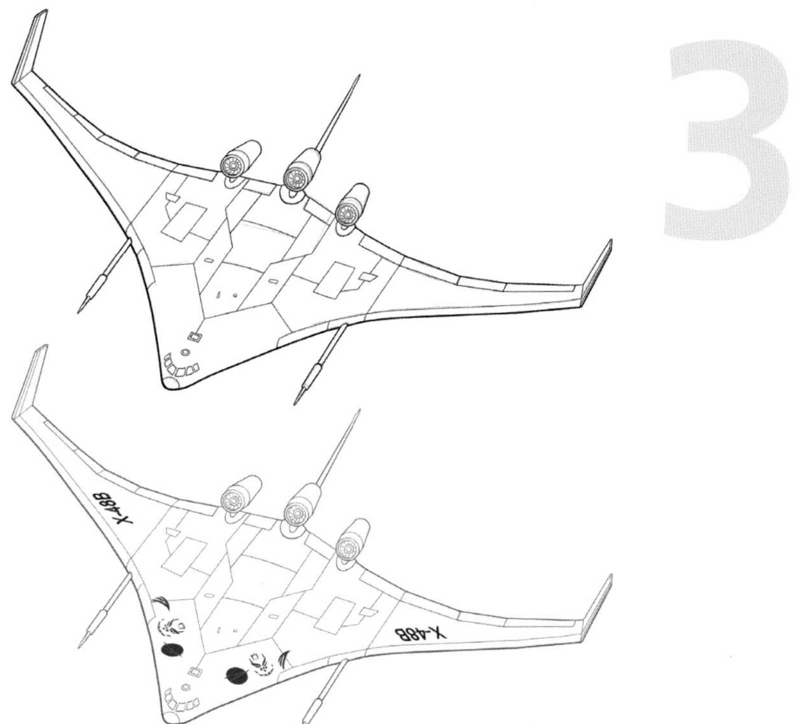


Practically all the inking was done with rulers or line tools in order to respect the technological and futuristic appearance of this aircraft. The few emblems of the fuselage can be seen below.

Pour conserver l'aspect technologique et futuriste de l'aéronef, utilisez des règles et outils de tracé pour presque toutes les lignes. Sur la partie inférieure, vous pouvez observer les quelques emblèmes de son fuselage.

Um den hochtechnologischen, futuristischen Look des Flugzeugs aufrechtzuerhalten, werden bei praktische allen Strichen der Tuschezeichnung Lineale bzw. Linien-Werkzeuge eingesetzt. In der unteren Abbildung sind die wenigen Symbole auf dem Rumpf zu sehen.

Om het technologische en futuristische aspect van het luchtschip te handhaven is gebruik gemaakt van linialen of andere hulpmiddelen bij praktisch alle inktstrepen. Aan de onderkant zijn de weinige emblemen van de romp te zien.

Para mantener el aspecto tecnológico y futurista de la aeronave se han utilizado reglas o herramientas de línea en la práctica totalidad de las tintas. En la parte inferior se observan los pocos emblemas de su fuselaje.

Per mantenere l'aspetto tecnologico e avveniristico del velivolo sono stati utilizzati righelli o strumenti linea per quasi tutte le linee. Nella parte inferiore si osservano i pochi simboli presenti sulla fusoliera.

Para manter o aspecto tecnológico e futurista da aeronave utilizaram-se réguas ou ferramentas geométricas em praticamente todas as tintas. Na parte inferior observam-se os poucos emblemas da sua fuselagem.

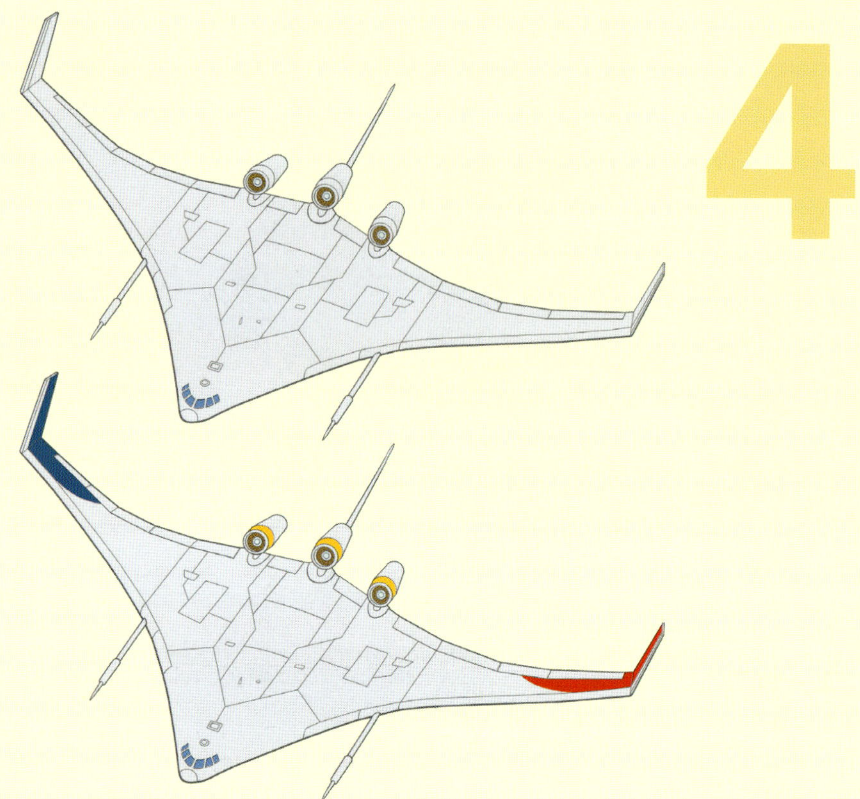

4

Gray as a base color gives the plane a cold, futuristic, and extra-terrestrial appearance. The colored designs below offer contrast and a humanizing touch to the aircraft.

La couleur grise donne à l'avion un aspect futuriste, froid et extraterrestre. Le design coloré de la partie inférieure apporte un contraste et donne à l'aéronef un aspect plus humain.

Die graue Grundfarbe verleiht dem Flugzeug ein kalt und außerirdisch wirkendes futuristisches Aussehen. Die Farbakzente der unteren Abbildung sorgen für einen ansprechenden Kontrast und lassen das Flugzeug weniger entmenschlicht wirken.

Door de grijze basiskleur ziet het vliegtuig er futuristisch, kil en buitenaards uit. De kleurontwerpen van de onderkant zorgen voor contrast en maken het luchtschip menselijker.

El color base gris le da al avión un aspecto futurista, frío y alienígena. Los diseños de color de la parte inferior aportan contraste y humanizan la aeronave.

Il colore di base grigio dà all'aereo un aspetto futuristico, freddo e alieno. I motivi di colore sulla parte inferiore aggiungono un certo contrasto e rendono il velivolo più umano.

A cor base cinzenta dá ao avião um aspecto futurista, frio e alienígena. Os desenhos de cor da parte inferior concedem contraste e humanizam a aeronave.

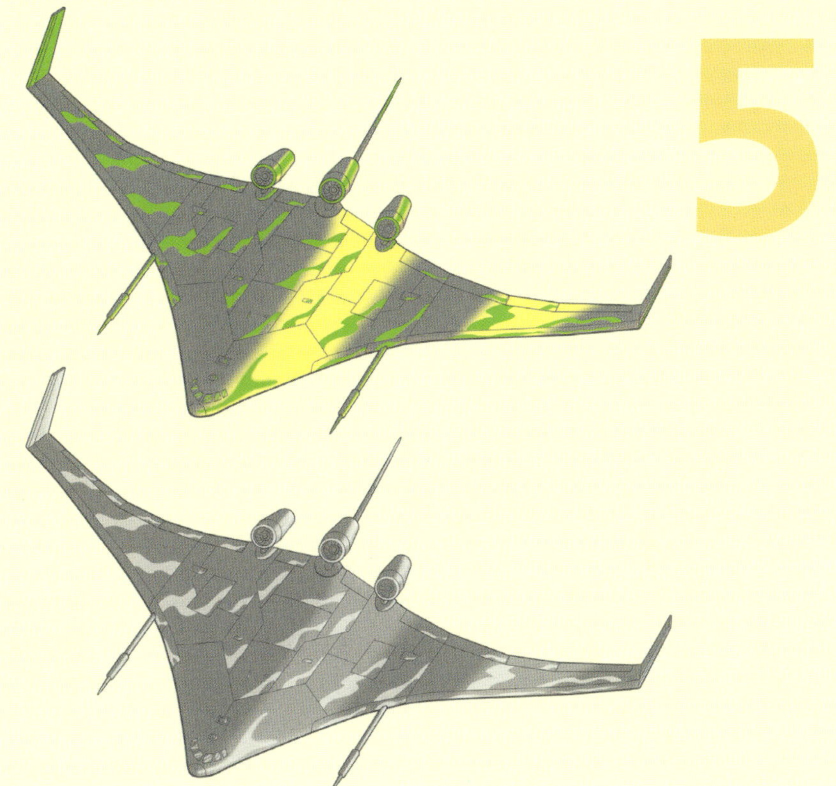

5

The longitudinal lighting layer adds volume, while the small details enrich the image. The result of turning both layers to white with different levels of opacity can be seen below.

La couche de lumière longitudinale apporte du volume tandis que les petits détails enrichissent la structure. Sur la partie inférieure, vous pouvez observer le résultat une fois les deux couches colorées en blanc avec des opacités différentes.

Die in Längsrichtung angeordneten Lichtbereiche verleihen der Darstellung Tiefe, während die kleinen Details das Bild bereichern. Unten ist das Ergebnis der Konvertierung beider Lichtebenen in Weiß (mit unterschiedlicher Transparenz) zu sehen.

De longitudinale lichtlaag zorgt voor volume terwijl de kleine details de figuur verrijken. Aan de onderkant kunnen we het resultaat zien nadat beide lagen naar wit zijn overgegaan met verschillende maten van opaciteit.

La capa de luces longitudinal aporta volumen, mientras que los pequeños detalles enriquecen la figura. En la parte inferior podemos ver el resultado de pasar ambas capas a blanco con opacidades diferentes.

Il livello di luci longitudinale aggiunge volume, mentre i piccoli dettagli arricchiscono il soggetto. Nella parte inferiore possiamo vedere il risultato ottenuto mettendo entrambi i livelli in bianco con opacità diverse.

A camada de luzes longitudinal concede volume, enquanto que os pequenos detalhes enriquecem a figura. Na parte inferior podemos ver o resultado de passar ambas as camadas para branco com opacidades diferentes.

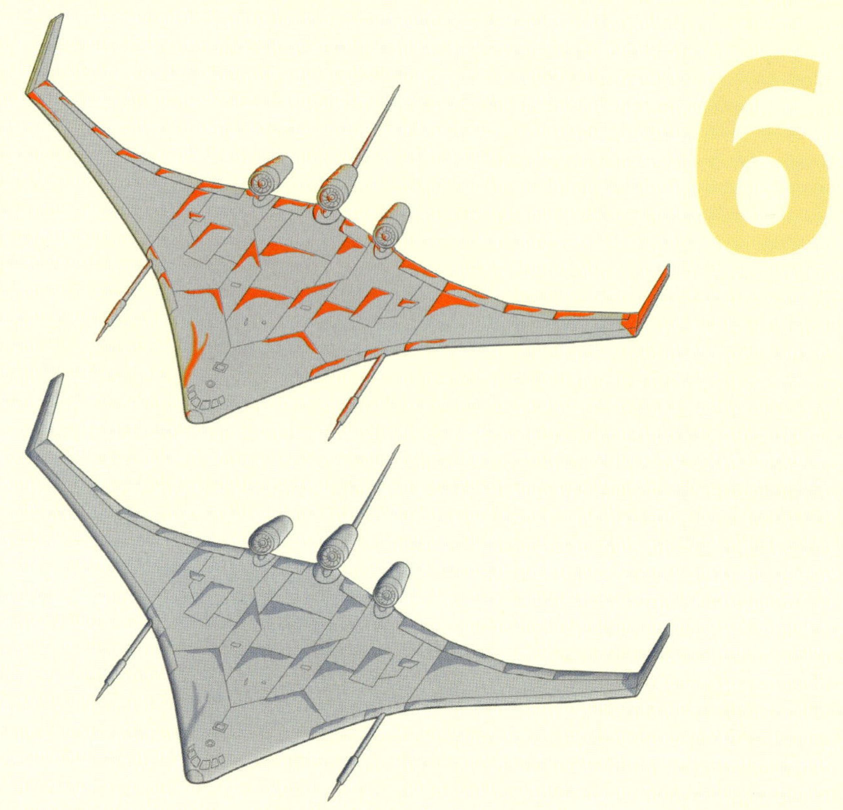

Only one layer is used for the shading, applying it to specific areas that are contrasted with the lighting. Below you can see the application of shading in violet with a low level of opacity.

Pour les ombres, utilisez une seule couche appliquée sur des zones concrètes qui s'opposent aux lumières. Sur la partie inférieure, vous pouvez observer l'application des ombres avec une couleur violette de faible opacité.

Für die Schatten wird lediglich eine Ebene verwendet, in der klar abgegrenzte dunklere Zonen mit den Lichtbereichen kontrastieren. Anschließend werden die Schattenbereiche in Violett konvertiert und recht transparent gestaltet.

Voor de schaduwen wordt slechts één laag gebruikt die op concrete zones tegenover de lichten worden aangebracht. Aan de onderkant kunnen we zien hoe de schaduwen zijn aangebracht met een paarse, enigszins doorzichtige kleur.

Para las sombras utilizamos sólo una capa, aplicada a zonas concretas que se contraponen con las luces. En la parte inferior podemos ver la aplicación de las sombras con un color violeta a baja opacidad.

Per le ombre utilizziamo soltanto un livello, applicato a zone specifiche che si contrappongono alle luci. Nella parte inferiore possiamo vedere l'applicazione delle ombre con un colore viola a bassa opacità.

Para as sombras utilizamos só uma camada, aplicada em zonas concretas que se contrapõem com as luzes. Na parte inferior podemos ver a aplicação das sombras com uma cor violeta com baixa opacidade.

# 7

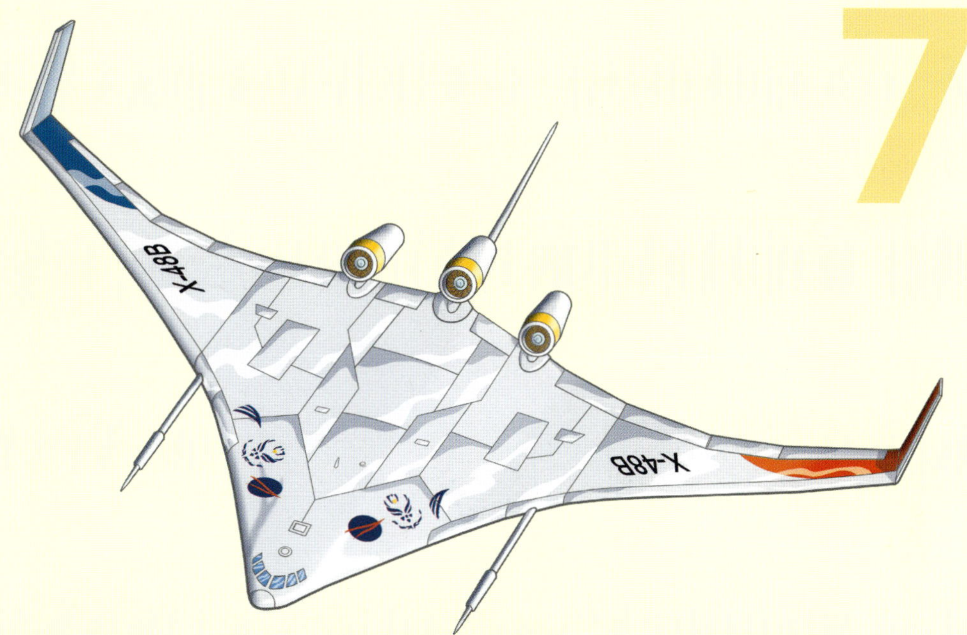


The finished drawing shows a light and futuristic aircraft that hints at a bright and hopeful future for aviation.

Le dessin final représente un aéronef futuriste et lumineux, présageant l'avenir brillant et prometteur de l'aviation.

Die fertige Zeichnung zeigt ein futuristisches, strahlendes Flugzeug, das für die strahlende, hoffnungsvolle Zukunft der Luftfahrt steht.

De afgeronde tekening toont een futuristisch en licht luchtschip dat een briljante en hoopgevende toekomst voor de luchtvaart van de toekomst voorspelt.

El dibujo acabado muestra una aeronave futurista y luminosa que insinúa un porvenir brillante y esperanzador para la aviación del futuro.

Il disegno finito mostra un velivolo futuristico e luminoso che suggerisce un avvenire brillante e pieno di speranza per l'aviazione.

O desenho acabado mostra uma aeronave futurista e luminosa que sugere um porvir brilhante e esperançoso para a aviação do futuro.

## Acknowledgments

Our thanks to Raquel González and Javier Pauner, whose collaboration was essential in producing this book.

## Remerciements

Merci à Raquel González et à Javier Pauner, dont la collaboration a été fondamentale pour la réalisation de ce livre.

## Danksagung

Vielen Dank an Raquel González und Javier Pauner, ohne deren Mitarbeit die Erstellung dieses Bandes nicht möglich gewesen wäre.

## Erkentelijkheid

Met dank aan Raquel González en Javier Pauner, wiens medewerking essentieel was voor het samenstellen van dit boekwerk.

## Agradecimientos

Gracias a Raquel González y a Javier Pauner, cuya colaboración fue fundamental para la realización de esta obra.

## Ringraziamenti

Grazie a Raquel González e a Javier Pauner, la cui collaborazione è stata fondamentale nella realizzazione di quest'opera.

## Agradecimentos

Obrigada a Raquel González e a Javier Pauner, cuja colaboração foi fundamental para a realização desta obra.